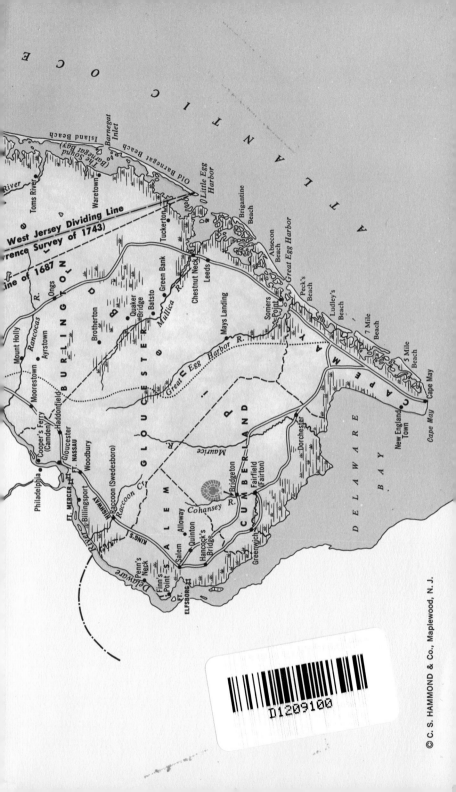

ATLANTIC OCE[AN]

West Jersey Dividing Line
[Law]rence Survey of 1743)
[Li]ne of 1687

River
Toms River
Waretown

The Sound
(Barnegat Bay)
Island Beach
Old Barnegat Beach
Barnegat Inlet

Little Egg Harbor
Tuckerton
Green Bank
Chestnut Neck
Leeds
Brigantine Beach
Absecon Beach
Great Egg Harbor

BURLINGTON
Mount Holly
Rancocas R.
Ongs
Brotherton
Ayrstown
Moorestown
Quaker Bridge
Batsto
Mullica R.
Mays Landing
Somers Point
Peck's Beach
Ludley's Beach
7 Mile Beach

GLOUCESTER
Haddonfield
Cooper's Ferry (Camden)
Gloucester
FT. NASSAU
Woodbury
Raccoon (Swedesboro)
Great Egg Harbor R.

CUMBERLAND
Maurice R.
Dorchester
New England Town
5 Mile Beach
Cape May

Philadelphia
FT. MERCER
Billingsport
Raccoon Cr.
Cohansey
Bridgeton
Fairfield (Fairton)
CAPE MAY

FT. NASSAU
KING'S HIGHWAY
SALEM
Alloway
Quinton
Hancock's Bridge
Greenwich
Cohansey R.

DELAWARE BAY

Delaware River
Penn's Neck
Finn's Point
FT. ELFSBORG
Salem

Cape May

© C. S. HAMMOND & Co., Maplewood, N. J.

D1209100

RUTGERS STUDIES IN HISTORY: NUMBER 6

EXPERIMENT IN INDEPENDENCE

F138
.M2 WITHDRAWN

Experiment in Independence

NEW JERSEY IN
THE CRITICAL PERIOD
1781-1789

****

RICHARD P. McCORMICK

Rutgers University Press

NEW BRUNSWICK, NEW JERSEY

1 9 5 0

Second Printing
Copyright 1950

By

THE TRUSTEES OF RUTGERS COLLEGE

in New Jersey

Library of Congress Catalog Card Number: 70-189316

ISBN: 0-8135-0729-4

ALL RIGHTS RESERVED

Manufactured in the United States of America

For those to whom
it meant the most
MOTHER
and
KATCH

22378

Preface

****

WHEN VIEWED solely from the narrow perspective of nationalism, the years between the Revolution and the Constitution appear clouded with discord and failure and offer a dramatic contrast to the climactic achievement of 1789. No balanced history of the era can be written, however, from such a partial and inappropriate frame of reference. A broader approach, which recognizes that the unique and significant characteristic of the "critical period" was the dominance of the states in their individual capacities, is needed. Temporarily endowed with full sovereignty, the several members of the feeble Confederation were at liberty to devise solutions to their local problems on their own initiative. Each was engaged in an experiment in independence at the same time that all were conscious of a common heritage and a common destiny.

The difficulties New Jersey encountered after making the transition from colonialism and strife to freedom and peace were broadly similar to those which confronted its sister states. The damages that had been sustained in a long and costly war had to be repaired, the political institutions essential to self-government under republican principles had to be preserved and perfected, and relations among the states had to be organized on a satisfactory basis. These matters, although seemingly in separate categories, were in fact so intimately connected that only by doing violence to the fabric of history can they be considered separately. It is the purpose of this study to examine the experience of New Jersey as it sought to meet these large problems and explain the circumstances that conditioned its attitude toward them. It should be recognized at the outset that New Jersey cannot be regarded as a "typical" state and that the unusual course which it pursued cannot readily be understood by mere reference to conventional interpretations.

A small state, situated between the principal commercial cities of the Confederation, split into two rival geographical divisions by historical, religious, economic, and cultural factors, without a frontier or a metropolis, a tidewater or a back country, New Jersey had no counterpart among the original states. The peculiar sectional cleavage between East and West Jersey, inherited from colonial times and aggravated by the war, constituted the main basis of political alignments. This divergence was particularly acute over financial questions, which were the paramount source of conflict throughout the period. Down to 1785, neither section possessed clearcut control of the government, but between that year and 1788, East Jersey was supreme by a narrow margin, and a series of popular or "radical" measures were enacted. After the adoption of the Federal Constitution, West Jersey, in alliance with the conservative minority in the east, came to power, and the pendulum swung to the right. Conspicuously exempt from sectional dispute was the subject of the strengthening of the union, on which all groups were in agreement.

A fair appraisal of the record of New Jersey in the postwar years reveals a balance heavily on the side of positive accomplishments. In spite of unsettled conditions, substantial progress was made in the ordinary tasks of economic, social, and cultural reconstruction. The crude political machinery established under the Constitution of 1776 successfully withstood the test of sectional strains. Self-government flourished to such an extent that the rule of the majority aroused the apprehensions of those who feared the consequences of unrestrained democracy. Extraordinary efforts were made to meet interest payments on the various types of public securities held within the state, with the result that the citizens paid heavier taxes than they had ever known before. Deflationary financial policies gave rise to popular demands for paper money, and the loan-office plan that was adopted to meet the critical currency shortage was a familiar expedient that had been employed effectively in the past. It was not a radical innovation but a time-tested remedy. Financial considerations motivated New Jersey to become a foremost advocate of a strengthened Confederation. What the state wanted most of all was a continental impost, which would mean an end to requisitions and the heavy tax burden which they entailed. The Constitution was welcomed by all classes because it promised such financial relief. The conservative minority gave the document enthusiastic approval for the added reason that it limited the power of the state legislature to enact laws detrimental to property rights.

It is a pleasure to record my indebtedness to all those individuals who by their aid and counsel have assisted me beyond my power to repay them. To the uniformly courteous and co-operative members of the staffs of the Friends Book Store, the Manuscripts Division of the Library of Congress, the Massachusetts Historical Society, the National Archives, the New Jersey Historical Society, the New Jersey State Library, the New York Historical Society, the New York Public Library, the Historical Society of Pennsylvania, the Princeton University Library, the Rutgers University Library, the Loeb

Library of the Stevens Institute of Technology, and the Surveyor-General's Office in Burlington, I am deeply obligated for services rendered. I am appreciative, too, of the financial assistance given me by the Rutgers University Research Council. My warmest personal thanks must be reserved for Professor Roy F. Nichols of the University of Pennsylvania, whose scholarly advice and friendly encouragement have meant much to me for many years, and for my indefatigable wife, who made this study her own.

Richard P. McCormick

RUTGERS UNIVERSITY
New Brunswick, New Jersey
December, 1949

Contents

****

		Page
I	Introduction to Independence	3
II	The Plight of the Loyalists	25
III	Social and Cultural Reconstruction	40
IV	Politics: the Rules and the Game	69
V	Business and the Government	103
VI	The Landed Interest	135
VII	Money: the Era of Deflation	158
VIII	Money: the Familiar Remedy	186
IX	New Jersey and the Confederation	218
X	New Jersey and the Constitution	252
XI	The Counterrevolution	280
XII	Conclusion	304
	Appendices	307
	Bibliography	309
	Index	327

KEY TO ABBREVIATIONS

****

DAB   —*Dictionary of American Biography*

HSP   —Historical Society of Pennsylvania

LC   —Manuscripts Division, Library of Congress

MHS   —Massachusetts Historical Society

NJHS   —New Jersey Historical Society

NJSL   —New Jersey State Library

NYHS   —New York Historical Society

NYPL   —New York Public Library

PNJHS—*Proceedings of the New Jersey Historical Society*

PUL   —Princeton University Library

RUL   —Rutgers University Library

SIT   —Stevens Institute of Technology

EXPERIMENT IN INDEPENDENCE

I

Introduction to Independence

★★★

REMOTE from the early scenes of conflict, New Jersey did not feel the full impact of the Revolution until the critical winter of 1776, when it was suddenly transformed into the principal theater of operations. The battles of Trenton, Princeton, and Monmouth, and the encampments made by Washington's main army within its borders throughout three winters, became conspicuous symbols of its deep involvement in the struggle. Aptly described as the "cockpit of the Revolution," this small state suffered more than its share of bloodshed and waste, with friend and foe alike contributing to the desolation. Bitter internecine strife between patriots and tories took its toll in many localities. Economic disorganization, together with political and social instability, left the lives of few citizens unaffected. As late as 1780, when the British made their final descent in force into the state, invasion was an imminent reality, and even after that date, while the enemy occupied New York it remained a constant threat. But the engagement at Springfield on June 23, 1781, marked the end of the active phase of the fight for independence in New Jersey, and although victory still seemed far distant, the ambiguous period of transition from war to peace had in fact begun.[1]

BETWEEN WAR AND PEACE

In the summer of 1781 the state for the last time witnessed the stirring scene of troops on their way to battle. Five years earlier the people of New Jersey had watched helplessly as the remnants of a beaten patriot army retreated before the superior might of the British under Howe and Cornwallis. Now they could take courage from the sight of two disciplined, well-equipped armies moving confidently to the offensive under the command of their familiar hero, General Washington. The French forces of the Count de Rochambeau and the Americans led by General Lincoln crossed the Hudson three days apart in the final week in August. Marching rapidly by separate routes through towns whose names were reminders of the grim year of defeat, they reached Trenton in less than ten days. From the Delaware they hastened on by water and by land to the Head of Elk and thence to the crucial siege of Yorktown. The tide of the war had changed.[2]

Seven weeks later the glorious news of the decisive defeat of Cornwallis was published in New Jersey's lone newspaper. In all sections of the state the event was signalized by enthusiastic celebrations. At Trenton, Governor William Livingston and the legislature attended services at the Presbyterian

[1] The best account of the war in New Jersey is Leonard Lundin, *Cockpit of the Revolution* (Princeton, 1940).

[2] Austin Scott, "Blazing the Way to Final Victory—1781," *PNJHS*, NS, VI (1921), pp. 1-10; John C. Fitzpatrick, ed., *The Writings of George Washington . . ., 1754-1799* (39 vol., Washington, D.C., 1931-1944), XXIII, pp. 6-7, 41-42, 59-60, 71-72; *New Jersey Gazette*, Aug. 29, Sept. 5, 1781; C. C. Robin, *New Travels through North-America . . .*, translated by Philip Freneau (Boston, 1784), pp. 37-38. Robin, who accompanied Rochambeau, was greatly impressed with the luxurious appearance of the New Jersey countryside. He noted that Trenton was the largest town the French had seen since leaving Providence.

Church, after which they assembled on the common to witness a discharge of cannon. This was followed by an "elegant entertainment" that included the customary thirteen toasts and ended early in the evening with a brilliant illumination. The citizenry of Princeton gathered on the green in front of Beekman's tavern to hear an "address suited to the institution of the day" delivered by a member of the college faculty, and in New Brunswick the leading gentlemen of the place met at a local hostelry "to spend an hour together in festivity and gladness." In mid-December all churches were called upon to observe a day of thanksgiving and praise for the recent success of American arms.[3]

Hopes were high for an early peace, but the period of waiting was to last for another year and a half. Early in 1782 one of New Jersey's leading statesmen expressed the belief that peace could not be won in "under two Years at least." [4] The legislature in May, 1782, disturbed by the arrival in New York of Sir Guy Carleton to replace the discredited Sir Henry Clinton as British commander, reasserted its determination to accept nothing less than complete independence. Convinced that the British, having failed to conquer by force of arms, were now seeking through subtlety to create divisions among the states and their allies, the lawmakers spiritedly declared their unwillingness to listen to any British proposals "except only thro' the intervention of Congress." Furthermore, they urged that peace should not be concluded separately by the states but only in conjunction with their companions in arms. Full support was pledged to Congress in prosecuting the war to a victorious end.[5]

[3] *New Jersey Gazette*, Oct. 24, 31, Nov. 7, 21, 1781.

[4] Elias Boudinot to Lewis Pintard, Feb. 5, 18, 1782. Boudinot Papers, II, HSP.

[5] *Votes and Proceedings of the General Assembly of the State of New Jersey, Fifth Session, Second Sitting*, pp. 12-13 (hereafter cited as *Votes and Proceedings*, 5-2). A new legislature met annually and in the years 1776 to 1789 customarily held more than one sitting.

In the meantime there were frequent reminders that the end of strife had not yet come, as civil dissension, refugee raids, British sorties, and privateering ventures enlivened the years after Yorktown. Monmouth County, in particular, was subjected to frequent alarms because of its exposed position and its internal disunity. Patriots and tories there plundered one another almost at will.[6] Ardent whigs banded themselves together in an association whose purpose it was to insure "that the helm of Government and all civil and military offices may be kept in the hands of such men as have been most instrumental in effecting the glorious revolution." These "Retaliators," as they were called, were pledged to support the laws of the state which inflicted penalties on tories, and to secure the banishment of all traitors. Led by Daniel Forman—onetime sheriff and justice of the peace—the group was accused of carrying on a virtual reign of terror in the county.[7] In September, 1782, protests were lodged with the legislature against the wanton and cruel actions of the band. Forman, in his judicial capacity, was charged with aiding and encouraging plundering. "Our doors have been forced open, our Houses rifled of Beds and other furniture, and Our Stock, and our Teams totally broke up," stated the injured petitioners. Moreover, it was reported that peaceful citizens were "taken by force of arms, on the Mandate of the Committee of Retaliation," and confined in the gaol, from which they could not be liberated even by *habeas corpus.* Similar complaints had been brought to the attention of the legislature at its previous session, but the supplicants had merely been referred to the normal protection of the laws.[8] Civil turmoil continued.

[6] Franklin Ellis, *History of Monmouth County, New Jersey* (Philadelphia, 1885), pp. 195 ff.

[7] Articles of Association of Inhabitants of Monmouth Co[unty] for united action against Tories, photostatic copy in Jersey Box, Misc., NYPL. The pact was signed by about two hundred men.

[8] Petition of certain inhabitants of Monmouth County, Sept. 2, 1782,

Raiding parties menaced the security of the frontier section of the state. From their stronghold on Sandy Hook—appropriately named "Refugee-Town"—renegade Americans carried out daring nocturnal forays against their former neighbors.[9] To their depredations were added those of the notorious "Pine Robbers," who plundered whig and tory alike from their hide-outs in the sparsely settled pine barrens of the shore region.[10] Burlington County was terrorized by John Bacon, who engaged in pitched battles with militia companies and survived capture until he was killed in April, 1783.[11] The Shrewsbury Quarterly Meeting of the Society of Friends was distressed in October, 1781, because a number of young Quakers who had fled to New York City, Long Island, and Staten Island "returned back & committed acts inconsistent with ... [their] peaceable principles & thereby Occasioned Public Scandal to the Society ..." [12] Large bands of refugees, supported by the Board of Associated Loyalists in New York and led by British officers, launched attacks against the state from bases in New York and Staten Island. Early in 1782, for example, three hundred of the enemy ascended the Raritan to New Brunswick, overwhelmed the feeble opposition of the inhabitants, and held complete possession of the town for an hour. When they departed, they took with them a number of prisoners and several whaleboats that had

---

East Jersey Manuscripts, NJHS; Petition of Inhabitants of Monmouth County, Sept., 1782, AM Papers, NJSL. A hearing was granted by the Assembly on this second plea. After listening for four days to testimony from both sides, the house decided that although it had been established that Forman was indeed the ringleader of the "Retaliators," his conduct did not justify impeachment. *Votes and Proceedings*, 7-1, pp. 23-33.

[9] *New Jersey Gazette*, Oct. 10, 1781, Feb. 13, 1782.

[10] Francis B. Lee, *New Jersey as a Colony and as a State* ... (4 vols., New York, 1903), pp. 94-95.

[11] *New Jersey Gazette*, Jan. 8, Apr. 9, 1783.

[12] Minutes of Shrewsbury Quarterly Meeting, Oct. 29, 1781, p. 114, Friends Book Store.

been employed in privateering.[13] A month later occurred the attack on the blockhouse at Toms River, which was to have international repercussions after Captain Charles Asgill was held as a hostage for the wanton murder of the American commander, Captain Joshua Huddy.[14]

Bold and plunder-seeking Americans engaged in innumerable raids that harassed the enemy on land and sea. Captain Adam Hyler of New Brunswick, with a small flotilla of armed boats, burned or captured ten British vessels in the six months after Yorktown and made his name feared as far distant as Long Island.[15] Equally daring was Captain Quigley, who in May, 1782, went in a small boat with three companions from Elizabeth Town to Staten Island, walked across the enemy-held island, captured a brig worth four thousand pounds, and sailed it to Little Egg Harbor as a prize.[16] Captain Hand of Cape May in the "Enterprise," Captain Smith of Gloucester in the "Dart," and a host of other aggressive privateers who put to sea from the many bays and inlets along the Jersey shore took a heavy toll of British shipping.[17] Not until the provisional treaty of peace arrived was New Jersey free from the alarms of war. The problem of defense continued to engross an important share of the energies of the legislature. Social tensions remained high. A wartime psychology still prevailed. Yorktown had

[13] *Archives of the State of New Jersey, Second Series* (5 vols., Trenton, 1901-1917), V, p. 358 (hereafter cited as *New Jersey Archives*, 2nd Ser.). "Credit is due to them for the execution of a well concerted plan," conceded the local militia commander, "and much credit is due to them for their humane treatment of the defenceless part of the community. No burnings or insults were permitted, and only two families were pillaged."

[14] *Ibid.*, pp. 400, 420, 437, 450; Lee, *History*, pp. 345 ff. The Toms River raid was in part in reprisal for the excesses of the "Retaliators."

[15] *New Jersey Archives*, 2nd Ser., V. pp. 306, 311, 320, 322, 425-26.

[16] *Ibid.*, pp. 449, 453.

[17] *Ibid.*, p. 453; Privateering bond of Jonathan Smith, Joshua Smith, and Elijah Clark, Oct. 24, 1782, Livingston Papers, MHS; Lundin, *Cockpit*, pp. 403-406.

brought relief from military pressure, but it had not brought an immediate restoration of domestic tranquillity.

As the long conflict approached its end, the chronic evil of illicit trade became so critical as to engage the principal attention of the authorities and to call forth special exertions on the part of loyal whigs. Commerce with the enemy in New York offered enticing rewards, for provisions could be exchanged there for specie or precious imported goods at a risk so small as to check only the most timorous. It was a relatively simple matter to pass through the thinly guarded lines in Bergen or Essex or to sail at night across the narrow reaches of New York Bay. A succession of stringent laws were passed to break up the nefarious traffic, but they were poorly enforced and scandalously ineffective.[18]

Late in the spring of 1782, coincident with the arrival in New York of the conciliatory Sir Guy Carleton and the temporary blockade of the Delaware by British cruisers, illegal trading grew to alarming proportions. Traders who had formerly been active in Philadelphia flocked to New Jersey to share in the bonanza. "Money is going from hence to New York to amounts almost incredible," wrote Abraham Clark from his seat in the Continental Congress, "and if not prevented will soon drain the Continent of all hard cash; we are with hasty strides ruining ourselves by this destructive commerce..."[19] Washington attempted to deal with the problem by ordering on May 10 that necessary communication with the enemy should be carried on only through Dobbs Ferry and not through Elizabeth Town, which was generally regarded as a center of contraband activities.[20] The legislature, prompted in part by Clark's warnings, enacted a new law in June to prevent intercourse with the enemy, at the

---

[18] Lundin, *Cockpit*, pp. 377–80.

[19] Clark to Caleb Camp, May 22, 1782, *PNJHS*, LI (1933), pp. 261–62.

[20] Fitzpatrick, *Writings*, XXIV, p. 376; *ibid.*, XXV, p. 6.

same time repealing a half dozen earlier laws on the subject.[21] Still the evil persisted.

Many saw in the lucrative commerce a "fiendish plot" to subdue America by draining off its currency for British gewgaws and trinkets. "What is become of our money?" asked "A Plain Farmer" in the columns of the *New Jersey Gazette*. "A few months ago we had plenty to pay our taxes and to answer other necessary purposes...Now it is gone. It is gone; and I will tell you where: It is gone to New-York to buy goods of those kinds which are not only useless, but ruinous to any people, and particularly to a plain, frugal people."[22] "Horatius" seconded this point of view, and, fearful that the magistrates could not execute the law because of "the number of miscreants concerned and associated in the said diabolical commerce," proposed that loyal whigs should form themselves into committees to aid in apprehending offenders.[23] Acting promptly on this suggestion, 153 inhabitants of Trenton and vicinity met on July 11 to draw up a declaration condemning British machinations and illegal traders and to arrange for a second meeting at the courthouse eight days later. At that time the declaration was formally adopted, and an "Association" was created for the purpose of joining with the regular authorities in preventing all dealings with the enemy. An executive committee composed of nine prominent citizens was empowered to act for the larger body.[24] Within the month similar Associations were formed

[21] *New Jersey Gazette*, July 3, 1782. Even the Quakers were not "clear" in the matter of dealing in illicit goods, as evidenced by their answers to the "Queries" in Quarterly Meetings. See the minutes of the Quarterly Meetings of Shrewsbury, Burlington, and Haddonfield Friends, Friends Book Store.

[22] *New Jersey Gazette*, June 26, 1782.

[23] *Ibid.*, July 3, 1782.

[24] *Ibid.*, July 17, 24, 1782. The main article in the declaration originally read: "We will avoid, as far as possible, all intercourse, communication and dealings with such as *have been*, or may be concerned in trading with the enemy, *or who have been*, or may be justly suspected

in Princeton, Nottingham, Bordentown, Burlington, Allentown, Amwell, and Kingwood, all of them closely modeled after the Trenton group.[25] In addition to the Associations, the Whig Societies that had been organized early in 1781 (principally in Somerset, Middlesex, and Monmouth Counties) to maintain the value of the state money, joined in the war against the traitorous profiteers.[26]

Despite the efforts of these self-constituted law-enforcing agencies, illicit trade continued to flourish. Only rarely, it would seem, was a dealer in contraband apprehended and convicted. So notorious did the traffic become that the French Minister lodged a vigorous protest against it with the Continental Congress. His letter was referred to a committee, which reported on October 30, 1782, "that a continuance of the flagitious clandestine commerce therein set forth between some of the Citizens of the State of Jersey and the Enemy cannot but be attended with the most destructive consequences . . ." The state was urged to attend to the matter, and a copy of the resolve was sent to the Commander-in-Chief.[27] Washington's response, in a letter to the Secretary at War, was brief and pointed, "I think myself bound to make the following remark: That the allotment of the whole Continental Army to that duty would not prevent the practice." [28] In December the legislature passed its eighth law to prevent illicit intercourse with the enemy, specifying among other

---

of being so concerned." The italicized words were omitted in the final form, indicating a disposition on the part of the Association to let bygones be bygones.

[25] *Ibid.*, Aug. 7, 14, 21, Sept. 4, 1782.

[26] *Ibid.*, Jan. 17, 1781, July 31, Sept. 4, 1782.

[27] *Journals of the Continental Congress* (34 vols., Washington, D.C., 1904-1937), XXIII, p. 697.

[28] Fitzpatrick, *Writings*, XXV, p. 322. In a letter to Governor Livingston, at this time, Washington wrote, "The evil complained of has been long growing, and has at length arisen to a height truly alarming." *Ibid.*, p. 337.

provisions that no cattle could be driven through Bergen without a passport.[29] Three months later Washington complained that the lines around New York were "completely broken down," and that those who had been commissioned to restrain the trade in contraband were actually conniving in it.[30]

As it became increasingly apparent that the war had run its course, rigorous whiggism succumbed to the desire for profits, and in the face of a strong demand for goods that were available in abundance in New York, legislation was powerless to prevent trade with the enemy.[31] The spirit of the times fostered a moral let-down. Men of enterprise were not disposed to permit either laws or patriotic scruples to prevent them from engaging in a lucrative commerce. The clandestine traffic with the British is but one illustration of the fact that economic life remained on an abnormal basis.

THE IMPACT OF VICTORY

Vague rumors of approaching peace began to reach America late in 1782. In the final week of that year Elias Boudinot—well informed because of his position as President of the Continental Congress—learned that Britain had on September 21 recognized the independence of the former colonies by sending Richard Oswald to treat with their commissioners. "The Rubicon is therefore Past," he exulted, "and I am happy that my Expectations are likely to be fulfilled . . ."[32] Two months of anxious waiting for news of the outcome of the negotiations followed. Then on March 12,

[29] *Acts of the General Assembly . . .*, compiled by Peter Wilson (Trenton, 1784), pp. 318-20.

[30] Washington to Secretary for Foreign Affairs, Mar. 19, 1783, Fitzpatrick, *Writings*, XXVI, p. 242.

[31] Robert A. East, *Business Enterprise in the American Revolutionary Era* (New York, 1938), p. 239. East notes a general tendency for businessmen to rush from war to profit-making enterprises.

[32] Boudinot to Lewis Pintard, Dec. 24, 1782, Boudinot Papers, II, HSP.

1783, Captain Joshua Barney arrived in Philadelphia with the provisional treaty that had been signed some three months before.[33] A copy of the document was at once forwarded to Governor Livingston by the Secretary for Foreign Affairs, who pessimistically observed that the conclusion of a treaty was still "very uncertain" and advised against any relaxation in war measures.[34] All doubts were soon dissipated, for on March 23 a French sloop arrived in Philadelphia with an authentic dispatch announcing that a general treaty of peace had been approved by all the belligerent powers on January 20.[35] Finally, on April 14, 1783, the Governor published the proclamation of the Continental Congress which declared that hostilities, after eight years, were at last at an end.[36] New Jersey was at peace.

The Governor's manifesto was greeted with celebrations in large towns and small hamlets throughout the state. In courthouse, tavern, and church, men gathered to solemnize the achievement of independence with orations, toasts, and thanksgiving. "The Treaty is universally applauded," wrote William Livingston to his son-in-law. William Paterson was more exact when he reported to his brother in New Orleans, "Everybody is pleased with the Peace except the Tories and Refugees, who are exceedingly clamorous and rail incessantly ag[ains]t the British King and Parliament."[37] Joy at the victorious termination of the war was equaled by fervent

[33] Edmund C. Burnett, *The Continental Congress* (New York, 1941), p. 563.

[34] Robert R. Livingston to Governor Livingston, Mar. 18, 1783, *Selections from the Correspondence of the Executive of New Jersey from 1776 to 1786* (Newark, 1848), pp. 330-31.

[35] *New Jersey Gazette*, Mar. 26, 1783; Elias Boudinot to General Washington, Mar. 23, 1783, J. J. Boudinot, ed., *The Life, Public Services, Addresses and Letters of Elias Boudinot* ... (Boston and New York, 1896), p. 302.

[36] *New Jersey Gazette*, Apr. 16, 1783.

[37] *Ibid.*, Apr. 16, 23, 1783; H. P. Johnston, ed., *Correspondence and Public Papers of John Jay* (4 vols., New York, 1890-1893), p. 46; Paterson Papers (Bancroft Transcripts), NYPL.

devotion to the *"Father and Deliverer"* of the new land.[38] When Washington in August, 1783, traveled to Princeton for an audience with the Continental Congress, he was greeted in every town through which he passed with effusive demonstrations of respect and gratitude.[39] He was, like the Declaration of Independence, already a symbol to the new nation.

The cessation of hostilities brought about an end of "the lines" and a reopening of communication with New York. For months Governor Livingston had been besieged with requests for special passes by countless men and women who wished for a variety of reasons to enter the city. Wives begged for permission to join husbands who had fled to serve their king, husbands longed to visit wives who had gone into the British lines for reasons of security, creditors were anxious lest their debtors should escape to England before discharging their obligations.[40] Cornelia Bell Paterson, wife of the state's attorney general, was pathetically eager to see her beloved brother, Andrew Bell, a tory in the British service. John Shaw pleaded for a pass when he learned that several men who owed him large sums were about to embark for England. Among them was "Mr. Mathews the Mayor." Henry Remsen wanted to collect debts aggregating twenty-two hundred pounds sterling.[41] All such requests were uniformly rejected by the firm governor, but after the proclamation of peace, the rush could not be restrained. Old contacts, inter-

---

[38] Reporting the sentiment of the people of the state, Elisha Boudinot wrote Washington, "There is scarcely a Man or Woman among them . . . but what have a Monument erected to you in their breasts, that can only be effaced with their lives." Boudinot, *Boudinot*, pp. 305-306.

[39] Fitzpatrick, *Writings*, XXVII, p. 113n.

[40] There are dozens of such letters in the William Livingston Transcripts, NJSL.

[41] "The Cornelia (Bell) Paterson Letters," *PNJHS*, XVI, pp. 186-201; John Shaw to Robert Morris, Apr. 14, 1783, Robert Morris Papers, RUL; Henry Remsen to William Livingston, Feb. 28, 1783, Livingston Papers, MHS.

rupted during the war years, were speedily resumed. Elias Boudinot, in the same letter in which he advised the authorities in New York of the arrival of the general treaty, took the opportunity to reaffirm his friendship for his old client, Lord Drummond, whose estate he had preserved from confiscation.[42] Traders flocked to the city to take advantage of the glutted markets and the low prices. Enterprising young lawyers moved there to participate in the boom times. William Paterson seriously considered taking such a step, but decided against it. "I wish to pass the Remainder of Life in Quietude & Peace," reasoned the future governor, "New York is at present a Scene of Confusion & Turbulence, and it is impossible to tell when it will settle down into Order and Composure." [43]

There was also an influx of visitors into New Jersey. Many British officers accepted the opportunity to assume the role of tourist before returning to Europe, and from all reports they were cordially received by their former enemies. Commodore Sir Edmund Assleck and a companion went to view the Passaic Falls, and on their return paid their respects to Governor Livingston at Elizabeth Town.[44] The observant Doctor Schoepf, chief surgeon to the Anspach troops, traveled without a pass through the state in the summer of 1783 and diligently recorded his valuable observations for posterity. Except for the "Musquetoes" and the overinquisitive tavernkeepers, he was favorably impressed with the treatment accorded him.[45] The Englishman, J. F. D. Smyth, was

[42] Boudinot to James Robinson, Mar. 24, 1783, Boudinot Papers, II, HSP.

[43] Paterson to Tom Paterson, May 12, 1783, Paterson Papers (Bancroft Transcripts), NYPL; Paterson to Andrew Bell, Feb. 27, 1784, Paterson Papers, Manuscripts Div., LC.

[44] John Livingston to Wm. Livingston, Aug. 24, 30, 1783; Livingston Papers, MHS.

[45] J. D. Schoepf, *Travels in the Confederation*, translated and edited by A. J. Morrison (2 vols., Philadelphia, 1911), I, pp. 11 ff.

another transient reporter who observed New Jersey as it emerged from the war.[46] The presence of the Continental Congress at Princeton throughout the summer of 1783 attracted a host of notables and gave a truly cosmopolitan air to the small college town.[47] Altogether the months immediately following the removal of barriers to communication were characterized by a high degree of social mobility.

Another immediate effect of the war's end was the retirement from public life of several distinguished figures who had played a conspicuous role during the revolutionary period. Having spent many years in the service of the state, during which time their personal fortunes were neglected, they were anxious to resume their trades or professions. Typical of this group was William Paterson, who in March, 1783, resigned his commission as attorney general:

> It was with Reluctance that I consented to be put in Nomination the last time; [he explained to the chairman of the joint meeting of the legislature]. Nothing could have prevailed upon me but a full conviction that it was my Duty to accept and continue in any Office in which my Country should place me during the War. The War is now at an End, it has terminated gloriously, and with it I wish to wind up my official Course & to return to private Life. My Reputation as a professional Man requires Study; my State of Health requires some more Repose than I have had for a few years past.[48]

Elias Boudinot waited only until the expiration of his term as President of the Congress to ask permission of the legislature to retire. "I am heartily tired of my station and rejoice at my

[46] J. F. D. Smyth, *Tour in the United States of America* ... (2 vols., London, 1784), II, pp. 395-401.

[47] Varnum L. Collins, *The Continental Congress at Princeton* (Princeton, 1908), pp. 113-16.

[48] Paterson to John Cox, Mar. 17, 1783, Paterson Papers, RUL.

approach to obscurity," he confided to a friend.[49] Robert Morris, the first chief justice of the state, was another who withdrew from politics once independence was assured.[50] William Churchill Houston, who had been four times elected to the Continental Congress, his colleague, John Witherspoon, and John Cox and John Stevens, both former vice presidents of the state, took little or no part in political affairs for some years after 1783. Not until the formation of a new government was in prospect did these influential leaders return to the public arena.

With independence assured, thoughtful men surveyed the present state of their new country and speculated about its future. Many of them were apprehensive and all recognized that the years ahead would impose difficult tests on the struggling republic. William Peartree Smith, who had lost a considerable personal estate in the war, saw little hope for the maintenance of self-government:

> And now ... all hands to work, [he wrote on learning that peace had come] to set all the parts of the Great acquired machine into some order which I fear is all going to Pieces, without sufficient force in the Commanding Spring ... All the inferior wheels will run into Confusion, and by and bye, some Master Hand will sieze it. So did a Cromwell; and if this should be necessary, as (inter nos et sub rosa) I think it will, God grant it may be the man who merits from the Country he has rescued—a Diadem.[51]

[49] Boudinot to the chairman of the joint meeting of the legislature, Oct. 29, 1783, Boudinot Papers, II, HSP; Boudinot to Robert R. Livingston, Oct. 23, 1783, Edmund C. Burnett, ed., *Letters of Members of the Continental Congress* (8 vols., Washington, D.C., 1921-1936), VII, p. 347.

[50] Robert Morris to Judge John Benson, Sept. 24, 1784, Robert Morris Papers, RUL.

[51] Smith to Elias Boudinot, Apr., 1783, *PNJHS*, IV (1849), p. 122. "... I don't know whether it would not have been best for us all," Smith wrote Boudinot on April 22, "had he [Washington] lain hold of the Helm; for I am confoundedly afraid the Stupid Crew will Sink the Ship, when escaped the Storm and got into safe port." *Ibid.*, p. 124.

Some months later Elias Boudinot was lamenting the fact that public affairs were "truly in a disagreeable situation." [52] The extravagance, speculation, and moral laxity of the times alarmed those who believed that the essence of republicanism was private virtue. Corrupt individuals would produce a corrupt society. The illustrious president of the College of New Jersey was not accustomed to injecting politics into his religious discourses, but in a sermon of thanksgiving in April, 1783, he felt it his duty to warn his audience of the pitfalls that surrounded them:

> ...let us guard against using our liberty as a cloke for licentiousness, and thus poisoning the blessing after we have attained it [he admonished]. Let us endeavour to bring into, and keep in credit and reputation, everything that may serve to give vigour to an equal republican constitution. Let us cherish a love of piety, order, industry and frugality. Let us check every disposition to luxury, effeminacy, and the pleasures of a dissipated life. Let us in public measures put honour upon modesty and self denial, which is the index of real merit. [53]

This comprehensive statement of the republican ideal was echoed by William Livingston; in the moving prose of which he was a master, he called upon the legislature to vindicate the judgment of Providence in the recent conflict by surmounting the obstacles that threatened continued progress:

> Perhaps at no perticular moment during our whole conflict with Great Britain, has there been a greater necessity than at the present juncture, for unanimity vigilance & exertion [he warned]. The glory we have acquired in the war will be resounded thro' the Universe. God forbid that we should ever tarnish its lustre by an unworthy conduct in

[52] Boudinot to Robert R. Livingston, Oct. 23, 1783, Burnett, *Letters*, VII, p. 347.

[53] John Witherspoon, *The Works of John Witherspoon, D.D.*,... (9 vols., Edinburgh, 1804), V, pp. 269-70.

times of peace... Let us now shew ourselves worthy of the
inestimable blessing of Freedom by an inflexible attachment to public Faith and national honour. Let us establish
our Character as a Sovereign State on the only durable Basis
of impartial and universal Justice. For whatever plausible
sophistry the artful may contrive, or the avaricious be ready
from self-interested motives, to adopt, we may depend upon
it that the observation of the wise man, will thro' all ages,
be found an uncontrovertible truth, that Righteousness Ex-
alteth a Nation, but that Sin (of which Injustice is one of
the most aggravated) is the reproach of any People.[54]

To men who were keenly aware of the importance of the
experiment that it inaugurated, the achievement of independence was a sobering event. Those who gave thought
to the future realized that the new state—and the Confederacy of which it was a member—had embarked on a
course that was not clearly charted. They sensed that the
years ahead would not be free of trials. The war had been
won, but the republican ideal had not yet been firmly established.

THE HERITAGE OF WAR

Peace was not to bring immediate tranquillity and prosperity to New Jersey. Eight years of warfare and internal
strife had left deep marks. Some were visible in the form of
ruined buildings, worthless money, and crippled men; others
could not easily be discerned, for they lay hidden within the
fabric of society. More was involved than those ordinary
concerns of reconstruction which confront any people at the
conclusion of a long and costly conflict. A novel experiment
in self-government was on trial. A new imperial order was
in the process of evolving. Republicanism was being tested.

Any generalizations regarding the effects of the war must
be preceded by the qualification that all sections and classes

[54] Message of Livingston to the legislature, May 19, 1783, Miscellaneous Manuscripts, NJSL.

in the state did not share equally the strains and burdens that it entailed. West Jersey, because of its influential Quaker minority, its remoteness from the principal scenes of conflict, and its predominantly rural character, was less affected than was East Jersey, which suffered heavily from invasions, from occupation by American and British forces, from internal discord, and from economic disorganization. The ardent whig minority contributed more than its quota of Continental troops, militiamen, supplies, taxes, loans, and public services, and its losses were correspondingly heavy. Similarly, the active loyalists paid a high price for their open stand against independence. Different economic, social, and cultural groups were influenced in widely varying degrees by the revolutionary struggle, which was to leave none of them completely untouched.

The devastation that resulted directly or indirectly from military operations was extensive. In 1782 an attempt was made to appraise the damages caused by British and American troops. The survey revealed that in Bergen, Essex, Middlesex, Somerset, and Burlington Counties alone there were almost two thousand instances of destruction attributable to the enemy, each case representing an average loss of more than a hundred pounds in specie. Middlesex was the chief victim, with 655 claims totaling over eighty thousand pounds. The depredations of the American soldiery were less numerous, although they were guilty of destroying the property of hundreds of individuals, particularly in Bergen and Morris.[55] Houses, churches, schools, stores, wharves, and

[55] A law of December 20, 1781, provided for the appointment of appraisers in each county to receive inventories of damages inflicted by both British and American troops. Partial records of this survey are contained in six bound volumes in the New Jersey State Library. Five volumes (Damages by British, 1776-1782) deal with Burlington, Bergen, Essex, Somerset, and Middlesex Counties; the sixth (Damages by Americans, 1776-1782) covers Bergen, Burlington, Somerset, Morris, and Hunterdon Counties. Carefully itemized lists accompany each claim. No compensation was ever granted to the claimants.

ships were ruined or pillaged, as were also cattle, libraries, crops, slaves, and household goods. Much of the energy of the state in the postwar years would have to be devoted to the plain task of rebuilding its physical plant.

The structure of society, too, had not gone unscathed. The flight of hundreds of loyalists, many of them members of the colonial aristocracy by virtue of their official positions, their English connections, or their landed wealth, had weakened the class to which they had belonged. The breaking-up of numerous large forfeited estates had a similar effect. The departure of the old leaders created opportunities for new men to take their places, men like William Paterson, Abraham Clark, and John Neilson. Society became more dynamic as sudden reversals of economic and political fortunes in the course of the war exalted some and humbled others. The spirit of the times created restiveness among the common people; small farmers, tenants, and mechanics were less disposed than formerly to accept their allotted subordinate position. Republican ideology, given currency by whig propagandists, Fourth of July orators, and anonymous newspaper essayists, awakened many to the vision of a better order of things.

Religious and cultural agencies emerged into the days of peace to find grave problems confronting them. Many congregations had lost their meetinghouses, their ministers, and a part of their membership. Divisions within and between denominations had been heightened by conflicting views on the dominant question of independence. Too, the years of strife, with their attendant psychology of instability, had fostered moral and theological laxity. The altered political situation seemed to make necessary drastic revisions in the forms of ecclesiastical organization. Educational agencies were also disrupted at the very time when republicanism was to place increased emphasis on their services. Precious libraries had been consumed in flames or pillaged, and a considerable body of cultured men and women had been driven out of the state. New ideas, the products of wartime experiences and of a widespread absorption in philosophical reflections, challenged familiar concepts and broadened intellectual horizons.

In no field, however, did the war produce greater dislocations than in the economic sphere. To the abnormal strains that resulted from the efforts to supply and finance the military machine were added the difficulties incident to the breakdown of established channels of trade. Certain enterprises had been artificially stimulated, a few had been curtailed. When the illicit and irregular commerce with the enemy came to an abrupt end with the peace, it was immediately apparent to discerning merchants that new barriers separated them from their customary markets. The landed interest, as represented by the proprietary boards of East and West Jersey, had suffered from the loyalism of several of its members, from confiscations, and from trespassers, and it was to be troubled as well by rebellious tenants, complications over clouded titles, and the competition of new lands in the West. Small farmers, who had exchanged their products for certificates of dubious value and paid heavier taxes than they had ever known, soon complained of their distress. Public creditors had abundant reasons for concern as they contemplated the probable fate of their piles of securities, worth but a part of their face amounts. All classes of people were vitally affected by the total derangement of the currency. In fact, no other topic aroused so much popular discussion or occasioned so much legislative activity as did the money question. It was the paramount economic problem.

New Jersey emerged from the war with an inherited set of political institutions that had been little altered in the transition from colonialism to independence. But although old forms were retained, the character of the government had been changed fundamentally by the removal of the restraining influence of British authority. The representatives of the people, in brief, were supreme. During the war, while domestic questions were of necessity subordinated to problems of defense, the nature of the new constitution was scarcely a subject of inquiry or controversy. The true testing period lay in the future. It remained to be determined whether unfettered legislative power was consonant with republicanism, whether the concept of limited government was to be abandoned or restored.

Nor did the structure of politics escape the impact of the Revolution. There was no distinct triumph of class or section, as was the case in many colonies, nor was there a clear-cut division of opposing forces into groups which can be described by the conventional labels "radical" or "conservative." [56] But the overweening prestige of the landed proprietors and others who had enjoyed executive favor was immediately lowered, and political instability brought new men to positions of leadership. These men were not drawn from the lowest ranks of society and were not extremists in their political and economic thinking. They were, however, sympathetic to republican ideology. Because of the increase in the number of elective officers and in the frequency of elections, and because of the greatly enlarged powers of the legislature, the franchise took on added significance. The ballot became a more direct and more potent instrument of change than it had been formerly, and it promised to give added weight to the influence of the whole people at the expense of the aristocratic few.

The war years had not been free from political dissension. On the contrary, there had been formidable obstacles to internal unity. A large segment of the population had remained cool toward independence and had seriously contested whig control of the government. The traditional cleavage between

[56] Merrill Jensen, *The Articles of Confederation* (Madison, 1940). Jensen gives an excellent discussion of political divisions within most of the states, but he entirely neglects New Jersey.

East Jersey and West Jersey persisted and grew even wider. Factionalism on the county level added zest to the competition for offices. Despite these bases of division, no formal party organizations had developed. The political scene was still confused and unpredictable at the arrival of peace.

II

The Plight of the Loyalists

****

THE termination of the war with England also brought to a decisive conclusion the internecine strife between whigs and tories that characterized the American Revolution. Victory for the cause of independence meant defeat for those who had openly or covertly opposed the break with the mother country. One of the immediate problems New Jersey faced, therefore, as it hailed the arrival of peace, was to determine what policies should be adopted toward those present and former citizens who had refused to participate in rebellion. Should such individuals be permitted to resume their former positions in society? What disposition should be made of the forfeited estates of avowed loyalists? The future political and civil status of the tories, too, was in doubt. It was to be more than a decade before these issues were fully resolved, and in the meantime the embers of internal dissension continued to smolder.

HOSTILITY AND HOSPITALITY

For many who had chosen to stand by their king, peace brought financial ruin and the dreary prospect of beginning life anew in some strange land. The number of men in New Jersey who were active in opposing the patriot cause cannot be ascertained with exactitude, but it certainly exceeded one thousand and may have been as high as five thousand. All segments of society were represented in this group—farmers, tailors, bakers, and weavers as well as lawyers, doctors, clergymen, and land magnates. They were principally from those sections of the state that had been most subjected to occupation by British troops. Most of them could be distinguished from their former neighbors only by the accident of their choice of the royal side; few had ever seen England. In the main those who openly espoused the loyalist cause by taking refuge in New York never returned to New Jersey but instead went to Canada at the conclusion of the war.[1] William Peartree Smith unsympathetically depicted their plight in doggerel verse:

> The Conscious Tory hangs his humbled Head,
> Or sneaks to Scotia with his axe and spade;
> Reluctant—there to weep 'mid Fogs or Frost—
> His Friends, his Family, his Country lost.
> There toils and sweats beneath inclement skies,
> Envies the once damn'd Rebel—curses George and dies.[2]

For years after the war had ended, enmity toward certain classes of tories persisted. With the depredations of the loyalist irregulars and the refuge bands still fresh in their memories, many people bitterly opposed the return to the state

[1] The most detailed survey of New Jersey loyalists is in E. A. Jones, *The Loyalists of New Jersey* ... (Newark, 1927). See also A. V. D. Honeyman, "Concerning the New Jersey Loyalists in the Revolution," *PNJHS*, LI (1933), pp. 117-33 and C. C. Vermeule, "The Active Loyalists of New Jersey," *PNJHS*, LII (1934), pp. 87-95. About four hundred New Jersey loyalists presented claims for their losses to the British government after the war, one-half of which were allowed. The largest payment was made to Daniel Coxe of Trenton, a distinguished lawyer and landowner, who received £9,997 on a claim for £41,305.

[2] Smith to Elias Boudinot, Apr., 1783, *PNJHS*, IV (1849), p. 122.

of those who had pillaged and murdered their neighbors in disregard of the rules of war. The publication of the provisional peace treaty provoked a storm of anti-tory sentiment. Articles Five and Six, which recommended that British adherents be permitted to remain in the states for twelve months in order to attempt to regain their forfeited property, aroused the particular hostility of ardent patriots. At the celebrations that heralded the end of hostilities, scathing denunciations of the banished renegades were mingled with toasts to liberty. Dire consequences were predicted for any who might be so foolhardy as to insist on the rights granted to them by the treaty. The recommendations of the Continental Congress, it was made plain, would not be heeded.[3] Several petitions were sent to the legislature praying that no tories should be allowed to return to their former houses. It was as "impossible for Fire and Water to unite, as to form an intimate Coalition between the Friends of freedom and the Vessels of slavery," read one impassioned plea. Another pointed out that even a temporary return of those who had been instrumental in multiplying the horrors of the late war "would involve the State in Feuds and Contentions," which could only terminate in bloodshed. Freedom and independence should not be shared with traitors.[4]

These violent outbursts, it should be noted, were directed not against tories in general but only against that group which had actively aided the enemy. Fear that such men might attempt to regain property that had fallen into the hands of patriots undoubtedly gave a strong impetus to the hate campaign. Certainly the greatest animosity was manifested in sections where confiscations had been most numerous. Only in rare instances, however, did the objectionable refugees

---

[3] *New Jersey Gazette,* Apr. 9, 16, 23, 1783.
[4] Memorial of freeholders of Bergen, May 3, 1783, Miscellaneous Manuscripts, NJSL; Petition of inhabitants of Essex, May 3, 1783, Loose Manuscripts, NJSL; *Votes and Proceedings,* 7-2, pp. 111-16.

attempt to resume their residence in the state. When they did, they were harshly treated by associations of fierce whigs, who insulted, abused, flogged, and tarred and feathered them, and even threatened them with the gallows. In Woodbridge, the local militia under General Nathaniel Heard were a law unto themselves in such matters, as were Forman's "Retaliators" in Monmouth.[5] "The Spirit of the People in this County is high"; observed William Paterson, "they seem determined not to suffer any of the Refugees to return & live among them—a few of them came over but they were immediately hunted back."[6] The climate of hatred was not short-lived. In 1786 a loyalist lady who contemplated legal action to regain her lost estate was advised by her counsel to "wait till the passions of the People ... [were] more cool." Even as late as 1787 the legislature was petitioned to banish from the state all men who had served with the British during the war. Periodic diatribes in the press evidenced continuing bitterness.[7]

On the other hand, tories who had played merely a passive role in the conflict were, in general, well treated. One of them, Frederick Smythe, former chief justice of the colony, took the precaution of obtaining special passes from the president of Pennsylvania, the governor of New Jersey, and the president of the Continental Congress before venturing on a business trip from New York to Philadelphia in September, 1783. He had been warned that he might expect trouble in crossing New Jersey. To his surprise, he made the journey

[5] Jones, *Loyalists*, pp. 108-13, 179-81; *Political Intelligencer*, June 22, July 13, 1784; Ellis Barron and Thomas Crowell, Jr. to William Livingston, June 15, 1784, Livingston Papers, MHS. Of 419 loyalists listed by Jones, scarcely a handful of those who might be described as "active" sought to return to the state.

[6] Paterson to Tom Paterson, May 12, 1783, Paterson Papers (Bancroft Transcripts), NYPL.

[7] Mary Poynton to Elias Boudinot, Apr. 21, 1786, Boudinot Papers, II, HSP; *Votes and Proceedings*, 11-2, p. 120; *Political Intelligencer*, Aug. 3, Oct. 19, Nov. 9, 1784, Sept. 14, 28, 1785.

without incident. "—either you have no Lyons in Jersey or they were all asleep," he wrote to a friend after he had reached his destination. "I never saw kinder looks, or experienced more civility from all who met me." Thomas Bradbury Chandler, Episcopal rector in Elizabeth Town before the Revolution, returned to the state from England in 1785 and was treated everywhere with respect. Andrew Bell, Dr. John Lawrence, and John Hinchman were others who were welcomed back. James Parker and Walter Rutherfurd, both of whom had been fined and imprisoned for their refusal to take the prescribed oath of abjuration and allegiance, very soon resumed their accustomed positions of influence in public affairs.[8]

Inoffensive tories were not only allowed to come back to New Jersey, they were even encouraged to do so. A well-planned campaign to foster their readmittance was launched in 1784. Its chief sponsors were John Rutherfurd, his loyalist father, and James Parker. As early as May, 1783, Rutherfurd had proposed that wealthy tory merchants should be invited to the state in order to contribute to the development of its commercial possibilities. Pointing out that such a policy had already been adopted by Connecticut, he urged his fellow citizens to seize the opportunity that was presented to them by passing an act of general amnesty.[9] For almost a year there was no further mention of the amnesty proposal. Then in April, 1784, there suddenly appeared in the New Brunswick *Political Intelligencer* a series of letters—probably

[8] Chandler to Rev. Dr. Maurice, Secretary of the Society for the Propagation of the Gospel, Oct. 3, 1785, SPG transcript in possession of Dr. Walter H. Stowe, New Brunswick, N. J.; Jones, *Loyalists*, pp. 25-26, 97-98, 125; Charles W. Parker, "Shipley—The Country Seat of a Jersey Loyalist," *PNJHS*, NS, XVI (1931).

[9] "Letters from John Rutherfurd to a member of the Assembly, May 16, 17, 1783," *PNJHS*, 2nd Ser., I (1867), pp. 177-82; "Mercator," *New Jersey Gazette*, June 4, 1783. Rutherfurd's letter was submitted to James Parker for his approval before it was published.

inspired by Rutherfurd and Parker—in which the project was enthusiastically revived.

Men of capital and talent were eager to settle in the state and bring about an end to its economic dependence on New York and Philadelphia, argued "Candidus." Christian sentiments, he added, dictated that erring expatriates should be forgiven. Sheppard Kollock and Shelly Arnett announced that their paper would welcome any essays that might "soften the minds of the citizens of America toward their unhappy brethren." A petition advocating hospitality toward those who were driven from other states was circulated in Middlesex and was signed by many leading men.[10] The merchants of the northern section of the state, who organized a committee for the promotion of trade, incorporated the plan in a comprehensive scheme of commercial expansion which they evolved.[11] On August 9, 1784, the mercantile group held a convention in New Brunswick and formally recommended a series of measures to the legislature, which was then meeting there. Among other things, they urged that two free ports should be established, in which citizenship should be granted to all except those who had been guilty of "licentious cruelty" in the late war. "If by the liberality of these terms a few men who have formerly entertained inimical wishes and intentions towards us, should gain admission," read their humble petition, "we doubt not your honor and spirit will remember that conquerors only can forgive . . ."[12] The free-port proposal was

[10] *Political Intelligencer*, Apr. 6, 13, 21, 1784.

[11] Robert Morris to John Rutherfurd, May 23, 1784, Morris to James Parker, John Neilson, and the committee for promotion of trade, Aug. 6, 1784, Robert Morris Papers, RUL. Morris was the counsel for the committee. For a discussion of the commercial projects favored by this group, see below, pp. 116-19.

[12] Petition of the deputies of the County of Morris, and towns of Elizabeth Town, Woodbridge, Perth Amboy, Piscataway, New Brunswick, Princeton, Trenton, and Lamberton, convened at New Brunswick, August 9, 1784, Loose Manuscripts, NJSL; *New Jersey Gazette*, Nov. 22, 1784. The chairman of the convention was the loyalist James Parker, who signed the petition.

adopted by the legislature with a minimum of opposition, and Perth Amboy and Burlington were named as the towns that were to be accorded special privileges. Any person who resided in either place for one month and engaged in trade was, after taking an oath of allegiance, to be given citizenship in the city. Only those who had been "guilty of licentious Cruelties in Plundering or Murder, contrary to the Usages of civilized Nations" were barred.[13] The effect of this law was negligible, for few if any tories accepted the proffered hand of friendship.

The partial act of amnesty was extremely limited in its application, but it reflected the mild attitude of the business community in particular and of the people in general toward former enemy adherents. The return of those who had worked actively against independence as well as of those who hoped to regain their forfeited property was firmly, and even violently, opposed. At the same time, little overt hostility was manifested toward loyalists who had played merely a passive role in the conflict.

THE SPOILS OF WAR

There was little inducement for many loyalists to return to their former homes, even had they been free to do so, for their property in most cases had long since been confiscated. The personal estates of those who joined the British were subject to forfeiture as early as August 1, 1777. A second law in April, 1778, established a procedure for determining who were offenders against the state and ordered that the personalty of such men be sold by three commissioners appointed for each county. These commissioners also leased the real estates of disloyal persons and collected any debts that were owed to them. In December of the same year the final

---

[13] *Votes and Proceedings*, 8-2, pp. 103-33; *Journal of the Proceedings of the Legislative-Council of the State of New-Jersey, Eighth Session, Second Sitting*, p. 18 (hereafter cited as *Journal of Council*, 8-2). *Acts of the Eighth General Assembly of the State of New Jersey, Second Sitting*, Act of Aug. 28, 1784 (hereafter cited as *Session Laws*, 8-2).

step in the process of confiscation was taken when it was decreed that "the Lands, Tenements, Hereditaments and Real Estates" of all convicted tories should be sold.[14] From this time until June, 1781, when the sales were temporarily suspended, hundreds of parcels of land were disposed of at public vendue.

In two and a half years the state realized almost £1,390,000 in continental currency from this fruitful source of revenue. More than half of the total came from Middlesex, Hunterdon, and Essex Counties; relatively small amounts were derived from that part of the state which lay south of Trenton.[15] The sales, it should be noted, took place during the period when the continental currency was depreciating

[14] Wilson, *Acts*, Act of July 5, 1777, Appendix IV, Act of April 18, 1778, pp. 43-52, Act of Dec. 11, 1778, pp. 67-75. In the case of a person suspected of disloyalty, the justice of the peace summoned a jury to hear the evidence furnished by the commissioners. If the jurors found the offender guilty, they certified this fact to the justice in the form of an inquisition. This inquisition was advertised and then was presented by the justice to the Inferior Court of Common Pleas, and the accused was given a final opportunity to contest the judgment. If the inquisition was not traversed, the court issued a writ to the commissioners directing the sale of the property. Provision was made for the payment by the state from the proceeds of the sale of any demands existing against the estate.

[15] These and subsequent figures on the amounts raised through the sale of confiscated estates were compiled from the confused reports made by the treasurer of the state to the legislature and printed in the *Votes and Proceedings*. They are probably not wholly accurate, but they furnish the only source available. The receipts reported by counties for the period December, 1778, to June, 1781, (omitting shillings and pence) were:

Middlesex .... £	451,929	Morris	62,380
Hunterdon ...	210,482	Gloucester ...	57,165
Essex	122,499	Salem	47,470
Monmouth ...	115,405	Burlington ...	47,413
Somerset	97,708	Cumberland ..	8,968
Bergen	96,768	Cape May	0
Sussex	71,123	Total	£1,388,910
			continental

rapidly from eight to one for specie to one hundred seventy-five to one. Consequently, the real return to the state in terms of hard money was but a small fraction—possibly 2 per cent—of the apparent return.[16] The judgment of a shrewd contemporary observer was correct when he stated that the confiscated property was "fooled away and turned to small account." It was doubtless a belated recognition of this fact that brought about the suspension of sales in June, 1781.[17]

With the arrival of peace, the question of what should be done with estates that still remained unsold became a lively topic of discussion. Considerable controversy centered around those articles of the treaty which made it incumbent on the Continental Congress to recommend to the states that they revise their confiscation laws and restore the property of loyalists who had not actually borne arms. The usually mild Dutch farmers of Bergen were appalled at this proposal, and immediately drafted a strongly worded memorial to the legislature on the subject. They implored their representatives not to "disgust their best friends by giving away the property of the State to miscreants who for a series of years have been preying on its vitals and fattening on its spoils." No leniency should be granted to "Traitors, Felons, Robbers, and

[16] "Horatius," 13, William Paterson Essays, RUL. Paterson estimated the loss to the state because of currency depreciation at over $300,000.

[17] John Rutherfurd, "Notes on the State of New Jersey," *PNJHS*, 2nd Ser., I, (1869), p. 82; Wilson, *Acts*, Act of June 26, 1781, p. 211. The peculations of the county commissioners, who made a practice of delaying their returns even beyond the allotted three-month period in order to take advantage of the depreciation of the currency, doubtless influenced the legislature in its decision. When in December, 1781, the commissioners were replaced by a single agent in each county, many of them were seriously delinquent in their accounts. Wilson, *Acts*, Act of Dec. 20, 1781, pp. 231-36. Governor Livingston condemned "the commissionaries for forfeited estates, who have plundered us of thousands by trading with the money, or converting it into real estate, and afterwards paying us at a great depreciation." Theodore Sedgwick, *A Memoir of the Life of William Livingston* (New York, 1833), pp. 392-93.

Murderers."[18] Loyal whigs did not wish to be denied the opportunity of exchanging their depreciated paper for good land. Speculators were eager to engage in a field of enterprise that promised large returns.[19] A principal item on the agenda of the legislature that met in October, 1783, therefore, was a bill to resume the sales of forfeited property. Passage of the measure was delayed for nearly a month while the Assembly and Council wrangled over the important matter of what should be accepted in payment. The lower house won out when the law, as finally enacted on December 16, specified that only state securities and specie would be accepted.[20]

Soon lengthy lists of properties were advertised for sale in the local newspapers. In Bergen alone the estates of 114 loyalists were placed on the auction block. In Sussex the discriminating bidder could choose among 121 tracts, including the extensive proprietorial holdings of Daniel Coxe, John Tabor-Kempe, Oliver Delancy, and Henry Cuyler. But scarcely had the vendues begun, when they were halted—"on account of numerous Frauds"—in August, 1784. Two years later they were resumed and were still proceeding when New Jersey entered the national period.[21] In the years from 1783

[18] Memorial of freeholders of Bergen to the legislature, May 3, 1783, Miscellaneous Manuscripts, NJSL. Similar sentiments were expressed in a petition of the same date from Essex. Petition of inhabitants of Essex, May 3, 1783, Loose Manuscripts, NJSL. In June the three Assemblymen from Monmouth felt called upon to issue a public denial of a rumor that they had introduced a bill to restore to tories their estates. *New Jersey Gazette*, June 25, 1783.

[19] Moore Furman to Col. John Neilson, Apr. 2, 1783; Neilson to Furman, Apr. 3, 1783, Neilson Papers, F 187, RUL.

[20] *Votes and Proceedings*, 8-1, pp. 33-72; *Journal of Council*, 8-1, pp. 17-25; Wilson, *Acts*, pp. 354-56. The Council, and a minority in the Assembly, wanted to make continental loan office certificates acceptable in payment for the lands. The Assembly favored what was undoubtedly the more popular course of receiving only state obligations, among which were the widely held officers' and soldiers' depreciation notes, militia notes, contractors certificates, and surplus certificates.

[21] *Political Intelligencer*, Feb. 24, Mar. 30, July 20, 1784; *New Jersey Gazette*, July 19, 1784; *Session Laws*, 8-2, Act of Aug. 9, 1784; *ibid.*, 10-3, Act of June 1, 1786.

to 1789, the sales yielded over £117,327, principally in state obligations of various kinds with a real value that was about 15 per cent of their nominal value.[22] Altogether the estates of at least five hundred active loyalists were confiscated and disposed of by New Jersey in the decade after 1778.[23] These properties were rich spoils of war for those who had given their support to independence. They also constituted a strong and enduring barrier to reconciliation between those who had chosen to give their allegiance to opposite causes in the recent conflict.

WHIGS AND TORIES

The issue of independence created a political cleavage within the state and gave rise to animosities that were to survive for more than a decade after the Revolution. Once the final tie with England had been severed, men were compelled to make a choice of sides, and the exigencies of the times required that only those who were willing to support the revolutionary cause should be permitted to enjoy full political freedom. As early as February, 1776, the franchise had been restricted to men who had signed the "Association." [24] After

[22] Receipts by counties were as follows:

Bergen	£ 43,557	Cape May	1,520
Middlesex	27,076	Burlington	1,396
Sussex	13,799	Morris	1,202
Monmouth	11,159	Gloucester	207
Essex	9,798	Cumberland	0
Hunterdon	4,785	Salem	0
Somerset	2,828	Total	£117,327
		(notes and certificates)	

[23] This conservative estimate is made on the basis of a study of newspaper advertisements of sales and of the reports of the state treasurer. See also "List of Estates Forfeited in Monmouth County, 1779-1784," *PNJHS*, NS, X (1925), pp. 318-21; Report by Samuel Forman on confiscated estates in Monmouth, 1779, Vault Manuscripts, NJSL; William H. Benedict, "Middlesex Forfeited Estates, 1778-1779," *PNJHS*, NS, XI (1926), pp, 396-97.

[24] *Minutes of the Provincial Congress and of the Council of Safety of the State of New Jersey* (Trenton, 1879), p. 430.

1777, all voters were obliged to take an oath of abjuration and allegiance, and persons who had joined or aided the enemy were barred from holding any office. Despite these legal precautions, the whigs were frequently hard pressed to maintain control, so numerous and active were the British sympathizers.

On occasion the patriots were forced to resort to outright electoral corruption to protect their interest. A convention of whigs meeting in Bergen County in 1782 petitioned the legislature to do away with the secret ballot on the ground that secrecy deprived them "of knowing the Necessity of Adjourning the Election, for the better purpose of guarding against the intrigues of the Disaffected." It was their proposal that all voting should be *viva voce;* otherwise, they explained, the government would "soon be Corrupted with that Political Pollution Which might in time prove the utter Ruin of the true Sons of Freedom." [25] This recommendation was promptly incorporated in a new election law, and it was hoped that with open voting the legislature might be preserved "pure and altogether uncontaminated with the least Blemish of Toryism or Anti-Republican Principles, the eternal pest of all free Governments." [26] The Whig Societies, the "Retaliators," and similar organizations frequently took drastic action to insure that true whigs alone should vote. Even the militia was employed to guard the polls against the disaffected.[27] The results were disappointing. "I have seen

[25] Petition of joint committee of the townships and precincts of New Jersey convened at Hoppers Town, Aug. 31, 1782, Loose Manuscripts, NJSL.

[26] *Session Laws,* 6-3, Act of Sept. 27, 1782. This law was repealed June 19, 1783.

[27] *New Jersey Gazette,* Jan. 17, 31, Mar. 14, 28, May 6, Oct. 31, 1781; Articles of Association of Inhabitants of Monmouth . . ., photostatic copy in Jersey Box, Misc., NYPL; *New Jersey Gazette,* Jan. 27, 1782; Petition of inhabitants of Burlington County, Oct. 25, 1783, AM Papers, NJSL; "Blawenburgh and Harlingen Records," *Somerset County Historical Quarterly,* IV (1915), pp. 119-20.

tories members of Congress," declared Governor Livingston, "judges upon tribunals, tories representatives in our Legislative councils, tories members of our Assemblies..." [28]

The return of peace did not bring about a removal of the disabilities that had been imposed on tories. On the contrary, the legislature was urged in the strongest terms to deny political freedom to "traitors." "These persons have made their election," protested one group of whigs, "...they ought not to participate, with us, [in] the enjoyment of that Freedom and Independence which they have endeavoured to destroy..." [29] "[They] will endeavour artfully to undermine our Establishment," warned the freeholders of Bergen, "and to intimidate our builders from proceeding in their work, untill they have wriggled themselves into the seat of government, when they may have an opportunity of subverting it." [30] The first postwar election law reflected these sentiments. Disqualified from holding any office and from voting in state elections were all those who had voluntarily taken refuge with the enemy, who had been adjudged guilty of treason, who had been fined or imprisoned for refusing to take the oath of abjuration and allegiance, or who had lost their estates through confiscation. In addition, all voters were required to take the prescribed loyalty oath if they were challenged by the election officials. [31] Thus were old bases of division perpetuated.

It soon became apparent that the whigs could not effectively prevent their erstwhile enemies from participating

[28] Sedgwick, *Memoir*, p. 393. See also Joseph Hugg to Livingston, Dec. 4, 1782, William Livingston Transcripts, NJSL.

[29] Petition of inhabitants of Essex, May 3, 1783, Loose Manuscripts, NJSL.

[30] Memorial of freeholders of Bergen, May 3, 1783, Manuscript Collection, NJSL. See also Lundin, *Cockpit*, p. 452.

[31] *Session Laws*, 8-1, Act of Dec. 16, 1783. The loophole in this law was the provision that voters must take the oath only if challenged. Negligent or partial election officials could—and did—permit avowed tories to vote.

in the government. Within a year after the peace treaty had been signed, for example, Robert Morris complained bitterly that a coroner in Bergen had placed on a jury in a suit involving a British subject twelve men who had never before taken the oath of allegiance.[32] In Burlington County in 1784 the "disaffected" overthrew the rebel party and sent a tory delegation to the legislature. They had been prevented from achieving victory the preceding year only because the whigs had called on the militia companies to control the polls.[33] Two of the legislators from Gloucester and one from Hunterdon were regarded with suspicion by ardent patriots.[34] By 1785 early supporters of the Revolution were decrying the fact that the tories and their Quaker allies were growing daily in political strength and that many former rebels were siding with them. "Depend upon it, my countrymen," warned "A Soldier," "these friends who are so base as to seek an asylum in that government which they have invoked heaven and earth to annihilate, are only waiting an opportunity to sting you imperceptibly to the heart." [35] There seemed to be some basis for such apprehension when Burlington and Perth Amboy were opened to refugees and when James Parker, an avowed loyalist, was elected mayor of the latter city by the legislature. Many die-hard Sons of Liberty found such actions extremely difficult to accept.[36]

But as the memories of the war grew dim and as new issues

[32] Robert Morris to Judge Benson, Sept. 24, 1784, Robert Morris Papers, RUL.

[33] William Livingston to Mrs. Livingston, Oct. 30, 1784, Livingston Papers, MHS; Petition of inhabitants of Burlington [Nov., 1784], AM Papers, NJSL; Petition of inhabitants of Burlington, Oct. 25, 1783. See below, pp. 91-3.

[34] William Livingston to Mrs. Livingston, Oct. 30, 1784, Livingston Papers, MHS; *New Jersey Gazette*, Oct. 2, 1782, Apr. 6, 13, 20, 26, 1784.

[35] *Political Intelligencer*, Feb. 1, Sept. 28, 1785; *New Jersey Gazette*, Oct. 10, 1785.

[36] "An Old Citizen," *New Jersey Gazette*, Oct. 11, 1784.

unconnected with independence emerged, the whig–tory cleavage became less and less significant. By 1788 sentiment within the state had undergone sufficient alteration to make possible the repeal of the restrictions that had been laid on the dissident loyalists. In November of that year a new election law swept away the oath requirement as well as the limitations on office-holding.[37] Officially, at least, political reconciliation had been accomplished, although tested whigs continued to dominate the councils of state as they had done since the commencement of the Revolution.

Within a relatively short span of years, and with a minimum of disorder, the barriers that had separated whigs and tories were broken down. Although there was to be no forgiveness for those who sought to recover their confiscated properties, there was no insurmountable antipathy displayed toward the large segment of the population that had hesitated to take the road that led to independence.

[37] *Session Laws*, 13-1, Act of Nov. 29, 1788. At the same time, Perth Amboy and Burlington, both of which had been conspicuous centers of toryism, were designated as the alternate state capitals.

III

Social and Cultural Reconstruction

★★★

THE Revolution was not accompanied by cataclysmic changes in the structure of society, but the familiar order was temporarily disarranged by the destruction and instability incident to the war. With the return of peace, the citizens of New Jersey faced the unspectacular task of rebuilding damaged social and cultural institutions at the same time that pressing economic and political concerns commanded a large share of public attention. Outside the sphere of governmental action, individuals in their private capacities energetically strove to reconstruct their religious, educational, fraternal, and professional organizations and to bring them into adjustment with the new conditions created by independence. As a result of their endeavors, a period of ferment and change became one of growth and accomplishment.

THE FABRIC OF SOCIETY

Reconstruction was in many ways complicated by the heterogeneity of the population of the state. The one hundred and thirty-five thousand white inhabitants in 1783 were a conglomeration of national and religious groups. Less than half were English in origin, and many of these had not come directly from across the sea but from New England; the characteristics they brought with them marked them as a group within the state. The Dutch, who comprised over one-sixth of the population, were the second most numerous stock. Most of them had moved from New York to settle in the valleys of the Raritan, the Hackensack, and the Passaic. Predominantly agriculturalists, they clung to their native speech and customs, gave indifferent support to their Reformed religion, and generally displayed little concern with political affairs. Close behind them in numbers were the Scotch and Scotch-Irish, whose vigorous Presbyterianism and conspicuous rebelliousness gave them an influence out of all proportion to their size. Some were descendants of the earliest settlers in East Jersey, but most were latecomers and were to be found principally on the poorer lands in the north central part of the state. The Germans, who in the main were also recent arrivals, constituted about one-tenth of the citizenry. Their principal strength was in the two northwestern counties of Hunterdon and Sussex, but they were represented as well among the iron miners in Morris and the glass workers in Salem. Esteemed for their industry and for their excellent agricultural methods, their chief interests were encompassed within the boundaries of their farms. Along the tributaries of the lower Delaware the Swedes had flourished and multiplied despite the failure of their nation's brief colonizing venture in the region. Together with the scattered French and Irish, they made up the tenth of the white population represented by minor stocks. Finally, there were some ten thousand Negroes, four-fifths of whom were slaves. They were confined chiefly to the northern half of the state and were heaviest in the Dutch counties of Bergen and Somerset.[1] People of the

[1] "Report of Committee on Linguistic and National Stocks in the Population of the United States," *Annual Report of the American His-*

same national background tended to settle together and so preserve the manners of their native country, but there was a considerable admixture in many counties, particularly in East Jersey.

New Jersey was one of the few states that had no frontier within its borders. Except for the unattractive region of the barren and sandy coastal plain, there was no area still unsettled. Approximately half of the people lived in the Delaware watershed, most of the remainder along the streams that flowed into the Newark and Raritan bays. Although there was no marked concentration within any one section, the route across the state from New York to Philadelphia was already somewhat more densely settled than any other portion. In this narrow corridor were located the principal towns of Newark, Elizabeth Town, Perth Amboy, New Brunswick, Trenton, and Burlington, no one of which contained over fifteen hundred inhabitants.[2] Here, too, were the leading churches, schools, libraries, newspapers, and other evidences of cultural development.

The economic basis of society was diversified agriculture. The average farmer worked his own holdings of under two hundred acres, aided by his family and perhaps by occasional hired men or a slave. Adhering in the main to the traditional four-field system, he did not specialize in the growing of one "cash crop"; instead he raised a variety of grains and also tended an orchard, a flock of sheep, a few head of cattle, some pigs, and a couple of horses. Self-sufficiency was a prime consideration. Much that was produced on the farm was con-

---

torical Association, 1931, I, *passim*; Jedidiah Morse, *The American Geography* (Elizabeth Town, 1789), pp. 286-92; Rutherfurd, "Notes," pp. 85-88; Witherspoon, *Works*, IX, p. 205. New Jersey had a lower percentage of English than any state except Pennsylvania, a higher proportion of Dutch than any state save New York. "Report of Committee ... National Stocks," pp. 124-25.

[2] List of Ratables, November 5, 1784, *Votes and Proceedings*, 9-1, p. 33; Morse, *Geography*, pp. 296-97.

sumed there or bartered within the neighborhood, but a portion went to market in exchange for a few necessities and for money with which to pay taxes and discharge debts. Convenient access to the centers of trade in Philadelphia and New York lifted the simple economy above the level of bare subsistence agriculture. Extremes of wealth or poverty were rare, for vast estates could seldom be made to yield a profit, and cheap land could be obtained readily by an industrious man. Accordingly, there was a fair degree of economic democracy.[3]

Another factor that had a deep influence on the social and cultural life of the state was the historic cleavage between East and West Jersey. Dating back more than a century to the division of the province between Sir George Carteret and the Quakers who had purchased the territory originally granted to Lord John Berkeley, the distinctive characteristics that marked each section had been perpetuated by pronounced differences in religion, in land systems, and in the national origins of the inhabitants. Moreover, the vestiges of separate governments lingered into the revolutionary era. West Jersey, with its dominant Quaker strain, its relatively homogeneous population, and its pronounced ruralness gave a greater appearance of stability than did East Jersey. The disunity of the state was further heightened by the attraction exerted on it by New York on the east and Philadelphia on the west. So persistent and real was the line that separated the two sections that it gave to the state a decidedly dual nature.[4]

[3] Rutherfurd, "Notes," pp. 81-87; Morse, *Geography*, pp. 287-89; Witherspoon, *Works*, IX, p. 202; Account Book of Robert Johnson of Salem, 1782-1790, RUL.

[4] Donald L. Kemmerer, *Path to Freedom* (Princeton, 1940), *passim*; Morse, *Geography*, p. 292. "The people of West-Jersey trade to Philadelphia," wrote Morse, "and of course imitate their fashions, and imbibe their manners. The inhabitants of East Jersey trade to New York, and regulate their fashions and manners according to those of New York."

The diversity of the people was accurately reflected in the variety of their religious beliefs. Most of them gave their allegiance to one of five major denominations—the Presbyterian, the Quaker, the Dutch Reformed, the Baptist, or the Anglican—and smaller numbers espoused the German Reformed, Lutheran, Swedish Lutheran, Moravian, and Methodist faiths. There was no organized Roman Catholic church. In general, tolerance and harmony maintained among the various Protestant groups, all of whom enjoyed complete liberty of conscience as well as full political rights. "We never hear of Disputes, Competitions or Jealousies among them," remarked one observer, and if he excepted the antagonism which sometimes developed between Quakers and Presbyterians and minor instances of hostility toward the struggling Methodists, his statement may be regarded as accurate.[5] Doubtless a large segment of the population attended no church, for not only were there areas where no facilities had as yet been provided to care for the spiritual needs of the inhabitants, but there were also certain national stocks, the Germans, for example, whose religious bodies were unable to furnish enough ministers to serve in the New World. The Swedish pastor, Nicholas Collin, ministered to men and women in Gloucester and Salem, to whom a yearly visit from a man of the cloth was a rarity. Similarly, the Reverend Uzal Ogden, Anglican missionary in Sussex, was appalled by the almost total lack of churches in that populous county.[6]

[5] Rutherfurd, "Notes," p. 88; Morse, *Geography*, pp. 292-93; William Livingston to Mathew Carey, Nov. 26, 1788, Livingston Papers, MHS.

[6] [Nicholas Collin] *The Journal and Biography of Nicholas Collin, 1746-1831*, translated by Amandus Johnson (Philadelphia, 1936), *passim*; Rev. Uzal Ogden to the Secretary of the Society for the Propagation of the Gospel, July 8, 1771, *PNJHS*, IV (1849), pp. 152-53; Nelson R. Burr, *Education in New Jersey, 1630-1871* (Princeton, 1942), pp. 92-94, 103. There were probably three times as many taverns in the state in 1784 as there were churches.

THE PROGRESS OF RELIGIOUS RECOVERY

As the war drew to a close, all denominations faced the task of putting their deranged affairs in order and of carrying forward their important work. Some sects had suffered heavier losses than others in the course of the conflict, but there were certain problems that were common to all. One of these was the general moral laxity and religious apathy that followed in the wake of a period during which spiritual concerns had of necessity been subordinated to secular interests. The destruction of church buildings, the departure of ministers into the army or into exile, and the disruption of congregations over the issue of independence all had telling effects on religious establishments, as did the dissemination of new doctrines, critical or revealed truth, and the demoralizing influence of military life. The complaint of one clergyman against "the cold Indifference with Respect to Religion which . . . always discovers itself amongst the greater Part of Mankind when *left to themselves*" was echoed by many of his calling. Ashbel Green, a student at the College of New Jersey, was shocked to discover that he was the only professor of religion among the undergraduates in that noted "Presbyterian seminary" and that many of his fellows were "grossly profane." Bishop Asbury in a trip through the state in 1787 received an unfavorable impression of its religious condition. Such diverse figures as Governor Livingston and the itinerant Quaker preacher, John Hunt, inveighed against the immorality and waywardness of the people.[7] From time to time there were reports of revivals in scattered localities. Newark

[7] "Additional Letters to the Reverend Abraham Beach, 1772-1791," edited by Rev. Walter H. Stowe, *Historical Magazine of the Protestant Episcopal Church*, V (1936), p. 133; Ashbel Green, *The Life of Ashbel Green* (New York, 1849), p. 133; John Atkinson, *Memorials of Methodism in New Jersey* . . . (Philadelphia, 1860), p. 366; *New Jersey Gazette*, Dec. 16, 1783; "John Hunt's Diary," edited by Edward A. Fuhlbruegge, *PNJHS*, LIII (1935), *passim.*

and Elizabeth Town in 1785 were stirred by the preaching of Uzal Ogden and his Presbyterian colleague, Dr. Alexander MacWhorter. A year later the little Baptist church at Mount Bethel in Somerset became the center of an awakening of spiritual fervor that soon spread to neighboring communities. But these instances were exceptional, and most congregations were occupied solely with problems of rehabilitation.[8]

The Presbyterian Church, the strongest and most influential in the state, had paid a heavy price for its ardent espousal of the revolutionary cause. From its ranks—both lay and clerical—had come the overwhelming majority of civil and military leaders, and the result was a necessary neglect of church affairs. The conspicuous patriotism of the sect had drawn upon it the particular hostility of the British, who left many of its meeting houses in ruins or severely damaged. In Elizabeth Town the building in which such notables as William Livingston, Elias Boudinot, Abraham Clark, and Jonathan Dayton worshiped had been burned by a party of refugees, and the beloved Pastor Caldwell had been slain.[9] The historic edifice in New Brunswick, once a center of "New Light" enthusiasm, had suffered a similar fate. Efforts to replace these structures were begun soon after the war ended, but funds could not at once be obtained for the purpose. Elizabeth Town resorted to the expedient of applying to the legislature for permission to raise money through a lottery.[10] A committee in New Brunswick launched an appeal for donations to "the benevolent of all Denominations," sending subscription lists as far distant as Boston with indifferent

[8] *Political Intelligencer*, Mar. 15, 1785; Morgan Edwards, *Materials Towards a History of the Baptists in New Jersey* (Philadelphia, 1792), II, p. 109; "The Diary of Joseph Lewis," *PNJHS*, LXII (1944), p. 171.

[9] Nicholas Murray, *Notes, Historical and Biographical Concerning Elizabethtown* ... (Elizabeth Town, 1844), pp. 110-11.

[10] Petition of the Trustees and Congregation of the 1st Presbyterian Church in Elizabeth Town, Nov. 25, 1784, Loose Manuscripts, NJSL.

success.[11] Despite the high cost of materials and the acute lack of money, both congregations proceeded slowly with the construction of new buildings, which by 1786 were sufficiently advanced to permit the resumption of services. Then recourse was had to a jointly sponsored lottery to secure the financial aid needed to bring about their completion.[12] There was a serious shortage of ministers to contend with as well. Some who had entered the army as chaplains did not return, few young men finished their training during the war years, and the poverty of many congregations made it difficult for them to support a pastor. The pulpits in both New Brunswick and Elizabeth Town were without settled ministers until 1786. As late as 1789 there were but twenty-five clergymen to supply over fifty congregations.[13] Organizational changes also followed in the wake of independence. When the constitution of the Presbyterian Church in America was adopted in May, 1788, and four synods were created to replace the single synod of New York and Philadelphia, the New Brunswick

[11] John Neilson to William Livingston, May 15, 1785, Livingston Papers, MHS; Proceedings of the Committee of the Presbyterian Church in N Brunswick Beginning 25 day of January 1784, Neilson Papers, F-56, RUL. "... the Presbyterian Church was destroyed by the British Army," read the address, "the late war has broken in upon the number and circumstances of the Members of it, and rendered us unable of ourselves, Notwithstanding our utmost exertions to build a House for the public worship of Almighty God . . ."

[12] Murray, *Notes*, p. 114; Rev. Robert Davidson, *A Historical Sketch of the First Presbyterian Church of the City of New Brunswick . . .* (New Brunswick, 1852), pp. 17-22; *Political Intelligencer*, June 7, 1786. The churches in Trenton and Princeton also sustained damages. John Hall, *History of the Presbyterian Church in Trenton, N. J. . . .* (2nd ed., Trenton, 1912), p. 162; Damages by British, 1776-1782, Middlesex County, NJSL.

[13] Murray, *Notes*, p. 111; Davidson, *Historical Sketch*, p. 25; Morse, *Geography*, p. 292; Rev. F. R. Brace, "New Jersey Chaplains in the Army of the Revolution," *PNJHS*, 3rd Ser., VI (1907), pp. 1-11; Charles Hodge, *The Constitutional History of the Presbyterian Church in the United States of America* (2 vols., Philadelphia, 1840), II, p. 162.

Presbytery became a part of the newly constituted Synod of New York and New Jersey. The state was not an ecclesiastical unit, however, for some congregations in the northernmost counties were assigned to the New York Presbytery and those in the southern counties to the Philadelphia Presbytery.[14]

Probably no religious body was more deeply affected by the war than was the Society of Friends, whose firm tenets on the subject of pacifism occasioned them peculiar difficulties. Their neutrality laid them open to the charge of toryism, especially in the early stages of the conflict, and there is little question that their conservative views made them opposed to the radical step of independence. Because of their great strength and influence in West Jersey, they were able to maintain their beliefs without bringing down upon themselves the fate they might have suffered had they been a helpless minority. They were fined, their property was seized, and they were sometimes abused, but they were not made the victims of wholesale persecutions nor were their services interrupted. A small number of their members, apparently less than one-tenth, failed to heed the "advices" respecting war and were disowned by their meetings, and others were guilty of excusable lapses in their testimony. But on the whole the Society adhered to its principles and in fact experienced a notable spiritual revival during its period of trial.[15]

The war years witnessed the development of active

[14] Green, *Ashbel Green*, p. 188; Hall, *History*, pp. 183-96; *Records of the Presbyterian Church in the United States of America* ... (Philadelphia, 1841), *passim*. In 1788 the New Brunswick Presbytery had the same number of ministers (fifteen) that it had had in 1773. *Records*, pp. 436-37, 541.

[15] Rufus M. Jones, *The Quakers in the American Colonies* (London, 1911), p. xxix; Lois Given, "The Burlington Friends in the American Revolution," typescript paper in possession of the author, Moorestown, N. J. The minutes of the Shrewsbury, Burlington, and Haddonfield Quarterly Meetings, now in the Friends Book Store, are the principal sources for the history of the Quakers in the war era.

humanitarian concerns among the Quakers. The three Quarterly Meetings in the state earnestly sought to bring about an end to slave-holding by their members, with the result that by 1783 few Friends owned slaves. Special meetings were held for Negroes as early as 1781 in the Burlington Quarter and schooling was provided for Negro children. A remarkable awakening of interest in education had as its goal the establishment of schools in every meeting. The widespread evil of intemperance was another matter that received attention. There are evidences that the "awakening" was accompanied by a growth in membership in the postwar decade. New monthly meetings were organized at Upper Evesham, Mansfield Neck, Upper Springfield, Greenwich, and Woodbury, and several meeting houses were constructed, including one at Burlington.[16]

The prospects of the Episcopal Church at the end of the war were, in the view of one of its clergymen, "exceedingly gloomy." [17] All but three of its ministers had departed from the state, and only one of those who remained had attempted to hold formal services. The Reverend Abraham Beach of New Brunswick closed his church on July 7, 1776, rather than omit the prescribed prayers for the King and, except for a brief period early in 1777 when the city was occupied by British troops, he did not reopen it until Christmas Day, 1780, when he reluctantly made the necessary revisions in the ritual.[18] Every congregation had been weakened by the loss

[16] Minutes of the Philadelphia Yearly Meeting, 1783-1788; Minutes of the Haddonfield Quarterly Meeting, 1783-1785, Friends Book Store. The largest and most vigorous of the Quarters was Burlington, which included over fifteen individual meetings. Shrewsbury was by far the smallest.

[17] "Additional Letters of the Reverend Abraham Beach, 1772-1791," edited by Rev. Walter H. Stowe, *Historical Magazine of the Protestant Episcopal Church*, V (1936), p. 133.

[18] Rev. Walter H. Stowe, "The Reverend Abraham Beach, D.D.," *Historical Magazine of the Protestant Episcopal Church*, III (1934), pp. 88-91.

of leading members. Many churches had been partially destroyed or had fallen into disrepair through long years of neglect. The building at Perth Amboy was in ruins and the one in New Brunswick needed extensive repairs. A grant of one hundred acres of land from the East Jersey Proprietors enabled the Perth Amboy congregation to begin the work of rehabilitating their structure, but their funds were soon exhausted. Both churches addressed unsuccessful appeals to the legislature for permission to hold a lottery.[19] The altered political situation made unlikely future financial support from the Society for the Propagation of the Gospel, which had contributed to the salaries of missionaries since 1702. Perhaps most serious of all, the denomination was left without direction or organization by the severance of the ties with England.[20]

New Jersey clergymen played a conspicuous role in the efforts to create an organization for the church. In September of 1783, the Reverend Abraham Beach in a letter to the

[19] Petition of the Church Wardens and Vestrymen of St. Peters Church in Perth Amboy to the East Jersey Proprietors, Apr. 16, 1785, New Jersey Manuscripts, I, NJHS; Petition of the Protestant Episcopal Church in Perth Amboy to the legislature, May, 1787; Petition of the Protestant Episcopal Church in New Brunswick to the legislature, May 17, 1786, Loose Manuscripts, NJSL.

[20] Stowe, "Abraham Beach," p. 91; Stowe, "Additional Letters," p. 137. The Reverend Dr. Chandler soon after his return to Elizabeth Town graphically described the plight of the church to the Secretary of the Venerable Society:

With regard to the *Church*, [he wrote on October 3, 1785] I fear that it has suffered more than the *State*, by the late revolution. It is no longer under the controll of British authority; it now wants the Support and patronage of the Society; it has lost a large proportion of its Clergy by death and expulsion, and their places are unsupplied; in many parts of the country, men of loose principles or of no principles, take the lead; and genuine Episcopacy, though the name is retained, is in danger of being sacrificed on the Altar of ecclesiastical republicanism.

SPG transcript in possession of Dr. Walter H. Stowe, New Brunswick, N. J.

Reverend Dr. William White of Philadelphia expressed the hope that members of the church "would interest themselves in its behalf, would endeavor to introduce Order and uniformity into it, and provide for a succession in the Ministry." Out of this correspondence developed the first postwar meeting of the Corporation for the Relief of Widows and Children of Clergymen in Christ's Church, New Brunswick, on May 11, 1784. This group, which included clergy and laity from New York, New Jersey, and Pennsylvania, determined to hold a second meeting at New York in October and appointed a committee of correspondence "for the purpose of forming a continental representation of the Episcopal Church and for the better management of the concerns of said Church." [21] At the New York conference it was agreed that a convention should be held in Philadelphia a year later to formulate a plan of union. Meanwhile the churches in New Jersey held their first state convention on July 6, 1785, at New Brunswick and resolved to adopt such proposals as the general body might devise.[22] The Philadelphia gathering, under the presidency of the liberal Dr. White, in addition to framing an ecclesiastical constitution, made drastic revisions in the Book of Common Prayer. These proceedings provoked an unfavorable reaction in the second New Jersey convention, which convened on May 16, 1786. Objecting to the "un-

[21] Stowe, "Abraham Beach," pp. 28-29; S. D. McConnell, *History of the American Episcopal Church* (New York, 1899), pp. 236-39. Beach was born in Connecticut in 1740, was graduated from Yale in 1757, and was ordained and appointed missionary at New Brunswick and Piscataway in 1767. In June, 1784, he was called to Trinity Church, New York, as assistant minister, but continued to participate in the New Jersey Conventions until 1787. In 1813 he resigned from his post at Trinity and returned to New Brunswick, where he died September 24, 1828.

[22] *Journals of the Conventions of the Protestant Episcopal Church of the State of New Jersey, 1785-1816* (New York, 1890), p. 4, Appendix I, pp. 21-22; *New Jersey Gazette*, Oct. 18, 1784. Three ministers and fourteen laymen representing eight churches were present at the New Brunswick convention.

reasonableness and irregularity" of the innovations, the group in a memorial to the general convention urged that body to act in such a manner as to "convince the world that it is their wish and intention to maintain the doctrines of the gospel, as now held by the Church of England, and to adhere to the liturgy of the said church, as far as shall be consistent with the American revolution and the constitution of the respective states." This document, which was acknowledged to have been "among the causes which prevented the disorganization of the American Church," championed the conservative position that was ultimately to prevail.[23] It had not been adopted without opposition, however, for the Reverend Uzal Ogden of Newark, whose Presbyterian leanings subsequently led to his suspension from the church, dissented vigorously from the "Memorial," maintaining that it did not accurately represent the views of many in the state.[24] The conflict between the conservatives and the liberals continued both in the local and general conventions until the two factions reached agreement on a plan of union and a prayer book at the Philadelphia Convention in 1789. By that date there were six ministers serving over fifteen active congregations in New Jersey.[25]

Independence brought no fundamental changes to the

[23] *Journals*, pp. 12-15. The authorship of the "Memorial of the New Jersey Convention" is generally attributed to the Rev. Dr. Thomas Bradbury Chandler. See Frank Gavin, "The Rev. Thomas Bradbury Chandler in the Light of his (Unpublished) Diary, 1777-85," reprinted from *Church History*, June, 1932, and Joseph Hooker, "Thomas Bradbury Chandler," *The Church Eclectic*, XVIII (1890). Chandler, one of the foremost men among the American clergy, had been a leading advocate of an American Episcopacy before the Revolution. He left Elizabeth Town in May, 1775, and soon sailed for England, where he remained until 1785. Suffering from cancer of the face, he could not resume in full his clerical functions after his return to New Jersey. The disease caused his death in 1790.

[24] Rev. Uzal Ogden and Mr. Patrick Dennis to Rev. Dr. William White, May 25, 1786, in *Journals*, pp. 585-87.

[25] *Ibid.*, pp. 16-79.

twenty-five Dutch Reformed Churches, although the war occasioned considerable material hardships because the membership was concentrated in regions where the desolation was heaviest. As early as 1771, when the Coetus and Conferentie parties healed the split which had divided the church for almost twenty years, the denomination had become largely independent of its connection with Holland. In 1784 the existing organization was formalized with the adoption of the names "synod" and "classis" to distinguish the general and subordinate ecclesiastical bodies, and four years later a special committee translated, modified, and published the doctrinal symbols and articles of government of the church. In the meantime Dr. John H. Livingston had been elected professor of theology to carry forward the training of new ministers.[26]

The Baptists emerged from the war virtually unaffected. Having long since made a satisfactory adjustment to the American environment, they needed to make no alteration in their form of government. The twenty-seven churches in New Jersey—three of which had been organized prior to 1700—were widely distributed from Cape May to Sussex, but they were conspicuously absent from the large towns. Their membership was composed in the main of small farmers, and perhaps for this reason they produced few outstanding personalities.[27]

[26] Edward T. Corwin, *A Manual of the Reformed Church in America, 1628-1902* (4th ed., New York, 1902), pp. 82-129; Rev. Abraham Messler, "The Hollanders in New Jersey," *PNJHS*, V (1850), pp. 69-89; Morse, *Geography*, p. 293. The Coetus was organized in 1737, and it sought gradually to increase the independence of the American churches. A conservative wing, the Conferentie, withdrew from the Coetus in 1755.

[27] Morgan Edwards, *Materials Toward a History of the Baptists in Jersey* (Philadelphia, 1792), *passim*. This remarkable book, which was the product of a visit by Edwards to all the churches in the state in 1789-1790, contains historical sketches and statistical information about every congregation. For a briefer statement, see Henry C. Vedder, *A History of the Baptists in the Middle States* (Philadelphia, 1898).

The rapid spread of Methodism was a phenomenon of the postwar decade. Gaining its first foothold in the state in 1770, the sect grew slowly at the start. But between 1780 and 1790 its membership increased remarkably from about one hundred and fifty to over twenty-three hundred. Its itinerant preachers, led by the fervent convert, Benjamin Abbott, and assisted by the frequent visits of Bishop Asbury, did their most effective work among the humbler folk in the rural areas of West Jersey, where religious facilities were extremely limited. In East Jersey they were able to make little progress in the face of opposition from the older denominations, although they did receive some encouragement in that region from the Episcopal clergy. Methodism, indeed, was the chief religious enthusiasm of the period.[28]

THE RESURGENCE OF INTELLECTUAL ACTIVITY

A heightened interest in education was one of many evidences of genuine cultural progress in the years following the Revolution. The "Great Awakening" of the 1740's had given a strong impetus to the establishment of schools, among them the College of New Jersey, Queen's College, and numerous academies, but the war had dispersed teachers and students and had forced the closing of many institutions. As soon as the fighting had receded from the state, however, people gave immediate attention to the restoration and expansion of educational facilities. Long before the churches had recovered from the effects of the conflict, the schools had fully made up their losses and had, in fact, surpassed their prewar status.

Common schools, where poorly qualified masters eked out a meager existence by instructing children of assorted ages in reading, writing, and arithmetic, were a familiar feature of

---

[28] John Atkinson, *Memorials of Methodism in New Jersey...* (Philadelphia, 1860), *passim;* Joseph S. Sickler, *The History of Salem County, New Jersey* (Salem, 1929), pp. 115-21.

the countryside. John Rutherfurd remarked in 1786 that there were "few Instances of a Farm house being more than two miles distant from a School." [29] Some were organized by groups of parents who were anxious that their offspring should have the rudiments of learning; others owed their origin to enterprising pedagogues, whose movements from place to place may be traced through their advertisements in the newspapers. In a few towns such as Newark, Woodbridge, and Piscataway, where the New England heritage was influential, schools received public support, but in most cases they were purely private agencies financed by tuition charges and by gifts from philanthropic donors.[30]

The Quaker schools were an important factor in West Jersey. Traditionally apathetic to education or at best in favor only of a "guarded" imparting of practical knowledge, the Friends had been stirred to activity on the eve of the Revolution by such discerning leaders as Anthony Benezet and John Woolman.[31] With the encouragement of the Philadelphia Yearly Meeting, committees were created in each Quarterly Meeting to press for the establishment of schools. The results of their work were apparent by 1786:

> In Burlington [read a report of the Yearly Meeting] some progress appears since last year. Funds being begun for the Support of Schools taught by Friends under the Inspection of Committees in several of the preparative Meetings ... In Glouc[este]r & Salem divers Lots of Ground have been procured & several School houses erected ... and two School Houses within the Compass of Rahway & Plainfield Mon[thl]y Meeting are mentioned.[32]

[29] Rutherfurd, "Notes," p. 89.

[30] Burr, *Education*, pp. 220 ff. See also the *New Jersey Gazette*, the *Political Intelligencer*, and the *New Jersey Journal* for the period.

[31] Jones, *Quakers*, p. xxix; Burr, *Education*, pp. 51-64; Thomas Woody, *Quaker Education in the Colony and State of New Jersey* (Philadelphia, 1923), pp. 18-27.

[32] Minutes of the Philadelphia Yearly Meeting, 1786, p. 96, Friends Book Store.

Useful learning was to be brought "not only to the Children of Friends of more easy Circumstances in Life but also to the offspring of such as are Poor and of the Black People ..." [33] By 1788 there were more than a dozen schools within the Burlington Quarter alone, and funds were being raised for five more.[34] These achievements were significant, for they marked something of a revolution in Quaker thinking and resulted in a multiplication of educational opportunities over a vast area of the state.

Grammar schools and their more highly developed counterparts, academies, increased in numbers by more than a third in the decade after 1780.[35] Outstanding among the new institutions was Trenton Academy, where students in 1782 could pursue a typical "English school" curriculum of reading, writing, arithmetic, and bookkeeping, or the academic course, which included English, Latin, Greek, geography, practical mathematics, natural philosophy, public speaking, "and the rudiments of any other branch of useful education." In 1785 a night school offering navigation and surveying as well as the "three R's" was added.[36] The older Hackensack Academy gave both elementary and college preparatory training, and in 1786 was the largest in the state with 140 scholars, many of them from New York. In 1788 the trustees ambitiously sought from the legislature the authority to grant

[33] Minutes of the Burlington Quarterly Meeting, Nov. 26, 1787, Friends Book Store.

[34] Minutes of the Burlington Quarterly Meeting, Aug, 25, 1788. The Haddonfield and Shrewsbury Quarters lagged behind prosperous Burlington but continued to make progress.

[35] Burr, *Education*, pp. 189-93; Morse, *Geography*, p. 284; Edwards, *Baptists*, pp. 122-23; *New Jersey Gazette*, Dec. 4, 1782, Apr. 28, 1785, Dec. 19, 1785; *Political Intelligencer*, Aug. 23, 1786. One or more schools were located in Hackensack, Trenton, Orange-Dale, Elizabeth Town, Burlington, Freehold, Princeton, New Brunswick, Salem, Bridgeton, Woodbury, Bordentown, Newark, Springfield, Perth Amboy, Lamington, and Allentown.

[36] *New Jersey Gazette*, Sept. 18, 1782, Dec. 23, 1783, Oct. 24, 1785, July 31, 1786; Hall, *Presbyterian Church*, pp. 197-98.

degrees, but their request was denied after it had precipitated a heated controversy in the press.[37] At Bordentown the universal genius of Burgess Allison attracted students from all parts of the country and from foreign lands. Most of these institutions owed their origin to the Presbyterian influence. Their masters and tutors were apt to be recent graduates of the College of New Jersey. They were not, however, sectarian or parochial schools, for they were open to all who could afford the modest tuition fees, and in some instances, at least, special funds were provided to subsidize the education of poor children.[38]

Education was not wholly restricted to the traditional types of institutions. Several evening schools gave adults an opportunity for self-improvement.[39] Vocal lessons were given by Aaron Ball and Amos Throop in Elizabeth Town.[40] Those with a desire to acquire the fundamentals of the newly popular French culture could study the language of Rousseau under authentic "monsieurs," who also imparted instruction in the most fashionable dances, graces, and manners and in drawing and fencing.[41] Nor were young females neglected. Mrs. Mease of London taught the girls of Princeton "tambouring, and every branch of useful and ornamental needle work, and a right pronunciation of their mother tounge," while her husband guided them in academic courses. Similar training was available in Trenton and Elizabeth Town and in

[37] Morse, *Geography*, p. 294; Diary of William North, 1786, NYHS; *New Jersey Journal*, Aug. 27, Sept. 3, 1788; Burr, *Education*, p. 193.

[38] [Moore Furman], *The Letters of Moore Furman* ... (New York, 1912), pp. 72-73.

[39] *New Jersey Gazette*, Dec. 5, 1781, Oct. 24, 1785; *Political Intelligencer*, Nov. 16, Dec. 28, 1784.

[40] *New Jersey Gazette*, Jan. 31, 1783; *Political Intelligencer*, May 24, 1786.

[41] *New Jersey Gazette*, Sept. 18, 1782, Jan. 29, 1783; *Political Intelligencer*, Nov. 11, 1783, Jan. 13, 1784, June 1, 1784.

the school conducted by the Moravian sisterhood at their little colony, Hope, in Hunterdon County.[42]

Unlike the lower schools and the academies, which experienced in the years after the peace a period of active expansion, the state's institutions of higher learning struggled for more than a decade to regain their prewar condition. Queen's College (now Rutgers University) had been forced to quit New Brunswick when the British occupied that town in 1776 and was able to keep going during the ensuing five years only because of the extraordinary fidelity of its young tutors. When it returned to its former home in 1781, it faced a precarious future.[43] Hampered by a chronic shortage of funds and deprived of the anticipated support of the Church that had been responsible for its founding, it nevertheless managed to keep going. In 1786, with the election of the renowned Jacob Rutsen Hardenbergh as the first regular president, it appeared to be on the way to some sort of stability. No students seem to have graduated in 1784, 1785, or 1786, but by 1789 there were ten who received their degrees at the impressive commencement ceremonies, a respectable number considering the difficulties that beset the college. Finally, however, an accumulation of misfortunes led to its closing in 1795; not until 1807 was it again revived.[44]

The College of New Jersey (Princeton University) was more successful in weathering the period of trial. Although its Nassau Hall had been heavily damaged by the British and its enrollment had dwindled to one-quarter of the normal

[42] *Brunswick Gazette*, Sept. 1, 1788; *New Jersey Gazette*, Mar. 30, 1784, Mar. 20, 1786; *New Jersey Journal*, Apr. 15, 1789.

[43] In 1781 the college received from the legislature a new charter, which voided a former requirement that ministers should not exceed one-third of the total number of trustees. Wilson, *Acts*, Act of June 5, 1781, pp. 192-93.

[44] William H. S. Demarest, *A History of Rutgers College, 1766-1924* (New Brunswick, 1924), pp. 110 ff.; Burr, *Education*, pp. 21-27.

figure, it soon showed signs of recovery. The trustees in 1781 decided that notwithstanding the "late desolation by the enemy, and the confusion of the times ... the whole former system might be reestablished," and took measures accordingly.[45] When an appeal to the legislature for financial aid was unsuccessful, President Witherspoon embarked for England in a vain effort to solicit aid. Despite these disappointments the remarkable Scotch educator, with the able assistance of his son-in-law, Dr. Samuel Stanhope Smith, gradually carried forward the work of reconstruction. The student body grew from around forty in 1782 to over twice that number in 1786, and by 1792 the largest class up to that time was graduated.[46]

Symptoms of cultural growth can be detected in fields other than education. Especially noteworthy were the developments in journalism. Prior to the Revolution, New Jersey had relied for its news on papers published in New York or Philadelphia. Early in 1778 Isaac Collins, with the encouragement of the legislature, established the *New Jersey Gazette* in Trenton; a year later Shepard Kollock began to issue the *New Jersey Journal* at Chatham. Thereafter the state was rarely without at least two weekly newspapers, and in 1787 there were four.[47] The journalistic ideal of the period was expressed by Kollock and his partner, Shelly Arnett, when they launched *The Political Intelligencer and New-Jersey Advertiser* at New Brunswick in 1783. "Neither diligence nor labour shall be wanting to render this paper a useful repository of knowledge, honour and entertainment," they announced,

---

[45] *New Jersey Gazette*, Oct. 10, 1781.

[46] Varnum L. Collins, *President Witherspoon, A Biography* (2 vols., Princeton, 1925), pp. 118-43; Green, *Ashbel Green*, p. 145; Schoepf, *Travels*, p. 41.

[47] *The New-Jersey Journal, and Political Intelligencer*; *The New Brunswick Gazette, and Weekly Monitor*; the *Princeton Packet*; and *The Trenton Weekly Mercury*. Thomas F. Gordon, *The History of New Jersey* ... (Trenton, 1834), p. 324.

"while vice, the bane of society, with its concomitant attendants, though cloathed with the garb of authority, will be branded with every mark of infamy."[48] Kollock, an ardent republican and the most successful printer of the period, later issued *The New-Jersey Journal, and Political Intelligencer,* which in 1787 had a circulation of a thousand, principally in the northern counties.[49] The importance of the role played by these papers, crude and inadequate as they were, in creating an informed public opinion and in giving currency to the ideas of the day can scarcely be exaggerated.

Eclectic magazines provided a varied literary diet for many. *The New Jersey Magazine and Monthly Advertiser* was a short-lived venture, but the substantial *Christian's, Scholar's and Farmer's Magazine* which Shepard Kollock printed at Elizabeth Town was a worthy representative of its type.[50] Carey's *American Museum,* to which Governor Livingston was a frequent contributor, had nearly a hundred subscribers in New Jersey, and Noah Webster's *American Magazine* probably had a place in popular favor.[51] Quantities of books, ranging from Buchan's *Family Physician* to Raynal's *The Revolution in America,* were offered for sale by several dealers through advertisements in the local papers. The legislature, recognizing that "Learning tends to the Embellishment of Human Nature, the Honour of the Nation, and the general Good of Mankind," and acknowledging that men of learning should enjoy the profit from their labors, enacted a law giving any American author the exclusive right to print

[48] *Political Intelligencer,* Oct. 14, 1783. Kollock in 1785 moved his press to Elizabeth Town. Arnett began publication of *The New Brunswick Gazette, and Weekly Monitor* in 1787.

[49] Walter R. Fee, *The Transition from Aristocracy to Democracy in New Jersey* (Somerville, 1933), p. 104.

[50] *The New Jersey Magazine* was published at New Brunswick by Frederick Quequelle and James Prange. There were but three issues from December, 1786, to February, 1787. Kollock's magazine was issued bi-monthly from April, 1789, to March, 1791.

[51] *American Museum,* II (1787), subscription list.

and sell his works within the state for a term of fourteen years.[52] Library companies at Burlington and Trenton provided a limited number of gentlemen with reading matter. In Elizabeth Town a circulating library containing several hundred volumes was organized by Shepard Kollock on a subscription plan in 1786.[53] Doubtless several individuals had private libraries comparable to that of Governor Livingston, which at his death numbered 552 volumes.[54]

The outstanding learned group in the state was the New Jersey Medical Society. Organized in 1766 as the first such body in the colonies, it held regular meetings until 1775, when the war brought its activities to a halt. It was revived in November, 1781, and thereafter its members met twice a year to discuss professional concerns.[55] One of its accomplishments was the securing of an act regulating the practice of medicine and providing for the licensing of doctors.[56] The Society heard "dissertations" on such subjects as "the Blood, and the changes it is capable of undergoing in diseases," "the Nature and Uses of Animal Secretion," and "the Chemical Principles of Bodies," the last being delivered by the learned

[52] Wilson, *Acts*, "An Act for the Promotion and Encouragement of Literature," May 27, 1783.

[53] Joshua Maddox Wallace was admitted to membership in the Burlington Library Company in 1786. Wallace Papers, IV, HSP; *A History of Trenton, 1679-1929*, published under the auspices of the Trenton Historical Society (2 vols., Princeton, 1929), pp. 755-56; *Political Intelligencer*, May 17, July 26, Aug. 2, 1786.

[54] Inventory of Livingston's library, 1790, Livingston Papers, MHS.

[55] "Philadelphus" in the *New Jersey Gazette*, Sept. 11, 1786, gives an excellent account of the origin of the Society. See also *The Rise, Minutes and Proceedings of the New Jersey Medical Society* (Newark, 1879), pp. 3-40; Stephen Wickes, *History of Medicine in New Jersey and of its Medical Men* (Newark, 1879), pp. 48-51.

[56] *Session Laws*, 8-1, Act of Nov. 26, 1783. The preamble justified the act by stating that "many ignorant and unskillful Persons do take upon themselves to administer Physick and Surgery ... to the endangering of the Lives and Limbs of the good Subjects of the ... [state]."

Dr. Jonathan Elmer. The causes of putrid fever, dropsy, and epilepsy were earnestly debated, difficult cases were considered, and prospective members were examined. There was correspondence with the Massachusetts Medical Society and with the Medical College of Philadelphia. In all, some fifty physicians attended the sessions of this active and progressive organization in the decade after 1781.[57] The "Trenton Society for Improvement in Useful Knowledge" and the "New Jersey Society for Promoting Agriculture, Commerce and Arts" were also in existence in these years, but little is known of their activities.[58]

Other groups, whose purposes were more social than cultural, gained prominence in the period. The convivial "Sons of St. Tammany" gathered annually on the first of May to toast their patron.[59] The conventions of the Society of Cincinnati brought together the leading military figures of the state for appropriate celebrations each Fourth of July,[60] many of the same men were instrumental in organizing the first Masonic Grand Lodge of New Jersey in December, 1786.[61]

[57] *Rise, Minutes and Proceedings,* pp. 39-77.

[58] *New Jersey Gazette,* Sept. 12, 1781, May 31, Dec. 31, 1784.

[59] The Constitution of the New Jersey Society of the sons of St. Tamminy No. 1, Society Collection, HSP; *New Jersey Gazette,* May 28, 1783.

[60] *New Jersey Gazette,* July 12, 1784, July 11, 1785, July 10, 1786; A list of the members of the Cincinnati Society in the State of New Jersey—July, 1788, D:227, NJHS.

[61] There were apparently seven lodges in the state in 1788. The political prominence of the Grand Lodge officers is worthy of notice. Grand Master David Brearly was chief justice of the Supreme Court, Deputy Grand Master Robert L. Hooper was vice president of the Legislative Council, Senior Grand Warden William Leddell was a former sheriff of Morris County, Junior Grand Warden Daniel Marsh was in the Assembly, Deputy Grand Secretary Maskell Ewing was clerk of the Assembly, and Grand Treasurer Joshua Corshon was sheriff of Hunterdon County. See David McGregor, "History of Freemasonry in New Jersey," *Proceedings of the Grand Lodge ... of Free and Accepted Masons for the State of New Jersey,* XL (1937), *passim.*

THE EMERGENCE OF HUMANITARIANISM

Humanitarian concerns, stimulated by the natural-rights ideology of the Revolution, were productive of significant social reforms. Slavery, in particular, was brought under attack. During the colonial period, a desire to encourage white immigration had led to the enactment of laws designed to limit the importation of Negroes, but there was little widespread criticism of slavery until the Society of Friends became aroused about the matter early in the second half of the eighteenth century. In 1774 slave holding was declared by the Quaker Yearly Meeting to be an offense against its discipline, and thereafter the sect was to work unremittingly for its extirpation.[62]

In the midst of the war the Quakers were joined in their crusade by those who believed that slavery was inconsistent with the doctrines enunciated in the Declaration of Independence. "A Friend to Justice" expressed this new point of view in a letter to the *New Jersey Gazette*:

A whig, Sir, [he wrote in 1780] abhors the very idea of slavery, let the colour or complexion of a slave be what it may. He is a friend to liberty, and a supporter of the rights of mankind universally, without any regard to partial interests or selfish views. Every pulse of his heart, beats for liberty . . .[63]

[62] Henry S. Cooley, *A Study of Slavery in New Jersey, Johns Hopkins Studies in History and Political Science,* 14th Series, ix-x (1896), pp. 9-17; Jones, *Quakers,* pp. 519-20; D. H. Gardner, "The Emancipation of Slaves in New Jersey," *PNJHS,* NS, XIV (1929), pp. 181-202. New Jersey in 1784 had close to ten thousand slaves, most of them being held in those sections of East Jersey where the Dutch were numerous. Only New York among the northern states had a larger number.

[63] *New Jersey Gazette,* Nov. 8, 1780. For similar views, see *ibid.,* Jan. 10, Mar. 21, 1781.

Governor William Livingston, who in 1778 had urged the legislature to take some steps toward eventual emancipation, repeatedly denounced slavery and gave his complete support to the abolition movement.[64] William Churchill Houston condemned the institution as "a Disgrace to any Government," and both Isaac Collins and Shepard Kollock used their newspapers to promote the cause of freedom. Thus the Quakers secured powerful allies.[65]

A petition to the legislature in 1781 sought gradual emancipation through a plan similar to that which had been adopted in Pennsylvania, but no action was taken and five years passed before the demand was renewed.[66] Then, early in 1786, after having received pleas from a "great number of inhabitants" at its previous session, the legislature passed an act to prevent the importation of slaves, authorize their manumission, and prevent their being abused. Especially significant is the statement in the preamble that the slave trade was contrary to "principles of humanity and justice." [67] This measure did not entirely suit the Friends and their associates, and they continued their campaign. The influential Philadelphia Quaker leader, James Pemberton, sought the aid of Governor Liv-

[64] Cooley, *Slavery*, p. 23; Sedgwick, *Memoir*, pp. 339-400; Livingston to James Pemberton, Oct. 20, 1788, Etting Collection, Old Congress, II, HSP.

[65] Essay on Taxation by W. C. Houston, May 14, 1782, Etting Collection, Old Congress, II, HSP; *New Jersey Gazette*, Mar. 5, 1785; *Political Intelligencer*, Mar. 15, 1786. For the Quaker attitude, see the minutes of the Burlington, Shrewsbury, and Haddonfield Quarterly Meetings, Friends Book Store.

[66] The petition, which was printed in the *New Jersey Gazette*, Mar. 21, 1781, referred to the Declaration of Independence in justifying the stand that all men should be free.

[67] *Session Laws*, 10-1, "An Act to prevent the Importation of Slaves into the State of New Jersey, and to authorize the Manumission of them under certain restrictions, and to prevent the Abuse of Slaves," Mar. 2, 1786; *Votes and Proceedings*, 10-1, pp. 15, 24; *ibid.*, 10-2, pp. 14-26; Cooley, *Slavery*, pp. 18 ff.

ingston, who explained why it was difficult to obtain an effective law:

> It was my wish to have gone farther. But however desirous the western part of New Jersey may be ... there are some of the northern counties whom too rapid progress in the business would furnish with an excuse to oppose it altogether.

He added the sage observation that political experience had taught him that it was wise to take what one could get rather than to seek the unobtainable.[68] Pemberton in his answer described the aims and tactics of the Quakers:

> A Deputation lately nominated by our religious Society will I expect in a few days wait on the General Assembly at Princetown with an address, and Petition on the interesting subject, which I wish may claim attention equal to its importance, but altho' from the circumstances of your northern counties, we may not obtain all we wish for, yet I hope the Legislature will be induced to repeal a clause in your late law which appears to be very objectionable, & that they will absolutely prohibite the equipment of Ships in any part of the State for the nefarious traffic to Africa, grant protection to the free blacks from kidnappers, and provide against the Separation of the nearest connections in life, ... and that such other regulations may take place in favour of the oppressed people, as are consistent with humanity, Justice, and the precepts of the Christian Religion.[69]

The Quaker petition, together with others from Hunterdon and Princeton, was presented to the Assembly early in November, 1788. A "Grand Committee" of thirteen was appointed to bring in a bill, which shuttled back and forth between the Assembly and the Council for three weeks before

[68] Livingston to James Pemberton, Oct. 20, 1788, Etting Collection, Old Congress, II, HSP.

[69] James Pemberton to William Livingston, Nov. 4, 1788, Livingston Papers, MHS.

it finally passed.[70] The new law accurately reflected the desires of the petitioners. In addition to providing for the forfeiture of all vessels engaged in the slave trade, it prohibited the removal of any slave from the state without his consent, unless his master was also leaving. Henceforth criminal offenses by Negroes and mulattoes were to be judged and punished in the same manner as those committed by white citizens. Furthermore, any slave born after 1788 was to be taught to read at the expense of his master before reaching the age of twenty-one.[71] That the Quakers were primarily responsible for this humanitarian act is incontrovertible, but the influence of those who believed that freedom and liberty were natural rights of all men was not inconsiderable.[72]

Also indicative of the new spirit of the times were the modifications that were made in the laws governing the descent of property. In 1784, limitations were placed on the ancient and aristocratic practice of creating perpetual estates "in tail." Thereafter any entailed property that had passed through one heir since the death of the testator was to become vested unconditionally in the possessor in fee simple. In effect, lands could not be entailed beyond one generation. This legislation was prompted in large part by the fact that heirs frequently resorted to the old English forms of recovery in order to break the entail and were put to great expense in the process. Moreover, there were those who believed that the custom was contrary to "the enlightened policy of the present

[70] *Votes and Proceedings*, 13-1, pp. 16-75. The vote on the measure in the Assembly was 24-14. In the minority were the entire delegations from the northern counties of Essex, Bergen, Somerset, and Sussex and one member each from Burlington and Cape May.

[71] *Session Laws*, 13-1, Act of Nov. 26, 1788.

[72] There is some evidence that societies for promoting the abolition of slavery were organized at Burlington (1783), Trenton (1786), and Princeton (1788). Cooley, *Slavery*, p. 23; Gardner, "Emancipation," pp. 11-12. For the attitude of the Presbyterian Church on the question at this time, see *Records of the Presbyterian Church*, pp. 539-40.

republican age." [73] The right of primogeniture, too, was altered. Prior to 1780 the whole estate of an intestate person had passed to the male heir, but legislation in that year provided for the division of the property among all the children, with the sons receiving two shares to one for each daughter. This reform, in the opinion of William Paterson, was in accord with "the genius of the government." [74]

Concern over the evil of intemperance was to be expected in a state where taverns were at least three times as numerous as churches and where the distillation of hard cider was a household art. The Quakers were foremost in condemning the use or sale of spirituous liquors, and their sentiments occasionally were echoed in other quarters, apparently with little effect. [75] The imprisonment of insolvent debtors struck at least one "Friend to Liberty" as being cruel and unreasonable. [76] No complaints seem to have been raised, however, against the barbarous criminal code, which still sanctioned the use of the pillory, the whipping post, and the branding iron. [77] Nor did William Livingston, vigorous defender of liberty that he was, have any scruples against purchasing the time of Irish and German indentured servants at so much a head. [78]

A review of the social and cultural aspects of the critical

[73] *Laws of the State of New Jersey*, compiled by William Paterson (Newark, 1800), Act of Aug. 26, 1784, pp. 53-54 and Act of Mar. 23, 1786, p. 78; "Aurelius," William Paterson Essays, RUL. The statute *de donis* remained in force in New Jersey until June 13, 1799, and entailed estates existed as conditional fees under the common law until 1820. William Griffith, *Annual Law Register of the United States*, IV (Burlington, 1822), p. 1261.

[74] Wilson, *Laws*, Act of May 24, 1780, pp. 125-26; "Aurelius," William Paterson Essays, RUL.

[75] Morse, *Geography*, p. 287; "John Hunt's Diary," *PNJHS*, LIII, p. 28; *New Jersey Gazette*, Mar. 23, 1784; *Brunswick Gazette*, Aug. 12, 1788.

[76] *Brunswick Gazette*, Sept. 9, 1788.

[77] *New Jersey Gazette*, Nov. 22, 1784, Aug. 1, 1785.

[78] Abraham Bancker to Livingston, Feb. 23, Mar. 12, 1784, Peter Wikoff to Livingston, Mar. 31, 1785, Livingston Papers, MHS.

period, therefore, does not disclose social disintegration or cultural stagnation. On the contrary, considerable progress was made in the rehabilitation and renovation of familiar institutions. Society, although not in a violent state of flux, exhibited vigorous symptoms of change as well as a sense of direction. The old order was not completely restored, for independence created demands and opportunities for development that had not existed previously. Reconstruction, then, was affected by the altered political situation and by the currency given to republican ideology.

IV

Politics: the Rules and the Game

★★★

WHILE social reconstruction was in progress, basic readjustments were taking place in the political life of the state. Independence had given to New Jersey—as well as to her sister states—complete freedom from the restraints of British authority and the opportunity to begin an experiment in self-rule in accordance with the principles of republicanism. Those citizens who were eligible to exercise the franchise now possessed virtually unlimited power within the state, and their will could not be denied by any external agency until the Federal Constitution became operative in 1789. The machinery through which the people were to manifest and effectuate their will acquired a new importance. On the character of the electoral process were to depend, in the final analysis, both the nature of the government and the direction that government would take.

THE MEANING OF SELF-GOVERNMENT

The new government bore strong external resemblances to the old. But it was fundamentally different in that it vested full sovereignty in the people. The majority could rule. As this fact became evident, a disagreement developed over the true meaning of republicanism. At issue was the question of whether or not the majority was bound to recognize any limitations of its powers.

Although familiar colonial institutions were retained in the government established by the constitution that the Provincial Congress drafted in 1776, some of them were drastically altered in their functions, and all were brought within range of popular control.[1] Members of the Council, sheriffs, and coroners, all of whom had formerly been named to office by the royal governor, now were elected directly by the qualified voters. The joint meeting of the Council and Assembly chose the governor, justices of the Supreme Court, and other officials who in the past had been appointive placemen. Annual elections were a significant innovation. The governor was given no executive powers, no veto, and no exclusive pardoning power. He presided over the Council and the Court of Errors and Appeals, and acted as chancellor, captain-general, and surrogate-general. The Supreme Court and all inferior courts were creatures of the legislature; the terms of all judicial officers were limited and their salaries might be reduced at any time.[2] Clearly the legislative branch enjoyed complete supremacy. There were but three restrictions on its power: it could not abolish annual elections, trial by jury, or religious liberty. Of the two houses, the Assembly was the more powerful, for it possessed the sole right to

[1] See Charles R. Erdman, *The New Jersey Constitution of 1776* (Princeton, 1929), for an able analysis of the document. Also of value is L. Q. C. Elmer, *The Constitution and Government of the Province and State of New Jersey* ... (Newark, 1872), ch. II.

[2] Chief Justice David Brearly was deeply concerned about the ability of the legislature to exert "improper influence" on the Supreme Court. He strongly urged that justices be given a fixed salary and that they be appointed for good behavior. Governor Livingston held similar views. Brearly to Livingston, Dec. 10, 1783, Livingston Papers, MHS; "Scipio" [Livingston], *New Jersey Gazette*, June 14, 1784.

initiate revenue bills, and it had three times the vote of the Council in joint meeting.

Some of the implications of these far-reaching changes in the form of government are obvious. Political influence could now be gained only by securing popular approval, not by gaining the favor of officials who were responsible to a governor or king. The methods by which the "Perth Amboy group" had wielded power in the pre-Revolutionary days were at an end.[3] Political contests henceforth would be between rival groups of citizens within the state, not between the people and the crown officials. Political activity took on increased zest and meaning with frequent elections, and the many perquisites at the disposal of the joint meeting offered tangible rewards to those who competed successfully for office. A loose constitution and an absence of external controls encouraged, or at least made possible, innovations and abrupt shifts in policy. Popular pressures, voiced through petitions, could scarcely be ignored. The electoral machinery, the key to the effectiveness of the representative process, assumed heightened significance.

That the newly gained liberty did not at once eventuate in "democratical license" may be attributed in large part to the restraining effect of republican theory. Emphasizing integrity, responsibility, virtue, and respect for property rights, and deploring excesses of factionalism and selfish abuses of power, this doctrine was invoked as a limitation on those who might attempt radical measures. William Paterson, whose political views were typical of those held by substantial citizens, defined this philosophy concisely. "Republicanism," he explained, "delights in virtue, which is an active principle, and excites to honesty and industry, and of course is opposed to idleness and sloth. The equalizing of property by the strong hand of power would be a tax upon the active and industrious man for the support of the sluggard . . . That nation, however," he con-

[3] Lundin, *Cockpit*, pp. 46-47.

ceded, "bids fairest to attain the summit of political prosperity and happiness, in which property, especially if it be of
a landed nature, is fairly equally diffused among the people."
A fundamental principle to be observed in legislation was that
"all Citizens of a State ought to be viewed with equal Eyes;
that one Order of *Citizens* ought not to be preferred to
another; that Property ought to be secured, and rendered
inviolate; that Industry ought to be encouraged." Fearing
the consequences of divisions within the state, it was natural
that he should subscribe to the view that "Party is the mad-
ness of many for the gain of the few." [4] John Witherspoon
adhered to the same creed. It was his belief that "in free
states, where the body of the people have the supreme power
properly in their own hands, and must be ultimately resorted
to on all great matters, if there be a general corruption of
manners, there can be nothing but confusion. So true is this
that civil liberty cannot be long preserved without virtue." [5]
Giving voice to his forebodings about the future in 1787,
Governor Livingston lamented, "We do not exhibit the virtue
that is necessary to support a republican government. . . ." [6]

There was not, of course, unanimous agreement on the
meaning of republicanism, particularly when the matter of
majority rule was considered in relation to a live issue. During the course of the heated controversy over the proposed
issuance of paper money, for example, "Curtius" argued
that while in general all laws should correspond with the
wishes of the majority, there were occasions when the legislature should disregard the *vox populi*. He stated the conservative position when he contended that "a virtuous legislature
will not, cannot listen to any proposition, however popular,
that came within the description of being *unjust*, impolitic or

[4] William Paterson Essays, RUL; Essay on Money, 1786, Paterson
Papers (Bancroft Transcripts), NYPL.
[5] Witherspoon, *Works*, V, p. 266.
[6] Sedgwick, *Memoir*, p. 403.

unnecessary . . ." [7] "Then we are not a republican government," countered "Willing to Learn," a paper-money advocate, "for the evident signification thereof is that the people (the majority of the people) bear rule, and it is for them to determine wether [*sic*] a proposition is *unjust, impolitic,* and *unnecessary* or not, . . . the plain definition of republican government is that every elector has a voice in every law which is made to govern him the same as if he personally sat in council . . ." [8] Such a statement as this was bound to alarm the man of property, for it implied that there was no limit to the power of "the people" and that mere numbers were to reign unchecked; this would not be republicanism but democracy, synonym for mob rule.[9] Subsequently, the course of events within the state was to convince the conservatives that a "true Republican constitution" could be restored only by vesting in the central government the power to restrain the states from passing laws that were violative of property rights.

CANDIDATES AND CAMPAIGNS

The nature of the government that developed after independence is only partially revealed in the constitution and in the political thought of the day. Of equal or even greater importance was the actual machinery through which the citizens, individually or in groups, expressed their will. Particular interest attaches to the manner in which the members of the legislature were chosen.

Each of the thirteen counties of the state elected one councilor and three assemblymen, with the result that Cape May's twenty-two hundred people had a representation equal to

[7] *Political Intelligencer*, Jan. 4, 1786.

[8] *Political Intelligencer*, Jan. 25, 1786. "Willing to Learn" was probably Abraham Clark, outstanding champion of the rights of the majority.

[9] "Fellow Citizen," *Political Intelligencer*, May 24, 1786.

Hunterdon's eighteen thousand.[10] The Constitution of 1776 continued the colonial requirement that members of the lower house must be worth five hundred pounds in real and personal property, fixed the qualifications for members of the upper house at twice that amount, and specified that all candidates must have been inhabitants of the county for one year.[11] These constitutional provisions were subsequently altered by legislative enactments. After 1777 an oath of abjuration and allegiance was exacted from all lawmakers, and in 1783 the residence requirement was extended to include two years in the state and seven years in the United States. Moreover, certain classes of tories were barred from office. These additional qualifications, which may be regarded as war measures, were all repealed in 1788.[12] In effect, any freeholder who owned a farm of around two hundred acres—or who possessed the equivalent in personal property—was eligible to sit in the Assembly.[13]

Candidates had to meet tests other than those prescribed by law. So strong was the prejudice against "those harpies the lawyers, the greatest curse New-Jersey experiences," as one vehement essayist characterized them, that they were practically excluded from running for office.[14] Quakers were debarred by the tenets of their sect from holding any position

[10] The Constitution of 1776 provided that the legislature might increase or diminish the number of assemblymen from any county "on the principles of more equal representation," but the whole number was never to be less than thirty-nine (Art. V). No changes were made, however, until 1797. Paterson, *Laws*, pp. 229-34.

[11] Constitution of 1776, Art. II. All legislators had to take an oath (or affirmation) not to repeal or annul the three inviolable sections of the constitution.

[12] *Session Laws*, 1-2, Act of June 4, 1777; *ibid.*, 8-1, Act of Dec. 16, 1783; *ibid.*, 13-1, Act of Nov. 29, 1788.

[13] Rutherfurd, "Notes," p. 84.

[14] "Atticus," *New Jersey Gazette*, July 4, 1787. William C. Houston remarked in 1779 that there was not "a single Gentleman of the Law in the Assembly." Houston to Robert Morris, Oct. 4, 1779, Houston-Morris Letters, RUL.

in the government under the penalty of being expelled from meeting. With some exceptions, this self-denying ordinance was effective.[15] It was advantageous to have been "an early and decided whig," or a militia officer. Justices of the peace were highly eligible, for they had unusual opportunities for "courting popularity to be chosen Assembly-men." [16] There was some prejudice against men of great wealth, although it was recognized that legislators should possess sufficient means to relieve them of the necessity of depending on their salaries.[17] In general the two houses were filled with prosperous farmers and a small number of merchants. The ideal representative, according to Governor Livingston, was one who would "detach himself from all partialities and county-interests, inconsistent with the common weal," promote the welfare of the whole state, be a model of morality, and never be "influenced in his suffrage by motives merely selfish or unworthy." Needless to say these high standards were not met.[18]

Candidates were selected and placed in nomination in a variety of ways. On rare occasions an ambitious office seeker would advertise in the press that in obedience to the earnest solicitations of his friends he had consented to let his name be brought before the public. Such "barefaced electioneering"

[15] Michenor, *Retrospect*, p. 274; Jones, *Quakers*, p. 443; Minutes of the Burlington Quarterly Meeting, Feb. 23, 1789. After 1784 Burlington was represented in the Assembly by delegations that were almost wholly Quaker.

[16] Sedgwick, *Memoir*, p. 394.

[17] "A Citizen of New Jersey," *New Jersey Gazette*, Oct. 10, 1785; "Blawenburgh and Harlingen Records," *Somerset County Historical Quarterly*, IV (1915), p. 120.

[18] [William Livingston], "Characteristics of a Good Assemblyman," *American Museum*, IV (1788), pp. 238-40. "I also inclose a piece describing the duties of an Assemblyman," Livingston wrote to the editor of the *Museum*, "by which, if our Legislators would regulate their conduct, I am persuaded we should have better Laws & less roguery than at present we are burdened with." Livingston to Matthew Carey, Aug. 19, 1788, Livingston Papers, MHS.

was vigorously condemned by some purists. "Art thou soliciting votes in a republican government, in which every
appointment ought freely and spontaneously to flow from
the people?" inquired one indignant whig, who was "fearful
of the pernicious consequences of making interest to obtain
publick offices." [19] Individuals, who usually chose to hide
their identity under a pseudonym, frequently recommended
whole tickets through the columns of the newspapers, at the
same time proclaiming the virtues of the nominees.[20] It was
not uncommon for small coteries of citizens, dissatisfied with
the trend of public affairs, to urge a man of "integrity, understanding, and steadiness" to enter the lists.[21] In many localities, it was customary for a group of voters to gather at a
convenient tavern several weeks before an election to agree
on a slate to which they might give their united support.[22] An
elaborate nominating machinery existed for a time in Somerset. In October, 1782, all the militia companies in the Eastern
and Western Precincts chose committees which met in convention and named three persons as their combined choice
for the legislature. At the same time a delegation was appointed to meet with a similar group from the Northern
Precinct on election day and attempt to settle on a mutually
satisfactory ticket. If the Northern Precinct was willing to
enter into the scheme, the other precincts agreed to drop one
of their men, but if no bargain could be concluded, the trio
selected by the convention would be backed.[23] Militia com-

[19] *New Jersey Gazette*, Aug. 14, 21, 28, 1782, Sept. 5, 19, 1785.

[20] *Ibid.*, Oct. 3, 1787, Oct. 8, 1788.

[21] Robert Morris to Peter Wilson, Sept. 24, 1784, Robert Morris
Papers, RUL; Anonymous to John Stevens, Sr., Oct. 1, 1784, Stevens
Papers, SIT.

[22] *New Jersey Gazette*, Sept. 4, 1782; *New Jersey Journal*, Sept.
24, 1788.

[23] "Blawenburgh and Harlingen Records," pp. 119-20. Apparently
the three precincts came to an agreement, for two of the three men
proposed by the convention—Schuurman and Longstreet—were
elected together with one "northerner," Edward Bunn.

panies in Burlington engaged in similar political activities, as did the "Retaliators" in Monmouth.[24] The experience that had been gained during the Revolutionary era in organizing local committees for a multiplicity of purposes doubtless familiarized men with the techniques of joint action.

The official process of nomination was simple and direct. On the day of an election any voter could propose a candidate, whose name—together with those of his competitors—would be "wrote in fair Characters under the Word Council or Assembly . . . and fixed up in full View at the Door of the House" where the poll was to be taken.[25] Unlike other parts of the electoral machinery, this procedure offered few possibilities for manipulation. In the Burlington election of 1783, however, the official ticket was "tore Down and Destroyed at Different Times" by one faction, with the result that "persons who came in order to give their Votes at Said Election not knowing of any other persons having been Set up did Give their Votes Contrary to their Inclinations." [26] Evidently men were frequently placed in nomination without their knowledge or consent, for there are numerous instances of successful candidates declining to serve.[27]

Pre-election campaigning was conducted under restrictions imposed by the dispersed nature of the population, the poorness of facilities for communication and travel, and the sentiment that aggressive vote-seeking was anti-republican. Too, the fact that there was prior to 1789 no state-wide canvass tended to confine electioneering to the local level. The weekly newspapers took little notice of political contests, possibly because it would have been impractical to follow events in

[24] Petition of the inhabitants of Burlington County, Oct. 25, 1783, AM Papers, NJSL.

[25] *Session Laws*, 8-1, Act of Dec. 16, 1783.

[26] Petition of inhabitants of Burlington County, Oct. 25, 1783, AM Papers, NJSL.

[27] *Votes and Proceedings*, 8-1, p. 14; *ibid*., 9-1, pp. 11, 67, 98; *ibid*., 10-1, p. 30.

each of the thirteen counties. Lists of opposing candidates were never published, and only rarely were there extended discussions of issues or personalities. Even such a critical election as that of 1785, which was to have an important effect on the paper-money question, failed to bring forth any marked flurry of journalistic energies and moved "Rusticus" to deplore the apathy and deadness of the press.[28] Contributions from the pen of a "Citizen of New Jersey" or a "Friend to Justice" occasionally drew the attention of the electorate to facts that should influence their decisions on men and measures and attacked the conduct of certain individuals, but the effectiveness of appeals of this kind was limited.[29] Probably the custom of "making interest," or securing pledges of support from "men of influence," was the commonest and most important form of campaign activity. Every community had its respected leaders, whose opinions carried weight with the multitudes. Correspondence or consultation among such figures was frequently sufficient to bring about a strong combination in behalf of a ticket. On the eve of a critical election in Hunterdon in 1784, an anonymous writer told John Stevens of the plans that were under way to bring about the success of his faction. "We have had several Conferences on the subject previous to fixing the ticket," he explained, "& I have the pleasure to assure you, that the Inhabitants of Trenton *Generally*, as well as those of the lower part of the County, with whom we have had an opportunity of Conversing, are for the Ticket, & seem determined to push the Candidates with all their Interest ... We are unwearied in our endeavours below, not doubting but that the good people of the middle & upper parts of the County, will heartily unite with us." A delegation was to "wait on

[28] *New Jersey Gazette*, Sept. 12, 1785.
[29] *Ibid.*, Sept. 25, 1782, Sept. 20, Oct. 11, 1784, Oct. 15, 1786; *Political Intelligencer*, Oct. 5, 19, 1784; *Brunswick Gazette*, Sept. 18, 1787.

Colonel Houghton in a few Days, & *if possible fix* him and his friends," and an address to the people was ready for distribution.[30] Personal solicitation by the candidates was common, and there is evidence that the practice of villifying and slandering opponents was widespread.[31] Party labels were seldom employed, although late in 1787 it was proposed that "the Foederalists should be distinguished hereafter by the name Washingtonians and the Antifoederalists by the name of Shayites..."[32]

Political techniques in the post-Revolutionary decade were not noticeably different from those that had been employed during the colonial period. Evidently the potentialities inherent in mass organization in a popular form of government did not immediately become apparent to the politicos. Party organization did not ascend above the level of local factionalism. To many, the very word "party" carried anti-republican connotations. Not until 1789, when the first state-wide election was held to choose the members of the first Congress, was the semblance of a state-wide political organization to appear.

THE ELECTORAL MACHINERY

Although independence did not at once produce significant innovations in the structure of politics, there were noteworthy developments in the machinery through which the will of the people was expressed. Annual elections, the increase in the number of elective offices, and the new importance that attached to the representative process after political freedom had become a reality, all contributed to a heightened interest

[30] Anonymous to John Stevens, Sr., Oct. 1, 1784, Stevens Papers, SIT.

[31] *New Jersey Journal*, Oct. 15, 1788; Message of Governor Livingston, *Minutes and Proceedings of the Council and General Assembly of the State of New Jersey in Joint Meeting*, Oct. 30, 1782 (hereafter cited as *Minutes of the Joint Meeting* with date).

[32] *New Jersey Journal*, Oct. 17, 1787.

in the electoral machinery. Between 1725 and the outbreak of
the Revolution there had been virtually no changes in the
laws regulating voting. The first fifteen years of independence, however, saw the passage of eight major acts dealing
with the subject.

Basic in any consideration of the machinery of self-
government is the matter of the franchise. For more than half
a century before the Revolution only freeholders (and house-
holders in the towns of Perth Amboy and Burlington) had
been privileged to vote for members of the Legislature.[33] But
the Provincial Congress on February 28, 1776, in response to
a demand from several counties, decided that it would be
"reasonable and expedient to extend the qualifications of
electors, to persons possessing certain degrees of property, as
well personal as real," and accordingly admitted to suffrage
individuals who were worth fifty pounds in personal estate.[34]
This action marked a fundamental departure from the concept
that political rights were connected with landed property.[35]
The practical effect of the change was unquestionably a great
increase in the number of eligible voters. The constitution that
was adopted a few months later was equally liberal in that it
enfranchised all inhabitants of full age who were worth "fifty
Pounds, Proclamation money, clear estate" and had been
resident in a county for one year.[36] These conditions were
repeated in subsequent laws and others were added. After
1777 voters were required to take an oath or affirmation of
abjuration and allegiance, and in 1783 those who had taken
refuge with the enemy, who had been fined or imprisoned

[33] A. E. McKinley, *The Suffrage Franchise in the Thirteen English Colonies in America* (Philadelphia, 1905), p. 257.

[34] *Acts of the General Assembly of the Province of New Jersey ...*,
compiled by Samuel Allinson (Burlington, 1776), p. 10; *Minutes
Provincial Congress*, pp. 5-6; D. L. Kemmerer, "The Suffrage Franchise in Colonial New Jersey," *PNJHS*, LII (1939), pp. 166-73.

[35] McKinley, *Suffrage*, pp. 240-41.

[36] Constitution of 1776, Art. IV.

for refusing to take the oath of allegiance, or whose property had been confiscated were disfranchised.[37] No distinctions were made as to sex or color and, until 1807, women and Negroes voted.[38]

It is probable that only a small fraction of adult white males were prevented from voting by the property qualification. Because of the currency depreciation and the legal tender laws, a man who had as little as one pound in hard money could at times fulfill the requirements. Indeed, he might "come to the Election in meer Radgs or Stark naked" and still escape challenge.[39] The proportion of those who were barred as a result of the provisions respecting allegiance cannot be estimated, but it must have been large, particularly during the war years.

The enforcement of the legal requirements governing the suffrage was largely at the discretion of the officials who conducted the elections, and there was wide latitude for frauds and abuses. An elector was not obliged to give evidence of his fitness unless he was challenged. If the inspectors were lax or if they were engaged in promoting the interests of certain candidates, they might accept the ballots of ineligible persons without question. In Burlington in 1782 it was claimed that individuals were allowed to vote "without the least Distinction or an attempt made to require the Fidelity of any Voter, except in one or two Instances where the Oaths of Government were required, at the same Time refused, notwithstanding [they] were permitted to give their votes..."

[37] *Session Laws*, 1-2, Act of June 4, 1777; *ibid.*, 8-1, Act of Dec. 16, 1786. The property qualification was defined as fifty pounds lawful money "clear estate." The restrictions on former tories were removed in 1788. *Session Laws*, 13-1, Act of Nov. 21, 1788.

[38] William A. Whitehead, "A Brief Statement on Female Suffrage," *PNJHS*, VIII (1856), pp. 101-105.

[39] Petition of the freeholders of the southern part of Somerset County, Feb. 12, 1783, East Jersey Manuscripts, NJHS.

Similar charges were made the following year.[40] Dishonest inspectors in Hunterdon in 1788 accepted ballots from persons under age, mulatto slaves, apprentice boys, and residents of other counties and states, as well as from those who lacked sufficient property.[41] Instances of this sort were not rare; they may even have been customary.[42]

Corrupt practices were facilitated by the fact that it was relatively easy for one party to gain complete control of the election machinery. The sheriff—unless he was himself a candidate—was the presiding official at the polls, but his power was exceeded by that of the inspectors, who were chosen by the voters when they came together on the first morning of the election. The inspectors in turn selected three clerks.[43] Thus the most numerous faction could readily fill all the positions with men favorable to its candidates. It was the inspectors who judged the qualifications of voters; in addition they decided when to open and close the poll, took custody of the ballot box, counted the ballots, and, with the sheriff, issued certificates of election. If, as was often the case, they were so unscrupulous as to use their authority in a partisan manner, they could manage affairs so as to produce a majority for their friends.[44]

The most important factor regulating the number of votes cast in any election was the accessibility of the polling place. In colonial times elections had been held customarily at the courthouses in each county, although the sheriff had the

[40] *Votes and Proceedings*, 7-1, p. 15; Petition of inhabitants of Burlington County, Oct. 25, 1783, AM Papers, NJSL.

[41] Petition of inhabitants of Hunterdon County, 1788, AM Papers, NJSL.

[42] See, for example, *Votes and Proceedings*, 7-1, p. 8; *ibid.*, 10-1, p. 23; *ibid.*, 12-1, p. 35; "Elector," *New Jersey Journal*, Sept. 30, 1789; "The Election," *Federal Post*, Nov. 18, 1788.

[43] *Session Laws*, 8-1, Act of Dec. 16, 1783.

[44] "Elector," *New Jersey Journal*, Sept. 30, 1789; *Votes and Proceedings*, 7-1, p. 8; Petition of inhabitants of Hunterdon County, 1788, AM Papers, NJSL.

authority, with the consent of the candidates, to move the poll from place to place.[45] After independence it became the practice to limit by law the places where, in addition to the county seat, votes might be received. There was a noticeable trend toward an increase in the number of polling places. Alternate locations were provided in three counties in 1779, in six counties in 1782, in eight counties in 1783, and in all thirteen counties in 1788. There were in 1779 only eighteen places where voters might cast their ballots for members of the legislature; a decade later there were fifty.[46] As a result of this development, many who had been unable to exercise their franchise because of the difficulties involved in travelling to the polls, now had a chance to participate in the choice of officials. No longer were small sections within each county able to dominate elections in practical violation of the principle of representation. Furthermore, with a geographical broadening of the electorate, new opportunities were created for experiments in political organization.

The question of where elections should be held vitally affected the interests of different groups or factions and provoked considerable controversy. So intense was the feeling in certain counties where the poll was unduly restricted to one area as to encourage secession movements.[47] The character of a legislative delegation could be drastically altered by a change in the location of the polls. Protests against the injustice of confining the poll to one or two designated towns were common. A typical complaint was embodied in a petition

[45] Allinson, *Acts*, Act of Aug. 13, 1725, pp. 69-70.

[46] *Session Laws*, 1-2, Act of June 4, 1777; Wilson, *Acts*, Acts of Sept. 27, 1782, June 19, 1783, Dec. 16, 1783; *Session Laws*, 13-1, Act of Nov. 29, 1788.

[47] Petition of freeholders of southern part of Somerset County, Feb. 12, 1783, East Jersey Manuscripts, NJHS; Petition of inhabitants of Gloucester County, May 15, 1786, Loose Manuscripts, NJSL; *Votes and Proceedings*, 11-2, p. 22; "The Schemer," *New Jersey Gazette*, Sept. 25, 1786.

from the inhabitants of the vicinity of Woodbridge in Middlesex to the legislature. Their plea read:

> That they from Experience find Many Inconveniencies Occationed by the Late act [of December 29, 1779] for regulating of Elections having fixed the Poll to be held at New Brunswick during the whole time of Elections. As the County is Divided by the river Rarriton, Many persons who would give their Votes in the Township or Neighbourhood were they reside Will not be at the Trouble and Expence of going a Distance from home, and Crossing a Ferry, to give their Votes at New Brunswick, which Barrs the Poorer Sort of People from Voteing. Your Petitinors Conceives that Neither the Candidates for Representatives, Nor those for the office of Sheriff have an Equal Chance, On account of the Poll being fixed at one place, And as your Petitioners have always, till Lately Enjoyed the Priviledge of having the Poll adjourned and removed from time to time, and place to place; within the County; They humbly pray that by a Suppliment to the Election act, they May again be vested with the Same Indulgence ...[48]

Several of the most respectable residents of New Brunswick signed a counterpetition opposing any change. The removal of the poll would be attended with "many disadvantages and much contention" and would not serve any good purpose, they maintained.[49] The people of Stafford and Dover townships in Monmouth complained that they did not have "an Opportunity of giveing their Votes on account of living so far Distant from the place of Election" and asked that the poll might be moved to Toms River.[50] The voters of Hunter-

[48] Petitions of the freeholders and inhabitants of Middlesex County, Sept. 1, 1782, AM Papers, NJSL.

[49] Petition of inhabitants of Middlesex, Sept. 24, 1782, AM Papers, NJSL. The election law of June 19, 1783, provided for the removal of the poll in Middlesex from New Brunswick to Bonhamtown and Cranberry.

[50] Petition of inhabitants of Stafford and Dover townships, May 15, 1786, AM Papers, NJSL. Elections were held only at Freehold.

don found the existing system of conducting elections "in many Instances extremely burthensome & Grievious and attended with a public & private Expence, and a waste of Time, that in a great measure obstructs & will finally ... destroy, if continued, the Execution of so Important an object." Their proposal was that elections should be held in each township and that the polls should all be closed on the same day.[51]

The movement for making the polls accessible to all the people undoubtedly was given impetus after 1788 by the introduction of state-wide elections for Congress. Early political alignments corresponded with the sectional division between East and West Jersey, and the contending factions, anxious to attract the maximum number of votes to their standards, were favorably inclined toward an extension of voting facilities. On the eve of the first Congressional contest the number of polling places in the state was suddenly increased from twenty-nine to fifty.[52] As a consequence of this action, many times the normal vote was cast in some counties.[53]

The legal provisions governing the movement of the poll gave to those in charge of the election important discretionary power. A majority of the inspectors could decline to permit the authorized adjournment from place to place and might do so if they were partial to a faction whose interests would be served by such a refusal. An instance of this type of

[51] Petition of inhabitants of Hunterdon County, May 25, 1787, AM Papers, NJSL. It was essentially this procedure that was finally adopted throughout the state in 1797. Paterson, *Laws*, Act of Feb. 23, 1797, pp. 229-34.

[52] *Session Laws*, 13-1, Act of Nov. 29, 1788.

[53] In Burlington, for example, 258 votes were cast at the single polling place in 1787. In the 1789 Congressional election 2,826 ballots were received at eight polling places. Henry C. Shinn, "An Early New Jersey Poll List," *Pennsylvania Magazine of History and Biography*, XLIV (1920), pp. 77-81; J. M. Wallace to Elias Boudinot, Mar. 9, 1790, Wallace Papers, IV, HSP.

manipulation occurred in Burlington in 1784. An anti-whig group managed to get its men chosen inspectors when the election began at the town of Burlington. These officials, who had "Previous to the poles being Opened Determined that it should not be removed, inasmuch as they Did not approve of the Law in that Respect," would not assent to a petition from the inhabitants of Bordentown asking that the poll be adjourned to their town.[54] Another technique was for the inspectors to make a tour of the county, taking in votes in the people's houses.[55] A timely closing of the poll could also affect the outcome of a contest.

During the postwar years there was no uniform mode of voting. Prior to the Revolution, the typical English custom of polling the electors by "the view," by show of hands, or by voice vote seems to have prevailed, and it was sanctioned by the ordinance of February 28, 1776.[56] In 1777, however, a new law specified that in the future all elections were to be by ballot, although exceptions were made for six counties. Five years later *viva voce* voting was temporarily decreed for all counties, apparently to enable the whigs to prevent their opponents from gaining control of the government.[57] Eight counties were authorized to employ the *viva voce* method by the act of December 16, 1783, and five of them continued the

[54] Petition of inhabitants of Burlington, Nov., 1784, AM Papers, NJSL. The petitioners observed that a majority of the inspectors "did not approve of any Law on the present Establishment during the War . . ." The election was upheld. *Votes and Proceedings*, 9-1, p. 17.

[55] "Elector," *New Jersey Journal*, Sept. 30, 1789.

[56] Allinson, *Acts*, Act of Aug. 13, 1725, pp. 69-70; C. F. Bishop, *History of Elections in the American Colonies* (New York, 1893), pp. 155-64. There is evidence that prior to 1702 some type of ballot may have been employed. *Ibid.*, pp. 166-67; McKinley, *Suffrage*, pp. 245-46.

[57] *Session Laws*, 6-3, Act of Sept. 27, 1782; Petition of joint committee of townships and precincts of New Jersey, Aug. 31, 1782, Loose Manuscripts, NJSL. This law was repealed June 19, 1783.

practice after the act of November 29, 1788.[58] East Jersey tended to favor the traditional system while West Jersey leaned toward the ballot. No satisfactory explanation of this divergence has been advanced, but it is possible that the difference was in some way related to the colonial experience of the two sections.[59]

Protests against the *viva voce* manner of voting were not uncommon. The lack of secrecy was productive of many evils, declared a number of inhabitants of Cumberland in a remonstrance to the legislature, because "men of large estates or who have many debtors may, & we presume, often do, influence a great many Voters in an Undue manner ..." Open voting wounded "the tender sensibilities of friendship" and occasioned the "exercise of the irascible & jealous passions." Electors in a republic should be free from all control by private interests and should be uninfluenced by fear, favor, or affection.[60] Similar views were held by the people of Gloucester, who deemed it "an essential privilege to vote by Ballot," and by some residents of Middlesex.[61]

Where ballots were used, the elector either wrote the names of the candidates he favored on a slip of paper or else accepted a written ticket that had been prepared in advance by one of the factions engaged in the contest. Although fines were levied against anyone who imposed on an illiterate

[58] The *viva voce* procedure was used in Essex, Morris, and Cape May from colonial times until after 1788, in Middlesex, Monmouth, and Cumberland until 1788, in Bergen after 1782, and in Sussex after 1783. Somerset, Burlington, Gloucester, Salem, and Hunterdon used the ballot after 1777, except in 1782. Bergen voted by ballot from 1777 to 1782, Sussex from 1777 to 1782 and in 1783.

[59] Lundin, *Cockpit*, p. 272n.

[60] Petition of inhabitants of Cumberland County, Nov. 7, 1786, AM Papers, NJSL; *Votes and Proceedings*, 11-2, p. 23.

[61] Petitions of inhabitants of Gloucester County, Sept. 26, 1782, AM Papers, NJSL; *Votes and Proceedings*, 7-1, p. 12; *ibid.*, 13-1, p. 26. On the other hand, the continuance of *viva voce* voting was urged in a petition from Essex. *Ibid.*, 7-1, p. 55.

person by giving him a ticket containing names other than those for whom he had asked, the ignorant were frequently tricked. "Tickets are often palmed upon such as cannot write nor read," claimed William Paterson, "by which means they sometimes vote *in* the person whom they intended to vote *out*." [62] Too, there was apparently nothing to prevent an inspector from unfolding and looking at a ballot and then inventing some pretext for refusing it.[63] The ballot was handed to one of the inspectors, who announced the name and residence of the voter and, if no objection was made put the ballot into a locked box. At the end of the election the tickets were taken from the box one at a time by an inspector who called out the names of the candidates and the office. The ticket was then passed to another inspector who went through the same procedure before delivering it to the sheriff to be filed. The tallies were kept by the clerks, and the final results were announced by the sheriff.[64]

The elections began on the second Tuesday in October and might continue for several days if the polls were moved to various towns within the county. The usual voting place was a tavern, whose facilities, it may be presumed, were used for more than the receiving of ballots. That the proceedings were apt to be tumultuous at times is apparent from the fact that it was thought necessary to penalize persons who appeared "with any Weapons of War" or who "put any of the Electors in Fear of personal Danger." Bribery and vote-

---

[62] "Aurelius," William Paterson Essays, RUL.

[63] William Paterson, Notes on contested election before the Assembly [1788], Paterson Papers, PUL. The cynical "Elector" advised those who wished to manipulate elections to have some hardy fellow with a club at the service of the inspectors so that "if any person offers any dirty, blotted ticket, which is not printed at your direction, he may drive him away or compel him to take such an one as you approve of, and give it in to the inspectors at the window." *New Jersey Journal*, Sept. 30, 1789.

[64] *Session Laws*, 1-2, Act of June 4, 1777; *ibid.*, 8-1, Act of Dec. 16, 1783.

buying were also prohibited. The art of electioneering was assiduously plied by the various candidates and their supporters, and if the enticement of intangible promises failed to win a convert, success might be had with beef and grog.[65] A primitive picture of the scene at the polls was recorded by an amateur poet in 1788.

> Zealous Patriots heading rabbles
> Orators promoting squabbles
> Free Electors always swilling
> Candidates not worth a shilling!
> Butchers, Farmers, and Carmen,
> Half-pay Officers and Chairmen
> Many Zealots, not worth nothing,
> Many perjured Persons voting;
> Candidates, with Tradesmen pissing,
> Cleaners, Bagpipes, Clapping, Hissing
> Warmes Friends in Opposition,
> Hottest Foes in Coalition!
> Open Houses, paid to tempt the
> Rotten Votes, with Bellies empty;
> Boxing, Drinking, Rhyming, Sweating;
> Fevers, Fractures, Inflamations,
> Bonefires, Squibs, Illuminations;
> Murd'rers, daring all detection,
> Pray, Gentlemen, how do you like the Election? [66]

Any generalizations regarding the size of the electorate in the post-Revolutionary decade are subject to many qualifications. The number of men voting at a given election was limited not so much by the stated property requirement—which in practice was probably not an important barrier—as it was by such factors as the honesty of the inspectors, the accessibility of the polls, the religious scruples of the Quakers,

[65] *Session Laws*, 8-1, Act of Dec. 16, 1783; "An Epigrim [*sic*] on the Middlesex Election," *Brunswick Gazette*, Oct. 21, 1789; "Diary of Joseph Lewis," *PNJHS*, LX (1942), p. 203.

[66] "The Election," *Federal Post*, Nov. 18, 1788.

and the amount of pressure exerted to "get out the vote." In Burlington County, about one-tenth of the adult white males participated in state elections. This small proportion may be explained by the fact that an influential clique was usually able to confine the poll to the city of Burlington. In the Congressional election of 1789, however, when votes were needed for the West Jersey ticket, Burlington managed to poll a vote equivalent to eight-tenths of the adult white males by receiving ballots in at least eight places around the county.[67] In Hunterdon, where ballots were used and the poll was opened at six different locations, from three-tenths to four-tenths of the adult white males customarily voted.[68] The proportion in Essex, stronghold of *viva voce* voting, rose as high as seven-tenths in 1785, and in the first Congressional contest, the vote cast was equal to nine-tenths of the adult white male population. This suspiciously high figure, like that in Burlington, was achieved as the result of wholesale frauds.[69] The potential electorate, then, included all but a small fraction—possibly as low as one-tenth—of the white males over twenty-one, but for a variety of reasons, only a minority of those who were eligible usually exercised their right of franchise.[70]

[67] These estimates are based on the assumption that white males over twenty-one constituted approximately one-fifth of the total white population. See p. 85n.

[68] *New Jersey Gazette*, Oct. 16, 1782, Oct. 24, 1785; *Political Intelligencer*, Oct. 26, 1784; *New Jersey Journal*, Feb. 25, 1789.

[69] *Political Intelligencer*, Oct. 26, 1785; Essex election return, Apr. 27, 1789, Livingston Papers, MHS.

[70] In 1797, William Paterson estimated the number of the electors in the state at thirty-five thousand. This was equivalent to 90 per cent of the adult white males. He stated further that seldom did more than one-third of the eligible voters go to the polls. "The office of sheriff," he wrote, "being of a lucrative nature, frequently calls forth great exertions, especially when the contest happens to exist between powerful and active competitors. In such cases I have known two thirds, three fourths, and sometimes five sixths of the electors brought into action." "Hortentius," No. 4, William Paterson Essays, RUL.

The several revisions in the election laws were notable elements in the efforts made by New Jersey to orient itself to the conditions created by independence. The electoral machinery was obviously crude and irregular, and it was an easy prey to corrupt influences. But during this period of transition and experimentation, there gradually emerged a trend toward uniformity, which was to be realized in large measure in 1797.[71] Moreover, the potential electorate was expanded as franchise qualifications were reduced and voting facilities were extended. More people were both eligible and able to vote in 1789 than in 1776. It could not be said that political power was restricted to an unrepresentative minority of the people. On the contrary, a high degree of popular government maintained.

CONTESTED ELECTIONS

In view of the many possibilities for corruption and manipulation inherent in the crude voting machinery, it is not surprising that scarcely a year passed without the legislature having to decide one or more cases of contested elections. Usually the protest was presented in the form of a petition signed by a large number of citizens asking that the election be set aside and a new one be held. Each house had the power under the constitution to judge "the qualifications and election" of its own members, and accordingly could hold hearings and summon witnesses. Only in rare instances were members who had been certified by the sheriff and inspectors unseated.

In Burlington County a long struggle between two factions, which may be loosely designated as the whigs and the "disaffected," gave rise to charges of illegality in three successive

[71] Paterson, *Laws*, Act of Feb. 22, 1797, pp. 229-34. With the township as the unit, all voting was to be by ballot and was to be completed within two days.

years. In 1782 the "disaffected" group achieved a victory by gaining control of the poll and permitting persons who were suspected of being tories to vote.[72] A year later the whigs organized in earnest. A few days before the election militia captains posted notices around the county asking their men to meet them at specified taverns in the town of Burlington on the morning the poll was to be opened. It is "as necessary in Peace to guard against the private as it was in War against the declared Enemies of Our Country," proclaimed the manifestoes.[73] Alerted in this manner, the companies gathered at the election place under arms, tore down the ticket which was put up by the "disaffected," and used "improper influences" to further the candidacy of their nominees.[74] The balloting continued for two days, and when the totals were announced, it appeared that the whigs had been able to muster some 180 votes to approximately 160 for their opponents.[75] Several petitions, signed by almost three hundred persons, were soon delivered to the legislature, which was asked to declare invalid the election of the councilor and two of the assemblymen. After a two-day hearing on the matter, that body came to the conclusion that the evidence presented was insufficient

[72] Petition of inhabitants of Burlington County, AM Papers, NJSL; *Votes and Proceedings*, 7-1, pp. 15, 24. The charges were dismissed by the Assembly when no one appeared to support them.

[73] Two notices by Capt. Curtis and Capt. Thomas, Oct. 9, 1783, AM Papers, NJSL.

[74] Petition of inhabitants of Burlington, Oct. 25, 1783, AM Papers, NJSL; *Votes and Proceedings*, 8-1, p. 18.

[75] Minute of the Burlington election, Oct. 14-15, 1783, signed by Joseph Bloomfield, Clayton Newbold, and Isaac Cogill, AM Papers, NJSL. The vote for councilor was: Peter Tallman, 173; John Coxe, 16; William Newbold, 158. For assemblymen: George Anderson, 337; Israel Shreve, 196; Caleb Shreve, 180; John Biddle, 160; Josiah Haines, 160; Thomas Fenimore, 10. The election of Anderson, who was acceptable to both factions, was not contested. According to the poll list, only 344 persons voted, yet the total vote for councilor indicates that there were 347 ballots cast. Poll list of Burlington election, October, 1783, AM Papers, NJSL.

to void the election.[76] The "disaffected" returned to power in 1784 over the protests of the whigs, who unsuccessfully sought to challenge their triumph by charging that the inspectors had refused to move the poll to Bordentown.[77]

The election in Hunterdon in October, 1788, was carried on in a manner so irregular as to arouse over two hundred petitioners to demand that it be set aside. The principal accusation was that "the Box which contained the votes ... [was] Intrusted into the hands of Certain Inspectors (who were deeply gained into the favour of Divers Candidates) & not secured as the Law directs, without Lock or Key, or any other kind of Security usually practised in Said County." Moreover, the complainants listed ten different categories of ineligible persons who had been unlawfully allowed to vote.[78] In the course of an extended hearing before the Assembly, in which William Paterson appeared for the defendants and Frederick Frelinghuysen for the plaintiffs, it was alleged that the ballot box had been intrusted to certain inspectors who had bet on one of the successful candidates, that the box was not locked as the law required but was merely fastened with a nail, that the box was actually transported from poll to poll by one of the candidates in his sulky, and that two hundred votes for one of the losers had been removed and replaced with a similar number for his opponent. Paterson in his defense stated that betting—unlike bribery—was no offense, that it was the duty of the sheriff to provide a proper ballot

[76] *Votes and Proceedings*, 8-1, pp. 6-27. Petition of sundry freeholders of Burlington, Nov. 11, 1783, AM Papers, NJSL.

[77] Petition of inhabitants of Burlington, [Nov., 1784]. AM Papers, NJSL; *Votes and Proceedings*, 9-1, pp. 12-17. The election was upheld by a vote of 21-6.

[78] Petitions of inhabitants of Hunterdon County, [Oct., 1788], AM Papers, NJSL; *Votes and Proceedings*, 13-1, p. 7. Counterpetitions signed by 348 men characterized the protest as "the offspring of Disappointed Expectations and abortive hopes" and asked that it be disregarded. Remonstrances of inhabitants of Hunterdon, Nov., 1788, AM Papers, NJSL.

box, that the box in fact had had no lock for four years, and that the box was at no time out of the custody of the inspectors. As for the charge that unqualified persons had voted, he maintained that final decisions on such questions rested with those who conducted the election. The skillful lawyer argued that the holding of a new election would only lead to more contention, "for severe Contests in Matters of this kind," he insisted, "occupy the Time and attention and interest and inflame the Passions of all the Competitors and their Adherents; they give a Keeness and Bitterness to the Spirit of Party, which seldom wears off for a Length of Years, and Sometimes continues and festers in the Bosom till the close of Life." [79] Impressed no doubt by Paterson's reasoning, the house ruled that there was not sufficient evidence of corruption and sustained the election.[80]

Of seven contested elections that were brought to the attention of the legislature between 1782 and 1788, in only one instance was a new election ordered. The Monmouth election in 1785 must have been flagrantly managed, for both houses unanimously refused to seat the men who were returned. Because the election of the sheriff was judged to be illegal and no effort had even been made to choose coroners, there was no officer to whom a writ could be directed, and it was necessary to enact a special law authorizing the clerk of the Court of Quarter Sessions to set in motion the machinery for a new election.[81] This case was exceptional. In general the

[79] William Paterson, Notes on contested election before the Assembly [1788], Paterson Papers, PUL.

[80] *Votes and Proceedings*, 13-1, pp. 7-14.

[81] *Ibid.*, 10-1, pp. 6-27; *Session Laws*, 10-1, Act of Nov. 5, 1785. In the runoff, Daniel Hendrickson, speaker of the preceding Assembly, and Doctor Thomas Henderson, a political power since the first days of the Revolution, were overthrown by the less well-known Peter Schenck and Joseph Stillwell. The redoubtable David Forman also went down to defeat. *New Jersey Gazette*, Dec. 5, 1785; Lundin, *Cockpit*, pp. 286-93. For other cases of contested elections, see *Votes and Proceedings*, 7-1, pp. 8-18; *ibid.*, 11-1, pp. 6-12.

legislators were accustomed to view with considerable tolerance evidence of corrupt practices at the polls.

ELECTIONS BY THE JOINT MEETING

Independence brought about not only an increase in the
number of offices at the gift of the people, but it resulted as
well in the transfer to their representatives of the appointive
power that had formerly been vested in the governor and
Council. Aside from sheriffs, coroners, and members of the
legislature, virtually all posts within the state were filled by
the two houses in joint meeting. That body chose the
governor, attorney general, secretary of state, treasurer,
justices of the Supreme Court, judges of the Courts of Common Pleas, justices of the peace, military and naval officers,
agents for confiscated estates, clerk of the Supreme Court, clerks
of the circuits, county clerks, and the mayors and aldermen of
certain cities. Possessed of the power of distributing a host of
offices (many of them lucrative), the legislators could now
attract to themselves political support by favoring their
friends. "Courting favor" and "making interest" took on a
new significance, for tangible rewards offered added zest to
factional contests.

The habitual choice of the joint meeting for governor was
William Livingston. Elected in 1776 as the first executive
under the recently adopted constitution, he was continued in
office each year until his death in 1790.[82] Known as "Old
Flint" because of his vigorous whiggism, he triumphed easily
over his opponents. During the war period his tenure was at
times challenged by a handful of men who were actuated by
personal animus or by tory sympathies, but no contender was
ever able to muster more than eight votes against him. In

[82] Richard P. McCormick, "The First Election of Governor Wil-
liam Livingston," *PNJHS*, LXV (1947), pp. 92-100; Margaret B.
Macmillan, *The War Governors in the American Revolution* (New
York, 1943), pp. 239 ff.; Sedgwick, *Memoir, passim*.

1783 the only dissident voice in the joint meeting was that of Samuel Tucker, whom Livingston despised and against whom he directed a series of scathing attacks in the columns of the *Gazette*.[83] General Elias Dayton, the state's outstanding military figure, was the nominee of the opposition in 1784. Livingston proudly described the circumstances of the election to his wife:

> The election of the officers of Government was finished last night. Mr. Cooper (who is this year returned as one of the Council for Gloucester) & Mr. Tucker, my implacable Enemies, set up General Dayton, who had their two votes, & those of two members of the assembly for the County of Burlington, [William Newbold and Clayton Newbold], both reputed Tories & those of a member of Gloucester [Thomas Clark] influenced by this Cooper: and this is all the interest they could make against me after the most indefatigable industry for that purpose. So that the general will make but an indifferent figure in the printed account of the votes with his five votes out of 43.[84]

Two years later his rival was Abraham Clark, who received but eight votes despite the fact that he was the acknowledged leader of the popular paper-money cause.[85] "I was happy to hear of your reelection for Governor," wrote the faithful Mrs. Livingston to her spouse, "I had my fears about it. God is better to us than our fears." [86] In 1787 only one vote was cast against Livingston, and in the two following years his

[83] *Minutes of the Joint Meeting*, Nov. 6, 1783. Writing under the pseudonym of "Scipio," Livingston accused Tucker of misconduct as treasurer of the state in 1776 and of having taken a "protection" from the British. The controversy was aired in the *New Jersey Gazette* for several months beginning in February, 1784.

[84] Livingston to Mrs. Livingston, Oct. 30, 1784, Livingston Papers, MHS; *Minutes of the Joint Meeting*, Oct. 29, 1784.

[85] *Ibid.*, Oct. 31, 1786. Seven of Clark's votes came from Somerset and Middlesex and one from Burlington.

[86] Susan Livingston to Livingston, Nov. 4, 1786, Livingston Papers, MHS.

election was unanimous.[87] The governorship was clearly not an object of factional contention.

The dozens of other offices at the disposal of the joint meeting were eagerly solicited, for they brought to the recipient either a good income from fees or political influence. Plurality of officeholding was common. Because former legislators had a near-monopoly on public employment, there was virtually an officeholding class, whose members seldom were without one or more positions in the state. It was a rare assemblyman who was not at one time or another a judge, a justice of the peace, or a clerk.[88] That the selection of minor judges was frequently governed by political considerations is apparent from the criticism leveled by "A Citizen of New Jersey" against the appointments made on one occasion in Hunterdon. ". . . few of them seem to arise either from the necessity of the appointment, or the abilities of the appointed," the writer complained, "but merely from a view to secure the members future elections." [89]

When an especially lucrative post became vacant, extraordinary exertions were made by candidates to win support in the joint meeting. William Churchill Houston had been dead less than three days when a host of competitors entered the lists for the clerkship of the Supreme Court, which he had held for seven years. Samuel Witham Stockton, clerk of Hunterdon County, rushed off a dispatch to the influential Elisha Boudinot and inclosed a number of letters to the assemblymen of Bergen, Essex, and Morris, informing them of his pretentions. "I wish you would get Judge Peck & Mr. McWhorter or whoever else with yourself you think proper

[87] *Minutes of the Joint Meeting*, Oct. 31, 1787, Oct. 31, 1788, Nov. 2, 1789.

[88] Colonel Joseph Hugg of Gloucester served on the Council, became judge of the Court of Common Pleas, clerk of the orphans' court, and surrogate and in 1785 was anxious to become county clerk. Richard Howell to R. S. Smith, Nov., 1788, Smith Papers, RUL.

[89] *New Jersey Gazette*, Oct. 10, 1785.

to speak particularly to Mr. Wilson & the Bergen Members & Essex & Mid[dlesex] if you see them," he implored. "Richard S[tockton] & [Frederick] Frelinghuysen will exert themselves much on this occasion, and the latter is to be at Bruns^k on ye 27th & will make a point of speaking to all he knows as they pass." One of Stockton's rivals, James Ewing, travelled through the state in his sulky "to make personal application to the members of the Assembly." Both men were doomed to disappointment, however, for the plum went to Major Richard Howell of Gloucester.[90] When the term of Bowes Reed, the perennial secretary of state, drew to a close a few weeks later, a newspaper correspondent inquired "for what reason that office (being *the most lucrative one* in the state of New-Jersey) should be always kept in the hands of one person: It is from a moderate calculation supposed to be worth from twelve to fifteen hundred [pounds] a year." The question, it would appear, was prompted by the "unprecedented" and "unjustifiable" conduct of the legislature in choosing Houston's successor.[91] Long tenure in office was common. James Mott was annually reelected treasurer for more than fifteen years, Joseph Bloomfield served for a decade as attorney general, Maskell Ewing was clerk of the Assembly for a score of years, Elisha Boudinot was a fixture as clerk of the circuits, James Ewing was repeatedly chosen auditor. Rotation in office was a principle foreign to a period which knew no state-wide organized political parties.[92]

[90] S. W. Stockton to Elisha Boudinot, Aug. 15, 23, 1788, Boudinot Letters, PUL; Stockton to Wm. Livingston, Aug. 16, 1788, Livingston Papers, MHS; *New Jersey Journal*, Sept. 10, 1788.

[91] *Federal Post*, Oct. 21, Nov. 4, 1788.

[92] In the decade 1780-1790, there was only one instance when the joint meeting failed to reelect the incumbent to one of the major state offices. In 1783 John Stevens, Jr., was replaced as treasurer by James Mott. *Minutes of the Joint Meeting*, Nov. 2, 1783.

BASES OF POLITICAL DIVISIONS

Because there were no state-wide elections prior to 1789, there was little incentive for the organization of state-wide political parties. The county was the basic political unit, and within each county local factions contended for dominance. There were many bases for intra-county divisions. Regional rivalry was pronounced in several counties, particularly in the larger ones and in those where the location of the polls gave to one section an unequal advantage. The principal towns were frequently regarded with jealousy and suspicion by rural communities. Differences in religion and in national origins also promoted antagonisms. In nearly every county the whig-tory split was a familiar element in factionalism. Alignments that had developed during the Revolution, when the cause of independence was the paramount issue, endured long after that issue had been resolved. Gradually, however, as new questions came to the fore, the wartime combinations gave way to others in which whiggism was not a major consideration.[93]

Outstanding personalities—"men of interest"—and their family connections were potent centers of political strength. The Huggs of Gloucester, the Smiths of Burlington, the Elmers of Cumberland, the Boudinots of Essex, and the Sinnicksons of Salem were able to exert a powerful influence over the voters of their counties. Individuals like Abraham Clark of Essex, James Schureman of Middlesex, and Benjamin Van Cleve of Hunterdon could command large personal followings. The weight of the prestige of such men was a valuable asset to any faction.

In addition to these local factors, which were most apparent on the county level, there were broad and significant divisions

---

[93] It should be noted that for more than a generation after the end of the Revolution, the Federalists were condemned by their opponents as being the party of toryism. Fee, *Transition*, p. 131.

within the state as a whole. In the legislature, where the majority interests of each county were represented, there was on almost all public questions a fundamental cleavage between the members from East Jersey and those from West Jersey. This was not the sectionalism of tidewater against backcountry, of plantation owners against yeomen, of a metropolis against the hinterlands, of a trading region against an agricultural region, or of an over-represented minority against an under-represented majority. Rather it was a sectionalism in which historical and cultural influences were as important as geographic and economic determinants.

Throughout the colonial period the marked differences between the two Jerseys had been maintained and had received explicit governmental recognition.[94] The Revolution, instead of bringing unity to the state, actually heightened the traditional duality. Noah Webster was one of many who observed that "the jealousies between East and West Jersey ... [were] almost az great az between the northern and suthern states, upon a question respecting the seet of government, or any other matter of little consequence to the union." [95] The Quakers and the Presbyterians were if anything more at odds than they had been formerly. The two proprietary boards revived and carried on their old disagreements. New York and Philadelphia continued to pull at either end of the state as they had in the past.

The war created new bases for sectional antagonism. It was East Jersey that had borne the brunt of the conflict, furnished the whig leadership, made the largest contributions to victory, and suffered the heaviest losses. In West Jersey the influential Quaker minority had adopted a negative or neutral attitude and had refused as a matter of principle to give aid to the

[94] The legislature met alternately at Perth Amboy and Burlington, and each division had equal representation and its own treasury.

[95] Noah Webster, *A Collection of Essays and Fugitive Writings on Moral, Historical, Political, and Literary Subjects* (Boston, 1790), p. 352.

rebel cause. Adhering to their religious scruples, they had balked at paying taxes for defraying military expenses and had likewise declined to receive the continental and state notes that were issued to finance the war. For many years after peace had been won, they kept up their opposition to taxation for paying war costs.[96] Thus while the northern part of the state was flooded with paper currency and certificates, received in payment for military supplies and services, the southern part had relatively little such paper in circulation. This peculiar financial condition was largely responsible for the divergent views held by the legislators from the two divisions on the vital money problem after 1783. So strong was the sectional cleavage that it tended to obscure class lines.

Nothing resembling a state-wide party organization developed prior to 1789. For that reason it is difficult to attach meaningful labels to the numerous individuals and groups that dominated the political scene. In view of the unusual sectionalism that formed the most obvious basis of political alignments, it is appropriate to use geographical terms to denote the principal contending factions. There was the West Jersey faction and the East Jersey faction. They took opposing stands on numerous public questions. In a loose sense, West Jersey was "conservative" and East Jersey was "radical," but these words have to be used cautiously and interpreted carefully. Moreover, conflict over domestic matters did not extend to what may be called continental concerns. Where questions respecting the Confederation were involved, harmony took the place of dissension.

Despite its many defects, the machinery that was developed in New Jersey after independence provided for the representation of the various classes and sections of the state in a more proportionate manner than did that which had prevailed before the Revolution. With the elimination of such

[96] Minutes of the Philadelphia Yearly Meeting, 1780-1789, pp. 14, 90, 99-101, 104, 110, 143, Friends Book Store.

inequitable features as the freehold suffrage requirement, infrequent elections, the appointive Council, and the interference of crown officials, there was increased opportunity for the will of the people to predominate in the determination of policy. There still remained, of course, formidable obstacles to true majority rule. The system of equal representation of all counties in the legislature, the crude electoral facilities, the limitations on the franchise, the property qualifications demanded of legislators, and the persistence of a deference toward members of the gentry operated to give undue weight to some minority groups. But self-government was indeed a reality. So real was it that by 1787 an influential body of the citizenry was fearful that republicanism had degenerated into democracy.

V

Business and the Government

A FLEXIBLE and independent government, responsive to popular pressures, encouraged different economic groups in the state to solicit legislation favorable to their interests. Merchants, landowners, security holders, and debtors all sought to influence public policy through the available political channels. The small but enterprising business community, free from British mercantilistic restraints but at the same time conscious of the existence of formidable barriers to economic progress, was especially concerned with the promotion of measures that would foster the development of commerce. Although little help could be expected from the impotent Congress of the Confederation, the legislature, it seemed, might do much to stimulate foreign trade by enacting appropriate regulations. A variety of proposals were advanced by the mercantile element to accomplish the desired objective, but these plans won only incomplete acceptance and were foredoomed to failure. The experience served to emphasize New Jersey's dependence on New York and Philadelphia markets and to accent the need for vesting in the central government comprehensive and exclusive authority over commerce.

THE VICISSITUDES OF COMMERCE

Prior to the Revolution, New Jersey had the smallest overseas trade of any colony with the possible exception of Delaware. Direct sailings for Europe were a rarity. A few sloops
laden with wheat, flour, rye, corn, pork, cattle, horses, butter,
and staves sailed to the West Indies and returned with such
commodities as sugar, rum, and wine. Flaxseed, potash, and
iron were sent to England to pay in part for heavy imports
of dry goods and tea.[1] Trade was not centered in any one
principal port but was carried on from a dozen or more towns,
many of which were accessible by water only to vessels that
were too small to attempt long voyages. Such a diffusion of
commercial activities did not favor the development of a
strong merchant class capable of providing the capital for
extensive foreign operations. Good markets and adequate
credit facilities were available near at hand in New York and
Philadelphia. It was to those cities that by far the greater
portion of the colony's exports was sent, and from them were
procured the necessities that could not be produced at home.[2]

The outbreak of war brought about the complete disruption
of normal trade. Embargoes were put into effect, imports
were cut off, New York was occupied by the British, many
merchants entered military service, and the seas became
unsafe for shipping. For a few years there was commercial
stagnation, but by 1780 there was a noticeable change. Imports again flowed into the country in a volume that may
have equalled prewar marks. New York was bulging with
British goods, much of which found its way into other states

---

[1] John Sheffield, *Observations on the Commerce of the United States*
(Dublin, 1784), Chart VIII; Rutherfurd, "Notes," pp. 82-83.

[2] Witherspoon, *Works*, IX, p. 206; East, *Business Enterprise*, p. 17;
Morse, *Geography*, p. 288; Petition of Citizens of Perth Amboy to
legislature, May 29, 1786, Manuscript Collection, NJSL.

through illicit channels.[3] French and Spanish specie provided the people with the means to supply themselves with the luxuries that they had long lacked. In New Jersey the stores were once again well stocked with imported articles of all descriptions. Those with money to buy could purchase sugar, tea, coffee, broadcloths, linens, silk handkerchiefs, hardware, glassware, knee buckles, snuff, tobacco, "and an assortment of other goods too tedious to mention." [4] The prosperity of the times motivated some fifty men and women in Essex alone to seek licenses as storekeepers in 1781.[5] Strenuous efforts were made to halt the spending spree, which was rapidly draining the country of its precious stock of hard cash, but the boom was not to end until money and credit were exhausted.[6]

With the arrival of peace, wartime restrictions on the movement of goods were lifted, and the principal merchants of the state—many of whom had done no private business during the war—looked forward eagerly and hopefully to the resumption of normal commerce. A week after the news of the definitive treaty reached New Jersey, Colonel John Neilson of New Brunswick and Moore Furman of Trenton were exchanging views on trade prospects. New York, they agreed, should provide a good market for foodstuffs. Neilson had a boat ready to convey produce there as soon as the communication should be opened.[7] The city was full to overflowing with the English wares that were still so much in demand, and it

---

[3] East, *Business Enterprise*, pp. 184, 244; Sheffield, *Observations*, Chart X.

[4] *New Jersey Gazette*, Dec. 27, 1780, Nov. 14, 1781, Aug. 14, 1782.

[5] Petitions to Justices of the Court of Common Pleas, Essex County, Jan.-Apr., 1781, Vault Manuscripts, NJSL.

[6] Webster, *Collection of Essays*, p. 188.

[7] Moore Furman to Col. John Neilson, Apr. 2, 1783; Neilson to Furman, Apr. 3, 1783, Neilson Papers, F 187, RUL; *New Jersey Gazette*, Apr. 9, 1783. Neilson advertised that after "six years attention to public business," he was returning to trade "as soon as regularity takes the place of confusion, with respect to commercial affairs."

was in need of provisions for its garrison. The Dutch farmers of Somerset were soon sending their flour down the Raritan and across to the metropolis, and were receiving in exchange satins and silks for their wives and daughters. Along the Delaware dozens of small boats were carrying wheat, corn, and pork to Philadelphia. The familiar colonial trade pattern was restored.[8]

Throughout 1784 and 1785, there were in each issue of the newspapers numerous advertisements of large assortments of European and West Indian goods. New York wholesalers solicited patronage and offered favorable credit terms.[9] There were more than three hundred and fifty shopkeepers in the state in 1784, the vast majority of whom relied on New York and Philadelphia for their wares.[10] Sales apparently held up well until the latter part of 1785, when there was an abrupt decline in the number of advertisements. Complaints of hard times became chronic, and the consumption of foreign luxuries was blamed for having drained the country of all of its hard money. "Gordius" in 1786 charged that the sorry economic plight of the state was directly attributable to the extravagant purchases of goods from the old enemy, Britain. Dead heroes, he exclaimed, cry out against such treason. Others accused "the American and European adventurers, who have imported about four times the quantity of goods the country can consume." Some went so far as to advocate the formation of committees and associations, as in the days of yore, to enforce a return to republican simplicity. Many were resentful of the "tribute" that was exacted by the merchants of the neighboring states.[11]

---

[8] *Ibid.*, Apr. 16, 1783; Robert Johnson Account Book, RUL; Schoepf, *Travels*, p. 23; Witherspoon, *Works*, IX, p. 207.

[9] *New Jersey Gazette*, 1783-1786; *Political Intelligencer*, 1783-1786.

[10] *Votes and Proceedings*, 9-1, p. 33.

[11] *Political Intelligencer*, Sept. 28, 1785, May 10, Sept. 20, Oct. 11, 1786; *New Jersey Journal*, Nov. 22, 1786, Jan. 24, 1787.

New Jersey was, in fact, experiencing the effects of the general economic depression that enveloped the country late in 1785. American merchants had overextended themselves in ordering British goods on credit. Soon they and their English correspondents discovered that the new country did not have the capacity to meet the obligations it had incurred. As early as the summer of 1784 one prudent London firm was declining any additional orders from America. Remittances from overseas were so far in arrears, they explained, that they could not obtain goods on favorable terms from the manufacturers, who required timely payments.[12] After conditions had begun to improve, a New York merchant gave to a colleague in Amsterdam a concise analysis of the factors responsible for the collapse of the trade boom:

> The want of regular Remittances from this Country to Europe since the Peace has very justly operated to restrain their Confidence in the American Merchants; this Difficulty has been owing in great Measure to the too extensive Credit given by the Importing Merchants here; to other Merchants & Shopkeepers their Customers, who in like manner have given Credit to the Consumer; & in consequence have been very difficient in their Payments; this kind of Business is however very nearly at an end; the Quantity of Goods imported here, this Year [1787] will be much reduced, the Business of course getting into fewer hands, not only the Profits will be more worth Attention, but by the Check to the Current of Credit the Importer will have it in his power to observe Punctuality in his Remittances.[13]

[12] Roger and Bromfield, London, to John Banks, Charleston, July 7, 1784, Miscellaneous Manuscripts, RUL. The British merchant, they wrote, "is avail'd of Credits from the Manufacturer yet in order to be serv'd on the best terms it is necessary to be making large Payments before they become due & of course it is absolutely requisite on their Part to receive an Advance in some Degree proportion'l to the Extent of them, which alone can enable them to act with advantage."

[13] Lewis Ogden, New York, to Messrs. Daniel Crommelin and Sons, Apr. 10, 1787, Letter Book of Lewis Ogden, 1787-1798, NYPL. For

The humble storekeepers as well as the capital merchants were adversely affected by the tightening of credit, and all faced a critical period of deflation and readjustment.

Many observers, failing to appreciate the fact that the depression was a general one and that its causes were international in scope, overemphasized certain local factors. Some claimed that middlemen in New York and Philadelphia by their heavy charges created an unfavorable balance of trade for New Jersey, which therefore sank more and more into debt.[14] Differences in exchange rates of currency, it was held, made it impossible to secure a fair price for Jersey produce in the neighboring cities. The expense of freightage reduced profits; prices for farm products were too low.[15] The duties levied by both Pennsylvania and New York on foreign imports came in for their share of criticism. It is doubtful that the state imposts, which did not affect American products, constituted a hindrance to the flow of goods between the states, but citizens of New Jersey were naturally resentful about contributing to the support of the neighboring governments.[16]

---

a typical case of a New Jersey merchant who had overextended himself, see the letters of James Parker to Stewart and Jones, New York merchants, in Stewart and Jones Papers, NYPL.

[14] Rutherfurd, "Notes," p. 182; John Beatty to William Livingston, Apr. 13, 1785, Livingston Papers, MHS; "A.Z., *Political Intelligencer*, Sept. 20, 1786.

[15] John Neilson to Abraham Lott, Sept. 4, 1785, Neilson Papers, F 141, RUL. "...we can make no remittance to New York, without the loss of the difference of the exchange with 2 to 10 pct added to it, in any produce which is at present brought to market," Neilson wrote, "for instance we pay 4/6 here for Corn which we can only get 4/6 in New York & must pay 3 bushels freight besides Measuring &c ..." Significantly Neilson makes no complaint against New York's impost or its clearance fees.

[16] On the matter of state tariffs, see Albert A. Giesecke, *American Commercial Regulation before 1789* (Philadelphia, 1910), pp. 125 ff.; Thomas B. Cochran, *New York in the Confederation* (Philadelphia, 1932), pp. 155n, 167n; E. Wilder Spaulding, *New York in*

Valiant efforts were made by a few merchants to break away from the disadvantageous and unprofitable trade with New York and Philadelphia by developing foreign connections. Although such ventures required more capital and involved greater risks than did domestic commerce, they promised large profits. Within a year or two after the peace, several vessels, some of them newly built, were making regular sailings from the Raritan and the Delaware to Europe and the West Indies.[17] John Neilson carried on a flourishing trade in flaxseed with England and Ireland, receiving British products in return.[18] For a time he secured fabulous prices for staves, flour, butter, bread, and hams at the tiny Dutch island of St. Eustatius. In 1786 superfine flour was selling there for nearly nine pounds a barrel while the New York price was only forty-five shillings. Usually payment was taken in rum and sugar. By 1788, however, this market had become less attractive. It was "overstocked with Provisions of every kind," and cargoes were spoiling before

---

the Critical Period, 1783-1789 (New York, 1932), pp. 153-59; Robert L. Brunhouse, *The Counter-Revolution in Pennsylvania* (Harrisburg, 1942), pp. 152-73; William Columbus Hunter, *The Commercial Policy of New Jersey Under the Confederation* (Princeton, 1922), pp. 25-31.

[17] *New Jersey Gazette,* Sept. 6, Oct. 25, 1784, Aug. 8, 1785, June 9, 1786; *Brunswick Gazette,* Sept. 18, Nov. 6, 1787; Neilson Papers, F 187, RUL. Neilson's ships were the "Betsey," "Aurora," "Jersey," and "Neptune." Moore Furman had interests in the "Trenton" and the "New Jersey."

[18] For details of Neilson's trading ventures, see Neilson Papers, F 51, RUL. Late in 1785, when Neilson was indebted to his London factors to the extent of almost twelve hundred pounds, they wrote to him: "We rest confidentially in Your Opinion to remit Us the whole of our account in the Course of this Fall & Winter—we are to the last Degree distress'd by the want of returns being made by our friends in America, & if this winter they should fail to remit us early and amply; many of our tradesmen & Manufacturers must be inevitably ruined, which God & our Correspondents avert!" Cruger, Lediard and Mullett to Neilson, Nov. 1, 1785.

they could be sold. A year later conditions were even worse.[19] Neilson's vessels also brought back wine from Madeira and salt from St. Ubes. On one voyage in 1784 his schooner "Neptune" visited Havana, Nassau, Charleston, Wilmington, and Newport.[20] Moore Furman was another merchant who engaged in trade both with Madeira and the West Indies.[21]

Foreign trade was subject to so many uncertainties that Jersey merchants with their small capital found it a hazardous business. Markets were unsteady and the perils of the sea were ever present. Neilson often suffered serious losses when his cargoes went unsold.[22] Soon after the adoption of the Constitution, he prudently withdrew from overseas enterprises and thereafter confined his dealings to the near and safe markets at New York.[23] The effort to create an independent foreign commerce for New Jersey failed.[24] The failure, however, could not in any way be attributed to the deficiencies of

[19] W. Stevenson and Co., St. Eustatius, to Neilson, Apr. 14, Sept. 4, 27, 1788, Mar. 25, 1789, Neilson Papers, F 51, RUL. "Our Market is much Overdone with American Provisions," Neilson's agent in St. Eustatius informed him in 1789, "the prices are low & much fear it will be some time before there is a change for the better."

[20] Moses Guest, *Poems...to which are annexed, Extracts from a Journal...* (Cincinnati, 1824), pp. 84-90.

[21] *New Jersey Gazette*, Aug. 8, 1785, June 9, 1786; James Searle, Bordentown, to John Searle, Madeira, June 17, 1787, Conarroe, I, HSP. Searle asked his brother in Madeira to send back some grapevines, carnations, and carnation seeds for Governor Livingston, an ardent horticulturist.

[22] Matthew Sleght to Neilson, Feb. 16, 1786; Thompson and Gordon to Neilson, July 12, 1788; Thomas Devereaux to Neilson, Sept. 15, 1787, Neilson Papers, F 51, RUL.

[23] Robert T. Thompson, *Colonel James Neilson: A Business Man of the Early Machine Age in New Jersey, 1784-1862* (New Brunswick, 1940), pp. 12-15.

[24] Phineas Bond correctly decided in 1787 that no port in the state was of enough consequence to justify the presence of a British agent. "Letters of Phineas Bond," *Annual Report of the American Historical Association*, 1896, I, p. 525.

the Confederation. Rather it was due to certain obvious weaknesses in the commercial position of the state.

THE MERCANTILE PROGRAM

New Jersey had entertained high hopes that independence would provide an opportunity to bring about an end to its long-standing commercial subservience to New York and Philadelphia. Governor Livingston expressed a common sentiment when in May, 1783, he urged the legislature to "give proper Encouragement to the Commerce of this State, and to prevent as far as possible our Neighbours from reaping those Profits on our Consumption of foreign Manufactures which might be secured to our own Citizens..."[25] Similar views were voiced at a public meeting in Newark. "...now is the time for New Jersey to push herself forward, and take her rank among the commercial states in our union," declared the assemblage.[26] Interested groups proposed various measures which, they thought, would further the attainment of the ambitious objective.

It was widely believed that the state would benefit by adopting a policy of free trade and by holding out inducements to wealthy merchants to settle there. This course of action was favored not only by those who were directly involved in trade but also by large landowners, who foresaw that commercial prosperity might attract immigrants and enhance real estate values, and by those who were sympathetic to the return of exiled tories.[27] John Rutherfurd in May, 1783, published two carefully prepared letters, ostensibly addressed to a member of the Assembly, in which he set forth in full the desirability of developing foreign commerce. In

[25] Message to legislature, May 19, 1783, Miscellaneous Manuscripts, NJSL.

[26] *New Jersey Gazette*, June 4, 1783.

[27] John Rutherfurd and James Parker were leading advocates of these proposals. John's father, Walter, and Parker were both proprietors of East Jersey and both had been loyalists (see pp. 29-31).

the past, he pointed out, local merchants had dealt almost exclusively with New York and Philadelphia, "and their Expences, Carriage, and loss of Time laid a charge on their Wares of at least 5 p cent. by this means," he claimed, "none of our Dealers grew considerable among us, and were unable to undertake foreign ventures." The time had come to alter this situation. The state should open its ports to the ships of all nations and cease to pay "tribute" to middlemen. Moreover, it should extend a welcome to wealthy merchants, regardless of their former political convictions, for their capital would greatly enrich the state.[28] On June 11, 1783, the legislature declared that all ports in the state should thereafter be open, an action which it doubtless would have taken without Rutherfurd's prompting.[29]

It soon became apparent that free trade would not suffice to extricate New Jersey from its difficulties. Within a few months the merchants in the eastern part of the state were complaining to the legislature about the drain of currency to New York and Philadelphia. "... the Confederation ... having committed the Power of regulating Commerce to the several States ...," read one petition, "this Evil will be increased unless Means are adopted to obviate it, because not only the ordinary Profits of Trade will center in those cities, but New Jersey will also be compelled to pay all such Duties as their respective Governments may think proper to impose, for the exclusive Emolument of New York and Pennsylvania."[30] A duty levied on commodities of foreign growth or manufacture imported into New Jersey from the neighboring

---

[28] "Letters from John Rutherfurd to a member of the Assembly, May 16, 17, 1783," *PNJHS*, 2nd Ser., I (1867), pp. 177-82; "Mercator," *New Jersey Gazette*, June 4, 1783.

[29] *Session Laws*, 7-2, Act of June 11, 1783. By the same law the Confederation was authorized to levy a continental impost.

[30] Early in 1784 both New York and Pennsylvania enacted tariff duties. Cochran, *Confederation*, p. 155n; Brunhouse, *Counter-Revolution*, p. 152.

states would "have every beneficial Effect." [31] This petition, and others of a similar tenor, were turned over to a special committee, which reported that, because of the importance of the subject and the likelihood that the Assembly would soon adjourn, no law could be passed. The whole question was therefore referred to the next sitting, "in order that more general Knowledge of Trade and Commerce" might be obtained.[32]

At each succeeding meeting of the legislature, the impost proposal was regularly revived, and each time action on the matter was postponed.[33] "It is true our wooden headed Assembly have referred over to the next session the Impost Bill, but it will assuredly pass then; if it does not we will have a trade without it," James Parker wrote angrily to John Rutherfurd in December, 1784.[34] In November, 1786, the Assembly delegated two members—Jonathan Dayton and Daniel Marsh of Essex—to study the problem and report their opinion at the next session. When the house again convened, the familiar bill was read once more and on May 24, 1787, a significant resolution, possibly framed by Dayton and Marsh, was adopted:

> *Ordered,* That as it is the Expectation and Wish of this House, that the Convention now holding in Philadelphia may, by the Establishment of an equal and general Com-

[31] *Votes and Proceedings,* 8-1, pp. 64-65; Petition of merchants and citizens to legislature, Dec. 12, 1783, Manuscript Collection, NJSL. Among the signers of this plea were Matthias Ogden, John Neilson, William Paterson, Jonathan Dayton, Elias Boudinot, Elisha Boudinot, and Elias Dayton. Several of these men were lawyers and were not themselves directly engaged in trade, but they were members of an enterprising group that consistently sought to expand business opportunities of all kinds. Most of them were later Federalists.

[32] *Votes and Proceedings,* 8-1, pp. 64-65, 76-77.

[33] *Ibid.,* 9-1, p. 73; *ibid.,* 10-1, p. 45; *ibid.,* 10-2, p. 68; *ibid.,* 10-3, p. 13; *ibid.,* 11-1, p. 62; *ibid.,* 11-2, p. 15; *ibid.,* 12-1, p. 7.

[34] Parker to Rutherfurd, Dec. 28, 1784, Miscellaneous Manuscripts, NYHS.

mercial System, render the Passing of this Bill altogether unnecessary, the further consideration of it be postponed to the next sitting.[35]

Here was a clear and authentic expression of New Jersey's sentiments on the subject of trade regulation and a forecast of its subsequent attitude toward the Constitution.

The nearest approach to an impost in New Jersey was a short-lived excise tax, which was enacted by the legislature in June, 1787.[36] This was primarily a financial expedient designed to obtain money to fill a requisition of the Continental Congress, but it contained as well some features that may be regarded as protective. Specific internal duties were levied on a long list of imported articles "sold or bartered by retail," and a 5 per cent *ad valorem* tax was laid on a few items such as fabrics, glassware, and iron and steel products. The excise did not apply to any articles produced or manufactured in the United States, with the sole exception of rum distilled from molasses. The revenue was to be raised by collectors in each county, who would purchase their offices at a public auction. Retailers were required to obtain licenses, post bonds, maintain detailed accounts, and answer inquiries under oath.

The excise law immediately aroused violent protests in all sections of the state. In several counties mass meetings were held and plans were made to obtain the speedy repeal of the measure.[37] Objections were directed mainly against the methods that had been provided for collecting the tax. The office of collector, which would not be filled by a vote of the people, would be "deemed intolerable under the most de-

[35] *Votes and Proceedings*, 11-2, p. 15. The measure met a similar fate when it was brought up again in October, 1787.

[36] *Ibid.*, 11-2, p. 27; *Journal of Council*, 11-2, p. 16; *Session Laws*, 11-2, Act of June 4, 1787. The measure passed by a narrow vote and received its strongest support from the East Jersey members.

[37] *Brunswick Gazette*, Aug. 13, 28, Sept. 14, 1787; *New Jersey Journal*, Aug. 29, Sept. 15, 1787.

spotic government," storekeepers would be put to great expense in keeping the required reports, and the inquisitorial powers of the excise officials would be violative of the rights of free people. When the day arrived to place the collector-ships up for sale, well-organized groups of citizens in some counties followed a prearranged plan to purchase the offices at a ridiculously low figure with the understanding that they would lie dormant.[38] In the face of such general opposition the law was manifestly unenforcible. This situation was glaringly apparent to the embarrassed legislators, and they promptly suspended the act when next they met in October, 1787.[39] The brief experiment with an indirect tariff was conspicuously unsuccessful.

The merchants failed utterly in their efforts to secure a tariff on foreign goods coming from other states. The legislature, in which the agrarian interest was dominant, was astute enough to realize that New Jersey did not have the ability to develop an independent overseas trade. It doubtless foresaw that while an impost might redound to the benefit of a few traders, it would in effect constitute a double tax on foreign wares and would therefore raise prices for the masses of the people without conferring any compensatory advantage. The widespread anger over the tariff policies of Pennsylvania and New York arose not so much out of resentment against the commercial superiority of those states as it did out of an appreciation of the indirect financial loss sustained by New Jersey. What was wanted was a Continental impost, which would give the Confederation revenues derived from a source

[38] The office brought £16 in Somerset, £17 in Essex, and the same amount in Burlington. In Hunterdon, Middlesex, and Monmouth, on the other hand, it went for prices ranging from a thousand to three thousand pounds. In Bergen, a gallows was erected to hang any man who should dare to offer a bid. *Brunswick Gazette*, Sept. 25, Oct. 9, 30, 1787; *New Jersey Journal*, Sept. 19, 26, Oct. 3, 1787.

[39] *Votes and Proceedings*, 12-1, pp. 9-27, 34; *Session Laws*, 12-1, Act of Nov. 2, 1787.

other than requisitions and would therefore operate to reduce the tax burden of the state.

The most elaborate scheme for the encouragement of trade to be brought before the legislature was the many-sided free-ports project. The proposal that certain ports should be made free and that special privileges should be granted to them had been broached first early in 1783, but there was little support for the plan until the summer of 1784.[40] Then in May of that year, the merchants in both divisions of the state, prompted by the receipt of a circular letter from the Philadelphia Merchants' Committee, formed themselves into an organization to take collective action on matters relating to commerce.[41] Soon a "Committee for the Promotion of Trade in New Jersey" was created with James Parker and John Neilson as its leading members.

During the summer the committee evolved an original and comprehensive plan, which was embodied in a bill drafted by Robert Morris (former chief justice and one of the inner circle of the East Jersey Proprietors) for submission to the legislature.[42] In soliciting the support of a Bergen assembly-

[40] "Genesea," *New Jersey Gazette*, May 21, 1783.

[41] *New Jersey Gazette*, May 17, 1784; Philadelphia Merchants' Committee to The Merchants in Massachusetts, Jan. 3, 1784, Society Collection, HSP; John Neilson to Col. Matthias Ogden, May 19, 1784, Neilson Papers, F 39, RUL. Neilson received the Philadelphia letter from Charles Pettit, one of its authors, but delayed calling the merchants together for several months because of "the detached Situation of that part of the Community in New Jersey and their feeble state when collected."

[42] Robert Morris to Messrs. Parker, Neilson and Committee, Aug. 6, 1784, Robert Morris Papers, RUL. Morris, who was the natural son of Robert Hunter Morris and a grandson of Governor Lewis Morris, served as the first chief justice of New Jersey from 1777 to 1779. A lawyer with an extensive practice, he was a member of the East Jersey Board of Proprietors and agent for the West Jersey Society. He was appointed to the Federal District Court under the Judiciary Act of 1789, and held office until his death in 1815. Robert Morris Papers, RUL.

man, Morris stressed the need for developing the foreign commerce of the state and explained the main features of the measure. "To effect the concentering Trade it is proposed to lay dutys on all imports not made into a few specified ports, with some other privileges of a trifling nature when compared with the first," he wrote, "which if executed will effect the object at this favorable season when New York & Pennsylvania have laid duties for us to pay." [43]

On August 5, 1784, the legislature met in special session at New Brunswick, and four days later there came together in the same town representatives of the merchants of Morris County, Woodbridge, Perth Amboy, New Brunswick, Piscataway, Elizabeth Town, Princeton, Trenton, and Lamberton "for the purpose of considering measures to be submitted to the Legislature on the subject of commerce." This convention drew up a petition in which it set forth its program. Situated between powerful neighbors, it maintained, the state could build up a foreign trade only by offering unusual inducements to merchants. Accordingly it recommended that two free ports, endowed with "the most ample immunities and privileges that may be useful for their own internal order and regulation," should be established for a term of twenty-five years. Duties should be levied on foreign products that were not imported into the state through the free ports. "This is necessary, for if a duty be not laid on all merchandise not immediately imported into this state, our neighbors will take advantage of this neglect and become our carriers . . ." Merchants in the free ports should be granted exemption from all state tariffs and from taxes on their vessels and stock. Citizenship should be granted on liberal terms; even former tories should be eligible.

There was need for haste in adopting these expedients. "As trade, since the last revolution, seems to be in a degree of

[43] Robert Morris to Adam Boyd, Aug. 8, 1784, Robert Morris Papers, RUL.

fluctuation, and has not yet determined itself to any permanent and exclusive marts," concluded the petitioners, "it appears to be the only remaining moment in which New Jersey can lay in her claim and exert her natural resources with success, to obtain her just proportion of general wealth and commerce of the continent." Perth Amboy and Trenton (with Lamberton) were proposed as the port towns.[44]

The petition was presented to the legislature, and within a few days Assemblyman Randolph of Middlesex introduced a free-port bill, possibly the one that had been drafted by Robert Morris.[45] Over the objections of the Hunterdon representatives, Burlington was substituted for Trenton in the measure, and it was passed by an overwhelming vote in both houses.[46] The law constituted Perth Amboy and Burlington free ports for twenty-five years, permitted any merchants— except those who had been guilty of "licentious Cruelties" as tories—to become citizens of the free cities after a residence of one month, exempted from duties all foreign goods landed at the ports, and excluded from taxation the stock, possessions, and vessels of merchants.[47] The act differed in one all-important respect from the original proposal, in that it made

[44] Petition of deputies of County of Morris, towns of Elizabeth Town, Woodbridge, Perth Amboy, Piscataway, New Brunswick, Princeton, Trenton, and Lamberton convened at New Brunswick, Aug. 9, 1784, Loose Manuscripts, NJSL; *New Jersey Gazette*, Nov. 22, 1784. It is important to notice the provisions respecting imposts. Former writers have neglected this aspect of the free-port project. See Hunter, *Commercial Policy*, pp. 27-28.

[45] *Votes and Proceedings*, 8-2, pp. 103, 110.

[46] *Ibid.*, 8-2, pp. 129, 132, 133; *Journal of Council*, 8-2, p. 18. The vote was 24 to 5 in the Assembly; 9 to 2 in the Council. Sectional lines were not drawn because each division received similar privileges. Both Trenton and Burlington submitted petitions to the legislature, each asking that it be given preference as a free port. *Votes and Proceedings*, 8-2, pp. 117, 120.

[47] *Session Laws*, 8-2, Act of Aug. 28, 1784. The exemption from duties did not apply to slaves or to such duties as might be levied by the United States.

no provisions whatsoever for laying imposts either on foreign goods brought in through other ports or on those imported from other states. This feature had evidently been stricken out in the Assembly. Consequently the so-called free ports were actually no more free with regard to tariff duties than were any others in the state.

More was involved in the free-ports project than the desire to encourage trade. The chief promoter of the plan was James Parker, and he was principally interested in restoring the fortunes of Perth Amboy, where he had extensive real estate holdings. Soon after the passage of the act he was industriously trying to sell dozens of lots along the waterfront there.[48] Moreover, Parker and the Rutherfurds were doubtless motivated by a desire to provide a haven for their loyalist friends. Not without reason did "An Old Citizen" complain: "It is too much, I cannot patiently reconcile myself to it. Burlington and Amboy, not noted for affection throughout the war, they must be free ports, not for merchandize only, but for Refugees ... [and] because they have not done us mischief enough we must pay their taxes!"[49] There was also the hope that companies of English merchants, attracted by the special privileges accorded to traders, might settle in the town, add to its wealth, and appreciate land values.[50] The

[48] *Political Intelligencer*, Oct. 14, 1784. "The proprietor of these lots is convinced that it would be greatly to his advantage to postpone this sale until next spring," Parker advertised, "but his zeal for the promotion of the commercial plan now happily begun in New-Jersey, induces him to take this method of removing the complaint made by numbers, that convenient lots to build upon cannot be had at a reasonable price." See also Parker to John Rutherfurd, Dec. 28, 1784, Miscellaneous Manuscripts, NYHS; Petition of James Parker to legislature, Mar. 21, 1786, Loose Manuscripts, NJSL.

[49] *New Jersey Gazette*, Oct. 11, 1784.

[50] Robert Morris to John Rutherfurd, May 23, 1784, Robert Morris Papers, RUL; Schoepf, *Travels*, p. 23. Parker advertised the advantages possessed by Perth Amboy as far distant as Kingston, Jamaica. Thomas Ryerson to Parker, July 6, 1785, James Parker Papers, RUL.

strongest impetus behind the measure came from the landed proprietors and merchants of East Jersey; the inclusion of a West Jersey port was probably dictated by political necessity.

There is no evidence that any of the objectives of the measure were attained. There was no sizable influx of "capital merchants" or of tories into the free towns, no increase in the volume of foreign trade, no real estate boom. Without the impost, the free-ports plan was vitiated from the start. But even if the measure as originally designed had been adopted, the results would probably not have been otherwise. The merchants of New Jersey found their best markets in New York and Philadelphia, and they could not—even with favorable legislation—build up a rival to those pre-eminent mercantile centers.[51]

New Jersey's commercial policy was a source of some annoyance to her neighbors, who saw their own tariff structures threatened by her zeal for free trade. New York, in particular, was irritated by the refusal of her would-be competitor to levy discriminatory duties on British products and vessels.[52] Accordingly, that state took appropriate measures to prevent the smuggling of foreign wares across her borders and, in 1785, taxed such goods at the same rate as those imported in English ships, unless the owner could satisfy the collector that they had been brought into the United States in an American ship.[53] Two years later, the New York legislature deemed it necessary to exact entrance

[51] Morse, *Geography*, p. 288; Hunter, *Commercial Policy*, pp. 30-31; Webster, *Collection of Essays*, p. 352. Early in 1786 James Parker himself had boats sailing twice a week from Perth Amboy to New York. *New Jersey Gazette*, Jan. 30, 1786.

[52] Most states levied such duties after the British West Indian trade was closed to American shipping in July, 1783. Giesecke, *Commercial Regulation*, pp. 127-29. For the New York acts, see Cochran, *Confederation*, pp. 167n, 168n.

[53] Edward Channing, *A History of the United States*, III (New York, 1912), p. 467; Hunter, *Commercial Policy*, p. 28.

and clearance fees from boats bound to and from Connecticut and New Jersey. The fees were four times greater if the freight consisted of foreign goods than if American products were carried.[54] New Jersey answered these retaliatory acts by imposing a tax of thirty pounds a month on the lighthouse that New York had erected on Sandy Hook. Recognizing that the collection of the assessment might be "too difficult in its Execution," the legislature authorized the local tax collector to call on the sheriff of Monmouth County for assistance.[55] The importance of this incident has been greatly exaggerated by writers who have been concerned with depicting the states as engaged in spiteful quarrels under the Confederation. Viewed from another perspective, it is surprising that the diverse policies pursued by New York and New Jersey did not result in a more serious clash than that represented by the petty lighthouse tax.

It is apparent that what may loosely be termed the "mercantile interest" was not able to command the sympathetic attention of the legislature for all of its requests for favorable laws. Free trade and free ports were solicited and obtained with a minimum of opposition. Within limits, there existed a genuine concern with the promotion of trade. But the legislators would not go all the way in yielding to demands for impost duties. Realizing that New Jersey because of its fundamental commercial weakness could derive no appreciable benefits from a state tariff, they were ardently in favor of a continental impost, which would bring financial relief from oppressive requisitions.[56] The various measures that were

[54] Channing, *History*, III, p. 467.

[55] *Session Laws*, 11-2, Act of June 7, 1787; *American Museum*, II (Dec., 1787), p. 601; *New Jersey Journal*, July 25, 1787. The tax was regularly collected for at least a year. Treasurer's Receipt Book, 1783-1789, PUL. In 1790 the four-acre tract on which the lighthouse stood was ceded by New Jersey to the Federal government. Paterson, *Laws*, p. 103.

[56] See below, pp. 233-44.

proposed for the advancement of commerce were not put forward by a strongly organized merchant faction, nor was there any recognized merchant bloc in the legislature. Rather they were formulated and fostered by a small group, many of whom—like James Parker—were concerned as much with real estate promotion as they were with trade. Sectional controversies, common on most issues, were avoided by a skillful policy of "log-rolling," which assured equal advantages to both divisions of the state.

THE INCORPORATION OF CITIES

In addition to sponsoring projects to enhance the foreign trade of the state, the merchants and their allies were interested also in securing for the principal towns a type of government favorable to their business activities. Prior to the Revolution, Perth Amboy, New Brunswick, Burlington, Elizabeth Town, and Trenton had been granted charters by the royal governors.[57] After independence had been attained, new and revised charters were sought from the legislature. The movement was fostered by the commercial elements because they wanted "a more effective local government than the town meeting; agrarian political opposition had to be segregated because trading privileges were needed."[58]

At the same session of the legislature that enacted the free-ports measure, Perth Amboy, Burlington, Trenton, and New Brunswick all petitioned for charters, but only the last had its plea granted. The preamble of the act of incorporation recited that New Brunswick promised in time to become a

[57] For a description of these early charters, see Austin Scott, "The Early Cities of New Jersey," *PNJHS*, IV (1887), pp. 151-73, and Joseph S. Davis, *Essays in the Earlier History of American Corporations*, I (Cambridge, 1917), pp. 57-69. According to Scott, there were nine incorporated cities in the colonies in 1750, five of which were in New Jersey.

[58] East, *Business Enterprise*, p. 267. The movement was not confined to New Jersey. In Connecticut, for example, five towns became chartered corporations during the Confederation period.

place of extensive trade and that, as a populous town, it required "many particular Regulations for preserving good Order and Government." The principal officers of the corporation were a president, a register, four directors, six assistants (who together made up the Common Council), a marshal, an assessor, and a collector, all of whom were to be elected annually by the inhabitants.[59] The city was given virtually complete control over its internal affairs. It had its own sheriff in the person of the marshal as well as its own court of record. In the Common Council was vested the power of raising taxes, regulating markets, and appointing subordinate officers. There is no question that the business community was accorded the kind of protection and encouragement that it deemed essential to its welfare.

Perth Amboy and Burlington were incorporated at the next sitting of the legislature.[60] In both charters it was provided that the principal officers—the mayor, the recorder, and the three aldermen—were to be appointed by the joint meeting of the legislature, and that the members of the Common Council, a sheriff, a coroner, and two constables were to be elected annually by the freemen. All persons, except those who had been guilty of cruel behavior during the war, were entitled to become citizens after a residence of one year, and foreigners were permitted to purchase and hold property. The privileges and exemptions conferred on merchants by the free-ports act were embodied in the two charters. The legislative, executive, and judicial powers of the governing bodies were similar to those specified for New Brunswick.[61]

In the forefront of the incorporation movement was the

[59] *Session Laws*, 8-2, Act of Sept. 1, 1784.

[60] *Ibid.*, 9-1, Acts of Dec. 21, 1784. The Assembly passed both measures unanimously. *Votes and Proceedings*, 9-1, pp. 39, 63, 87.

[61] The borough of Elizabeth was incorporated November 28, 1789. Trenton was not incorporated until November 13, 1792, two years after it had become the capital of the State. Paterson, *Laws*, pp. 94-99, 116-18.

familiar figure of James Parker, who led the way with his plans for making Perth Amboy the commercial metropolis of the state.[62] Firm was his conviction that Amboy would "yet be the cornerstone of the building or the building ... [would] never be of any consequences." [63] It is not surprising that he should have expected to become mayor of the municipality in whose behalf he had worked so effectively. In November, 1785, at a meeting of the citizens of Perth Amboy, he was unanimously recommended to the joint meeting for the first post in the city, but because he had refused to take the oath of allegiance during the war, he was barred from holding any office. Undismayed by this barrier, Parker in a lengthy petition to the legislature pointed to the services he had rendered the state by promoting the plan of commercial development and asked that a special act be passed to qualify him for the mayoralty. With a minimum of opposition, the legislature enacted his request into law, after which the joint meeting elected him mayor.[64]

[62] At the conclusion of the legislative session in December, 1784, Parker noted in his account book his lobbying expenses:

Paid on Accot of Charter and Impost Bill	
sending Express to Gloucester	£ 2.10.0
for paper	0. 3.9
[Isaac] Collins printing Free port Law	1. 7.6
Copying Charter for printing	1.10.0
Exp at Witts [tavern]	9.16.0
Do at Williams	2. 3.5
Do at Smiths	0.15.0
Do at Sundries	0.12.0
Chargeable to this Account	£*19. 7.8*

[63] Parker to John Stevens, Sr., [1784?], Stevens Papers, SIT.

[64] Representation and petition of James Parker, Mar. 21, 1786, Loose Manuscripts, NJSL. Parker mentioned that he had "a very considerable interest in landed property in almost every County." *Votes and Proceedings*, 10-2, p. 82; *New Jersey Gazette*, Mar. 27, 1786; *Minutes of the Joint Meeting*, June 1, 1786. Evidently Perth Amboy had no mayor between the time of its incorporation in December, 1784, and the election of Parker in June, 1786.

It was Parker, too, who provoked a heated competition among the principal towns for the honor of becoming the capital of the state. Before the war the legislature had met alternately at Perth Amboy and Burlington, but after the outbreak of the Revolution it had no fixed place of residence. Holding its sessions in various commodious taverns, it seldom convened twice in succession in the same place.[65] When in 1786 it was proposed that the sittings should be held at Burlington and New Brunswick, Parker launched a determined campaign to bring about a return to colonial practice. Confident that the legislators would be "deaf to the Persuasions and Insinuations of crafty and designing men that may prefer their own Temporary Interest to the Publick and permanent advantages of the State," he urged the appropriateness of making the free port on the Raritan a seat of government.[66] Although he was unsuccessful in achieving his main objective at this time, he did frustrate the ambitions of New Brunswick, which had gone so far as to raise a subscription for constructing a suitable building. Parker considered his partial victory remarkable in view of the fact that his enemies had attempted to injure him by maliciously circulating the report that he had opposed any observance of the Fourth of July in the state convention of the Episcopal Church.[67]

The rivalry between the two Middlesex cities continued, with New Brunswick vigorously pressing its claim in a petition

[65] A familiar appropriation item at the close of each session was a sum to cover the expense of carting the records of the two houses of the legislature from place to place.

[66] Petition of citizens of Perth Amboy, May 29, 1786, Manuscript Collection, NJSL.

[67] Parker to Hon. John Stevens, May 29, 1786, Stevens Papers, SIT; *Journals of the Convention*, pp. 582-87. Parker begged Stevens to speak "to the Western Members—to the Eastern Members & every person out of doors" that he thought might have some influence on the legislature.

to the legislature in which it stressed its favorable location as well as its "plentiful markets and salubrious air." "...in a republic like this, it is not the interest or local situation of those who possess the honorable or lucrative offices of state," argued the Brunswickers insinuatingly, "but the convenience and advantage of the people at large which first bespeaks the attention of the legislature." [68] The lawmakers, however, were unable throughout several sittings to come to any agreement on the question. Those from the northern and southern extremities of the state wanted a single capital, preferably Trenton, while others clung to the old idea of two sites, one in each division.[69] Not until late in 1788 was the matter decided. Incorporated in an election law enacted in November of that year was the provision that in the future the legislature should meet alternately at Perth Amboy and Burlington.[70] But this return to the old order was destined to be of brief duration, for late in 1790 Trenton was designated as the permanent capital of the state.[71]

The movement for the incorporation of cities and the competition over the location of the capital both evidenced the aggressive interest of the business community in matters relating to its welfare. Although small in numbers, the merchants and their associates were an active and influential group in seeking special legislation. They did not play a dominant

[68] Petition to legislature, [1787], Neilson Papers, F 70, RUL.

[69] *Votes and Proceedings*, 12-2, pp. 17-29.

[70] *Session Laws*, 13-1, Act of Nov. 29, 1788. This plan was to become effective in October, 1789. In preparation for the return of the legislature to Amboy, James Parker supervised the repair of the old building that had been used before the Revolution, and commissioned William Dunlap, the noted historian of the American stage, to paint a coat of arms which was to be hung over the speaker's chair. Parker to Dunlap, Oct. 12, 1789, Parker Papers, NJHS.

[71] Paterson, *Laws*, p. 104. Although evidence on the point is lacking, it is not improbable that the hope that Trenton might be selected as the Federal capital had some effect in postponing the choice of that place as the state capital.

role in politics, but they nevertheless frequently found the means to gain their ends.

Trade was the principal occupation of men of business, but manufacturing was sufficiently developed to merit some consideration. Iron works in several counties gave promise of a prosperous growth. In hundreds of small establishments the production of shoes, glassware, lumber, cloth, and flour was carried on. Along almost every stream, mill wheels furnished power for a variety of purposes. Some men of vision, realizing that farming and commerce were not to bring great wealth to the state, saw that the future of New Jersey lay in the field of industry and urged that increased attention be given to this branch of economic endeavor.[72]

The iron industry had its origins at Shrewsbury in Monmouth County in the middle of the seventeenth century. During the early part of the following century, the rich hematite and magnetite mines in Morris, Bergen, and Sussex, and the bog ores in Gloucester and Burlington, began to be exploited. Dozens of furnaces and forges were erected in the wildest areas of the state, where fuel and water power were available in abundance.[73] In the two decades before the Revolution the industry underwent vast expansion. The fabulous Peter Hasenclever, backed by an English syndicate known as the London Company, spent over fifty thousand pounds in developing three tremendous works in Bergen County at Ringwood, Longpond, and Charlottenburg; and Charles Read and his associates built plants at Batsto, Taun-

---

[72] Rutherfurd, "Notes," p. 85; *New Jersey Journal*, Feb. 14, Sept. 12, 1787.

[73] J. L. Bishop, *A History of American Manufacturers from 1608 to 1860* ... (Philadelphia, 1866), pp. 539-46, 548-50; Charles S. Boyer, *Early Forges and Furnaces in New Jersey* (Philadelphia, 1931), pp. 1-2.

ton, Atsion, and Aetna in Burlington County. Other out-standing enterprises were the Andover, Oxford, Mount Hope, Sharpsborough, Union, Hibernia, and Speedwell fur-naces in Morris, Sussex, and Hunterdon Counties.[74]

Most of these establishments were engaged during the war in turning out badly needed munitions and implements for the Continental Army, but with the return of peace, the industry entered a period of chaos. Unsound financing, crude organization, and muddled ownership brought failure or paralysis to several works. The affairs of the London Company were in hopeless disorder after the death in 1780 of Robert Erskine, manager of the mining properties, and all operations were apparently at a standstill until the beginning of the nineteenth century.[75] The large-scale Burlington projects, disrupted by the bankruptcy and death of Charles Read in 1773, passed into the hands of separate proprietors and functioned only intermittently after 1783. The loyalism of their owners was responsible for the closing down of the Union and Andover furnaces.

In 1784 there were reportedly six furnaces and more than fifty forges and bloomeries in the state, but it is doubtful whether half of them were actually functioning.[76] The leading iron-master was John Jacob Faesch, a native of Switzerland and onetime superintendent for the London Company, who successfully ran the Mount Hope furnace from 1772 until his death in 1799 and for a time leased the Hibernia

[74] *Ibid.*, *passim*; Albert H. Heusser, *The Forgotten General, Robert Erskine, F. R. S.* (Paterson, 1928), pp. 23-26; J. F. Tuttle, "Hibernia Furnace and the Surrounding Country in the Revolutionary War," *PNJHS*, 2nd Ser., VI (1881), pp. 148-73; C. R. Woodward, *Ploughs and Politicks* (New Brunswick, 1941), pp. 86-96.

[75] Robert Lettis Hooper and his wife, who was Erskine's widow, were empowered to manage the company's affairs by the legislature on June 20, 1782. Heusser, *Forgotten General*, pp. 189-93; Wilson, *Acts*, pp. 271-72. Hooper subsequently became involved in numerous law-suits. Account Book of Robert Morris, Robert Morris Papers, RUL.

[76] *Votes and Proceedings*, 9-1, p. 23; Rutherfurd, "Notes," p. 86.

works.[77] In 1784 Faesch took over the slitting mill that had been erected by Samuel Ogden at Boonton in 1770 in defiance of British regulations. A number of trip hammers were installed, and later a forge was added.[78] The Hibernia establishment, after some years of idleness pending the settlement of Lord Sterling's involved estate, came under the control of Benjamin Thompson, who in 1788 purchased over five thousand acres of timberland from the East Jersey proprietors to meet fuel needs.[79] The noted Batsto furnace, in which Quartermaster General Nathanael Greene and his two deputies, John Cox and Charles Pettit, held interests, was put into blast in 1784, principally, it would appear, in an effort to attract a buyer for the works.[80] Numerous individual forges, some of which obtained their pig iron from Pennsylvania, survived the years of confusion with a minimum of difficulty, for they did not require the large amounts of capital needed for a furnace and all its attendant facilities.

Although mismanagement and disorganization were probably the chief causes of the depressed condition of the industry, there were other factors which bore a share of the responsibility. Reckless use of timber, consumed in enormous quantities in the form of charcoal, was a chronic evil; when no more wood was available within convenient distance,

---

[77] J. F. Tuttle, "The Early History of Morris County, New Jersey," *PNJHS*, 2nd Ser., I (1867), pp. 37-38; Boyer, *Forges and Furnaces*, pp. 136-39.

[78] Samuel Ogden to General Nathanael Greene, Feb. 29, 1784, Ely Collection, NJHS. Ogden moved to New York, leaving his business in the hands of Faesch.

[79] Minutes of the East Jersey Proprietors, Sept. 13, 1786, Sept. 12, 1788 (draft copies by James Parker), PUL.

[80] Charles Pettit to General Greene, Mar. 5, 1780, Miscellaneous Manuscripts, RUL; Pettit to Joseph Reed, May 15, 1784, Joseph Reed Papers, XI, NYHS. The works were advertised as comprising a furnace, a new forge with four fires, a slitting mill, and a rolling mill. *Pennsylvania Packet*, Apr. 15, 1784. The Taunton works were for sale in 1785. *New Jersey Gazette*, Apr. 25, 1785.

operations became unprofitable. The observant Dr. Schoepf noted that after exhausting a forest of twenty thousand acres in a dozen years, the Union furnace had to be abandoned. Batsto faced similar difficulties.[81] The high cost of provisions and of labor, the "ungenerous and impolitic mode of taxing manufactures," and the exorbitant prices exacted by the masters of slitting mills were also cited as reasons for the stagnation which seemed to prevail. Too, the New Jersey works faced stiff competition from Pennsylvania and from England.[82]

Unlike the merchants, the iron manufacturers were not very active in seeking aid or protection from the state. They did not constitute a powerful or unified group politically, although many of them occupied public offices. John Cox and Robert Lettis Hooper each filled the post of vice-president of the Council; Thomas Reynolds, Anthony Sharp, Jacob Arnold, Hugh Hughes, and Mark Thompson were members of the legislature; John Jacob Faesch, Thomas Anderson, and Reynolds sat in the convention that ratified the Constitution; and Joseph Bloomfield was attorney-general. Bloomfield, who operated a nail factory in company with John Little at Burlington, did solicit a duty on nails and exemption of his workmen from military service, but his request was not granted.[83] Nothing came of the suggestion of "Cadmus" that the state should give premiums to foster the industry, reduce taxes, and adopt measures to insure good quality in iron products.[84]

[81] Schoepf, *Travels*, p. 37; Charles Pettit to General Greene, Mar. 5, 1780. Miscellaneous Manuscripts, RUL; Arthur C. Bining, *Pennsylvania Iron Manufacture in the Eighteenth Century* (Harrisburg, 1938), p. 75.

[82] "Cadmus," *New Jersey Journal*, May 23, 1787; Rutherford, "Notes," p. 86.

[83] *Votes and Proceedings*, 11-2, p. 9; Bloomfield to Little, May, 1787, Emmet Collection, NYPL; *Federal Post*, Nov. 25, 1788.

[84] *New Jersey Journal*, May 23, 1787.

There are definite indications that by 1789 the iron industry had weathered the postwar crisis and had recovered its losses. In addition to eight furnaces and eighty forges and bloomeries, the state had several nail factories and slitting mills, a steel plant, a plating forge, and an air furnace that was chiefly employed in casting kettles. In Morris County alone there were seven mines, two furnaces, two rolling and slitting mills, and about thirty active forges. Production was adequate to furnish enough iron implements to meet local needs and to permit some exports to the West Indies.[85]

Far from insignificant in the economy of the state were the hundreds of mills of different types that were engaged in the processing of raw materials. More than three hundred sawmills, operating principally in sparsely settled areas, furnished lumber for the iron works and for shipment to New York and the West Indies. Five hundred gristmills turned out thousands of barrels of flour and meal. In 1789 there were over one hundred and forty such establishments along the numerous streams in Sussex and Hunterdon alone. Some forty fulling-mills did a flourishing business dressing cloth woven by skilled weavers or by diligent matrons. The more enterprising fullers sent wagons on scheduled trips through the countryside to pick up and deliver the cloth at specified places. The tanning of leather was carried on extensively, and Newark especially was noted for its shoes and other leather products.[86]

The feeble beginnings of the factory system may be detected in the postwar decade. There was a glassworks in

---

[85] *Votes and Proceedings*, 14-2, pp. 32-33; Phineas Bond to Duke of Leeds, Encl. 22, "Letters of Phineas Bond," p. 652; Witherspoon, *Works*, IX, p. 206; Morse, *Geography*, p. 288. Morse estimated the output of iron in 1789 at twelve hundred tons of pig and twelve hundred tons of bar iron a year.

[86] *Votes and Proceedings*, 9-1, p. 33; *ibid.*, 14-2, pp. 32-33; *New Jersey Journal*, Nov. 8, 15, 1786; Joseph Atkinson, *The History of Newark* (Newark, 1878), p. 146.

Salem County and another at Woodbury, where green bottles were made in large quantities and unsuccessful experiments were conducted in producing window glass.[87] Richard Way Furman late in 1785 advertised his intention of opening a factory at Trenton to produce boots, shoes, and slippers.[88] Abraham Egbert erected a tobacco manufactory at Springfield to supply cut or roll tobacco "at the New York price or below."[89] In Sussex County there was a "new building for the purpose of making pot-ash, in the manufactory of which the owners had already made considerable advances."[90] A half dozen breweries catered to the popular taste for malt beverages.

Efforts to stimulate manufacturing were not lacking. A group of men in Morris and Essex, motivated by patriotic as well as economic motives, proposed to form a joint-stock company in 1787 to bring financial support to iron and stock-raising projects. "After what has been said on the subject," wrote one of their number, "it may be unnecessary to add anything more, unless that we ought to view ourselves as young beginners in the world, whose all is at stake, and that it depends upon our virtue and good economy, whether we shall be a prosperous and happy nation, or sink into all the meanness of abject slavery, disgrace and contempt."[91] John Rutherfurd was convinced that "unless we manufacture more and import less, we must ever be a very poor state."[92] Particular emphasis was placed upon the desirability of increasing the domestic production of wool and flax in order to lessen dependence on foreign sources for cloth. The Newark

---

[87] Collin, *Journal*, p. 282; *American Museum*, III (June, 1788), p. 593; "Letters of Phineas Bond," p. 652.

[88] *New Jersey Gazette*, Dec. 19, 1785.

[89] *New Jersey Journal*, Nov. 15, 1786.

[90] *Columbian Magazine*, II (Sept., 1788), p. 502.

[91] *New Jersey Journal*, Feb. 14, June 13, 1785. It would seem that the venture was never brought to maturity.

[92] Rutherfurd, "Notes," p. 85.

town meeting in 1788 went so far as to vote premiums to encourage wool raising. "A Zealous Columbian" came forth with the idea that poor taxes might be used to establish woolen and linen manufactories, which could be staffed by paupers and minor criminals.[93] Altogether there were numerous signs of a vigorous interest in the expansion of manufacturing enterprises. That these new currents had been set in motion or at least been given added force by the psychology of change that was a part of the Revolution seems highly probable.

The economy of the postwar years was characterized then, by a brief inflationary boom, followed by a severe trade depression which lasted until around 1787. The period of hard times was the result of broad economic causes, but the confused monetary situation undoubtedly contributed to the general distress. The mercantile group in New Jersey, at first optimistic over commercial prospects and inclined toward a policy of free trade, soon discovered that familiar markets yielded small profits and that a direct overseas trade could be built up only with the aid of a tariff that would discriminate against goods imported from neighboring states. Their persistent efforts to secure such a tariff, coupled with the free-ports plan, failed because the dominant agrarian interest in the state was more concerned with securing relief from taxation through the adoption of a continental impost.

The business community, scattered though it was and weak in political power, was nevertheless able to secure legislative consideration for several of its demands. It was particularly successful in obtaining favorable charters of incorporation for the principal towns, and it achieved a hollow victory in having Perth Amboy and Burlington designated as free ports. Had the merchants and their allies been concentrated in one metropolis, as they were in New York and Pennsylvania,

[93] Atkinson, *Newark*, p. 151; Witherspoon, *Works*, IX, p. 206; *New Jersey Journal*, Sept. 12, 1787.

their influence would doubtless have been greater than it was.

Industry, particularly iron mining and manufacturing, was affected adversely by the transition from war to peace and by the prevalent economic slowdown. Tentative feelers were put forth for governmental assistance, with no significant results. There was, however, a growing awareness that the economic future of the state lay in fields other than agriculture and trade.

VI

The Landed Interest

★★★

L IKE the business community, the landed proprietors constituted a recognizable economic group whose influence was apparent in the sphere of government. The Board of Proprietors of East Jersey and the Council of Proprietors of West Jersey, although weakened in personnel and prestige by the Revolution, still were composed of individuals whose political weight was commensurate with the large stake that they had in society. Both groups demonstrated their vitality in the postwar years and adapted themselves to the altered political situation. Their future was not promising, however, for their residual holdings were but a fraction of what they had once been and new types of enterprise were soon to reduce the relative importance of landed wealth. Too, their political effectiveness was lessened because the two bodies for many years engaged in a bitter rivalry for legislative favor instead of combining their forces behind common objectives.

THE OLD ORDER REVIVES

Throughout the colonial period the proprietors had occupied positions of leadership in determining the course of public affairs. They customarily dominated the Council and held many of the chief civil positions. Their proprietary ownership of the land in their respective divisions placed them at the apex of the economic structure. Aside from the royal officials, probably no group had a stronger attachment to the *status quo*.[1] The extent to which they were affected by the war is therefore of particular interest.

This is not the place to attempt even a cursory description of the complicated proprietary system, but it is necessary to recognize that the setup in East Jersey differed in important respects from that in West Jersey. In the latter division the shares of propriety, one hundred in number, were very early divided into minute fractions. With the exception of the large block of twenty-two shares in the possession of the West Jersey Society and the several shares under the control of the Penn and Coxe families, few individuals held more than a thirty-second of a propriety. This amount permitted the holder to participate in the annual election of the Council of Proprietors, which was composed of five members chosen from Burlington and four from Gloucester. The total number of whole shares in East Jersey was twenty-four, and the process of subdivision was never carried so far there as in West Jersey. Owners of one-fourth of a share were entitled to sit on the Board. The East Jersey proprietors tended to have much larger holdings than did their counterparts in the other division, and they were far less representative of the general population. Most of them were men of considerable prominence in public life. In West Jersey, relations between the proprietors and the masses of the people were in the main harmonious, but in East Jersey there had been almost con-

---

[1] For descriptions of the proprietary system, see Edwin P. Tanner, *The Province of New Jersey, 1664-1738* (New York, 1908), and Edgar J. Fisher, *New Jersey as a Royal Province, 1738-1776* (New York, 1911).

tinual contention between proprietary and anti-proprietary factions.

The East Jersey proprietors were totally disorganized by the Revolution. Most members of the Board, many of whom were royal officials, were hostile to the cause of independence and left the province to serve their king.[2] Several lost their properties through confiscation and never returned to the state. The political power of the group was irreparably damaged. Even though the proprietors were represented on the Council by John Stevens, in the Continental Congress by Elias Boudinot, on the Supreme Court by Robert Morris, and in the army by Lord Stirling, they never again held the preeminent position in public affairs that they did before independence. With its personnel and records dispersed, the Board for all practical purposes ceased to exist and held no regular meetings for six years after 1776.[3] In the interim the affairs of the proprietors fell into disorder, trespasses on the unallocated lands went undetected, and the future of the group was clouded in uncertainty.

Fortunately for the perpetuation of the Board there remained in New Jersey a small but vigorous nucleus composed of James Parker, Walter Rutherfurd, and John Stevens, all of whom were anxious to re-establish the proprietary organization as soon as possible. Stimulated by the aggressive encroachments of the West Jersey proprietors upon their lands, a remnant of the old Board came together in Morristown in April, 1782, and after resolving to take steps to recover the

---

[2] Among those who remained loyal to Britain were James Parker, Cortlandt Skinner, John Smyth (the principal officers of the Board), Walter Rutherfurd, Henry Cuyler, John L. Johnston, Heathcote Johnston, David Ogden, Stephen Skinner, and Oliver DeLancey. John Stevens, Lord Stirling, Elias Boudinot, and William Burnet became whigs. Lundin, *Cockpit*, pp. 46n, 82; Jones, *Loyalists, passim.*

[3] William Roome, *The Early Days and Early Surveys of East New Jersey* (Morristown, 1883), p. 50. A rump board met at Freehold in August, 1778. Lundin, *Cockpit*, pp. 446-47.

scattered records, adjourned to meet in Princeton in June.[4] At this second meeting the decision was made to reopen the surveyor-general's office for the purpose of receiving and recording surveys. John Stevens, Jr., was appointed deputy surveyor-general and was instructed to make his headquarters at Trenton.[5] In September, 1784, the Board was fully reconstituted, new officers were elected, and the surveyor-general's office was returned to Perth Amboy.[6]

There were many urgent matters that demanded the attention of the reorganized proprietors. They discovered that daring men had taken advantage of the wartime confusion to steal timber from the undistributed lands and that others had seized the opportunity to stop paying rents. "Wherever I turn my Eyes as a Landlord or as a Proprietor of Lands in Common or unlocated the greatest Destruction presents itself," lamented James Parker, "and such a licentious Behavior in the people in general that Really people who have not their Interests immediately under their Eyes have but a very gloomy prospect."[7] Tenants in many places refused to renew their

[4] Roome, *Early Days*, p. 50. The attempt to secure the proprietary records, the bulk of which were in New York, was unsuccessful in 1782. Lundin, *Cockpit*, pp. 447-48. A second effort early in 1783 also met with failure. Not until 1785 were the records finally returned to Perth Amboy. Day Book of John Stevens, 1782-1783, Memorial to Sir Guy Carleton, Feb. 27, 1783, John Smyth to Sir Guy Carleton, Mar. 1, 1783, Stevens Papers, SIT; *New Jersey Gazette*, June 20, 1785.

[5] Instructions for John Stevens, Jr., prepared by Lord Stirling, June 6, 1782, Stevens Papers, SIT; *New Jersey Gazette*, June 19, 1782.

[6] Day Book of John Stevens, Sept., 1784, Stevens Papers, SIT; *Political Intelligencer*, Sept. 21, 1784; *New Jersey Gazette*, Sept. 27, 1784. The new officers of the Board were John Stevens, president; William Burnet, vice-president; John Rutherford, surveyor-general; and James Parker, register. Others who were regular attendants at the meetings, which were held in April and September, were Azariah Dunham, John Johnston, John L. Johnston, Walter Rutherfurd, John Parker, Robert Morris, John Rattoone, and John Stevens, Jr.

[7] Parker to John Stevens, Sr., Jan. 11, 1786, Stevens Papers, SIT. Earlier Parker had complained that "all the landings in the country

leases and entered into pacts to stand by one another against their landlords.[8] Only by resorting to countless lawsuits could the proprietors protect their interests.

The long-standing controversy with the Elizabeth Town Associates, which had disturbed the peace of the colony from the earliest days, was once more revived.[9] Late in 1783 John Stevens approached Abraham Clark with the suggestion that the contending parties should meet and endeavor to arrive at some agreement. Clark responded that the Elizabeth Town committee, "sensible of the benefit the whole State would derive from the Settlement of such an important controversie, and influenced by the most pacifick disposition," was willing to enter into conversations.[10] In March, 1784, Stevens and Walter Rutherfurd travelled to Elizabeth Town for the appointed conference. The proprietors offered to confirm a compromise plan that they had put forward prior to the war, and the committee replied with a counterproposal. After some discussion, it was apparent that no solution to the historic quarrel could be reached, and there the negotiations ended.[11] But

from Shrewsbury to South River . . . [were] full of wood and timber pillaged off the common lands of the proprietors." Parker to Stevens, [1784?], Stevens Papers, SIT.

[8] Cornelius Haring to Robert Morris, Apr. 30, 1786, Robert Morris Papers, RUL; Richard P. McCormick, "The West Jersey Estate of Sir Robert Barker," *PNJHS*, LXIV (1946), pp. 14-15.

[9] The Elizabeth Town Associates derived their title from an Indian purchase made with official sanction before Berkeley and Carteret established control over New Jersey. Subsequently the East Jersey proprietors contested the Elizabeth Town claim and repeatedly sought to have it invalidated. The controversy reached something of a climax two decades before the Revolution, when preparations were made for carrying the case to the Court of Chancery, but the dispute never came before the court. For the involved history of the problem, see Tanner, *Province*, pp. 80-96, 660-67; Fisher, *Royal Province*, pp. 176-206.

[10] Abraham Clark to James Parker, Nov. 10, 1783, New Jersey Manuscripts, III, NJHS.

[11] Day Book of John Stevens, Mar. 11, 1784, Stevens Papers, SIT. Evidently the committee proposed in substance that the holders of lands under either party "as far westward as the Society Tract and

although the bases of the dispute were not eliminated and minor clashes subsequently arose between individual proprietors and their old adversaries, the conflict never assumed major proportions and was not a significant factor, as it once had been, in disturbing the political unity of East Jersey.[12]

A principal concern of the proprietors was, of course, the management and distribution of lands that had not as yet been surveyed to individuals. There still remained in East Jersey vast tracts in Monmouth, Sussex, Morris, and Bergen Counties that had never been taken up under patents. Most of this acreage was of little value, and rights of location could be obtained for as little as four dollars an acre.[13] Early in 1785 consideration was given to the advisability of declaring a dividend to enable each shareholder to survey a proportionate amount of the unappropriated stock of lands. The subject was discussed at the April meeting, and in September it was decided that a division should be made of forty-five hundred acres to each whole propriety.[14] Immediately there was a rush to obtain rights of location; within six months John Stevens, President of the Board, had signed almost a hundred and fifty warrants.[15]

Eastward to the old Town Lotts below the first Mountain" should pay ten pounds per hundred acres. See also James Parker to John Stevens, [Mar., 1784?], Stevens Papers, SIT.

[12] James Parker experienced difficulties with Elizabeth Town claimants in 1787. See papers relating to the Peapack Patent, Parker Papers, NJHS.

[13] Rutherfurd, "Notes," p. 79. A right of location entitled the holder to survey a given quantity of land.

[14] Walter Rutherfurd to John Stevens, Jan. 3, 1785, Stevens Papers, SIT; *New Jersey Gazette*, June 20, 1785; *Political Intelligencer*, June 15, 1785; Roome, *Early Days*, p. 38. This was the fourth dividend to be declared by the proprietors.

[15] Day Book of John Stevens, Stevens Papers, SIT. Between November 16, 1785 and September 12, 1789, Stevens signed about 215 warrants, which authorized the holders to survey amounts varying from a few to as many as eleven thousand acres. The dividend apparently reduced the value of the rights to $2.50 an acre. Rutherfurd, "Notes," p. 79.

Another significant accomplishment of the Board was the liquidation of the troublesome Ramapo tract, which the proprietors had acquired in common around 1750. Prior to the Revolution, unsuccessful efforts had been made to sell these lands, located principally in the northern parts of the present counties of Bergen and Passaic. During the war the tenants who resided on the tract stopped paying their rents, and after the return of peace they refused to acknowledge the title of the proprietors.[16] A special committee appointed by the Board to deal with this problem was able to persuade the recalcitrants to renew their old leases by agreeing to forgive all arrearages.[17] The next step was to arrange for the division of the tract, which had not been a source of profit under the system of joint ownership. In September and December of 1790 allotments were made on the basis of approximately 191 acres (valued at £346) to each one-fourth of a propriety.[18]

[16] Roome, *Early Days*, pp. 31-35.

[17] For the details of this arrangement, see the Romapock Papers, Manuscript Division, LC. The proprietors' committee consisted of Azariah Dunham, John Stevens, Jr., and John Rutherfurd.

[18] See Romapock Papers, Parker Papers, NJHS. The entire tract of 18,341 acres was valued at £33,245.3.6. The relative size of the holdings of each proprietor is indicated by the value of the allotment that each received (shillings and pence omitted):

James Parker	£2,701	P. V. B. Livingston	£ 988
R. R. Livingston	2,839	Trustee of Henry	
Wm. Burnet	1,285	Cuyler, Jr.	675
J. & E. Stevens &		Isaac Sharp Assigns	332
J. Stevens, Jr.	2,696	Joseph Sharp Assigns	345
Robert Morris	1,296	Andrew Johnston	1,017
Robert Morris &		W. and C. Rutherfurd	671
John DeLancey	1,348	Estate of Azariah	
John Reid	1,363	Dunham	375
Trustees of Henry		Estate of David Knott	366
Cuyler, Sr.	1,529	Estate of I. Bland	388
Theoph. Bache &		Earl of Perth	1,061
John Rattoone	1,322	Richard Morris	334
Richard Penn	1,389	R. Morris, Assigns of J.	
Elisha Boudinot &		Barton, E. Lawrence	323
R. R. Livingston	1,370		

The proprietors were also engaged on occasion in soliciting special laws to protect their interests or facilitate their operations. Largely through the efforts of the indefatigable James Parker, whose lobbying activities rarely met with failure, they were usually able to induce the legislature to heed their requests. One such act established a simple method by which the state might sell confiscated shares of propriety.[19] Another provided an entirely new procedure for partitioning lands that were held by joint tenants or tenants in common to replace the complicated and expensive practice that had long been followed.[20] A third was designed to reduce the number of controversies over conflicting claims to lands by setting forth certain definite limitations on lawsuits respecting titles.[21]

Despite their apparently dismal situation at the end of the war, the East Jersey proprietors made remarkable progress in re-establishing their organization, repairing their losses, and regaining their influence. Their power was never again to be as great as it had been in colonial times, for their landholdings had shrunk to a small fraction of what they had once been and their political strength had been seriously impaired by the loyalism of some of their number and by the elimination of the appointive Council. But they still included among their members men of wealth, ability, and prestige, who with their many connections were always able to command a respectful following.

Assigns of J. Barton and		Isabella Kearney and	
Richard Ashfield .... £ 343		others and P. Knott .. £ 667	
T. Bache, J. Rattoone,		James Parker and others . 1,000	
and Estate of		Kenneth Hankinson 344	
A. Dunham 332			

[19] Walter Rutherfurd to John Stevens, Jan. 3, 1785, Stevens Papers, SIT; *Session Laws*, 10-3, Act of June 1, 1786.

[20] James Parker to John Stevens, Nov. 18, 1786, Walter Rutherfurd to John Stevens, Feb. 5, 1788, Stevens Papers, SIT; Paterson, *Laws*, pp. 89-91.

[21] *Session Laws*, 11-2, Act of June 5, 1787.

Unlike the proprietors of East Jersey, those of West Jersey were little affected by the war. Their leaders, although not distinguished for their whiggism, were nevertheless not active tories, with the notable exception of Daniel Coxe. Less conspicuous in public life than the principal proprietors in East Jersey, they managed to avoid becoming involved in the public turmoils of the period. Throughout the Revolution the Council of Proprietors met regularly in February, May, August, and November at Burlington. The personnel of the body underwent few changes; the annual elections were evidently a formality.[22] In the years after 1782 the group had as its main concern a conflict with East Jersey over the true location of the boundary line between the two divisions.

The West Jersey Society, an English organization which owned outright some one hundred and seventeen thousand acres of surveyed land, and possessed in addition rights of location entitling it to over a hundred and three thousand acres more, sustained some losses when its extensive holdings were neglected for many years during the war.[23] Its American agent, John Hunt, died in Virginia in 1778, and there was no one to replace him until late in 1780 when Joseph Reed, Pres-

[22] Minutes of the Meetings of the Proprietors of West Jersey, Books C and D, Surveyor-General's Office, Burlington (hereafter cited as West Jersey Minutes). The members of the Council in 1776 were John Monrow, Abraham Hewlings, Thomas Rodman, Daniel Ellis, William Smith, Samuel Clements, Isaac Kay, Thomas Clark, and John Estaugh. Six years later Monrow, Clements, and Estaugh had been replaced by John Bispham, John Bispham, Jr., and John Estaugh Hopkins. Daniel Ellis was the perennial clerk of the Council. Hewlings and Rodman between them held the presidency for over two decades.
[23] The Society, whose headquarters were in London, purchased from Dr. Daniel Coxe in 1691 more than twenty proprieties and became the largest single shareholder in West Jersey. Tanner, *Province*, pp. 17 ff.; John Clement, *Notes and Memoranda Relating to the West New Jersey Society* . . . (Camden, 1886), *passim*. In addition to its West Jersey land the Society had smaller holdings in East Jersey and in Pennsylvania. Estimate by Mr. Hopkins, enclosed in letter to Robert Morris, Feb. 1, 1786, Robert Morris Papers, RUL.

ident of the Supreme Executive Council of Pennsylvania and a principal shareholder in the Society, took it upon himself to act as Hunt's successor. A year later he had himself vested with powers of agency by a special act of the New Jersey legislature.[24] As he entered upon his self-appointed duties, Reed discovered that the Society lands, which he described as being "of a miserable Quality, loaded with Taxes, disputed Lines & inhabited by some of the most unprincipled Wretches on Earth," were in a sorry state. Portions had been sold to discharge tax delinquencies, squatters had established themselves in many places, and vast quantities of timber had been stolen. He accordingly named James Butland of Philadelphia as his deputy and instructed him to try to lease lands to persons who were on the premises and to prevent waste by seizing any tar, shingles, or boards cut on Society property.[25]

Butland experienced great difficulty in getting the squatters to take leases and met with only indifferent success in stopping thievery. He was made the victim of "a most outrageous and riotous assault" by a group of worthies in Gloucester who resented his appearance in their midst.[26] His negotiations with Joseph Ball, who, as the manager of the Batsto Iron Works, was engaged in making wholesale shipments of lumber appropriated from the Society's lands to New York, netted him a small payment and more threats against his life.[27]

In 1784 Reed went to London, evidently with the intention of arranging for the purchase of all of the Society's interests as a speculative venture. His scheme came to nought, how-

[24] Reed purchased seventy-five shares in the Society in 1773. Joseph Reed to Robert Morris, June 8, 1784, Joseph Reed Papers, NYHS; *New Jersey Archives*, 2nd Ser., V, pp. 132-33, 170; Wilson, *Acts*, pp. 217-18; Mr. Lane to Robert Morris, July 25, 1784, Robert Morris Papers, RUL.

[25] Affidavit of James Butland, [1784], Robert Morris Papers, RUL.

[26] Broadside advertisement by Joseph Reed, Oct. 30, 1783, RUL.

[27] *New Jersey Archives*, 2nd Ser., V, pp. 132-33; Deposition of James Butland, Oct. 21, 1782, Robert Morris Papers, RUL.

ever, when he was unable to induce either William Bingham or Jeremiah Wadsworth to furnish the necessary financial backing. Soon after he arrived in London the officers of the Society, who received him in a manner that was anything but cordial, selected Robert Morris to act as their attorney in America, and Reed returned home bitterly disappointed with the results of his mission.[28]

Morris served his clients with his customary energy, but was able to accomplish little because his powers for some years were limited merely to transmitting proposals, together with his recommendations, to England. He could not sell lands; neither could he draw on the Society for money.[29] In 1787 he endeavored to dispose of all the Society's holdings for eighteen thousand pounds to William Bingham, a founder of the Bank of North America and a man of considerable property, the purchaser to pay all claims against the estate. But the negotiations fell through when Bingham objected to the terms.[30] Apparently no large sales were made until 1801, when a tract at Egg Harbor was sold for twenty-five thousand dollars. Shortly thereafter Morris was replaced by Phineas Bond as the Society's agent.[31]

[28] Power of attorney to Robert Morris, July 21, 1784, Robert Morris Papers, RUL. For the story of Reed's activities in London, see his letter book, pp. 141-87, in NYHS. Reed's biographer mentions only that he had "some business relations connected with a land company, known as the West Jersey Company." William B. Reed, *Life and Correspondence of Joseph Reed*, II (Philadelphia, 1847), p. 397.

[29] Memorandum by Robert Morris, Nov. 17, 1784, Morris to John Rutherfurd, July 28, 1786, Robert Morris Papers, RUL.

[30] Morris to Bingham, Sept. 22, Nov. 11, 1787, Robert Morris Papers, RUL.

[31] Morris to James Boggs, Dec. 13, 1801, Robert Morris Papers, RUL. The West Jersey Society, dissatisfied with the terms of the transaction, subsequently brought suit against Morris. Clement erroneously gives the dates of Morris' agency as 1787-1793. Clement, *West Jersey Society*, pp. 31-32. The Society's rights in New Jersey were purchased by Benjamin B. Cooper in 1814. *Ibid.*, p. 32.

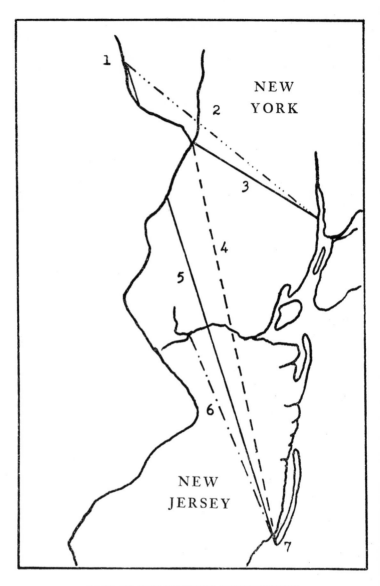

MAP OF THE DIVIDING-LINE DISPUTE

1 North Station Point, 41°, 40″   4 Proposed New Division Line
2 N.Y.–N.J. Boundary before 1769   5 Lawrence's Line (1743)
3 N.Y.–N.J. Boundary after 1769   6 Keith's Line (1687)
                7 Little Egg Harbor Station Point

THE DIVIDING-LINE CONTROVERSY

Absorbing much of the energies of both the East and West Jersey proprietors in the postwar years was a complicated dispute over the location of the boundary line between the two divisions. Inasmuch as the power of deciding the controversy rested with the legislature, each faction strove to enlist the unanimous support of the representatives from its section. The effect, therefore, was the aggravation of the traditional internal split within the state. Moreover, the conflict tended to keep the conservative landed interest divided for many years and had incalculable political consequences. From 1782 to 1786 the matter was constantly before the legislature, and while it did not arouse considerable popular attention, it was to many prominent figures an issue of paramount importance.

The dispute had its origins in the fact that no dividing line had ever been explicitly accepted by both proprietary groups. It was agreed that the line should run from Little Egg Harbor to the northwestern extremity of the state, but this north station point had not been officially located.[32] The East Jersey proprietors in 1743, acting on their own initiative, delegated John Lawrence to survey a line from Little Egg Harbor to a point on the Delaware in latitude 41 degrees, 40 minutes. The West Jersey proprietors never formally recognized this boundary, although they did give it tacit acknowledgment in authorizing surveys. When in 1769 a royal commission charged with determining the boundary between New York

---

[32] Early grants describing the boundaries of New Jersey and of East Jersey fixed the north station on the "northernmost branch of the said Bay or River of Delaware which is in fourtie one degrees and fourtie minutes of lattitude . . ." This description was confusing in that the northernmost branch of the Delaware was not in the latitude set forth. The question subsequently became whether to accept the branch or the latitude as the determining factor. Fisher, *Royal Province*, pp. 210 ff.

and New Jersey established the north station point at the junction of the Mackhackimack and the Delaware in latitude 41 degrees, 21 minutes, 37 seconds, the basis was laid for an attack upon the validity of Lawrence's line. The new station point was several miles south and east of the old one, and if a line was run to it from Little Egg Harbor, it would lie to the eastward of Lawrence's line, with which it formed an acute angle. It was to be the contention of West Jersey that such a line should be drawn and that the lands "within the angle"— amounting to over four hundred and twenty-five thousand acres—should properly belong to West Jersey.[33]

Soon after the decision of the royal commission had been confirmed by the legislatures of New York and New Jersey, the West Jersey Council of Proprietors set about making good its claim to the territory within the angle by issuing warrants for land in the disputed region. But when its surveyors attempted to carry out their functions, they were forcibly restrained from doing so by militant East Jersey agents who smashed their compasses and broke their chains.[34] Overtures were then made to the East Jersey proprietors for a peaceful settlement of the issue, without results. In the meantime, recourse was had to the legislature, which was asked to pass a law authorizing a special commission to run a true division line. It was specified that whichever group of proprietors might be found to have taken more than its share of lands, according to the new boundary, should compensate the other,

---

[33] The conflicting arguments respecting the dividing line are detailed in *The Petitions and Memorials of the Proprietors of West and East-Jersey to the Legislature of New Jersey* . . . (New York, 1784 and 1786) and in *A Concise View of the Controversy between the Proprietors of East and West-Jersey* . . . (Philadelphia, 1785). The former was prepared by the East Jersey proprietors and the latter by the West Jersey proprietors.

[34] For an interesting account of the misfortunes that befell Ebenezer Cowell, a deputy-surveyor from West Jersey, see West Jersey Minutes, Book C, Dec. 7, 1774.

and that the titles of *bona fide* settlers should not be disturbed.[35] With the Revolution impending, no action was taken to effectuate this plan.

During the war, while the East Jersey Board was in eclipse, the West Jersey Council took the opportunity to authorize numerous surveys in the angle.[36] This area, much of which had never been patented, held strong attractions, for there was practically no desirable land remaining unallocated to the west of Lawrence's line.[37] Realizing that their encroachments would not go unchallenged, the western proprietors made timely preparations for defending their pretentions. At a meeting in Burlington in February, 1782, they appointed a five-man committee, composed of Joseph Reed, Jonathan D. Sergeant, Clement Biddle, Daniel Ellis, and Ebenezer Cowell, to manage their interests in the matter; and they sent an ultimatum to Parker, Stevens, and Rutherfurd of the eastern proprietors: if a satisfactory answer to the terms of settlement that had been proposed originally in 1775 was not promptly received, the western proprietors would renew their appeal to the legislature.[38]

The members of the West Jersey committee were an interesting group. Joseph Reed, aide and confidante of Washington and former chief executive of Pennsylvania, had been

[35] Petition of West Jersey Proprietors to Governor and Legislature, Jan. 25, 1775, in *Petitions and Memorials*, pp. 5-10.

[36] Interestingly enough, John Stevens was among those who purchased West Jersey rights for land in the angle. He secured a thousand acres for £120 in 1775. Day Book of John Stevens, Mar. 12, 1783, Stevens Papers, SIT.

[37] Rutherfurd, "Notes," p. 79; West Jersey Minutes, Book C, *passim*. Angle surveys were clearly designated as such in the West Jersey records.

[38] (Copy) Minute of meeting of General Proprietors of West Jersey at home of James Edsall, Feb. 6, 1782, Nelson Manuscripts, 354, NJHS. Strangely enough, this minute does not appear in the West Jersey minute book in Burlington, yet corroboratory evidence suggests its authenticity. See *New Jersey Gazette*, Jan. 16, 1782.

born in Trenton but had settled in Philadelphia in 1770. He was a brother of Bowes Reed, the secretary of state in New Jersey. Sergeant left New Jersey in 1777, after having sat in the Provincial Congress and the Continental Congress, and became attorney general of Pennsylvania and a leader, with Reed, of the Radical party there. Born in Philadelphia of old West Jersey stock, Biddle served under General Greene as Commissary General of Forage and was a merchant, importer, and broker with family connections in Burlington. Cowell was deputy surveyor-general of West Jersey, and Daniel Ellis was the clerk of the Council of Proprietors.[39] Reed, Sergeant, and Biddle had never before played a prominent role in proprietary affairs. Probably they became involved at this time because of the speculative possibilities offered by the venture.[40]

The response of the East Jersey proprietors to the ultimatum sent by their adversaries was a flat refusal to consider any alteration in the division line based on the change in the north station point.[41] Accordingly, the West Jersey committee prepared a petition to the legislature asking that the division line be determined by neutral commissioners and that they be granted "a recompence in value of land, from the general stock of the Eastern proprietors" for those tracts within the angle which had already been taken up under East Jersey surveys.[42] Much to their disappointment, the Assembly re-

[39] There are adequate sketches of Reed, Sergeant, and Biddle in the *DAB* and of Cowell in Hall, *Presbyterian Church*, p. 141.

[40] Reed and Sergeant were paid handsomely for their legal services to the committee. West Jersey Minutes, Book D, Nov. 2, 1784.

[41] Draft of letter from East Jersey proprietors to West Jersey proprietors, June 6, 1782, Stevens Papers, SIT.

[42] Petition of West Jersey proprietors, Nov. 18, 1782, Manuscript Collection, NJSL. West Jersey did not propose to appropriate the lands held under East Jersey by *bona fide* settlers, but did wish to receive an equivalent acreage elsewhere in East Jersey by way of compensation. The petitioners suggested that the Ramapo Tract could be used for this purpose.

jected their plea in November, 1782, by a large majority.[43] Undaunted by this defeat, however, they were again before the legislature in June, 1783, with the draft of a bill embodying their demands.[44]

In the meantime the Eastern proprietors were not idle. John Rutherfurd, in consultation with William Paterson and William Churchill Houston, was delegated to prepare a memorial in defense of the eastern proprietors' position.[45] This lengthy document, which was read in the Assembly in June, 1783, at the same time that West Jersey renewed its petition, recited the history of the division-line controversy from 1664 to the moment and argued for the perpetuation of Lawrence's line. It was charged that "certain persons [Reed, Sergeant, and Biddle?] having of late introduced themselves into the councils of the West-Jersey proprietors" were responsible for deluding with their "alluring suggestions" the majority of the proprietors and inducing them to pursue an attack on a boundary which had been recognized for decades. A change in the line would result in "the industrious farmer being ousted of the possession of his land . . . [and] the laborious tradesman being torn from his valuable buildings." As to the proposal that the legislature should intervene in the dispute, the memorialists believed it to be "a settled maxim of government, that the legislature of a state, ought never to interfere in the private disputes of individuals, where the

[43] *Votes and Proceedings*, 7-1, p. 42. The vote was 22 to 11, with members divided largely along sectional lines.

[44] *New Jersey Gazette*, Feb. 12, 1783; Petition of West Jersey proprietors, May 26, 1783, Manuscript Collection, NJSL.

[45] Day Book of John Stevens, Mar. 12, 1783, Stevens Papers SIT; Account of John Rutherfurd with the East Jersey proprietors in connection with the dispute with West Jersey over the dividing line, [1784], East Jersey Manuscripts, 131, NJHS. There is abundant evidence that the principal author of the *Petitions and Memorials*, printed by Shepard Kollock in New York in 1784 and reprinted with additions in 1786, was John Rutherfurd. Day Book of John Stevens, Aug. 3, 1784.

courts of law and equity ... [were] adequate to the cognizance thereof, except where all the parties, affected thereby, do agree thereto and solicit such a mode of settlement." Lawrence's line should be confirmed, or if this line was not clear, commissioners should be appointed to run a line from Little Egg Harbor to the old station point.[46]

The legislature took no action on the petitions until December, 1783, when it resolved to permit the western proprietors to introduce a bill at the next sitting, which convened in August, 1784.[47] On the eve of the session, the western proprietors met and decided that it would be "absolutely Necessary for Some person to go with the Bill as Soon as Possible in order to forward the passing of it," and Biddle and Cowell, who were chosen for this important errand, were instructed to "Endeavour as much as Possible with the Members to forward the Passing of said bill." [48] When the bill was delivered to the Assembly, James Parker and John Stevens in a brief petition asked that a hearing be held on the measure at some future date, and the Assembly scheduled the event for the following session.[49]

Both sides made elaborate preparations for the hearing. The legal staff of the West Jersey committee, which in addition to Reed and Sergeant included Joseph Bloomfield, attorney general of the state, and the future chief justice, James Kinsey, carefully brought together all the evidence they could find bearing on the controversy.[50] William Pater-

---

[46] Memorial and representation of the East Jersey proprietors, May 25, 1783, Manuscript Collection, NJSL; *Petitions and Memorials*, pp. 14-40.

[47] *New Jersey Gazette*, Jan. 27, 1784.

[48] Order of Council of Proprietors, Aug. 5, 1784, Ellis Papers, NYHS.

[49] Petition of James Parker and John Stevens, Aug. 11, 1784, Manuscript Collection, NJSL; Day Book of John Stevens, Aug. 3, 1784; *Votes and Proceedings*, 8-2, p. 110.

[50] Daniel Ellis to Ebenezer Cowell and Clement Biddle, Oct. 18, 1784, Ellis Papers, NYHS.

son, William Churchill Houston, Robert Morris, and John Rutherfurd were similarly occupied in the interests of East Jersey. Each party had numerous petitions favorable to its cause drawn up and distributed among the farmers who resided in the disputed area.[51]

Early in November, 1784, the legislature listened for three days to the arguments of the opposing counsel. Jonathan D. Sergeant, urging the enactment of the bill sponsored by the West Jersey proprietors, stressed the necessity of placing the dispute before special commissioners, who would give an impartial decision on the division line. William Paterson vigorously denounced this proposal. "Better that a private Individual should suffer, be ruined," he declaimed, "than that Trial by jury [should be] infringed, and [the] Const^{n} torn up by its very roots." [52] At the conclusion of the debate, the Assembly rejected the bill by the narrow margin of seventeen to sixteen, with the Speaker, Hendrickson of Monmouth, casting the deciding vote. Moses Bloomfield of Middlesex, whose son was deeply interested in the passage of the measure, was the lone eastern representative to vote in the affirmative. The only negative votes among the western members came from Anthony Sharp of Salem, whose family had extensive interests in East Jersey, and Benjamin Van Cleve of Hunterdon.[53]

Unwilling to accept this defeat as final, the West Jersey proprietors in April, 1785, resolved to continue their fight.

[51] Day Book of John Stevens, Oct. 20, 1784, Stevens Papers, SIT; Petition of citizens living near the dividing line, Nov. 5, 1784, Loose Manuscripts, NJSL; Petition and remonstrance of inhabitants of Somerset County, [1784], Manuscript Collection, NJSL.

[52] Minutes of a hearing on a bill presented by the proprietors of West New Jersey [in Paterson's hand], Nov. 2, 1784, Paterson Papers, PUL. Robert Morris, Gouverneur Morris, and Joseph Bloomfield also appeared.

[53] *Votes and Proceedings*, 9-1, p. 14. Two weeks later Hendrickson resigned as Speaker because of "ill health" and Van Cleve replaced him. Several West Jersey members were absent.

Plans were made for again bringing the matter before the legislature and for answering the East Jersey *Petitions and Memorials*. This latter task was entrusted to Richard Stockton, son of the "Signer," who replaced the deceased Joseph Reed on the special committee. Concern was expressed about the announced intention of the eastern proprietors to declare a dividend, and an advertisement was placed in the *New Jersey Gazette* warning prospective purchasers of East Jersey rights not to survey lands within the angle.[54] On November 18, 1785, the Assembly for the second time granted the persistent controversialists leave to bring in their familiar bill at the next sitting.[55] On the following day the East Jersey proprietors submitted a counterpetition, in which they accused their antagonists of being "swayed by the persuasions of designing men" and of having fraudulently peddled, throughout the state, rights of location for lands in the angle.[56]

Looking forward anxiously to the second hearing before the legislature, Daniel Ellis, clerk of the western proprietors, realistically viewed the prospects of success. "The Fear seems to be," he explained to his associates, "Wether we Shall be able to get a Quorum of the Council in Our Favour, for the Eastern Proprietors are Indefatagable in Trying all Methods

[54] Minutes of meeting of West Jersey proprietors, Apr. 11, 1785, Nelson Manuscripts, 354, NJHS; *New Jersey Gazette*, Mar. 7, Apr. 25, 1785. The authorship of *A Concise View of the Controversy between the Proprietors of East and West-Jersey* (Philadelphia, 1785), which was West Jersey's answer to the *Petitions and Memorials*, has usually been attributed to Ebenezer Cowell. It would seem, however, that Richard Stockton, who at the April meeting was "requested to Draw an answer to the pamphlet Published by the Eastern proprietors and Send the Draught thereof for the approbation of Messrs. Kinsey and Sergeant," was really the author.

[55] *Votes and Proceedings*, 10-1, pp. 37, 45; Daniel Ellis to Ebenezer Cowell and Clement Biddle, Nov. 21, 1785, Ellis Papers, NYHS. The vote was 21 to 11.

[56] *Petitions and Memorials*, pp. 78-96.

they Possibly Can to Defeat us. It behoves the Western Proprietors," he added, "to Exert themselves and to Get the Western Members to attend at the Next Sitting and use their Endeavours with the Council so as to Get a Quorum in our favour, otherwise it will have to be done all over again and perhaps we may not have so favourable an opportunity again." [57] Copies of the desired bill were printed for distribution to the members of the legislature, and Ebenezer Cowell was sent up to Sussex to secure signatures to a petition.[58]

In February, 1786, the Assembly set aside five days to listen to the counsel for each faction, as they once more presented the usual arguments for and against the appointment of a commission to survey a new division line. When the vote was taken, the bill was rejected, twenty-three to thirteen. The minority was made up entirely of western members. Voting with the eastern representatives were five assemblymen from Sussex and Hunterdon and one from Cape May.[59] After four years of unremitting efforts to obtain the legislation that would have given them almost a half-million acres, the West Jersey proprietors had gained nothing.

Despite their many setbacks, however, they did not relinquish their claim to the disputed lands. Turning from the legislature to the courts, they brought ejectment suits against those whose titles were based on East Jersey surveys within the angle. The members of the East Jersey Board met this

[57] Ellis to Cowell and Biddle, Nov. 21, 1785, Ellis Papers, NYHS.
[58] Ellis to Cowell and Biddle, Dec. 8, 1785, Ellis Papers, NYHS; Petition of citizens near the line of partition, [1786], Manuscript Collection, NJSL.
[59] *Votes and Proceedings*, 10-2, pp. 19-20. A recent political revolution in Hunterdon had resulted in the ousting of Samuel Tucker, enemy of the Eastern proprietors, and in the conversion of his erstwhile colleague, John Lambert, to the eastern viewpoint. The shift in the position of the Sussex members may have been related to the fact that in the alignment on the paper-money question, which was then being agitated, Sussex was tied to East Jersey.

threat by resolving to undertake the defense of such actions at their common expense.[60] But neither side could long afford to engage in an interminable series of tedious and expensive lawsuits, the results of which were limited and inconclusive, and soon the controversy became quiescent. The matter was revived briefly in 1795 when the western proprietors reasserted their claim to the lands within the angle and threatened once more to seek a remedy for the alleged trespasses on their domain. To this challenge the eastern magnates issued a prompt rejoinder, charging a designing minority with being responsible for renewing the agitation.[61] As late as 1886 the old dispute was still capable of being revived.[62]

Bitterly at odds over the dividing-line question, the landed interest for many years after the war did not constitute a united political force. Instead of combining, as they might have been expected to do, in strong opposition to growing radical tendencies, the two proprietary groups expended much of their political strength in contending with one another. The repercussions of this situation were particularly important in East Jersey. It was in that section that agrarian measures had their greatest support. If the eastern proprietors had chosen to exert their considerable influence on the side of conservatism, they might have been able to restrain the popular tide. But they were desperately in need of the backing of the eastern legislators and could not afford to antag-

[60] West Jersey Minutes, Book D, May 3, 1786; East Jersey Minutes, Sept. 16, 1786.

[61] *An Address from the Council of Proprietors of the Western Division of New Jersey, to the Occupiers of Lands Within the Angle. To which are added Remarks on the said Address by Aristides* (n.p., 1795).

[62] *Report of the Committee of the Council of Proprietors of West New Jersey in relation to the Province Line between East and West New Jersey* (Camden, 1888). East Jersey was accused of "granting rights for location on Long Beach west of the dividing line . . ."

onize them by attempting to balk their favorite projects.[63] It is perhaps significant that after 1786, when the proprietary quarrel subsided, the conservatives in both divisions coalesced and the temper of the legislature underwent a decided change.

[63] A careful study of the correspondence of John Stevens, Sr., James Parker, and Robert Morris reveals surprisingly little comment on such matters as paper money, tender laws, and debtor laws, all of which were of outstanding public interest.

VII

Money: the Era of Deflation

****

M ERCANTILE projects and proprietary disputes were concerns of the few. They did not raise issues that aroused widespread popular interest. Financial problems stimulated more public controversy and absorbed more legislative energy in the troubled eighties than did any others. They arose in the main out of attempts to rehabilitate a currency system that had been totally deranged by the expedients that had been adopted under the pressure of military necessity. Also involved was the matter of servicing a debt which, in view of the available resources, seemed staggering. Every citizen, wealthy or poor, was directly affected by the decisions that were made respecting money, taxation, public securities, and measures for the relief of debtors. Understandably enough, rival economic groups within the state held opposing views on these vital questions, and they sought to utilize the existing political processes to have enacted such laws as they deemed essential to their welfare. Under these conditions, the sensitivity of the machinery of self-government to popular pressures was to be tested thoroughly, and some of the basic implications of majority rule were to become apparent.

THE FATE OF THE NEW EMISSION

A momentous turning point in Continental finance, which was to have important repercussions in New Jersey, occurred early in 1780. On March 18, the Continental Congress reluctantly but courageously came to the conclusion that the paper bills of credit upon which it had so long relied to finance the war must be abandoned. Accordingly, that body decided to call in the printing-press money by taxes at its current value, which was somewhat arbitrarily fixed at forty to one for specie. Thus by one stroke a nominal debt of two hundred million dollars was reduced to five million dollars. The depreciated bills were to be destroyed and replaced by new ones issued on the credit of the individual states in the proportion of one for every twenty of the old that they turned in to the Continental collectors. Each state was to provide for the redemption of its own "new emission" money within six years. Although viewed by some as a faithless act of repudiation, this measure was intended to substitute for the depreciated "continental" a contracted and stable currency.[1]

In order to understand the consequences of this action in New Jersey, it is necessary to summarize briefly the condition of the currency in the state at the time. In comparison with other states, New Jersey was relatively deficient in paper money when Congress set in motion its deflationary program. By 1780 the various issues of loan-office money and bills of credit that had been emitted by New Jersey both before and after Independence had been withdrawn from circulation.[2] The volume of Continental bills cannot be estimated with

---

[1] *Journals of the Continental Congress*, XVI, pp. 263-67; Burnett, *Continental Congress*, p. 426; C. J. Bullock, *The Finances of the United States from 1775 to 1789* . . . (Madison, 1895), p. 137; William C. Houston to Robert Morris, May 6, 1780, Houston-Morris Letters, RUL.

[2] E. A. Fuhlbruegge, "New Jersey Finances During the American Revolution," *PNJHS*, LV (1937), p. 174.

exactitude, but the amount was probably not far from seven million dollars, which at the current rate of exchange had a specie value of about one hundred and forty thousand dollars. This was a relatively small sum and was, in fact, only two-thirds of the quota that the state was expected to draw in by taxes under the retirement plan.[3] Gold and silver coin, introduced by the French army, by the Spanish trade, and by illicit dealings with the enemy, was becoming available and was to comprise a large part of the circulating medium for the next two or three years, until it was drained away by heavy taxes and by an unfavorable trade balance.[4] The factor that rendered the monetary situation critical in the extreme, however, was the enormous quantity of certificates that had been received in payment for the provisions and services furnished to the Continental troops.

In the first years of the war, New Jersey had been paid in cash for goods sold to the army during its lengthy residences within the state, and money was plentiful. But when the army took up its winter quarters at Morristown late in 1779, the financial resources of the Confederation were at a low ebb. Instead of cash, the farmers and artisans who supplied the forlorn army were given certificates, which they could ill refuse to accept, by both state and Continental purchasing agents. These paper promises to pay, given by a government that was all but bankrupt, were worth only a small fraction of their nominal value of several millions of dollars. Other states might and did avoid exchanging their products for the unwelcome certificates, but New Jersey had no alternative but to take them. "This then," wrote Governor Liv-

---

[3] New Jersey's quota was $11,700,000, of which less than seven million dollars could be raised. *American State Papers, Finance*, I, p. 58.

[4] Webster, *Collection of Essays*, p. 109; *New Jersey Gazette*, June 26, 1782; Fuhlbruegge, "New Jersey Finances," p. 175. Between June 21, 1781 and June 9, 1783, taxes levied in specie came to the extraordinary total of £305,930. See Appendix I.

ingston, "is the present situation of New-Jersey, drained. of supplies, drained of cash, over-run with certificates, and burdened with taxes; as a state indebted to the continent, at the same time that the continent is immensely indebted to the individuals which compose it."[5] This description, it should be noted, applied with special force to the northern counties, for the southern part of the state was remote from the site of the main encampments. Moreover many of the Quakers were reluctant to contribute their produce to the military machine. "Unequally exposed & harrassed," observed Robert Morris, "we are too hot on one side & too cold on tother . . ."[6] The uneven distribution of certificates was to have a significant effect on the attitude of the two sections on financial questions.

The legislature quickly demonstrated its willingness to co-operate fully in the new financial plan, and on June 9, 1780, made provision for redeeming the proportion of Continental bills assigned to it and for putting the new money into circulation.[7] A tax of ten million dollars in continental was levied; as the old bills were brought in, they were deposited with the Continental Loan Office, from which new emission bills were received in the ratio of one for twenty. After the bills had been signed and numbered, four-tenths of them were returned to the Loan Office, where they became available for Continental expenditures. The remaining six-tenths were delivered to the state treasurer. Bearing 5 per cent interest, the new emission was to be retired by taxes in six annual installments and was declared to be legal tender equal to specie. The rate of exchange between continental and new emission bills was explicitly fixed at forty to one.

Under the terms of this arrangement, New Jersey was

[5] "Scipio" [William Livingston], *New Jersey Gazette*, Oct. 28, Nov. 1, 1780.
[6] Morris to William C. Houston, Oct. 8, 1780, Houston-Morris Letters, RUL.
[7] *Session Laws*, 4-2, Act of June 9, 1780.

entitled to a maximum of six hundred thousand dollars in new money, but because less than two-thirds of the state's quota of continental bills was collected, the actual amount of new emission did not exceed $336,000. Of this sum not more than $291,000 was ever issued; the rest was cancelled as soon as it was received.[8] In effect then, seven million dollars in Continental currency was replaced by $291,000 in state money.

Soon after the new emission began to come off the printing presses, complaints were made that inasmuch as none of the new bills were in denominations under one dollar, people would be inconvenienced in paying their taxes and debts. To meet this justifiable criticism, the legislature on January 9, 1781, authorized the issuance of eighty thousand dollars in denominations ranging from six pence to seven shillings and six pence. This fractional currency, which was made legal tender, was supposed to be sunk by taxes in equal installments in 1786 and 1787.[9] Although not properly considered new emission, these bills of credit were subsequently treated in much the same manner as the bills of June 8, 1780.

Those who had hoped that with the adoption of the new currency system the era of depreciation and fluctuation had been brought to an end were doomed to early disappointment. Scarcely had the new emission been put into circulation when it began to fall in value. This condition was attributable mainly to the fact that the forty-to-one rate of exchange with continental fixed by law was artificial and erroneous, for continental was in fact currently valued in June, 1780, at about sixty to one and was destined to go much lower still.

---

[8] John Stevens, Jr., Treasurer, "To the Citizens of New Jersey," *New Jersey Gazette*, Apr. 16, 1783; *American State Papers, Finance*, I, p. 58.

[9] *Session Laws*, 5-1, Act of Jan. 9, 1781. The new-emission bills were in denominations of $20, $8, $7, $5, $4, $3, $2, $1. Those of January 9, 1781 were in denominations of 7/6, 6/, 5/, 4/, 3/9, 3/6, 2/6, 1/6, 1/, 9d, and 6d.

In its decline, continental dragged the new emission down.[10] The refusal of many merchants, of the Quakers, and of tradesmen in neighboring states to place full confidence in the money was another factor that made for depreciation.[11] Too, the great increase in the amount of specie, brought into the state by the profitable traffic with the enemy, probably made the paper less acceptable than it otherwise would have been. Finally, there were the speculators, who were provided with enticing opportunities for manipulation because of the differences in rates of exchange from state to state, and who bore no small share of the responsibility for the difficulties which beset the new emission.[12] Within less than a year, the state money was being reckoned generally at three to one for specie in spite of the tender laws.

Efforts were made to halt the depreciation, with little success. In November, 1780, the unfortunate forty-to-one proportion was abandoned, and the governor and his Privy Council were authorized to proclaim a new rate of exchange based on current values.[13] The ratio was set at seventy-five to one in November, 1780, at one hundred and fifty to one in April, 1781, and at one hundred and seventy-five to one in June.[14] In the meantime the numerous Whig Societies in the northern part of the state interested themselves in the matter.

[10] "Scipio" [William Livingston], *New Jersey Gazette*, Nov. 1, 1780; Bullock, *Finances*, p. 133.

[11] "A Tradesman of New Jersey," *New Jersey Gazette*, May 23, 1781; *Political Intelligencer*, Feb. 1, 1785.

[12] Burnett, *Continental Congress*, p. 510; "A Whig Freeholder," *New Jersey Gazette*, June 6, 1781.

[13] *Session Laws*, 5-1, Act of Nov. 17, 1780. In January, 1781, continental was declared to be legal tender for debts at its current value only. Wilson, *Acts*, Act of Jan. 5, 1781, p. 157.

[14] *New Jersey Gazette*, Mar. 7, May 5, June 6, 1781. The seventy-five-to-one ratio was maintained for five months, despite the fact that during this period depreciation was proceeding rapidly. Probably the main reason why no change was made was that Pennsylvania adhered to this ratio. "Scipio" [William Livingston], *New Jersey Gazette*, Apr. 25, 1781; "Silentio," *New Jersey Gazette*, Mar. 7, 1781.

"*Resolved unanimously,*" declared the group in Monmouth, "That we use our utmost endeavours to support the credit of the paper currency of this state, and to execute the law strictly against every person who shall, to our knowledge attempt to depreciate it." [15] But no measures, official or otherwise, could give the new emission a value equal to specie, and in June, 1781, the legislature, recognizing that compulsory laws had answered no good purpose, repealed the acts that had made the money legal tender. Some protection was afforded to debtors by the provision that any creditor who before May 1, 1782, sought to exact payment for a debt contracted prior to the removal of tender could be forced to accept the state bills at their face value.[16] Six months later the government admitted its complete inability to maintain the value of the new emission when it directed the treasurer to pay out the bills at the current exchange rate of three for one.[17]

After this open acknowledgment had been made of the fact that the state paper had depreciated, the basis was laid for a major controversy over the question of whether the bills should be redeemed at par, in accordance with the promise on their faces, or at their actual worth. For more than two years, this subject was hotly debated both in and out of the legislature. Foremost among those who argued that the money should be redeemed at its current value were the spokesmen of West Jersey, whose constituents had relatively little new emission and who were anxious to have the state debt reduced at the lowest cost to themselves. On the opposite side were most of the conservative whigs of East Jersey and the public creditors.

[15] *New Jersey Gazette*, May 16, 1781; "A True Patriot," *New Jersey Gazette*, Apr. 11, 1781.

[16] Wilson, *Acts*, Act of June 13, 1781, pp. 197-98. This action was in part a result of the recommendation made by the Continental Congress on March 16 that all states repeal their tender laws. Burnett, *Continental Congress*, p. 512.

[17] *Votes and Proceedings*, 6-1, p. 76.

The issue emerged into prominence soon after the two houses convened in the fall of 1782. By that time $130,000 of new emission had already been brought in by taxes and cancelled in accordance with the plan that had been adopted in June, 1780, and the legislature was expected to levy a new tax to retire the next scheduled installment.[18] But when a bill for this purpose was introduced, it was defeated by the narrow margin of nineteen to eighteen. All but four of the negative votes came from West Jersey members, who opposed the measure because it called for redemption at par. Most of the assemblymen from the western division had given their support to an amendment which would have authorized payment of the tax in specie at the ratio of one to three for paper, but this proposal, too, was beaten.[19] Unable to come to an agreement on the question, the lawmakers adjourned without having enacted any tax law. They did, however, instruct the treasurer not to issue any more of the state money until $122,-540 (approximately the amount outstanding) had been cancelled.[20]

The inconclusive outcome of the contest over the tax bill stimulated rival groups to resort to the familiar device of circulating petitions in support of their respective positions. Almost five hundred citizens in Essex called upon the legislature to adhere to the pledge printed on the face of the new emission by redeeming the money at its nominal value. They expressed their alarm at the growing popularity of the doctrine "That future Assemblies are not bound by the Acts of former Ones," pointing out that such heresies would destroy all public and private virtue. Those patriots who had "trusted the Public, Particularly in the most critical and trying times, ought not to be Consigned to Injury and distress." Similar

[18] *New Jersey Gazette*, Aug. 29, 1781; John Stevens, Jr., "To the Citizens of New Jersey," *New Jersey Gazette*, Apr. 16, 1783.

[19] *Votes and Proceedings*, 7-1, pp. 60-63.

[20] *Ibid.*, 7-1, pp. 85, 88.

pleas were signed by men of substance in Middlesex and Hunterdon.[21]

The proponents of depreciation were even more active in defending their cause. A petition drawn up by some of the wealthiest men in Salem observed that inasmuch as the new emission had been paid out of the treasury at the ratio of three to one for specie ever since December, 1781, there was no reason why it should not be received at the same proportion in tax payments. Remarking that state bills were scarce in their region, they asked "why the honest and industrious part of the Community should be put to the Trouble and Expense of travelling to Trenton, where the greater Part of the State Money centers, in order to procure it, or pay an advance of twenty-five per Cent on the real Exchange to obtain it at Home, which is about the average of what it costs us." They charged that the present holders of the money were speculators who had acquired it at a low rate and were now hoping to realize a profit of 200 per cent on their investment.[22] The inhabitants of Gloucester, too, complained of the difficulty of obtaining new emission and asked that they be permitted to pay their tax in specie at one for three.[23] From Hunterdon came a vigorous protest, signed by 793 individuals, against "Exactions made to Inhance the Fortunes of Individuals." [24] The Burlington Grand Jury was outspoken in requesting that the money be called in at no greater value

[21] Petition of inhabitants of Essex, May 5, 1783, AM Papers, NJSL; Petition of Middlesex subscribers, Jan. 24, 1783, Loose Manuscripts, NJSL; Petition of Hunterdon subscribers, [Jan., 1783], Vault Manuscripts, NJSL; *Votes and Proceedings*, 7-2, p. 113.

[22] Representation and remonstrances of Salem inhabitants, [1783], Loose Manuscripts, NJSL. Among the signers were Andrew Sinnickson, Robert Johnson, Anthony Keasby, and Ephraim Lloyd, all of whom were men of means.

[23] Petition of Gloucester inhabitants, May 24, 1783, AM Papers, NJSL.

[24] Petitions of Hunterdon inhabitants, [1783], Loose Manuscripts, NJSL.

than it had been paid out of the treasury.[25] In New Brunswick the Athenian Society, a local discussion club with its headquarters at Queen's College, earnestly debated the subject "Whether the State money should be redeemed at its nominal value or at its present depreciated State" without arriving at any decision.[26]

The legislators came together in a special sitting in May, 1783, and renewed their wrangling over the redemption question. Several bills were proposed in attempts to come to some acceptable compromise on the matter, but the end result was the referral of the whole problem to the next session.[27] When the legislature met after the October elections, the advocates of repudiation were in control of the Assembly. All but two of the West Jersey members joined with six from East Jersey on December 19 to pass a bill authorizing a tax of ten thousand pounds in specie to redeem thirty thousand pounds in bills of credit.[28] On the following day the Council promptly rejected the measure by a vote of seven to four.[29] Reduced to its simplest terms, the contest was now between the creditor interest of East Jersey on the one side and the creditor interest of West Jersey, abetted by the "poorer sort" in both divisions, on the other. In August, 1784, the Assembly once more passed its redemption bill by an overwhelming vote, but again the Council prevented it from becoming law.[30]

During the brief election campaign in October, 1784, the

[25] *Votes and Proceedings*, 7-2, p. 97. The same stand was taken by 464 petitioners from Sussex, 469 from Essex, and 198 from Somerset. *Ibid.*, pp. 97-98.

[26] Transactions of the Athenian Society, Feb. 19, 1783, RUL.

[27] *Votes and Proceedings*, 7-2, pp. 115-30.

[28] *Ibid.*, 8-1, p. 75. The vote was twenty to eleven.

[29] *Journal of Council*, 8-1, p. 31. Only one West Jersey member voted with the majority.

[30] *Votes and Proceedings*, 8-2, p. 114; *Journal of Council*, 8-2, p. 18.

seven councilors who had negatived the will of the Assembly were both defended and attacked for their action. The electors were strongly advised to replace the men who had prevented the redemption of the state money at its current rate. On the other hand, a self-styled "Friend to Justice" expressed the hope that the Council would "never again suffer the state to be stigmatized with the opprobious epithet of leaving their worthy creditors to the levity of merciless debtors, or robbing their constituents of two-thirds of their cash."[31] The verdict at the polls brought eight new men to the Council and drastically altered the complexion of that body.

When the Assembly in December, 1784, passed a bill to raise ten thousand pounds to be used in redeeming thirty thousand pounds in new emission, the Council promptly gave its approval.[32] The ten-thousand-pound tax was payable either in specie or in paper at a ratio of three to one. The treasurer was directed to exchange a dollar in coin for every three dollars in new emission that was tendered to him and to retain the bills for cancellation.[33] Repudiation had triumphed. Momentarily united in victory were the conservative, hard-money spokesmen of West Jersey and the future leaders of the radical, paper-money faction from East Jersey, including the popular champion, Abraham Clark.

The strange spectacle of legislators from the southern part of the state arrayed on the side of depreciation is readily explained. The new emission had been issued while the war was in progress, and much of it went for the purchase of

[31] *Political Intelligencer*, Oct. 5, 19, 1784.

[32] *Votes and Proceedings*, 9-1, p. 77; *Journal of Council*, 9-1, p. 38. In the majority were the four West Jersey councilors and those from Middlesex, Monmouth, and Somerset. The minority consisted of the members from Bergen, Essex, Morris, and Sussex.

[33] *Session Laws*, 9-1, Act of Dec. 21, 1784. Thus the effect of the law was to call out of circulation eighty thousand dollars in state money at a three-to-one depreciation.

military supplies. Consequently it was generally refused by the Quakers and did not circulate in large quantities in West Jersey. Because most of the money was held by public creditors in the northern counties, West Jersey was naturally not averse to paying off this state obligation at one-third of the face value.[34] As for those representatives from East Jersey who sided with the majority, they were apparently convinced that it would be impolitic and unjust to enrich a minority by redeeming at its nominal value money that had unquestionably undergone considerable depreciation. Too, some felt that it would be better to receive at least one dollar in specie for three of the bills than to get nothing.[35] The substantial public creditors, those who held large sums of new emission, and those who deprecated the breach of faith committed by the legislature felt themselves affected adversely. "I have seen," lamented Governor Livingston, who had suffered heavy losses through depreciation, "paper money emitted by a Legislature that solemnly promised to redeem it, that afterwards depreciated it themselves—and I therefore believe I shall never see the honest redemption of it."[36] William Paterson sarcastically characterized the act of repudiation as "a master stroke in politicks ... a splendid display of legislative honesty and skill!"[37] Henceforth the customary opposition of the creditor interest to paper money was to be reinforced by the conviction that the legislature could not be trusted to adhere to its promises, that public contracts might be voided by a simple majority vote, and that the rights of property, in fact, were insecure in an unrestricted democracy.

[34] *Political Intelligencer*, Feb. 5, 1785; Representation and remonstrance of Salem inhabitants, [1783], Loose Manuscripts, NJSL.

[35] "Willing to Learn" [Abraham Clark?], *Political Intelligencer*, Dec. 21, 1785.

[36] Sedgwick, *Memoir*, p. 394; Frank Monaghan, "Unpublished Correspondence of William Livingston and John Jay," *PNJHS*, LII (1934), p. 152.

[37] "Horatius," 14, William Paterson Essays, RUL.

While the long debate was in progress over the manner of redeeming the new emission, the money was being retired steadily. Of the total of $291,000 that had been issued, $130,000 had been cancelled by June, 1782, and at the end of 1784 the amount in circulation did not exceed $115,000. By 1790 all but about 5 per cent of the bills had been destroyed. The removal from circulation of the fractional currency did not begin until December, 1784, and by 1790 almost one-half of this money had been burned.[38] The marked contraction of the paper currency between 1780 and 1784, taken together with the decline in the quantity of specie toward the end of that period, brought complaints about the scarcity of money and soon led to another episode of inflation.

Contributing to the deflationary process were the unusually heavy taxes. Down to the end of 1779, tax levies in the state had amounted to less than $270,000 in continental money and certificates. In the next two years, because of heavy requisitions by the Continental Congress, twenty-two million dollars in continental was called for, although not much more than half of this sum was collected.[39] Between September, 1781, and January, 1784, there fell due a total of $706,664 in state money and certificates and $815,816 in specie. On the whole the record of collections was remarkable. By November, 1784, the actual returns to the treasury came to $645,776 in state money and certificates and $730,888 in

[38] John Stevens, Jr., "To the Citizens of New Jersey," *New Jersey Gazette*, Apr. 16, 1783; *Votes and Proceedings*, 7-1, pp. 85, 88; *ibid.*, 9-1, p. 91; *ibid.*, 10-1, pp. 19-21; *ibid.*, 11-1, pp. 26, 28; *ibid.*, 11-2, pp. 26-27; *ibid.*, 13-1, p. 20; Report of Samuel Tucker and James Ewing, Jan. 9, 1783, AM Papers, NJSL; Report of R. Hoops and D. Newbold, Nov. 9, 1790, AM Papers, NJSL.

[39] Fuhlbruegge, "New Jersey Finances," pp. 175-78; "An Account of Taxes raised in the State of New Jersey from Aug. 1, 1778, to Jan. 1, 1784," prepared by James Mott, treasurer, May 17, 1792, Robert Morris Papers, RUL. Reduced to specie at forty to one, these taxes amounted to $550,000.

specie.[40] The bulk of the receipts were used to meet the requisitions of Congress, and much of the remainder went to pay the interest on public debts. Judged by any standard, these exactions were extraordinary, and because of the nature of the tax system, they fell with special severity on the farmer. Unlike many other states, New Jersey had no revenue-producing tariff or saleable public lands. Overburdened with taxes and acutely conscious of the currency shortage, there is little wonder that the harassed agrarians were to turn to paper money early in 1785 for the amelioration of their financial difficulties.

THE PLIGHT OF THE PUBLIC CREDITORS

A public concern no less pressing than the money problem was the matter of making provision for the various types of government securities and promises-to-pay that had been issued so freely to finance the war. Representing in their entirety a sum far larger than all the specie and bills of credit in circulation, these debts fell into three separate categories. First, there were the obligations owed by the United States to individuals within the state. In this class were the notes of the Continental Loan Office, the certificates given by the Continental quartermasters and commissaries in payment for supplies and services, and the final settlement notes that were given to the officers and soldiers from New Jersey in the Continental Army for their arrears of pay and subsistence.[41] Secondly, there were the debts owed by the state to its own

[40] See Appendix I for a full statement of tax receipts. The staggering amount of these taxes should be emphasized. After the adoption of the Federal Constitution there was a precipitant decline in state taxes, which even as late as 1840 seldom exceeded thirty thousand dollars a year.

[41] A. S. Bolles, *The Financial History of the United States from 1774 to 1789 ...* (New York, 1884), pp. 259-64, 281-83, 316; Wilson, *Acts*, Act of Dec. 20, 1783, pp. 363-77; *American State Papers, Finance*, I, p. 30.

citizens. These were principally the notes that had been given to the soldiers to make up the losses that they had suffered because of the depreciation of the money in which they had been paid and the notes that were given in settlement of the pay of militiamen.[42] Finally, there were debts incurred by the state for which partial reimbursement was anticipated from the Congress when the accounts of all the states should be balanced and settled. In this group were the certificates that had been distributed by local contractors or purchasing agents in compensation for military supplies.[43]

The amounts of these several kinds of obligations in existence at any one time cannot in most cases be determined. During the last years of the war, immense quantities of certificates were made receivable for taxes, and they were acceptable also in payment for confiscated estates, fines, and other debts due to the state. Because of the confusion attendant on keeping accounts, it is impossible even to estimate how large a portion of the certificates were retired in this manner.[44] No more reliable information can be obtained than that embodied in Hamilton's report on the state and national debts in 1790.

[42] Wilson, *Acts*, Act of Jan. 6, 1781, pp. 159-63; *Session Laws*, 8-1, Act of Dec. 20, 1783; *Votes and Proceedings*, 10-2, p. 78; *American State Papers, Finance*, I, p. 31.

[43] *Votes and Proceedings*, 10-2, p. 78; Wilson, *Acts*, Act of Dec. 29, 1779, pp. 114-17. For more than a year, beginning late in 1779, the burden of supplying the Army was thrown on the states under a system of "specific supply." In filling its quota of provisions, services, and other items, the state authorized contractors in each county to issue certificates in return for goods. Ultimately the accounts of the states were supposed to be adjusted and balanced. *Journals of the Continental Congress*, XV, p. 1377; L. C. Hatch, *The Administration of the Continental Army* (New York, 1904), p. 104 ff.

[44] A committee of the legislature, appointed August 30, 1784, to examine the accounts of the treasurer and determine the amount of certificates that had been brought in, reported that the books were so irregular that nothing could be learned from them, and advised that it would only be burdening the state with unnecessary expense to continue with the investigation. Report of Commissioners [1785], AM Papers, NJSL.

At that date the United States owed to citizens of New Jersey $2,431,845, of which $1,121,360 represented Continental Loan Office notes, $917,968 liquidated quartermasters' and commissaries' certificates, and the remainder soldiers' final settlement notes. New Jersey thus held about one-eleventh of the total domestic debt, a disproportionately large sum for so small a state. The state debts totaled $788,680, of which $324,056 represented obligations for which the state had expected some reimbursement from the United States but which it had, in fact, itself assumed. This state debt of New Jersey, which was only one-thirtieth of the aggregate of state debts, was extremely small.[45]

The indebtedness that had been incurred by both the Continental Congress and the state gave rise to a numerous class of public creditors, who were deeply concerned that measures should be devised to discharge the interest, at least, on the obligations. Unless some steps were taken in this direction, a vast amount of paper assets would be rendered valueless. When it became evident that the Confederation would not be able to meet its financial obligations, New Jersey ambitiously concocted its own plan for satisfying the demands of the Continental creditors and wrestled as well with the task of reducing the tangled state debt to a semblance of order to the end that it, too, might be serviced. Having assumed these weighty responsibilities, the state in effect declared its financial independence of the Confederation.

The sequence of events that led up to the taking over by the state of the burden of making interest payments to Continental creditors began in 1782. Unable to rely any longer on foreign bills of exchange to meet the charges on the Continental Loan Office certificates, the Congress in September, 1782, made an emergency requisition on the states for funds with which to still the clamor of the security holders. It was specifically provided that the money raised would be used for

[45] *American State Papers, Finance,* I, pp. 30-31.

interest payments in each state before any sums were forwarded to the Continental treasury.[46] The legislature that met in October, 1782, failed to take any action on this request, and its neglect thoroughly aroused the public creditors, who set about impressing their representatives with the necessity of attending to the matter. Meetings were called to "determine on such modes of application as ... [might] be judged most proper, to induce the Legislature to take up the business as early in the sessions as possible."[47] Petitions calling for the fulfillment of the requisition were drawn up in several counties. Unless some means were found to maintain interest payments, "great Numbers of the most early & decided Supporters of American Liberty and of the most helpless Members of the Community" would suffer.[48]

Evidently this campaign was not without effect, for in June, 1783, both houses by unanimous vote approved the desired tax law.[49] Out of a total of $242,480 payable in specie and bank notes, $56,000 was to be deposited with Joseph Borden, Continental Loan Officer for New Jersey, for the purpose of discharging one year's interest on loan office certificates and other liquidated debts due from the United States to inhabitants of the state.[50] Six months later a significant amendment to this act directed the treasurer not to turn over any money to the loan officer but instead to pay it out directly

[46] *Journals of the Continental Congress*, XXII, p. 447; *ibid.*, XXIII, pp. 545-46, 555, 564-71; Bolles, *Financial History*, pp. 262-63, 313. New Jersey's quota of the requisition was sixty-six thousand dollars.

[47] *New Jersey Gazette*, Nov. 27, 1782.

[48] Petition of Middlesex subscribers, Jan. 24, 1783, Loose Manuscripts, NJSL; Petition of Hunterdon subscribers, [Jan., 1783], Vault Manuscripts, NJSL; Petition of inhabitants of Essex, May 5, 1783, AM Papers, NJSL. These were the same petitioners who had asked for the redemption of the state money at its full value.

[49] *Votes and Proceedings*, 7-2, p. 112; *Journal of Council*, 7-2, p. 52.

[50] *Session Laws*, 7-2, Act of June 9, 1783. Of the remaining sum, $80,827 was to go to the Continental treasury for prior requisitions, and the rest was reserved for state expenses.

to the security holders.[51] Henceforth New Jersey was not to authorize the payment of any money whatsoever to the Continental government.

While the state was preparing to embark on its independent course, the Congress had been at work on a "strange, though artful, plan of finance," which blossomed to maturity on April 18, 1783.[52] Combining a number of familiar ingredients, which taken together were expected to be palatable to all the states, the scheme represented the noblest effort ever made by the Confederation to provide a solution for its financial weaknesses. The states were asked to vest in the Congress the power to levy import duties for a term of twenty-five years, the proceeds to be applied solely to payments on the debt. At the same time they were to raise through taxes, apportioned on a more equitable basis than that laid down in Article VIII, a supplemental revenue of one and a half million dollars for the same term of years and for the same purpose as the impost. Finally, it was once more recommended that those states which had claims to the western territory should make acceptable cessions in accordance with prior resolutions of the Congress. This "Grand Financial Plan" possessed many virtues, but one insuperable defect was the clause reading: "That none of the preceding resolutions shall take effect until all of them shall be acceded to by every state."[53] Needless to say, unanimous approval was never secured.

Although no state was more favorable to an impost, to western cessions, and to adequate provisions for debt servicing, New Jersey took a highly realistic attitude toward the resolutions of April 18, 1783, and acted on the correct assumption that they would not be adopted with the required

[51] *Ibid.*, 8-1, Act of Dec. 16, 1783. This action was taken at the same time that the state decided to follow its own course in making interest payments to Continental creditors.

[52] Burnett, *Letters*, VII, pp. 122-24.

[53] *Journals of the Continental Congress*, XXIV, pp. 257-61.

unanimity. The legislature promptly gave its consent to the levying of a Continental tariff and to the altering of Article VIII, but delayed action on the supplemental revenues until the end of the year.[54] Then, on December 20, an act was passed which was ostensibly based on the recommendation of Congress but which actually marked a definite break between the state and the Confederation.[55]

The law stated that for the term of twenty-five years the sum of $83,358—which was the quota of New Jersey under the resolutions of April 18, 1783—should be raised in taxes for the purpose of paying the interest and principal of debts due from the United States to inhabitants of the state. Acknowledging that it would be impractical to bring in this amount in specie because of the scarcity of gold and silver, the law provided for the printing of $83,358 in paper money. This "revenue money," as it came to be called, was to be receivable for the tax equal in value to specie. Most important of all, the act declared that it would be "highly proper and just that those Citizens who contribute their Proportion of said Revenue, and at the same time are Creditors of the United States, should receive out of such Revenues the Advantages expressly intended thereby," and directed the treasurer to pay out the money to local creditors instead of forwarding it to the Continental treasury. As soon as the bills were ready, one year's interest was to be paid on the loan certificates and on the liquidated quartermaster and commissary certificates. After the first year's tax had been received, interest would be paid on these certificates as well as on the final settlement notes that had been issued to the soldiers of the Jersey Line. The possessors of these obligations were required

[54] *Votes and Proceedings*, 7-2, pp. 130-31; *Journal of Council*, 7-2, pp. 52, 63; Wilson, *Acts*, Act of June 11, 1783, pp. 329-30, Act of July 17, 1783, pp. 333-34.

[55] *Votes and Proceedings*, 8-1, p. 72; *Journal of Council*, 8-1, p. 31. The vote in the Assembly was twenty-three to ten; the vote in the Council, eight to three. All of the negative votes came from West Jersey members.

to take an oath that the certificates had been the property of an inhabitant of the state on May 1, 1783, and had not since belonged to an inhabitant of any other state.[56] Thus the owners of Continental securities were assured of an annual income in a type of money which was expected to maintain its value because it would be called in each year in taxes.

At the time the law was passed, interest was payable only on the loan-office certificates, for the quartermaster and commissary certificates had not yet been liquidated and the soldiers' final settlement notes had not been issued. Congress as early as June 12, 1780, had authorized the appointment of commissioners who were to visit each state and examine and adjust accounts and two years later had renewed and amplified the powers of these agents.[57] But it was not until November, 1783, that a commissioner, Benjamin Thompson, took up his duties in New Jersey.[58] For the next two years

[56] Wilson, *Acts*, "An Act for raising a Revenue of £31,259.5.0 [$83,358] per Annum, for the term of twenty-five Years, for the Purpose of paying the Interest and Principal of Debts due from the United States, agreeably to a Recommendation of Congress of the 18th day of April, 1783, and for appropriating the same," Dec. 20, 1783, pp. 363-77. A plan similar in principle to this had been proposed by Governor Livingston three years earlier. "Scipio" [William Livingston], *New Jersey Gazette*, Nov. 1, 1780. The revenue money, printed by Isaac Collins in denominations ranging from £6 to 2/6, was ready for distribution in May, 1784. Certificate of James Mott and James Ewing, April, 1784, Livingston Papers, MHS; *New Jersey Gazette*, May 17, 1784.

[57] *Journals of the Continental Congress*, XVII, pp. 504-505; *ibid.*, XXII, pp. 83-86, 102-104. By a resolution of February 20, 1782, the commissioners were authorized to liquidate and settle in specie value "all certificates given for supplies by public officers to individuals, and other claims against the United States by individuals for supplies furnished the army, the transportation thereof and contingent expenses thereon . . ." A single commissioner was to be nominated for each state by the Superintendent of Finance and approved by the state. Other commissioners were delegated to settle the accounts of the five major departments.

[58] *Votes and Proceedings*, 6-1, p. 18; Wilson, *Acts*, Act of June 15, 1782, pp. 269-70; *Votes and Proceedings*, 8-1, pp. 13, 15. The nomination of Thompson was approved by the legislature, November 8, 1783.

he travelled from county to county exchanging new securities, which became known as "Thompson's notes," for the old certificates according to an established rate of depreciation. Thompson's notes bore 6 per cent interest, which was payable by the state under the act of December 20, 1783.[59] In February, 1784, after months of delay, the final settlement notes—also called "Pierce's notes"—were at last ready for distribution, and they, too, were soon drawing 6 per cent interest.[60]

Having made its own provisions for its Continental creditors at considerable expense to the taxpayers of the state, New Jersey felt no further obligation to contribute financially to the Confederation. It was not disposed to burden its citizens with additional levies while other states relied on revenues from tariffs and western lands, revenues that properly belonged to the general government, to pay the Continental requisitions. Convinced of the justness of its stand, the legislature in December, 1784, ordered the treasurer not to deliver any more money to the United States' treasury until all the states had approved the Continental impost and the plan for establishing supplemental funds for a term of twenty-five years.[61] This clear statement of policy was not to be altered so long as the Confederation lasted.

[59] *Ibid.*, 9-1, pp. 98, 100; *New Jersey Gazette*, Dec. 16, 1783; Benjamin Thompson to Governor Livingston, Oct. 22, 1785, Manuscript Collection, NJSL; *Journals of the Continental Congress*, XXVII, pp. 540–45.
 [60] *New Jersey Gazette*, Feb. 10, 1784, Aug. 22, 1785; *Political Intelligencer*, Feb. 24, 1784.
 [61] *Votes and Proceedings*, 9-1, p. 57; *Journal of Council*, 9-1, p. 99; *Session Laws*, 9-1, Act of Dec. 23, 1784. By the same law, the treasurer was directed not to pay any interest on the commutation notes that had been granted to army officers in lieu of the half-pay for five years that had been promised them. New Jersey steadfastly refused to accept the commutation plan, even though it had been adopted by the Congress. Burnett, *Continental Congress*, p. 568; *Votes and Proceedings*, 8-1, p. 69; *Correspondence ... Executive*, pp. 267-68, 325-26.

The state creditors did not fare so well as those who held Continental securities. Payments were made on the soldiers' depreciation notes beginning in 1782.[62] But it was not until 1787 that adequate arrangements were made for paying interest on the county contractors' notes and the militia notes.[63] This long delay was in part caused by the uncertain status of the contractors' certificates, which were not wholly state obligations, and by the time required to liquidate and settle the muddled accounts.[64]

Seemingly the arrangements that had been made for servicing the public debt were highly favorable to the creditors. But there was no guarantee that the legislature might not at some future date repudiate the whole plan, just as it had repudiated the promise to redeem the new emission at full value. The representatives of the people could undo what they had done. What security was there, then, for men of property under popular government?

DEBTORS AND CREDITORS

Attentive as the legislature was to the welfare of the public creditors, it was far from neglectful of the interests of the private debtors. The repeal of the tender laws, the contraction of the currency, and the imposition of heavy taxes all contributed to render it difficult for those who had borrowed money during the war years to discharge their obligations. Particularly unfortunate were the individuals whose chief assets were certificates, which made a poor substitute for cash. Plagued by their distressed constituents, the legislators devised numerous legal expedients to provide relief for those who were threatened with insolvency.

[62] *Votes and Proceedings*, 7-1, p. 81; *ibid.*, 8-1, p. 59.
[63] *Session Laws*, 6-2, Act of June 22, 1782; *ibid.*, 8-1, Act of Dec. 20, 1783; *ibid.*, 9-2, Act of Dec. 8, 1784; Wilson, *Acts*, Act of Jan. 6, 1781, pp. 159-63.
[64] See Appendix II for a detailed account of interest payments.

Although the tender laws were repealed in June, 1781, creditors were restrained from bringing immediate suit against their debtors by the stipulation that they might be compelled to accept paper money at its nominal value for one year.[65] Once this time limit had expired, men who had successfully avoided receiving payment in depreciated currency while it had been a legal tender set about attempting to collect in hard money.[66] A flood of lawsuits was the result. Immediately the debtors complained against the expense of defending actions in court, and in response to their pleas, the legislature enacted a law which permitted local justices of the peace to decide cases involving less than twelve pounds, authorized a stay of execution for three months in actions above six pounds, and prevented the Supreme Court from handling suits where the consideration was under fifty pounds.[67]

The "£12 law" provided cheap justice, but it did not stop creditors from obtaining judgments by the scores. It was not long before the gaols throughout the state were filled with insolvents, unable to obtain their releases until they somehow raised the money to pay their debts. To rescue these hapless individuals from their humiliating confinement, the legislature in 1783 revived and amended a colonial bankruptcy act. Any debtor who could obtain the consent of the major portion of his creditors could turn over to them his entire real and personal property, except for some clothes, tools, and a bed, and obtain his freedom.[68] Some conserv-

[65] Wilson, *Acts*, Act of June 13, 1781, pp. 197-98.

[66] A group of creditors in Middlesex County freely admitted that many of "the most Valuable Inhabitants; Consistent with Justice & Virtue Evaded the Receiving Continental, when it was far Depreciated." Petition of Middlesex inhabitants, Oct. 29, 1784, Loose Manuscripts, NJSL.

[67] Wilson, *Acts*, Act of June 5, 1782, pp. 263-64. A supplement to this law was passed December 23, 1784. *Session Laws*, 9-1, Act of Dec. 23, 1784.

[68] Allinson, *Acts*, Act of Dec. 21, 1771, pp. 356-63; *Session Laws*, 7-2, Act of June 18, 1783; *Votes and Proceedings*, 7-2, pp. 134, 143;

atives professed to be shocked at this general extension of bankruptcy privileges, which under English practice were confined to merchants, but an effort by the Council to repeal the law was defeated in the Assembly.[69]

As the prosecutions for debts continued, courts and lawyers naturally became the targets of popular criticism. The belief was widespread that lawsuits were "attended with many unnecessary Customs and Forms, both tedious and expensive." Consequently there was strong support for an "Act for regulating and shortening Proceedings in the Courts of Law," framed by Abraham Clark, a bitter foe of the legal profession.[70] This act drastically altered and simplified legal procedure, sought to eliminate costly delays and pettifogging quibbles, and fixed a rigid schedule of fees. Viewed with contempt by the members of the bar, it drew forth the protests of those who looked to the courts as the firm safeguard of property rights.[71]

Considerable controversy centered around the manner in which debts that had been contracted during the period of fluctuating currency values should be paid off after the legal tender laws had been repealed. In June, 1781, the legislature adopted a standard scale of depreciation, which was to be applied in discharging debts incurred in Continental money between 1777 and 1780.[72] But this measure was regarded

Journal of Council, 7-2, p. 64. This act had been passed by the Assembly in November, 1782, but it had been unanimously negatived by the Council. *Votes and Proceedings*, 7-1, p. 37; *Journal of Council*, 7-1, p. 27.

[69] "Scipio" [William Livingston], *New Jersey Gazette*, Mar. 2, 1784; "Multitude," *New Jersey Gazette*, Oct. 11, 1784; *Journal of Council*, 8-1, p. 16; *Votes and Proceedings*, 8-1, p. 44.

[70] *Ibid.*, 8-2, p. 101; *Journal of Council*, 8-2, p. 19; *Session Laws*, 8-2, Act of Aug. 30, 1784. The bill received unanimous approval in the Assembly and had only two opponents in the Council.

[71] "Multitude," *New Jersey Gazette*, Oct. 11, 1784; Sedgwick, *Memoir*, pp. 394-95; Elmer, *Constitutions*, p. 45.

[72] *Session Laws*, 5-2, Act of June 22, 1781. The tender laws were repealed June 13, 1781.

with disfavor by debtors because of its rigidity and its limited application. Moreover, it operated to the advantage of creditors who had illegally evaded receiving payments on their loans while money was cheap.

In answer to popular demand, an act was passed in June, 1783, which gave the courts the power to apply equity in arriving at decisions respecting the settlement of debts contracted before June 13, 1781. Too, any creditor who had declined to accept paper money could be paid off in state obligations if he attempted to collect within a year.[73] Even this law did not go far enough to suit the debtor group, and in September, 1784, another, and more drastic, expedient was adopted.[74] If any creditor who had taken refuge with the British or who had refused paper money while it was a legal tender took action against his debtor, the latter could offer any kind of public securities at their specie value in payment.[75]

The securities-tender law was violently condemned both in the press and in petitions by angry creditors throughout the state.[76] It was unjust, asserted a number of substantial men in Hunterdon, that debtors should be encouraged to defraud their creditors by paying off their obligations in

[73] *Votes and Proceedings*, 7-2, pp. 102-104, 146; *Journal of Council*, 7-2, p. 63; Wilson, *Acts*, Act of June 18, 1783.

[74] *Votes and Proceedings*, 8-2, pp. 128, 144; *Journal of Council*, 8-2, p. 23. The vote was twenty-one to seven in the Assembly, seven to three in the Council.

[75] *Session Laws*, 8-2, "An Act for the Relief of Persons holding Publick Securities, and for other Purposes therein mentioned," Sept. 4, 1784. The act provided also that anyone who was indebted to a person who had taken refuge with the British or who had refused paper money should be relieved of interest payments between 1776 and 1783 and that, if the plaintiff in any action in debt refused to stay proceedings for one year, the defendant might tender securities in discharge of the obligation.

[76] *New Jersey Gazette*, Sept. 20, Oct. 4, 11, Dec. 6, 1784; *Political Intelligencer*, Oct. 5, 1784; *Votes and Proceedings*, 9-1, pp. 19-21.

securities that were worth only one-sixth of their face value.[77] Andrew Sinnickson, Samuel Leake, Clement Hall, and other Salem conservatives contended that the act was "founded not upon the principles of Justice, but upon the Right of Conquest and upon the Right of the Sword; because no other Reason can be given, why the Act . . . was passed than because the Legislature had the Power and Will to enact such a Law."[78] The "morals of the People will thereby be more contaminated in one year, than all the Clergy in New Jersey will be able to heal in three Score and ten," read an appeal from Essex.[79] No merchant could sell his goods, complained the leading citizens of New Brunswick, without being liable to have certificates imposed on him. ". . . by that Law men of property are prevented from coming into our State—by it our Credit is Ruined with the neighbouring States, and we must be Dispised by foreign powers," they lamented.[80] Proponents of the measure expressed their surprise at the "strong & Violent struggles" that were made against it, and they solemnly warned that its repeal would "sink or Incapacitate so many of the Virtuous Citizens . . . that we should be in Danger of Gradually sinking into a state of Oppression and tyranny."[81]

A bill to repeal the objectionable law was passed by the conservative Council that took office after the October elections,

[77] Petition of inhabitants of Hunterdon, Nov. 4, 1784, Loose Manuscripts, NJSL.

[78] Petition of Salem subscribers, Oct. 12, 1784, Loose Manuscripts, NJSL.

[79] Petition of Essex subscribers, [Oct., 1784], Loose Manuscripts, NJSL. Among the signers were Jonathan Dayton, Elias Dayton, Matthias Williamson, Isaac Woodruff, and other men of means.

[80] Petition of Middlesex inhabitants, Oct. 29, 1784, Loose Manuscripts, NJSL.

[81] Petition of Morris subscribers, [1784], Loose Manuscripts, NJSL. This petition was signed by about a hundred and fifty men, among them Jacob Green, Presbyterian minister and onetime member of the Provincial Congress, Ellis Cook, a member of the Assembly for more than a decade, and Silas Condict, who had served both in the legislature and in the Continental Congress.

but it was easily defeated by the Assembly.[82] When the two houses threatened to become deadlocked over the issue, a compromise was devised. The securities-tender law was repealed as "injurious to the good Citizens of this State." At the same time, however, the act of June 18, 1783, was extended to apply to debts that had been contracted prior to the war, and debtors were excused from paying interest on sums that they had borrowed since 1776 if the creditor had spurned paper money.[83]

The several laws that were passed for the purpose of aiding distressed debtors were profoundly disturbing to men who held the rights of property in high respect. Such expedients, which were merely the precursors of others yet to come, seriously impaired the validity of private contracts. They were not calculated to enhance the faith of the conservatives in the efficacy of majority rule.

In the realm of financial affairs the closing years of the war were characterized by the adoption of policies that were bound to arouse general discontent among those in the lower ranks of society. At the same time, creditor groups were dealt with in such a manner that they could feel little security as they looked to the future. High taxes and the abrupt contraction of the currency produced deflationary conditions. An uncertain and inadequate debt-servicing program and a series of acts for the relief of debtors were injurious to public and private credit. The economic situation was so confused and so critical that desperate remedies were improvised with slight regard for their long-range effects.

Taken altogether, the series of financial measures that received legislative approval between 1780 and 1784 seem remarkable for their inconsistency. With bewildering impar-

[82] *Journal of Council*, 9-1, p. 14; *Votes and Proceedings*, 9-1, p. 36.
[83] *Ibid.*, 9-1, pp. 39, 62; *Journal of Council*, 9-1, pp. 24, 25; *Session Laws*, 9-1, Act of Dec. 8, 1784.

tiality, the lawmakers apparently tried to serve the interests of the most diverse elements within the state. The Assembly that was elected in October, 1783, for example, approved a plan for the payment of interest to public creditors, initiated a bill for the retirement of the state money at a depreciated rate, and went to extraordinary lengths to assist debtors. These conflicting acts were in part, no doubt, the result of bargains between rival factions, and in part the products of sheer muddledom in the face of various pressures.[84] They were also the outgrowth of unusual and unstable political alignments.

There was no clear-cut array of political forces on the money question. Serious divisions existed within both East Jersey and West Jersey. For a brief period the non-security-holding conservatives in West Jersey made common cause with the "poorer sort" from East Jersey in the contest over the redemption of the new emission. Controlling the Assembly, this combination was frustrated until after the election in October, 1784, by a Council in which the whig-public-creditor interest was dominant. The trend over the four-year period was toward the decline of the old whig faction in West Jersey and the rise of the agrarian strength in East Jersey. With the removal of the state-money question from the scene at the end of 1784, the break between the two sections became well defined, East Jersey gained supremacy, and politics entered a new phase as economic discontent reached a peak.

[84] Robert Morris, a conservative, sound-money man, blamed "that excentric genius," Abraham Clark, for the "inconsistency of some of the late measures of Government." Morris to Peter Wilson, Sept. 24, 1784, Robert Morris Papers, RUL.

VIII

Money: the Familiar Remedy

****

ECONOMIC depression, coupled with the deflationary financial policies that were adopted after 1780, produced widespread popular discontent and created an irresistible demand in the mid-eighties for an "increase in the circulating medium." The controversy that ensued exceeded in virulence any that were carried on during the stormy postwar decade, for basic political as well as economic issues were involved. In essence, there was raised the question of whether minority rights, and particularly property rights, could be transgressed at the will of the majority. Could the debtor use the power of his ballot to better his condition at the expense of his creditor? The answer was that under the form of government established by the Constitution of 1776 he could. "Democratical license," it would seem, recognized no bounds. To the discerning man of substance, this was an alarming situation, which must be corrected by the imposition of restraints upon the *vox populi*. Otherwise mob rule would bring about the destruction of all vestiges of honor, morality, and virtue.

AGRARIAN DISCONTENT

There were grounds for the general belief that there was a scarcity of money by the end of 1784. Continental bills had long since been retired and the total of state bills of credit and revenue money did not exceed $280,000, or two dollars *per capita*.[1] Gold and silver coin, which had been available in abundance two years before, was now extremely scarce.[2] Money from other states did not flow into New Jersey in any considerable amounts.[3] Moreover, because of the trade depression and the tightening of credit, the money in existence did not circulate rapidly.

Heightening the awareness of the money shortage were the heavy taxes, the proceeds of which went principally to public creditors in the form of interest payments. Levies during 1785 came to a total of $190,000 in revenue money and bills of credit, an amount equal to two-thirds of all the state money.[4] When attempts were made to collect these dues, many were unable to meet their assessments, and arrearages piled up. A year later the distress was so apparent that the legislature, recognizing that it would be "altogether impracticable if not impossible" to bring in the scheduled taxes within the period fixed by law, prolonged the date when the returns must be made.[5] Collectors and delinquents alike were

[1] There were in circulation $115,000 in new emission, $80,000 in fractional currency, and $83,360 in revenue money.

[2] Wilson, *Acts*, Act of Dec. 20, 1783, Sec. 23.

[3] Robert Morris to William C. Houston, Apr. 25, 1785, Houston-Morris Letters, RUL. Morris, who at the time was in New York, reported that counterfeit coins were in circulation there. But he remarked that there was slight chance that New Jersey would be victimized, "there being little danger that either true or false money should travel thither from hence."

[4] Eighty thousand dollars of this $190,000 was to be cancelled, $83,360 was to be paid to the public creditors, and the rest was to be used for the expenses of government. See Appendix I.

[5] *Session Laws*, 11-1, Act of Nov. 7, 1786.

castigated in the press, but receipts continued to lag.[6] Up in Morris County, the Reverend Mr. Johnes took the occasion to preach a sermon from Matthew 22:21. Joseph Lewis, landowner, minor official, and speculator, reported the event approvingly in his diary. "In the discourse," wrote Lewis, "he said that the payment of taxes as well as debts was to be included as meant and intended in the command of rendering to Caesar the things that are Caesars. Some of the people were offended, but others thot it a good discourse & a seasonable reproof from the pulpit & among the latter was the most thinking part of the society." [7]

Short of cash and burdened with taxes, the ordinary citizen was oppressed also by the weight of private debts. The war years had been characterized by the prevalence of a speculative psychology among all classes. Money, though uncertain in value, was plentiful, and there were alluring opportunities for reaping vast profits from shrewd and daring ventures. Under such circumstances, many individuals overextended themselves and emerged from the era of inflation saddled with debts. Especially hard pressed were those who had bought land on credit while money was cheap.[8] A fondness for imported fineries was responsible for the financial difficulties of others. Large numbers were simply the innocent victims of the unpredictable currency gyrations. Whatever the cause, there was a debtor group of sufficient size and importance to induce the legislature to enact several measures for their relief.

The depressed state of business and agriculture was appar-

---

[6] *New Jersey Gazette*, Jan. 31, 1785, July 29, Aug. 21, 1786.

[7] "Diary of Joseph Lewis," *PNJHS*, LX (1942), p. 62.

[8] Gordon, *History*, p. 325. To judge from the advertisements in the newspapers, land sales continued at a brisk rate down to 1785, when the volume declined noticeably.

ent by 1785.[9] Trade entered a period of stagnation, occasioned by the exhaustion of credit. The iron industry was in the doldrums. Markets for farm products became less attractive than they had been formerly. To add to their difficulties, the farmers had to contend with the ravages of the Hessian fly, which completely devastated the wheat crop over extensive areas of the state. The destructive effects of the insect were noticed first in the eastern counties in the summer of 1786, and within two years no part of the state was free of the scourge. Crop losses were severe, even though rye was substituted for wheat in the afflicted regions.[10] The declining productivity of lands, long abused by crude and wasteful methods of husbandry, meant reduced yields and smaller incomes. Wheat harvests of six bushels to the acre were common; excellent husbandmen raised no more than fourteen bushels.[11] Marginal farmers, unable to make a living on depleted soil, emigrated from the state to seek better lands elsewhere.[12]

Hard times and heavy taxes brought evidence of growing

[9] "The fact was," summarized Ashbel Green in looking back upon the period, "that the whole community was in a state of suffering and depression." Green, *Life*, p. 161.

[10] The newspapers and periodicals of the period contain dozens of articles on the fly and on the efforts that were made to devise measures for its control. The problem assumed such magnitude that in June, 1788, the importation of American grain into Great Britain was prohibited by a royal proclamation. The best accounts are Asa Fitch, "The Hessian Fly," *Transactions of the New York State Agricultural Society*, VI (1846), pp. 316-73, and the article on the Hessian fly in the *Encyclopaedia Britannica*, VIII (3rd edition, London, 1797). See also the "Letters of Phineas Bond," pp. 565-604; *American Museum*, I (1787), pp. 133-38, 291-93, 456-59; *New Jersey Gazette*, July 3, 1786; *New Jersey Journal*, June 25, 1788; *Brunswick Gazette*, July 26, Sept. 27, 1787, May 6, July 8, 1788, Jan. 20, 1789.

[11] Rutherfurd, "Notes," pp. 81-82; Schoepf, *Travels*, p. 45; *American Husbandry*, edited by Harry C. Carman (New York, 1939), pp. 97-110; Robert Johnson Account Book, RUL.

[12] Rutherfurd, "Notes," p. 81.

restiveness among the people. Usually this feeling of distress found expression in appeals to the legislature for laws in behalf of debtors or for the issuance of paper money. In some cases, however, there were overt acts of violence committed by men whose economic plight made them desperate. Morris County, in particular, was the scene of mass disorders. "A spirit of rebellion or uneasiness subsists in the greatest part of the community," recorded Joseph Lewis early in 1785. "They alledge that Congress & our Legislature have done great Injustice by not paying them for the services & produce furnished the army & c. They therefore rise in opposition to authority by refusing to pay their taxes, an instance of which appeared...in Mendham, where an attempt was made by a constable to sell some property at vendue which he had distrained for taxes, but a party (who had previously prepared clubs & c) would not suffer anyone to make a bid..." [13] Justice Symmes of the Supreme Court was of the opinion "that if the Grand Jury should indict some of the Ringleaders of the Mobs which ... [were] so troublesome in that County by their violently opposing the levying or collecting of taxes it would be of salutary effect." [14] Instances of this sort were evidently ·rare, but they constituted a disturbing warning that the popular temper was becoming aroused.

The moneyless host was not slow to propound a remedy for its economic ills. The remedy was in no sense novel or untried; it had been applied frequently and with good results in the past, with the approval of virtually all segments of society. Throughout the colonial period, paper money had taken the place of the nonexistent specie. On no less than four occasions between 1723 and 1774, loan-office money, issued on landed security in amounts ranging from twenty thousand to a hundred thousand pounds, had been put in circulation. If the colony had had its way, there would have been many more

[13] "Diary of Joseph Lewis," *PNJHS*, LX (1942), p. 61.
[14] Minutes of the Governor's Privy Council, Mar. 16, 1785, NJSL.

such instances. There were nineteen issues of bills of credit, which were retired by taxation over extended periods. During the Seven Years War, almost three hundred and fifty thousand pounds of this type of currency were printed.[15] From all accounts, the colonial paper held its value well. This fact was conceded even by such sound-money advocates as John Rutherfurd, William Livingston, William Paterson, and John Witherspoon.[16] Furthermore, these familiar monetary expedients had been found to be an admirable substitute for taxes.[17] In view of the weight of colonial experience, it was to be expected that there should be demands for paper money in the distressed mid-eighties. The unusual feature of the postwar monetary controversy was not the revival of loan-office proposals but rather the stubborn opposition which those proposals encountered. It is the attitude of the conservatives, rather than of the so-called radicals, that is in need of explanation.

[15] G. V. Werner, "The Fiscal History of Colonial New Jersey," Rutgers M.A. Thesis, 1934, RUL; Donald L. Kemmerer, "The Colonial Loan-Office System in New Jersey," *Journal of Political Economy*, XLVII (1939), pp. 867-74. Extended treatment of these issues may be found in Donald L. Kemmerer, *Path to Freedom* (Princeton, 1940), and in the works of Tanner and Fisher.

[16] Rutherfurd, "Notes," pp. 79-80; "Scipio" [William Livingston], *New Jersey Gazette*, Nov. 1, 1780; [William Paterson], Two articles on paper money, May, 1786, Paterson Papers (Bancroft Transcripts), NYPL; Witherspoon, *Works*, IX, p. 54; R. Wayne Parker, "Taxes and Money in New Jersey Before the Revolution," *PNJHS*, 2nd Ser., VII (1883), pp. 143-57; Fisher, *Royal Province*, p. 302. For a wholly sympathetic re-appraisal of the colonial loan-office plan, see the excellent article of Richard A. Lester, "Currency Issues to Overcome Depressions in Delaware, New Jersey, New York and Maryland, 1715-1737," *Journal of Political Economy*, XLVII (1939), pp. 182-217.

[17] The interest received on the loan-office money, for example, was sufficient to pay all the expenses of government for sixteen years after 1735. Kemmerer, *Freedom*, p. 145.

THE GREAT DEBATE

Agitation for the issuance of paper money assumed concrete form late in the summer of 1784. When the legislature came together in special session in New Brunswick in August of that year, it received petitions from four counties—Monmouth, Morris, Somerset, and Burlington—asking that currency be emitted on loan. These pleas were summarily referred to the next session, which was to meet in October.[18] At that time additional petitions were introduced from Sussex, Salem, and Essex, and a motion to appoint a committee to bring in a paper-money bill failed of passage by only two votes.[19] Late in December the legislature adjourned; it held no further sittings during the remaining ten months of its term.

The election of October, 1785, brought about a change in the alignment of the contending forces in both houses. Sixteen new men were sent to the Assembly and eight to the Council. The paper-money cause gained two assemblymen in Somerset and one in Middlesex, and it maintained its strength in the other counties of East Jersey and in Sussex and Hunterdon. In the Council, new members from Essex, Monmouth, Hunterdon, and Morris were to give their support to the loan-office measure. From the five lower counties of West Jersey came delegations that were all but unanimously against paper money, as were three assemblymen from the Dutch county of Bergen. To judge from the newspapers, the canvass was a singularly unexciting one. In fact, "Rusticus" lamented

---

[18] *Votes and Proceedings*, 8-2, pp. 99, 113. As early as December, 1783, the loan-office plan was a topic of public discussion. Jacobus Lake to Cornelius Ten Broeck, Dec. 15, 1783, "Blawenburgh and Harlingen Records," pp. 121-22.

[19] *Votes and Proceedings*, 9-1, pp. 9, 30-35. Opposed to the motion were nine members from West Jersey, six from Middlesex, Somerset, and Bergen, and Abraham Clark of Essex.

the political apathy which seemingly prevailed and criticized the "deadness of the press." [20]

Within a week after the newly elected Assembly had organized, a four-man committee was appointed to draft a loan-office bill.[21] Three weeks later the measure met its first major test when the house voted by a respectable majority to agree to the title of an "Act to strike £100,000 in bills of credit..."[22] Then, with the passage of the bill seemingly assured, Abraham Clark sponsored a motion to refer it to a committee, which would bring in a report at the next sitting. Over the opposition of the most ardent paper-money advocates, this resolution was adopted, and three days later the session adjourned.[23] The motives which prompted Clark, the acknowledged leader of the paper-money bloc, to resort to tactics of delay are unknown, but it is possible that he hoped to build up greater popular enthusiasm for the proposal in order to influence the decision of the Council, which contained a majority hostile to the plan.

While the Assembly was engaged in these preliminary maneuvers, the newspapers suddenly broke out with a rash of articles on the money question, and for the ensuing six months there was scarcely an issue that did not contain one or more diatribes on the subject. The outstanding proponent of inflation was "Willing to Learn"; in a series of ably written essays he defended the loan-office project and endeavored to answer the countless objections that were levelled against it.[24]

[20] *New Jersey Gazette*, Sept. 12, 1785. There was no discussion whatsoever of the loan-office proposal in the press at this time.

[21] *Votes and Proceedings*, 10-1, pp. 14, 17.

[22] *Ibid.*, 10-1, pp. 73-77. The vote was nineteen to twelve. In the minority were ten members from West Jersey, together with Schureman of Middlesex and Blauvelt of Bergen. Sussex, Morris, Somerset, Essex, and Hunterdon voted solidly in the affirmative.

[23] *Ibid.*, 10-1, pp. 76, 78.

[24] Between December 14, 1785, and April 26, 1786, "Willing to Learn," whose style and opinions were those of Abraham Clark, published ten pieces in the *Political Intelligencer*.

Paper money, he argued, should be emitted in the familiar colonial fashion in the form of mortgage-loans at 6 per cent interest on landed security. The bills should be legal tender and should be paid back in annual installments over a twenty-year period. If the borrower became delinquent in his payments, his land could be sold by the state. This plan, he maintained, would bring relief to those who were threatened with bankruptcy, enable creditors to collect their debts, reduce the burden on the courts, furnish people with the means to pay their taxes, permit the state to discharge the interest on its securities, and restore public credit. It would be a blow to speculators, lawyers, and sheriffs. Finally, the interest would be sufficient to support the normal costs of government. Countering the charge that the legislature could depreciate the money, "Willing to Learn" insisted that there was a difference "between money let out upon loan, and money emitted to support a war, or to pay any state debts whatever..." He was not concerned, he stated in response to another criticism, that the money should circulate beyond the borders of New Jersey, for this would only encourage extravagance and put the state in debt to its neighbors. Even Britain did not allow specie to be exported. To those who held that the constitution should be amended to prevent the further emission of paper currency, he retorted that in a republican government it was up to the majority of the people to enact whatever law they thought proper.

"Willing to Learn" was seconded by several less persistent essayists. "Tim Candid," in a beautifully written piece, castigated usurers and misers and called upon the legislature to be the "guardian of the weak" rather than an "instrument of oppression." [25] In a similar vein, "A Farmer" condemned "self-interested speculators... lawyers, who glory in the guinea fee,... [and] hard hearted creditors." [26] "Sinceras"

[25] *New Jersey Gazette*, Feb. 6, 1786.
[26] *Ibid.*

and "A Friend to Liberty" reminded their readers that paper money had enjoyed favor before the war and that it had not depreciated.[27] There was little discussion of the mechanics of the plan, presumably because there was general acquaintance with it.

For every article in favor of the loan office, there were four in opposition. The argument that recurred most frequently was that the representatives of the people could not be trusted to adhere to their promises, that they would—as they had done during the war—depreciate the state money in complete violation of all legal pledges. The experience with continental and with the new emission had convinced creditors that there was "no security or stability in any species of paper currency" as long as the legislature could alter its value. The loan office was attacked not so much on the basis of its economic shortcomings as it was on political grounds. Behind the fear of paper money was the fear of unrestrained majority rule. Democracy, as well as money, was the issue.[28]

No one was more vehement than Governor Livingston in criticizing the loan-office plan. Writing under the appropriate pseudonym, "Primitive Whig," he fervently denounced what he termed, "a design to perpetuate our national disgrace by prevailing upon our legislature to enable *him that is unjust to be unjust still and him that is filthy to be filthy still;* and him that has been a great rogue during the lawful tender of depreciated continental currency, to be a still greater rogue than he ever was." "The interest of the creditor," he asserted, "coincides with that of the community. Not so the interest of the debtor . . . Surely therefore the self-interest of one is just

---

[27] *Political Intelligencer*, Jan. 25, Feb. 8, 1786.

[28] For examples of this attitude, see "A Native of New Jersey," *New Jersey Gazette*, Nov. 14, 1785; "Homo," *New Jersey Gazette*, Dec. 26, 1785; "Curtius," *Political Intelligencer*, Jan. 4, 1786; "Eugenia," *New Jersey Gazette*, Jan. 23, 30, Feb. 13, 1786; "Disconsolate Widow," *Political Intelligencer*, Feb. 22, 1786; Rutherfurd, "Notes," p. 83.

and laudable: that of the other is knavish and infamous." He prayed for the time when "no cozening, trickish, fraudulent scoundrel ... [would] be able to plead legal protection for his cozenage, tricks, frauds and rascality" and questioned whether laws that rendered property insecure were constitutional.[29]

William Paterson, probably the most successful lawyer in the state, was another who entered the lists. "An Encrease of Paper-Money," he predicted, "especially if it be a Tender, will destroy what little Credit is left, will bewilder Conscience in the Mazes of dishonest Speculation, will allure some and constrain others into the Perpetration of Knavish acts, will turn Vice into a legal Virtue, and sanctify Iniquity by Law." It would be the "height of political Frenzy to order a new Emission of Paper, and by the compulsive Edict of Law to make it pass in Payment equal to gold and silver." [30] President Witherspoon of Princeton, in a pamphlet which appeared in several editions, expounded hard-money doctrines but admitted that the issuance of loan-office money might be expedient, provided it was not made legal tender or used to pay public debts.[31]

Some of the sound-money men declared that there was in reality no shortage of currency, that there was on the contrary plenty of specie in the country. It would not circulate, however, so long as the legislature persisted in passing laws by which creditors could be defrauded. The fact that the prices of agricultural products and of labor remained high was convincing evidence that money was not scarce. Honesty, in-

[29] "Primitive Whig," *New Jersey Gazette*, Jan. 9, 16, 23, 30, Feb. 6, 13, 1786; Sedgwick, *Memoir*, p. 249.

[30] Two articles on paper money, May, 1786, Paterson Papers (Bancroft Transcripts), NYPL. Paterson conceded that the colonial paper money had retained its value, but he pointed to the depreciation of the new emission as an example of the untrustworthiness of the legislature.

[31] "Essay on Money," Witherspoon, *Works*, IX, pp. 9-65; *American Museum*, II (1788), pp. 47-73; Collins, *Witherspoon*, I, pp. 256-57.

dustry, and good faith, rather than ruinous inflation, were the great needs of the times.[32] It is not likely that this mode of reasoning was persuasive to the farmer who was being pressed by the tax collector and the sheriff.

While the great debate over the money question raged in the newspapers, the legislature gathered in Trenton in mid-February, 1786, to resume consideration of the loan-office bill. Recognizing that the session would be of great interest to the public, the editors of both the *New Jersey Gazette* and the *Political Intelligencer* announced that they would print in full the *Votes and Proceedings* of the Assembly.[33] As the law-makers took up their tasks, they had little doubt of the sentiment of their constituents, for they received an unprecedented number of petitions from every county in the state praying for and against the emission of paper currency. Altogether there were at least one hundred and forty such petitions

---

[32] "A Native of New Jersey," *New Jersey Gazette*, Nov. 14, 1785; "Curtius," *Political Intelligencer*, Jan. 4, 1786; "Mechanic," *Political Intelligencer*, Jan. 18, Feb. 8, 1786. There is no question that prices were well above the prewar level. In fact, it is difficult to reconcile price movements in the postwar years with the fluctuations in currency. The price of wheat in Somerset County, for example, held fairly steady at seven shillings nine pence a bushel from 1784 through 1788, with the exception of a decline to seven shillings six pence in 1786. In Salem County, wheat declined from around eight shillings in 1784 to six shillings in 1788, although the price in 1785 was eight shillings four pence. Neither the monetary deflation of 1783-1786 nor the inflation of 1787 seems to have had the effect that might have been expected. Accounts of the prices of wheat, rye, and Indian corn in Somerset County, 1766-1789, Ten Eyck Paper, 289, RUL; Robert Johnson Account Book, RUL. It is of interest that the emission of two hundred thousand pounds in paper money in New York in 1786 did not interrupt the downward trend of prices there. The same situation is observable in Pennsylvania. Spaulding, *New York*, pp. 148-49; Brunhouse, *Counter-Revolution*, pp. 171-72; Arthur H. Cole, *Wholesale Commodity Prices in the United States, 1700-1861* (Cambridge, 1938), pp. 14-16, 43-44.

[33] *New Jersey Gazette*, Feb. 27, 1786; *Political Intelligencer*, Mar. 1, 1786.

signed by over ten thousand citizens. A tabulation of the various pleas showed a two-to-one majority for some form of paper money, with almost forty-seven hundred asking for legal-tender loan-office money.[34] The demands for inflation were not confined to the northern counties. From Burlington, Gloucester, and Salem there came nearly as many petitions in favor of a new emission as there were opposed. Support for the measure was decidedly lacking only in Bergen, Cumberland, and Cape May.[35] The people had made their will known in what amounted virtually to a popular referendum. It remained for their representatives to obey or disregard their mandate.

On February 21, Abraham Clark of Essex reported to the Assembly the controversial bill that had been committed to his care at the conclusion of the previous session, and during the month-long debate that followed, it was Clark who played the leading role as the generalissimo of the paper-money forces.[36] Sixty years old at the time, Clark had behind him over twenty years of almost uninterrupted officeholding. Austere in appearance and manner, he nevertheless enjoyed the confidence of the people. He was, in the eyes of his oppo-

---

[34] *Votes and Proceedings*, 10-2, pp. 6-36. As arranged by the Council, the sentiments expressed in the petitions were divided as follows:

For loan-office money without tender	1,348
For loan-office money with tender	4,684
For revenue money	391
For revenue money with tender	535
Against paper money of any kind	2,925
For a circulating medium without tender	101
For a circulating medium with tender	233
Total	*10,217*

Journal of Council, 10-2, p. 22.

[35] *Votes and Proceedings*, 10-2, pp. 6-36. Hunterdon filed the greatest number of petitions in favor of more money, and following in order were Middlesex, Somerset, Essex, and Morris. Middlesex sent in the most petitions against the loan office.

[36] *Ibid.*, 10-1, p. 78; *ibid.*, 10-2, p. 15.

nents, a crafty, eccentric, erratic demagogue, who was accustomed to speak in the legislature "with all the solemnity of a Priest in his countenance, with his head encircled with the glimmering of light . . ." [37] Actually he was a professional politician, who was usually to be found on the side of "popular measures" in the best traditions of his craft. [38] Heading the opposition was James Schureman, thirty-year-old merchant from New Brunswick. A graduate of Queen's College, Schureman had been a militia officer during the war and had distinguished himself as one of the captors of the noted British raider, Colonel Simcoe. He began his political career in the Assembly in 1783, and subsequently served in the Continental Congress, in the House of Representatives, and in the Senate. With his inherited Dutch conservatism and his substantial mercantile interests, he became a staunch Federalist and remained one until his death in 1824. [39]

Before the session was two weeks old, it was apparent that the paper-money bloc was in the majority in the Assembly by the close margin of one—and perhaps two—votes. [40] All the

[37] "A Farmer," *Political Intelligencer*, May 31, 1786.

[38] There is no adequate biography of Clark, and few of his letters have been preserved. There are brief sketches in Edwin F. Hatfield, *History of Elizabeth, New Jersey* (New York, 1868), pp. 586-88; *Dictionary of American Biography*, IV, pp. 118-19; Etting Collection, Sketches, HSP; Ann Hart Clark, *Abraham Clark* (San Francisco, 1923).

[39] Richard Wynkoop, *Schuremans of New Jersey* (2nd ed., New York, 1902), pp. 35-40.

[40] The pro-loan forces had a solid bloc of a minimum of nineteen members, made up of three men each from Essex, Monmouth, Somerset, Morris, and Sussex, two from Middlesex, one from Hunterdon, and one from Cape May. The anti-loan faction had a minimum of seventeen adherents, with three each from Bergen, Burlington, Gloucester, and Cumberland, two from Salem, two from Cape May, and one (Schureman) from Middlesex. John Lambert of Hunterdon vacillated but eventually sided with the majority. Benjamin Van Cleve of Hunterdon, the Speaker, did not vote, and one of the seats was vacant as the result of the death of Anthony Sharp of Salem. *Votes and Proceedings*, 10-2, pp. 21-78.

members from the northward of Trenton, with the conspicuous exception of the Bergen delegation and Schureman of Middlesex, were arrayed on one side. All those from the southern counties, exclusive of John Baker of Cape May, were on the other. The divergence of the Bergen members is accounted for by the preponderance in that county of the Dutch, who were firm believers in hard money.[41] That the assemblymen chosen from the lower half of the state should have been so uniformly opposed to paper money, despite the indications that a considerable number of their constituents favored inflation, is explainable partly on the grounds of the limited voting facilities that existed in that area. Because there were but seven polling places in the five lower counties, it was inconvenient and difficult for the "poorer sort" to vote. Moreover, the elections were held in the principal towns, where the conservative strength was greatest.[42]

The strategy of the anti-loan-office faction in the Assembly was to attempt to attach amendments to Clark's bill in order to make it less objectionable. At least a dozen were offered. Among the more important were those which provided that the money should be used solely to pay the interest on the state debt; that state securities as well as land should be accepted as collateral for loans; that the mortgages should be made assignable to any individual who would purchase them from the state; that counties which did not elect to receive their quota of the money should not be compelled to do so; and, most important of all, that the money should not be a legal tender. Every one of these proposals was promptly voted down by the determined, well-organized paper-money

[41] Somerset also had a large Dutch population, but political dominance there was exercised by the non-Dutch elements, particularly the Scotch-Irish. The latter group was favored because the one polling place in the county was located in the region in which it was most numerous.

[42] There were twenty-two polling places in the eight northern counties. *Session Laws*, 8-1, Act of Dec. 6, 1783.

bloc.[43] On March 9, the measure was brought to a vote and was passed, twenty to seventeen.[44]

The bill next went to the Council, where it encountered stiff resistance and met with an eight-to-five defeat.[45] Returned to the lower house, it was quickly repassed by the same margin as before and was sent again to the upper chamber. There it was once more rejected, this time, however, by a seven-to-six vote. Robert Lettis Hooper, vice president of the Council and a representative from the ardently pro-loan county of Hunterdon, had changed his mind.[46] On the following day the legislature, apparently deadlocked, adjourned.

Both factions realized that a final decision had not yet been reached. There was no let-up in the barrage of newspaper articles. Petitions continued to circulate. In Essex, delegates from each ward in the county gathered at Samuel Smith's tavern in Elizabeth Town to "agree upon some pointed instructions to their own members in the legislature." [47] At the annual town meeting in Newark on March 14, the assembled citizens unanimously adopted a resolution declaring that "the Issuing of Paper Money upon Loan would be of great advantage to this State, Expecially to the eastern Division of it . . ." Noting the deadlock between the Council and Assembly, they proposed as a compromise a law which would permit the original holders of public securities to

[43] *Votes and Proceedings*, 10-2, pp. 21-33.

[44] *Ibid.*, 10-2, pp. 43-44. In the minority were the representatives from the lower counties (except Baker), the Bergen delegation, and Schureman.

[45] Voting against the bill were Haring (Bergen), Newbold (Burlington), Clark (Gloucester), Mayhew (Salem), Eldridge (Cape May), Samuel Ogden (Cumberland), Hooper (Hunterdon), and Hoops (Sussex). The members from Essex, Middlesex, Somerset, Monmouth, and Morris voted affirmatively. *Journal of Council*, 10-2, pp. 24-25.

[46] *Votes and Proceedings*, 10-2, pp. 78-82; *Journal of Council*, 10-2, p. 41.

[47] *Political Intelligencer*, May 10, 1786.

borrow loan-office money on their securities in the same manner that landowners could borrow by mortgaging their lands. Instructions embodying these resolves were sent to the Essex representatives in the legislature.[48] When Benjamin Van Cleve, the Speaker of the Assembly, issued a call for a special session to convene on May 15 in New Brunswick, even Governor Livingston was ready to concede that the time had come for the advocates of sound money to capitulate.[49]

Meeting in the main room of James Drake's tavern, the lower house passed the loan-office bill on May 22 and forwarded it to the Council, which had its headquarters at the hostelry of Thomas Egbert.[50] Four days later the upper house enacted the measure into law by a vote of seven to six. Peter Haring, councilor from Bergen, had shifted from the negative to the affirmative. The *vox populi* had triumphed.[51]

The loan-office act, which took up twenty pages in the published *Session Laws*, was patterned closely after the colonial models.[52] The sum of one hundred thousand pounds ($266,-

[48] *Records of the Town of Newark, New Jersey* . . . (Newark, N. J., *1864*), pp. 162-63.

[49] ". . . I think the petitioners for paper money ought to be gratified," the governor wrote to Van Cleve, "and that such a measure would really relieve many honest people in distress, who ought undoubtedly to be relieved, as far as can be effected without injury to the commonwealth." Sedgwick, *Memoir*, pp. 397-98.

[50] *Votes and Proceedings*, 10-3, pp. 4-8. The vote was twenty-one to seven, with several West Jersey members abstaining. In the majority were the familiar nineteen who constituted the paper-money bloc, together with two representatives from Bergen, Terhune and Nicoll.

[51] *Journal of Council*, 10-3, p. 7. The reason for the change in the attitude of the Bergen members is obscure. That their conversion was not unpopular is evidenced by the fact that Haring, Terhune, and Nicoll were reelected in October, 1786. Blauvelt, who abstained from voting, was not returned. Governor Livingston, who customarily presided over the Council, was absent when the final vote was taken.

[52] *Session Laws*, 10-3, "An Act for striking and making current £100,000 in Bills of Credit, to be let out on Loan, and directing the Mode for sinking the same," May 26, 1786. For the colonial acts, see Kemmerer, "Colonial Loan-Office System," *passim*.

667) was to be printed in denominations from one shilling to six pounds. Under the supervision of loan-office commissioners, chosen by the justices and freeholders in each county, the money was to be lent in amounts under a hundred pounds to borrowers who could furnish at least double security in the form of a mortgage on lands, lots, or houses. Each county was given a quota of money, and if the demand exceeded the allotment, the amount available to individual borrowers was to be reduced proportionately. The bills were to be lent for twelve years at 6 per cent interest annually; after seven years they were to be paid back in five yearly installments and then destroyed. Interest receipts were to go into the state treasury for regular governmental expenditures. If the borrower failed to meet his payments of interest or principal, the state could foreclose and sell the property. The money was made full legal tender for all debts, public and private, and specific penalties were provided to enforce its acceptance.[53]

The loan offices in the several counties began their operations in November and December, 1786.[54] In Gloucester County over two hundred applicants, most of whom sought to borrow the maximum of a hundred pounds, besieged the commissioners. After spending several days in examining the claims, the officials disqualified some thirty individuals, mainly on the basis that the security offered was inadequate. They then decided to allot no more than fifty pounds to any one

[53] A week after the enactment of the loan-office measure, the legislature made the revenue money that had been issued under the law of December 20, 1783, full legal tender. *Votes and Proceedings*, 10-3, p. 25; *Journal of Council*, 10-3, p. 10; *Session Laws*, 10-3, Act of June 1, 1786.

[54] In some counties the justices and freeholders neglected to appoint loan-office commissioners within the time specified, apparently to defeat the intent of the act. To meet this challenge, the legislature charged the sheriff with making the appointments. *Session Laws*, 11-1, Act of Nov. 3, 1786.

person.[55] There were about four hundred and twenty requests for loans in Morris County, with the result that the most that any borrower could obtain was nineteen pounds.[56] In Somerset County one hundred and seventy-five applicants were awarded sums varying between twenty-six and one hundred pounds.[57] It is evident that the loan office did not bring direct financial relief to the poorest segment of society, for only those possessing a moderate quantity of land, unencumbered with prior mortgages, were eligible to receive the new bills. The landless mechanic, the tenant, and the insolvent debtor were excluded from the benefits of the act, although they may have profited indirectly from the increase in the money supply.

With the passage of the loan-office measure, debate over the money question abruptly subsided. Even the election that was held in October, 1786, did not bring forth any public discussion of the subject that a few months before had been uppermost in the popular mind. There were no marked changes in the composition of the newly chosen legislature, although both Clark and Schureman had gone on to the Continental Congress. Confronted with a "general dearth of news," Shepard Kollock filled the columns of his *New Jersey Journal* with Carver's *Travels Through the Interior Parts of this Continent*.[58] For almost two years, until the adoption of the Federal Constitution was assured, New Jersey was to be free from controversy over the matter of currency.

With the return of paper money and tender laws in 1786

---

[55] Gloucester Loan-Office Book, NJSL. The great number of applicants is of particular interest in view of the adamant opposition of the Gloucester legislators to the loan-office bill. Curiously enough, among the borrowers were Joseph Ellis and Franklin Davenport, both of whom were foes of paper money in the legislature.

[56] "Diary of Joseph Lewis," *PNJHS*, LXI (1943), p. 50.

[57] Somerset County Loan-Office Book, NJSL. The commonest amount was £52. Ephraim Martin, councilor from Somerset, was among the borrowers.

[58] *New Jersey Journal*, Nov. 8, 1786.

came additional acts for the relief of debtors. To hostile observers it seemed that the legislature was determined to devise
every possible expedient to reduce men of property to a
level with those who had none.[59] One such measure, designed
to prevent the sale of a debtor's estate at a fraction of its real
worth to satisfy claims against it, was the so-called "bull law,"
introduced by Abraham Clark and enacted in March by the
same bloc that favored the loan office.[60] Creditors were obliged
to accept at an appraised value sufficient goods, chattels, or
land to make up the sum of the debt. Characterized by its
opponents as being "in direct contravention of contracts, and
in open violation of every principle of honor, honesty, and
good faith," the act aroused so much criticism that it was repealed in November.[61]

Further steps were taken also to ease the plight of "insolvent debtors confined in gaol." Under the law of June, 1783,
such men had been permitted to obtain the privileges of bankruptcy only with the consent of a majority of their creditors.
In many cases, however, the requisite approval could not be
obtained. To meet this situation, it was decreed in June, 1786,
that the insolvent might petition for bankruptcy on his own
initiative, unless his creditors agreed to pay three shillings, six
pence to the gaolkeeper for his support.[62] Efforts by the As-

---

[59] William Livingston, "Strictures of Lilliput," *American Museum*,
IX (1791), pp. 239-41.

[60] *Votes and Proceedings*, 10-2, pp. 61, 74, 85; *Journal of Council*,
10-2, p. 42; *Session Laws*, 10-2, Act of Mar. 23, 1786. "Wheras [*sic*]
by Reason of the Scarcity of Cash," read the preamble to the law,
"many Persons' Estates or Effects are sold by Sheriffs or Coroners on
Writs of Fieri Facias much below their real Value, to the great Loss,
and in some Cases to the utter Ruin, of the Debtors against whom
such Writs are issued..."

[61] "Horatius," 15, William Paterson Essays, RUL; *Votes and Proceedings*, 11-1, p. 36; *Journal of Council*, 11-1, p. 24; *Session Laws*,
11-1, Act of Nov. 22, 1786.

[62] *Ibid.*, 10-3, Act of June 1, 1786. This act had passed the Assembly in March, but it had met with defeat in the Council. *Votes and
Proceedings*, 10-2, pp. 75, 85; *Journal of Council*, 10-2, p. 41.

sembly to enact a law "for the Stay of Execution in civil Actions," sponsored by Abraham Clark, were twice frustrated by the Council.[63]

The political combination of the seven northern counties, which were united in support of paper money, achieved a decisive triumph in 1786. The loan-office plan that was enacted can scarcely be called radical, for it was essentially the same expedient that had been employed on numerous occasions in the past. It was the familiar remedy for a shortage of currency. Conservatives were opposed to the measure because they had learned from recent experiences that a legislature sensitive to popular pressures could not be relied upon to maintain public faith.

THE DEBT PROBLEM

At the same time that the spectacular controversy over the money issue was in progress, the legislature was engaged in no less significant deliberations respecting the handling of public debts. The state, in December, 1783, had adopted the policy of paying the interest on Continental securities owned by its citizens, but this plan had to be re-examined in 1786 after the Confederation made a gesture toward assuming the burden. Also demanding consideration was the matter of funding and servicing the various classes of state debts. Responsibility for determining the solution to these important financial problems rested largely with the dominant paper-money bloc from the northern counties, and that faction was to demonstrate that its "radicalism" did not extend to the repudiation of governmental obligations. On the contrary, it displayed a zealous concern for the welfare of the security-holders—and particularly for the speculators—among its constituents.

The largest item of the state debt consisted of the certificates that had been given by county contractors in payment for

[63] *Votes and Proceedings*, 10-2, pp. 61, 74, 85, 87; *Journal of Council*, 10-2, p. 44.

military articles when the system of specific supply was in effect. The Continental Congress had promised that eventually the accounts of the several states would be settled and compared and that those states which had contributed more than their share would be reimbursed.[64] For several years no effective steps were taken to accomplish such a settlement. Finally, in October, 1785, Benjamin Thompson, the commissioner of accounts in New Jersey, urged Governor Livingston to request the legislature to adopt some method of determining the amount of the expenditures made by the state on behalf of the United States.[65] Because they had been put into circulation during a period when prices were erratic, the certificates would have to be liquidated according to some standard scale of depreciation before there could be any accurate estimate of their true aggregate value.

A plan for carrying out this complicated operation was devised by the legislature in November.[66] A special commissioner, Silas Condict, was instructed to visit each county and exchange newly printed state notes (Condict's notes) bearing 6 per cent interest for the certificates at their adjusted value. Interest payments on the old certificates were stopped.[67] Condict was directed to complete this herculean task by October 1, 1786, but he encountered so many difficulties that the time limit was subsequently extended to April 1, 1787.[68] Not until

[64] *Journals of the Continental Congress*, XV, p. 1377.

[65] Benjamin Thompson to Governor Livingston, Oct. 22, 1785, Manuscript Collection, NJSL. Thompson expected that he would soon complete his work in settling the accounts of individuals against the United States, and he looked forward to dealing next with accounts of the state.

[66] *Votes and Proceedings*, 10-1, pp. 76, 81; *Journal of Council*, 10-1, p. 29; *Session Laws*, 10-1, Act of Nov. 28, 1785.

[67] *Votes and Proceedings*, 10-1, pp. 82, 83.

[68] Silas Condict to Benjamin Van Cleve, Feb. 11, 1786, Manuscript Collection, NJSL; *Votes and Proceedings*, 11-1, pp. 62, 71; *Session Laws*, 11-1, Act of Nov. 27, 1786. Many certificate holders neglected to effect the exchange within the allotted period. *Votes and Proceed-*

September, 1788, were the final accounts of the state ready for submission to the Continental Congress, which could do nothing more than transmit them to its successor.[69]

While the contractor's certificates were in the process of being liquidated, the legislature attempted to formulate a long-range policy toward the state's debts. Interest payments were far in arrears, not only on the certificates but also on the soldiers' depreciation notes and on the militia notes, and no arrangements whatsoever had been made for paying off the principal. A committee of the Assembly, headed by Abraham Clark, surveyed the various categories of indebtedness in March, 1786, and concluded that it would be inadvisable to make provision for one type of obligation until like provisions could be made for all. Nothing should be done, therefore, until Condict had finished his work. Then all the confiscated estates and public barracks should be sold, and state securities should be received in payment. If any debts still remained, they should be discharged through taxes. The house agreed to this report, which called for no immediate action of any kind.[70]

The early months of 1786 witnessed also a series of significant decisions regarding the treatment of Continental creditors. In September, 1785, the Continental Congress called on the states for three million dollars, two-thirds of which was to be applied toward discharging the interest on the domestic debt. Incorporated in the requisition was the stipulation that no state was to be given credit for any interest payments it might make to its citizens after January 1, 1786.[71] Compliance with this

---

ings, 12-1, pp. 33, 64; James Mott to Ephraim Harris, Nov. 5, 1787, AM Papers, NJSL.

[69] *Votes and Proceedings,* 10-3, p. 21; Aaron Dunham to Ephraim Harris, Nov. 5, 1787, Aug. 28, 1788, AM Papers, NJSL; *Journals of the Continental Congress,* XXXIV, p. 568.

[70] *Votes and Proceedings,* 10-2, p. 78.

[71] *Journals of the Continental Congress,* XXIX, pp. 765-71. The full story of New Jersey's response to this requisition is related in chapter IX, pp. 233-44.

requisition would mean the disruption of the plan that the state had adopted in December, 1783. Noncompliance, on the other hand, would subject the state to the penalty of being deprived of credit for the sums that it might pay to holders of Continental securities. The dilemma was a serious one, and the legislature evidently was at a loss what to do. Consideration of the requisition was postponed in November, 1785, but the treasurer was ordered to cease interest payments on loan-office certificates and other liquidated debts of the United States.[72] The period of hesitation came to an end on February 20, 1786, however, when the Assembly by a near-unanimous vote approved a resolution that had been drafted by the irrepressible Abraham Clark in which the state in no uncertain terms declined to honor the requisition.[73] Two days later the treasurer was directed to resume interest payments.[74] New Jersey had reaffirmed the state's financial independence of the Confederation and at the same time reasserted its intention of meeting the demands of its own continental creditors.

Then came the problem of raising sufficient funds to finance the debt-servicing program. The annual "revenue tax" of £31,259.5 brought in enough money to pay less than two-thirds of the interest due on the continental securities, and no provision had as yet been made for the state creditors.[75] In May, 1786, the Council took the initiative in proposing that a joint committee of the two houses should confer on the debt question. The group was charged specifically with considering "The late Requisition of Congress, the Fulfillment of our Public Engagements, the making Provision for the Payment of Interest on State Debts, in order to do Justice to State Creditors,

---

[72] *Votes and Proceedings,* 10-1, pp. 28, 82.

[73] *Ibid.,* 10-2, pp. 12-13. The vote was thirty-two to three.

[74] *Ibid.,* 10-2, p. 17.

[75] The "revenue tax," it will be recalled, had been based not on the amount of securities in the state, but on the quota assigned New Jersey in the requisition of April 18, 1783. See pp. 176-7.

and to restore Public Credit; and the adopting Measures to raise a Revenue, by Impost and Excise, in order to make Taxation more equal, by releasing the Land-Holders, in placing the Burthen on Superfluities..." [76] The committee met on May 23 and reported on May 27, the day after the passage of the loan-office act. It recommended that a tax of £10,419.15 should be levied, in addition to the "revenue tax," to be applied toward discharging the interest on continental securities, that the revenue money should be made legal tender, that the confiscated estates and public barracks should be sold for state securities, and that money should be raised by an impost. [77] Acting on these proposals in part, the legislature made the revenue money legal tender on the same basis as the loan-office bills and authorized the sale of the remaining confiscated estates and public barracks. [78] Nothing was done about the impost or the additional tax. Whether the broad assurances to the public creditors contained in the committee's report were intended primarily to influence the Council in favor of the loan-office bill is impossible to determine, but it is not improbable that some such devious motives were involved. In any event, there seems to be no adequate explanation of the failure of the Assembly to implement the report that it adopted.

Similar maneuvers were indulged in by the lawmakers at their succeeding session. Once more the lower house repeated its refusal to honor a requisition of the Continental Congress

[76] *Votes and Proceedings*, 10-3, p. 8. The three members of the Council who were appointed to the committee, Kitchell (Morris), Martin (Somerset), and Ogden (Essex), were firm supporters of the loan office, as were two of the five members (Abraham Clark and John Starke) from the Assembly.

[77] *Ibid.*, 10-3, p. 18.

[78] *Ibid.*, 10-3, pp. 23-29; *Session Laws*, 10-3, Acts of June 1, 1786. Concern was expressed in some quarters that the revenue money might depreciate after it was made legal tender, but this was not immediately the case. *New Jersey Journal*, July 12, 19, Oct. 25, 1786.

that was to be used for payments on the domestic debt. Noting that "it must be very unimportant to Congress if the public Creditors are satisfied, and they exonerated, in what manner it be done," the Assembly approved a committee report that called for an increase in the revenue tax.[79] A bill for this purpose was introduced, read, and referred to the next sitting without a record vote.[80] The same treatment was accorded an impost bill, in lieu of which a tax was levied on ferries, stages, and taverns.[81] After this second glaring example of temporization, it is not surprising that John Cox, a substantial security holder, should have condemned the "stupid Assembly" for its failure to do justice to the public creditors in the state.[82]

In May, 1787, the Assembly, for what proved to be the last time, again focused its attention on the debt problem through the medium of a grand committee of thirteen members, one from each county. It was the ambitious recommendation of this group that the continental debt within the state should be funded to the extent of £537,567 by the issuance of new certificates, and that the "revenue tax" should be increased to fifty thousand pounds, the proceeds of which would be applied toward the payment of interest on both continental and state securities.[83] This report was brought to

---

[79] *Votes and Proceedings*, 11-1, pp. 30-32. The vote was twenty-one to seventeen, with most of the West Jersey members in the minority.

[80] *Ibid.*, 11-1, p. 62.

[81] *Ibid.*, 11-1, pp. 62, 65, 69; *Journal of Council*, 11-1, p. 29; *Session Laws*, 11-1, Act of Nov. 24, 1786.

[82] John Cox to John Stevens, Jr., Dec. 17, 1786, Stevens Papers, SIT.

[83] *Votes and Proceedings*, 11-2, pp. 16-17. The arithmetic of this proposal requires some explanation. Interest payments at 6 per cent on the state debt of £295,755 would come to £17,745. This sum deducted from £50,000 would leave £32,255, an amount equal to 6 per cent of £537,567. The total of the continental debt in New Jersey (1790) was actually above £900,000. *American State Papers, Finance*, I, p. 30.

a vote on May 25 and was defeated by a twenty-to-eighteen division. Opposed to the funding plan were fifteen members from West Jersey and five from Bergen, Essex, Middlesex, and Monmouth.[84] Next, there was introduced a bill to raise £17,745 for servicing the state debt, practically all of which had now been liquidated. After two weeks of discussion, the sum was reduced to £12,500 and the act was passed.[85] The treasurer was instructed to pay interest annually on soldiers' depreciation notes, militia notes, Condict's notes, and notes that had been given to persons who had claims against forfeited estates. Any person making application for interest had to testify that the certificates which he held had been the property of a citizen of New Jersey before May 1, 1787, and had not since belonged to an inhabitant of any other state. After years of delay, the state creditors were at last to receive an income from their depreciated securities.

Out of the bewildering welter of reports, resolutions, and votes on the debt question, it is possible to deduce some broad conclusions respecting the positions taken by various sections and groups in the state. The geographical distribution of securities was responsible for much of the difference of opinion manifested by the legislators. On the basis of the best evidence available, it is strikingly apparent that the overwhelming bulk of public securities, both state and continental, were held by residents of the northern half of the state. The majority of the security holders lived within a radius of ten miles of a line drawn from Burlington to Newark. With the

[84] *Votes and Proceedings,* 11-2, p. 19.

[85] *Ibid.,* 11-2, pp. 19-41; *Journal of Council,* 11-2, p. 21; *Session Laws,* 11-2, "An Act to raise the Sum of £12,500 per Annum, for the Term of twenty-two years, for the Purpose of paying the interest on the Debt due from this State to the Inhabitants thereof," June 7, 1787. The vote in the Assembly was twenty-seven to nine; in the Council, nine to three. Nine of the twelve opposing votes were cast by West Jersey members.

exception of the town of Burlington, there were relatively few public creditors south of Trenton.[86] In view of this condition, it is understandable that the representatives from the southern counties should have been strongly opposed to paying additional state taxes for servicing the continental debt. They were willing that New Jersey should contribute its proportionate quota toward meeting the financial obligations of the Confederation, but they would not consent to do more than that.[87] It follows that they would welcome the establishment of a central government capable of assuming the debt burden. It was for this reason, among others, that the non-security-holding regions of New Jersey were to give their ardent approval to the Federal Constitution.

The favorable consideration given by the representatives from the northern counties to proposals for making more

[86] These generalizations are based on an analysis of the subscriptions made to the Federal loans for funding the national and state debts. For the holders of state securities, see "Subscriptions toward a Loan to the United States as proposed by the Act of Congress of the 4th of August, 1790, in the Office of James Ewing, commissioner of Loans in the State of New Jersey, payable in Certificates of the Debt of the State of New Jersey," NJHS. The records dealing with subscriptions of continental securities are fragmentary. Apparently the only ones that have survived are those that list the owners of the funded 3 per cent stock, which comprised approximately one-third of the total domestic funded debt. See New Jersey Loan Office, Ledger C-2, Domestic Debt, Holdings of 3% Stock (Funded 3% Stock), July 1, 1791, National Archives. See also *Records of the Town of Newark*, pp. 162-63.

[87] For examples of this attitude, see *Votes and Proceedings*, 10-1, p. 28; *ibid.*, 10-2, p. 74; *ibid.*, 11-1, pp. 32, 63; *ibid.*, 11-2, p. 19. Again it should be pointed out that New Jersey's holdings of continental securities were disproportionately large. Consequently if the state assumed the entire burden of interest charges on the continental debt, it would have to raise a greater sum through taxes than would be required to meet a requisition of the Continental Congress for the same purpose. To be specific, New Jersey's share of the requisition of April 18, 1783, was £31,259.5, but nearly twice that sum would be needed to discharge the demands of continental security holders in the state.

adequate provision for continental creditors indicates that the advocates of paper money and of debtor laws were anything but hostile to the security holders, who were an important element among their constituents. True, they chose their own means of satisfying the creditors, many of whom would have preferred to rely on the Confederation rather than on the state. But although they were adamant in their refusal to honor the requisitions of the Continental Congress as long as that body lacked the power to levy an impost, they nevertheless met faithfully the obligations that the state had assumed in December, 1783, under the "revenue tax" plan and made gestures toward increasing that tax.[88] There was relatively little disagreement over the course of action to be followed with regard to the state debt. West Jersey, which during the period of the controversy over the retirement of the new emission had displayed a repudiationist attitude, subsequently became less solidly opposed to providing for the debts that had been contracted by the state.[89] The extent of this conversion was apparent in the vote on the £12,500 tax, when all but nine of the western members registered their approval of the act. The legislators from the security-holding

[88] *Ibid.*, 10-3, p. 18; *ibid.*, 11-1, pp. 30-32; *ibid.*, 11-2, pp. 16-19. If full information about the public-creditor group was available, it might be possible to make a distinction between the views of "original holders" and of those who had obtained securities at a later date and at a depreciated price. The former, who would be most anxious to recover the principal amount of their investment, probably placed their chief reliance in a strengthened Confederation, while the latter, content with a return of 20 per cent or more each year on their speculative purchases, were satisfied with the income guaranteed by the state. There are indications that an "understanding" existed between the speculators and the paper-money men. "Radical" Essex County, for example, was represented in the legislature by Jonathan Dayton, a notorious speculator, by his brother-in-law, Matthias Ogden, and by his associate in the Miami purchase, Daniel Marsh. Moreover, Dayton was closely identified politically with Abraham Clark, with whom his name was linked in the Congressional campaign of 1789.

[89] "Monitor," *Political Intelligencer*, May 10, 1786.

northern counties were almost to a man in favor of the measure.[90]

The public creditor in New Jersey was not the neglected figure that he was in many other states. His situation was not entirely to his liking, but under the circumstances it was not as bad as it might have been. Those who had obtained their securities at a depreciated price profited handsomely by their speculation, and there were many in this class. Throughout the postwar years there was an active market for securities at quotations ranging from three to seven shillings in the pound. Over a period of time, there was a tendency toward a concentration of the holdings of notes and certificates in the hands of a relatively small number of individuals. Such men as John Cox, Jacques Voorhees, and Joseph Lewis, and many others, were busily engaged in buying up securities whenever the opportunity presented itself.[91] New York brokers advertised their offers of high prices for state and continental securities in New Jersey newspapers.[92] As early as 1784 there were complaints that the soldiers' depreciation notes were being engrossed by "Col. N., Maj. O., and Wagonmaster G, and Quartermaster Q, and Deputy &c. &c., &c. all of the staff" and by "traders and monopolizers, who were making their fortunes while the brave soldiers were freely bleeding in their defence." [93] The citizens of Orange-Dale in Essex County at a public meeting in April, 1787, deplored the fact that the state securities were possessed by a few men, who

[90] *Votes and Proceedings*, 11-2, p. 41; *Journal of Council*, 11-2, p. 21. It is not unlikely, however, that the reduction in the amount of the tax from £17,745 to £12,500 was made at the insistence of West Jersey.

[91] Brockholst Livingston to William Livingston, Nov. 11, 1783, Livingston Papers, MHS; "Diary of Joseph Lewis," *PNJHS*, LX (1942), pp. 60, 136; Abraham Lott to John Neilson, Mar. 24, 1786, Neilson Papers, F 141, RUL.

[92] *Political Intelligencer*, Nov. 16, 1785, Feb. 1, 1786.

[93] "A True Watchman," *Political Intelligencer*, June 15, 1784.

had obtained them at a price far below their nominal value.[94] Speculation was not the only factor that motivated purchasers of securities. They were deemed to be a good investment. Elias Boudinot, a shrewd businessman, decided to sell some of his own property and that of a friend for certificates in 1786. He reasoned that income from the land did not exceed 2 per cent, whereas the interest on the certificates was 6 per cent.[95] Doubtless the "little man," who was forced to part with his depreciation notes, militia notes, Thompson's notes, or Condict's notes for a few shillings in the pound, was the heavy loser, for he not only surrendered all hope of recovering his principal, but he also paid the bulk of the taxes that went to service the debt.

After a broad survey of the measures that New Jersey adopted to meet its grave financial problems, certain conclusions seem inescapable. It is impossible, for one thing, to agree with such earlier writers as Fiske and McLaughlin who, on the basis of inadequate studies, characterized the paper-money movement as "political quackery" and described the advocates of inflation as including "the unhappy and deluded . . . [and] all those uneasy elements that opposed the extension of federal authority and believed in law only as a means of securing some selfish and niggardly end." [96] There

[94] *New Jersey Journal*, May 2, 1787. The assemblage declared "that any person who speculates in public securities, is not a proper person to represent the good people of this county in either house of Assembly." Unquestionably this attack was levelled against Jonathan Dayton, who in 1790 held over eleven thousand pounds in state securities.

[95] Elias Boudinot to James Cuthbert, Aug. 2, 1786, Boudinot Letters, PUL. Boudinot noted that "the Certificates still kept looking up, & were not growing worse, and that in all probability the Interest . . . [would] be punctually paid . . ."

[96] John Fiske, *The Critical Period of American History, 1783-1789* (Boston and New York, 1888), p. 160; Andrew C. McLaughlin, *The Confederation and the Constitution, 1783-1789* (New York, 1905), p. 141. Competent modern studies of the money question are sadly lacking. It is curious that such dated and uncritical works as those of Phillips, Gouge, Sumner, and Hepburn, for example, have so long been accepted as standard references.

can be little question that the monetary situation in 1786 called for some remedy. Under the type of popular government that existed in the state, the legislators had to take steps to relieve the economic distress that had developed out of the rapid contraction of the currency supply. They turned to a device, the loan office, with which they were thoroughly familiar and which they knew had worked effectively in the colonial period. They were not radicals, they were not indulging in "mad reasonings," they were not proposing an innovation or a vague panacea.

The opposition to the loan office was surprising. It can be explained principally on the basis that conservative men of property distrusted the popularly controlled legislature, which they believed would not adhere to its promises. "Democratical license" was their great fear. Because of their lack of confidence in majority rule, they later welcomed the imposition by the Federal government of important restrictions upon the powers of the states.

Equally as significant in the financial field as the loan-office plan were the unique arrangements that were made for discharging the interest due on continental securities. Although New Jersey for adequate reasons refused to honor the requisitions of Congress, it demonstrated its willingness to assume an extremely heavy tax burden in order to satisfy the demands of public creditors. Paper money was not synonymous with repudiation.

IX

New Jersey and the Confederation

★★

NEW JERSEY was seriously divided on most questions of internal policy, but it was firmly united in its attitude toward the Confederation. From the first it took an advanced position in demanding that the central government should be strengthened in important respects. It was particularly concerned that the Continental Congress should have full control over western lands and power to regulate trade and levy imposts. These views arose largely out of financial considerations. It was obvious that if Congress was granted revenues from land sales and from tariff duties, it would not have to rely so heavily upon requisitions, which New Jersey—lacking western lands or foreign commerce—could meet only through the imposition of oppressive taxes. Too, a prosperous Confederation would be able to pay its debts, and New Jersey was a public-creditor state. Moreover, as a small state, New Jersey, through confederation, would assume political equality with her powerful neighbors.

The most comprehensive statement of New Jersey's views on the Confederation was made in a "Representation" drafted by a joint committee of the legislature and sent to the Continental Congress on June 16, 1778. Several objections were offered to the proposed Articles of Confederation. During the succeeding decade, the state consistently maintained the sentiments embodied in the "Representation." [1] In the first place, criticism was levelled against the omission of any requirement that delegates take an oath to assent to no vote or proceeding which might violate the Confederation. Next, it was asserted that "the sole and exclusive power of regulating the trade of the United States with foreign nations ought to be clearly vested in Congress" and that funds derived from customs duties should be appropriated for general concerns. The boundaries of all states should be determined within five years after the final ratification of the Articles. Disappointment was expressed at the lack of provisions for the disposal of the former crown lands, which should "belong to the Congress in trust for the use and benefit of the United States." "Shall such States as are shut out by situation from availing themselves of the least advantage from this quarter," it was asked, "be left to sink under an enormous debt, whilst others are enabled in a short period to replace all their expenditures from the hard earnings of the whole Confederacy?" The "Representation" also contained pleas that a large standing army should be specifically prohibited, that quotas of men and money should be adjusted every five years, that land forces should be furnished in proportion to the whole number of inhabitants, and that a three-fourths vote should continue to be required on major questions even if there should be an increase in the number of states. Congress was urged to embody these recommendations in a revision of the Articles, "by which means we apprehend the mutual interest of all the States will be better

---

[1] *Votes and Proceedings*, 2-2, pp. 90, 143-48; *Journals of the Continental Congress*, XI, pp. 648-51. The joint committee was appointed March 25, and it reported June 15, 1778.

secured and promoted," concluded the appeal, "and the Legislature of this State will then be justified in ratifying the same."

The "Representation" received the attention of Congress, but that body declined to make any alterations in its handiwork.[2] Convinced of the "Justice and Equity" of its objections, New Jersey nevertheless agreed to ratify the Articles in November, 1778.[3] In doing so, however, it relinquished none of its contentions, but it recognized that "every separate and State-Interest ought to be postponed to the public Good." It confidently expected that time would operate to remove the inequalities of which it complained, and it never neglected an opportunity to promote its conception of a satisfactory basis of union.

WESTERN LANDS

A small, "landless" state, with well-defined boundaries, New Jersey was vitally interested in the lengthy controversy over the fate of the western lands. Taking the stand that the title to all lands that had belonged to the crown of Great Britain descended to the states in common after Independence, it insisted that, in effect, all the region west of the Alleghenies was the property of the United States. Because this conception comprehended not only the territory north of the Ohio River but also that to the south—in which lay the unconfirmed grants of the Indiana and Vandalia companies—New Jersey became the bitterest foe of Virginia's extensive and exclusive claims and the staunchest champion of the speculative land companies.[4]

New Jersey's motives are readily ascertained. The state

[2] *Ibid.*, XI, p. 651.

[3] *Votes and Proceedings*, 3-1, pp. 16-17, 21-22, 29; Wilson, *Acts*, Act of Nov. 20, 1778, pp. 61-62.

[4] Thomas P. Abernethy, *Western Lands and The American Revolution* (New York, 1937), pp. 363-65.

wanted to obtain, either directly or through the Confederation, its proportionate share of the former crown lands. It
regarded the western territory as a source of revenue and as
a field for speculation, and it wanted to participate in both.[5]
Public creditors hoped that returns from land sales would
enable the Confederation to discharge its debts.[6] Undoubtedly there was involved also jealousy of those states
which had vast, unsettled domains.[7] Reinforcing the stubborn opposition that New Jersey made to the pretensions of
Virginia was the influence of the indefatigable agents of the
Indiana Company, two of whom—William Trent and
George Morgan—were temporary citizens of the state.[8] Too,
there was the sincere conviction that the union would be

[5] Prior to the Revolution, the "landless" middle colonies had favored
limiting the bounds of the "landed" colonies and placing the western
region under the control of the crown. Their position after Independence, therefore, was not novel. See Merrill Jensen, "The Cession of the
Old Northwest," *Mississippi Valley Historical Review*, XXIII (June,
1936), pp. 27-48.

[6] "I have been tracing out ye Boundaries of ye United States upon
some maps I have," wrote William P. Smith to Elias Boudinot on
April 22, 1783, "It contains an amazing Extent of Territory ... I am
sorry the Spaniards have such a Slice at ye Western Extremity. But sure
there are Acres enough now to pay just debts." *PNJHS*, IV (1849),
p. 124.

[7] James Madison, "Observations on Vermont and Territorial Claims
[May 1, 1782]," Burnett, *Letters*, VI, p. 341.

[8] The Indiana Company had an equitable claim to approximately
three and one-half million acres in what is now West Virginia. This
claim was based upon a grant from the Six Nations at the Treaty of
Fort Stanwix (1768). It was never confirmed by the crown, and repeated efforts for over thirty years to gain recognition from Virginia
met with failure. For the fullest account of the Indiana Company, see
George E. Lewis, *The Indiana Company, 1763-1798* (Glendale,
1941). Also of value are A. T. Volwiler, *George Croghan and the
Westward Movement, 1741-1782* (Cleveland, 1926), and Max
Savelle, *George Morgan, Colony Builder* (New York, 1932). There
are satisfactory sketches of William Trent and George Morgan in the
DAB.

strengthened if Congress was given control over the disputed area.[9]

After the initial protest in the "Representation" of June 16, 1778, New Jersey made no further official pronouncement on the land question until the end of 1780. In the interim, Virginia had opened a land office in the territory south of the Ohio, the Indiana Company had memorialized Congress to recognize its rights, and Congress had recommended that the landed states make liberal cessions of their western claims.[10] It was at this juncture that the legislature received petitions from "sundry inhabitants" remonstrating against the sale of western lands by any one state and asking that Congress be entreated to "open an Office for the Sale and appropriation of the said Lands; the Proceeds to be applied to carry on and terminate the War, to aid the Funds, and establish the Credit of the publick Finances; and, by constituting a Common Interest, to render the Union firm and lasting..."[11] In response to these appeals, the Assembly appointed a committee to investigate the complaints and suggest a course of action. At the head of the group was placed William Trent, a leading member of the Indiana Company and its most persistent lobbyist, who was serving his first and only term in the legislature.[12] The committee

[9] Robert Morris to William C. Houston, Feb. 8, 1780, Houston-Morris Letters, RUL; *Votes and Proceedings*, 7-2, pp. 136-37.

[10] Abernethy, *Western Lands*, pp. 217-29, 238-39, 242-43; Lewis, *Indiana Company*, pp. 221-22, 225-34; Jensen, "Land Cessions," pp. 39-41.

[11] *Votes and Proceedings*, 5-1, pp. 77-78. George Morgan was probably, with Trent, the chief instigator of these petitions. Savelle, *Morgan*, p. 102.

[12] Trent, whose residence is usually given as Trenton, was elected from Burlington County. Apparently he was living in Nottingham township in 1779. *New Jersey Archives*, 2nd Ser., IV, pp. 77-78. One of Trent's colleagues from Burlington was William Hough, who may have been related to John Hough, a friend of another prominent Indiana claimant, Samuel Wharton. Lewis, *Indiana Company*, p. 202.

reported that the prayer of the petitioners should be granted, declared that the crown lands rightfully belonged to all the states in common, and entered into a detailed historical argument to show the falsity of Virginia's claims.[13] The house accepted the report and instructed the committee to prepare a representation to Congress. In this document, which was approved December 29, 1780, the state expressed its "utmost Surprise" at the sale of crown lands "for the separate Emolument of any State" and placed its trust in "the watchfull Care, the Wisdom, Justice and Firmness of Congress" to safeguard the rights of the union.[14]

Early in January, 1781, Virginia offered to cede to the United States her claim to the region north of the Ohio River on the condition that prior grants to private persons, either from the Indians or from the King, would be voided.[15] The terms of the cession met with little favor among the landless states, who prevented its acceptance for more than three years. New Jersey was incensed because the region south of the Ohio was not included. The legislature on October 4, 1781, drafted a set of instructions to the delegates in Congress, directing them to join with the delegates from other interested states in opposing the cession and condemning the "partial concessions" made by the Old Dominion. At the same time, a speedy and impartial hearing on the Indiana matter was demanded.[16] A year later the state was

[13] *Votes and Proceedings*, 5-1, pp. 77-78. The report bears evidence of Morgan's and Trent's handiwork, particularly in the section dealing with the significance of Virginia's acknowledgment of the Treaty of Fort Stanwix.

[14] "Representation and Remonstrance," Dec. 29, 1780, *Votes and Proceedings*, 5-1, pp. 78, 90-91.

[15] *Journals of the Continental Congress*, XXV, pp. 560-62.

[16] *Votes and Proceedings*, 5-3, p. 25. On November 3 a committee of Congress recommended against the acceptance of Virginia's cession and upheld the claims of the Indiana Company. Merrill Jensen, "The Creation of the National Domain, 1781-1784," *Mississippi Valley Historical Review*, XXVI (Dec., 1939), p. 330.

instrumental in bringing about the defeat in Congress of a compromise proposal, and the problem remained unsettled when the war ended.[17]

Interest in the land question revived with the return of peace. As the need for revenue became increasingly pressing, Congress renewed its efforts to come to some agreement on the issue. In New Jersey, hundreds of individuals petitioned the legislature to insist once more upon the right of the Confederation to the crown lands.[18] "Equality," writing in the *New Jersey Gazette*, argued that the state should have "its dividend of those countries lately ceded to the United States by the King of England; or an equal benefit from the sales thereof, in proportion to its quota of the expenses of the war." Otherwise New Jersey would be "deserted of its citizens, and beggared of its cash, while those who remain[ed] in the state must be rendered bankrupt by the publick debt."[19] When Congress in June took under consideration a committee report that tacitly excluded the pretensions of the land companies, the legislature for the fourth time made its views known.[20] "We cannot be silent," read a "Representation and Remonstrance" adopted June 14, 1783, "while viewing one State [Virginia] aggrandizing herself by the unjust Detention of the Property which has been procured by the common Blood and Treasure of the whole, and which, on every Principle of Reason and Justice, is vested in Congress for the Use and general Benefit of the Union they represent."[21] Whether or not this contention

[17] *Journals of the Continental Congress*, XXIII, pp. 552-53, 604-606.

[18] *Votes and Proceedings*, 7-2, pp. 98, 113, 128. The petitions came from Sussex, Morris, and Essex counties.

[19] *New Jersey Gazette*, May 28, 1783. Similar views were expressed by "Genesea," *New Jersey Gazette*, May 21, 1783.

[20] James Madison to Edmund Randolph, June 10, 1783, Burnett, *Letters*, VII, p. 187.

[21] *Votes and Proceedings*, 7-2, pp. 136-37; *Journals of the Continental Congress*, XXIV, pp. 408-409.

was just, it soon became apparent that the political tide was running against New Jersey.

On September 13, 1783, over the objections of the delegates from New Jersey and Maryland, Congress set forth the terms on which it would accept the cession of Virginia's claims.[22] Virginia promptly complied with the new conditions, and on March 1, 1784, Congress prepared to acknowledge the cession. John Beatty of New Jersey attempted to attach a proviso which would have specifically denied that acceptance of the grant implied "any opinion or decision of Congress respecting the extent or validity of the claim of the Commonwealth of Virginia, to western territory, by charter or otherwise," but his motion was supported only by New Jersey, Pennsylvania, and Rhode Island. Then the cession was formally approved, with New Jersey alone in opposition.[23] The controversy over the disposition of the crown lands had at last been settled.

On the same day, Congress dealt a hard blow to the Indiana claimants. Foreseeing the adverse effect that the acceptance of the Virginia cession would have on the claims of the Indiana Company, Colonel George Morgan of Princeton, a prominent member of the company, had asked the New Jersey legislature in December, 1783, to appoint him an official agent of the state for the purpose of making a further appeal to Congress. His prayer was granted, and he was formally commissioned.[24] His petition to Congress on February 26, 1784, recited the familiar history of the Indiana controversy,

---

[22] *Ibid.*, XXV, pp. 560-63. Virginia was asked to withdraw its condition respecting the invalidation of prior grants to private persons but was tacitly assured that such grants would not be recognized. This was a blow to the Illinois-Wabash speculators, many of whom resided in Maryland. New Jersey's objection was to the size of the cession.

[23] *Ibid.*, XXVI, pp. 113-17.

[24] *Votes and Proceedings*, 8-1, pp. 73-74; William Livingston to Col. George Morgan, Dec. 18, 1783, Papers of the Continental Congress, 42, V, Manuscripts Division, LC; Savelle, *Morgan*, pp. 105-106.

declared that a dispute now existed between New Jersey and Virginia over the matter, and called for a hearing "agreeably to the Ninth Article of Confederation & perpetual Union," which provided for the settlement of conflicts between states.[25] Congress, however, refused to take any action on the grounds that "the lands lay within the limits of Virginia and could be affected by the decision of no other tribunal, but of the Courts within the State."[26]

Thus New Jersey suffered a double defeat on the matter of the crown lands and on the case of the Indiana Company. That the verdicts were received with bad grace is evidenced by the fact that the legislature as late as March, 1786, instructed its delegates in Congress not to vote for any resolution that would charge the state with expense in gaining possession of, or in defending former crown lands claimed by, or which might accrue to, the exclusive benefit of any state.[27] The extent to which the Indiana intrigue may have influenced New Jersey to adopt the extreme position that it did on the land problem is uncertain. It is hardly conceivable that such individuals as Trent and Morgan could have foisted their views on the legislature if that body held opposing sentiments. No one was more radical on the subject of the crown lands than Abraham Clark, yet there is no evidence to indicate that he was associated with any speculative enterprises. The same might be said of many other prominent

[25] Petition of Col. George Morgan, Agent for the State of New Jersey, Feb. 26, 1784, Papers of the Continental Congress, 42, V, Manuscripts Division, LC. Jensen pictures Morgan as "one of the most powerful influences in New Jersey politics..." Jensen, "National Domain," p. 325n. I know of no evidence to support such a characterization. See Savelle, *Morgan, passim.*

[26] *Journals of the Continental Congress*, XXVI, pp. 110-11; Samuel Hardy to the Governor of Virginia, Benjamin Harrison, Mar. 12, 1784, Burnett, *Letters*, VII, p. 468. For the subsequent history of the Indiana Company, see Lewis, *Indiana Company*, pp. 271-93.

[27] *Votes and Proceedings*, 10-2, pp. 29-30.

figures.[28] In all probability the state patronized the cause of the Indiana proprietors for the reason that that cause coincided with its own broad interests.

Once it had been determined that the western territory was to be under the control of the central government, New Jersey, unlike many of the "Eastern" states, was anxious to have the region opened to settlement under favorable conditions. This attitude was particularly manifest in the course that the state followed on the critical Mississippi question. John Jay in his negotiations with the Spanish chargé d'affaires, Don Diego de Gardoqui, had been instructed by Congress in August, 1785, to insist upon the free navigation of the river, which had been closed by Spain the preceding year.[29] When Jay became convinced that such a concession was unobtainable and that commercial privileges beneficial to the North might be secured if the Mississippi matter was dropped, he sought to have his instructions altered. There ensued a controversy that threatened to disrupt the union, with the North and the South violently at odds. The North was willing to sacrifice the West if it could enhance its foreign commerce, while the South was the ardent champion of the new region. Also involved was the desire of some groups in the North to restrict western expansion, which they feared would drain off population from the seaboard states and depress land values.[30] The northern states achieved an indecisive victory in August, 1786, when by a vote of seven to five Congress acceded to Jay's request. Two of the New Jersey delegates, Josiah Hornblower and Lambert Cadwallader, sided with

---

[28] For the attitudes of William C. Houston and Robert Morris, both of whom believed firmly that New Jersey's stand was wholly justified, see Houston to Morris, Oct. 2, Nov. 27, 1779, Mar. 6, 1780, and Morris to Houston, Nov. 3, 1779, Feb. 8, 1780, Houston-Morris Letters, RUL.

[29] Burnett, *Continental Congress*, pp. 654-59; Samuel F. Bemis, *Pinckney's Treaty* (Baltimore, 1926), p. 29.

[30] *Ibid.*, pp. 92-102; Burnett, *Continental Congress*, pp. 655-59.

the majority, while the third, John Cleves Symmes, broke with his colleagues.[31]

Some southerners saw in this action the hint of a design to break up the Confederation. James Monroe was convinced that such a plot could be forestalled only by winning over New Jersey and Pennsylvania. Accordingly, he confided his suspicions to James Madison and asked him to get Abraham Clark, then with Madison at Annapolis, to use his influence to bring about a reversal of the state's position as expressed in the recent vote.[32] Madison communicated with Clark and received assurances that the needful would be done.[33] On November 23, both houses of the legislature adopted the report of a committee headed by Jonathan Dayton which instructed the delegates in Congress to oppose any proposition for yielding the navigation of the Mississippi. "We believe," read the instructions, "that the Value of the western Country, on the Sales of which we rely for the Discharge of our numerous Debts, is in some Degree dependant upon the free Navigation of this important River. The Cession of a disputed Right when once made, is not easily reclaimed. And whether the Court of Madrid asks or intends it for the Benefit of its own Subjects, or to barter with Britain, the Step will be equally imprudent, and the Inconvenience equally great." [34] This decisive utterance was heartening to the southern forces and discouraging to Secretary Jay,

---

[31] *Journals of the Continental Congress*, XXXI, pp. 575-76; Charles Thompson, Minutes of Proceedings in the Committee of the Whole, Aug. 18, 1786, Burnett, *Letters*, VIII, p. 439.

[32] James Monroe to James Madison, Sept. 12, 1786, S. M. Hamilton, ed., *The Writings of James Monroe* (New York, 1900), I, p. 169. Monroe remarked that Clark "put Hornblower in Congress & may turn him out . . ."

[33] Abraham Clark to James Madison, Nov. 23, 1786, Burnett, *Letters*, VIII, pp. 512-512n. Apparently John Cleves Symmes also brought the matter to the attention of the New Jersey legislature. James Monroe to James Madison, Oct. 7, 1786, *ibid.*, VIII, p. 476.

[34] *Votes and Proceedings*, 11-1, p. 75.

who prudently recognized the rise of popular opposition to his course and eventually decided to leave the whole problem to the new government under the Constitution.[35]

New Jersey diverged from the other northern states on this significant issue in part because, unlike most of them, it possessed no extensive foreign trade and had no public lands within its borders.[36] Consequently it was not greatly influenced by commercial considerations nor was it apprehensive about declining land values. It was, as has been stated before, concerned that the central government should derive a revenue from land sales. Moreover, both John Cleves Symmes and Jonathan Dayton, who played key roles in bringing about a clear definition of the official policy of the state, were personally attracted to the speculative opportunities in the West and appreciated the importance of the Mississippi question.

It became apparent after Congress opened the West to settlement that the extraordinary interest manifested by New Jersey in the fate of the western domain went beyond mere concern for the financial welfare of the Confederation or for the rights of the Indiana claimants. Land-hungry farmers and enterprising speculators alike were strongly attracted to the Ohio region by the promise of homes and fortunes. Ever since the end of the war, there had been a steady exodus of emigrants from the worn-out farms of the state to the frontiers of New York and Pennsylvania and to the vast trans-Allegheny country.[37] With the creation of

[35] James Madison to Thomas Jefferson, Feb. 11, 1787, Burnett, *Letters*, VIII, pp. 539-40; Bemis, *Pinckney's Treaty*, pp. 114-16.

[36] James Madison to Thomas Jefferson, Mar. 19, 1787, Madison to Governor Randolph, Apr. 2, 1787, Burnett, *Letters*, VIII, p. 570.

[37] W. F. Dunaway, "The English Settlers in Colonial Pennsylvania," *Pennsylvania Magazine of History and Biography*, LII (1928), p. 331; Morse, *Geography*, pp. 185-86; Minor Swick, "A Dutch Emigration from the Raritan Valley to New York State in 1785 and Later," *Somerset County Historical Quarterly*, IV (1915), pp. 21-25; "Letters of Phineas Bond," pp. 585, 642, 645; Memoir of Benjamin Van

the Northwest Territory, new impetus was given to the westward movement and capitalistic land companies were formed to solicit large grants from Congress.

As early as the spring of 1786, plans for the organization of a company of "adventurers into the western world," patterned after the recently formed Ohio Company of New England, were under discussion in New Jersey.[38] More than a year later, John Cleves Symmes after a trip to the Ohio region entered into negotiations with Congress for the purchase of a million-acre tract on the Miami River.[39] A former member of the legislature, Supreme Court justice, and delegate to Congress, Symmes possessed practical experience in public affairs and the daring and vision necessary to carry out his project. Allied with him in the enterprise were many of the most influential men in the state, including Elias Boudinot, Jonathan Dayton, General Elias Dayton, Matthias Ogden, Daniel Marsh (all of Elizabeth Town), Elisha Boudinot, and Joseph Bloomfield.[40] The grant secured, Symmes and his associates in November, 1787, advertised

Cleve, copied by M. S. Simpson, NYHS; Israel Shreve, "Journal from Jersey to the Monongahela," *Pennsylvania Magazine of History and Biography*, LII (1928), pp. 193-203; *New Jersey Gazette*, Apr. 18, 1785; *New Jersey Journal*, Mar. 19, 1788.

[38] "The Man at the Mast Head" (Morristown) in the *Political Intelligencer*, April 12, 1786, advised those who were interested in "promoting a respectable emigration from New-Jersey, into the country on the North-west of the river Ohio," to meet at the courthouses in each county and name committees to correspond with similar committees in other counties on a united plan of action. A meeting was actually held in Morris County in June, and another was planned in August. It is not improbable that this project was related to the subsequent activities of John Cleves Symmes, who resided in Morris County. *New Jersey Journal*, July 5, 1786.

[39] *Journals of the Continental Congress*, XXIII, pp. 509n, 512, 594.

[40] The best source for Symmes' Miami venture is Beverly W. Bond, ed., *The Correspondence of John Cleves Symmes* (New York, 1926). See also Charles H. Winfield, "Life and Public Services of John Cleves Symmes," *PNJHS*, 2nd Ser., V (1877), pp. 22-43.

the terms on which they would sell lands to prospective settlers, and appointed agents in all parts of the state to dispose
of warrants.[41] The proposals met with a ready response, particularly on the part of monied speculators in East Jersey,
and success seemed assured. Shares in the reserved lands on
the Great Miami River were eagerly bought up and, despite
complaints from some wary individuals about the purchase
terms, warrants were also in demand.[42] As soon as the first
installment had been paid on the Miami grant, Symmes,
who had been named one of the three judges of the Northwest Territory, prepared to lead an expedition to the region,
and on July 1, 1788, the emigrant caravan set forth from
Morristown.[43] Although financial difficulties subsequently

[41] Bond, *Correspondence*, pp. 7-11; *New Jersey Journal*, Sept. 5,
1787; "Avice au Public," Manuscripts D:53, NJHS. The roster of
Symmes' agents included many of the political and economic leaders
of the state, among whom were Joseph Bloomfield, Eli Elmer, Franklin
Davenport, Samuel Witham Stockton, Richard Stockton, Archibald
Mercer, Major William Lowrey, Thomas Anderson, Joseph Lewis,
Daniel Marsh, Elias Dayton, and John Burnet. *Brunswick Gazette*,
Jan. 8, 1788. It is noteworthy that a considerable number of those
interested in the Miami venture were Masons. McGregor, "Freema-
sonry," pp. 160-61.

[42] Bond, *Correspondence*, pp. 1-10; *New Jersey Journal*, Feb. 20,
Mar. 5, 12, 19, 1788; "Diary of Joseph Lewis," *PNJHS*, LXII
(1944), p. 40. The shareholders in the reserved lands (with the
shares each held) were:

Matthias Ogden	1	Timothy Jones	1
John N. Cummings	2	Thomas Kinney	1
Daniel Marsh	2	Daniel Tuttle	1
Elisha Boudinot	2	William Bradford	1
Matthias Denman	2	Daniel Symmes (?)	1
Silas Howell	1	Nathan Camp (?)	1
Dr. William Burnet	2	John Cleves Symmes	2 (?)
Israel Canfield	1	Elias Boudinot	2 (?)

"Copy of the original Account between the Proprietors of the Miami
reserved Township as settled by me by Virtue of a Power of Attorney
for that purpose from John Cleves Symmes, Esq.," Elias Boudinot's
ledger, pp. 102-103, NYPL.

[43] Burnett, *Continental Congress*, p. 659n; *New Jersey Journal*,
June 18, 1788.

arose and plagued Symmes until his death, his colony pros-
pered and grew.[44]

The Miami Associates were not alone in New Jersey in
seeking western land grants. The New Jersey Land Society,
prompted by George Morgan and composed mainly of residents of West Jersey, memorialized Congress in May, 1788,
for the right to purchase two million acres between the Mississippi and the River Au Vase on terms similar to those
which had been allowed to other companies.[45] The negotiations fell through, however, when the Treasury Board
recommended contractual arrangements that were wholly
unsatisfactory to the Society, which soon was dissolved.[46]
After meeting with failure in his dealings with Congress,
Morgan undertook to found a colony at New Madrid in the
Spanish Territory west of the Mississippi.[47] A group of men
from Elizabeth Town and vicinity, among whom were
Elias Boudinot and Jonathan Dayton, formed the East Jersey Company and contemplated buying two million acres
on the Little Miami River, but this project never progressed

[44] Winfield, "Symmes," pp. 30-42; Bond, *Correspondence, passim.*

[45] *Brunswick Gazette*, May 27, 1788; *Journals of the Continental
Congress*, XXIV, p. 152. For the memorial, dated May 1, 1788, and
other documents relating to the negotiations, see Papers of the Con-
tinental Congress, 41, VI, Manuscripts Division, LC. The signers of
the memorial were William, Cleayton, and Joseph Newbold, John
Cox, Joseph Bloomfield, Joel Gibbs, and Daniel Vardon of Burlington
County; Isaac Smith, Samuel W. Stockton, Aaron Dunham, and David
Brearly of Trenton; George Morgan, Richard Stockton, Frederick
Frelinghuysen, and Henry Vandike of Somerset County; Enist Van
Winkle of Spotswood, and William Edgar of New York City.

[46] *Journals of the Continental Congress*, XXXIV, pp. 213-17, 371-
73, 467-68, 525-26.

[47] Handbill of George Morgan, Oct. 3, 1788, Papers of the Continental Congress, 78, XVI, Manuscripts Division, LC; Israel Shreve
to John Phillips, Dec. 18, 1788, Dreer Collection, HSP; James Madison to John Brown, Jan. 21, 1789, Copy of original in possession of
John Scott Brown, Louisville, Ky., RŪL; A. P. Whitaker, *The Spanish
American Frontier: 1783-1795* (Boston, 1927), pp. 128, 158; Savelle,
Morgan, pp. 200-28.

beyond the embryonic state.[48] These several enterprises testify to the interest in the West that existed in New Jersey, and they help to explain the attitude of the state toward western problems as well as toward larger questions relating to the character of the central government. As citizens of a "landless" state, those individuals who were desirous of participating in speculation in western lands would naturally be averse to the disruption of the union, for only through the union could they be assured of the opportunity of sharing fully in the exploitation of the West.

CONTINENTAL FINANCES: IMPOST AND REQUISITIONS

In no field did the Confederation display its ineptitude more glaringly and disastrously than in that of finance. Although capable of incurring enormous debts, it lacked the ability to raise even a fraction of the money required to meet its mounting obligations. Its impotence can be attributed primarily to the fact that it was compelled to rely for its support on requisitions, which were inequitable in their incidence and impossible to collect. New Jersey was foremost in condemning this system and in urging that the Continental Congress should be empowered to levy duties on imports. Having little foreign trade of its own and paying large sums indirectly into the coffers of the customs houses of New York and Pennsylvania, the state would have much to gain and nothing to lose by the adoption of a continental impost. So convinced was New Jersey of the injustice of the operation of requisitions that it early resolved to withhold all financial contributions from the Confederation until the impost plan was accepted. In accordance with this conviction, it flatly refused to honor the requisition of 1785 and thereby precipitated a crisis which was an important link in the chain of events leading up to the drafting of the Constitution.

New Jersey first made the proposal that Congress should

[48] Bond, *Correspondence*, pp. 11, 26n.

have the power to tax imports and apply the revenues obtained to defray the common expenses of the Confederation when it stated its objections to the Articles in June, 1778.[49] The suggestion met a cool reception, and it was sidetracked for two years while Congress resorted to the dubious expedients of foreign and domestic loans and paper-money issues. In 1780, when it became evident that the continental currency had reached the limit of its usefulness and that financial reforms were imperative, Congress somewhat hesitantly toyed with the idea of levying an impost. After months of consideration and the usual series of committee reports, the delegates on February 3, 1781, took the momentous step of recommending that the states vest in Congress the power to levy a 5 per cent *ad valorem* duty on certain imported articles and on prize goods, the proceeds to be used to service the continental debt and pay for the war.[50] New Jersey's response to this request was prompt and unequivocal. On May 25, 1781, the legislature enacted a law granting to Congress all that it asked, and then waited hopefully for the other states to give their assent.[51] Eleven states acted affirmatively on the proposal, and for a while the prospects seemed encouraging, but the obstinate refusal of Rhode Island to fall in line blocked the measure.[52]

The impost plan gained in favor despite this initial setback, and it was revived and in a modified form was incorporated in the ingenious financial plan adopted by Congress on April 18,

[49] *Votes and Proceedings*, 2-2, pp. 143-46; *Journals of the Continental Congress*, XI, pp. 648-51.

[50] Burnett, *Continental Congress*, pp. 475-81; *Journals of the Continental Congress*, XIX, pp. 112-13. John Witherspoon of New Jersey had moved that Congress should be vested with the power of "superintending the commercial relations of every state" and also with the exclusive right to lay duties on all imported articles with the consent of nine states. His extreme proposal, however, received little support. *Ibid.*, XIX, p. 110.

[51] Wilson, *Acts*, Act of May 25, 1781, pp. 191-92.

[52] Burnett, *Continental Congress*, pp. 530-33.

1783.[53] The consent of all the states for this, as well as for the other elements in the plan, was required before the impost could become effective. Again New Jersey was quick to express her approval in June, 1783.[54] When it seemed likely that unanimous agreement on the measure would not be forthcoming, the legislature, "desirous of promoting the said Mode of Revenue, which they conceive[d] so essentially necessary for the Good of the Union," passed a supplementary act authorizing Congress to institute the duties whenever eleven states should approve.[55] Months lengthened into years, however, and Congress waited in vain for thirteen states to agree to the augmentation of its powers. At the beginning of 1786, only eight had complied and two—New York and Georgia—had rejected the proposal.[56] Five years had gone by since the impost idea had first been broached officially and still the Confederation remained wholly dependent on requisitions, a mode of raising revenue which had been demonstrated to be entirely inadequate.

New Jersey in the meantime had decided to remain financially aloof from the Confederation until Congress should be empowered to lay duties on imports. This policy actually was adopted in December, 1783, and was explicitly affirmed on December 23, 1784.[57] The full significance of this attitude was

[53] *Journals of the Continental Congress*, XXIV, pp. 257-61. See above, pp. 176-77. The proposal was that specific duties should be placed on a selected list of articles and 5 per cent *ad valorem* duties on all others for a period of twenty-five years. The proceeds were to be applied only toward discharging the interest and principal on the public debt. Customs collectors would be appointed by the states but would be amenable to and removable by Congress.

[54] *Votes and Proceedings*, 7-2, p. 130; *Journal of Council*, 7-2, p. 52; Wilson, *Acts*, Act of June 11, 1783, pp. 329-30. By the same law, all the ports in the state were declared free pending the adoption of the impost.

[55] *Session Laws*, 9-1, Act of Dec. 23, 1784.

[56] *Journals of the Continental Congress*, XXX, pp. 7-8.

[57] See above, pp. 177-78.

not immediately apparent, for between October, 1782, and September, 1785, Congress issued no new requisitions, although in April, 1784, it did call upon the states to complete payments on half of the eight-million-dollar requisition that had been submitted in October, 1781.[58] Early in 1785, however, Congress felt compelled to resort once more to a plea for funds, ". . . the Idea of an Impost for Foederal purposes, seems almost wholly Extinguished," sadly commented one of the New Jersey delegates, "& the Mode of raising Money by Requisition & for quotaing the National Debt, may continue for some years to come."[59] "We stand like Tantalus to our Chin in water, and are notwithstanding perishing with thirst," lamented another. "But perhaps, as it often happens, these Difficulties will bring us sooner into the proper Systems and Forms of political Administration . . ."[60] His forecast was soon to be realized. On September 27, 1785, Congress authorized a requisition for three million dollars, one-third of which was payable in specie and the remainder in indents, that is, certificates given for the interest due on the liquidated and loan-office debts. The interest certificates were not to be issued unless a state complied fully with the requisition. Moreover, interest payments made by any state on its own account after January 1, 1786, were not to be credited as a future charge against the United States. New Jersey's quota was $166,716.[61] The requisition came before the legislature early in November and, on the motion of Abraham Clark, was referred to the next sitting.

In a highly important letter to two of New Jersey's dele-

[58] Bolles, *Financial History*, pp. 307-23; *Journals of the Continental Congress*, XXVI, pp. 301-309, 312-14.

[59] John Beatty to William Livingston, Apr. 13, 1785, Livingston Papers, MHS.

[60] William C. Houston to William Livingston, Feb. 17, 1785, Livingston Papers, MHS.

[61] *Journals of the Continental Congress*, XXIX, pp. 765-71. See above, pp. 208-209.

gates in Congress, Clark set forth in detail "Several weighty objections" to the requisition.[62]

> First [he began] It is either a designed Scheme to Supercede the Necessity of a general Impost, or if not designed, will Assuredly have that effect...I am fully persuaded this Scheme is by some intended to give a final Stab to the impost, tho' not long since it was the General opinion, not only of Congress, but all cool and considerate Men, that an impost was the only practicable means of procuring money to pay the Interest of our foreign Debt, and that it is the most easy and equitable mode of raising a revenue; but now, contrary to the experience of all Nations, we are to Obtain the Necessary supplies only by Taxation...New York and Pennsylvania can raise their Quota of specie by State imposts, to which our Citizens by trading with them will contribute as much as theirs in proportion to their Numbers, and after all will have the full Quota of this state to pay besides: This is a burden too unequal and grievous for this State to submit to.

Next, Clark contended that the quota assigned to the state was too high, but subsequently he retracted this charge.[63] In the third place, he pointed out that interest certificates given on commutation notes would be indistinguishable from any others, and that New Jersey had repeatedly refused to acknowledge any obligation to contribute toward the payment of such notes. His fourth objection was to the prohibition laid on the issuance of interest certificates in any state that declined to comply with the requisition. This would be an unjust discrimination among public creditors. "They [the creditors] Loaned their money in their private Capacity to Congress," he insisted, "it was then of no Consequences where

[62] Abraham Clark to John Cleves Symmes and Josiah Hornblower, Dec. 9, 1785, Miscellaneous Manuscripts, RUL. Symmes and Hornblower were told to make whatever use they thought proper of the letter.

[63] "A Fellow Citizen" [Abraham Clark], *Political Intelligencer*, Feb. 8, 1786.

he resided ... It was no Stipulation in the contract that they were to be paid only in Case the Legislature of the State where they resided should in all cases follow the dictates of Congress..." Finally, he condemned the provision that no state was to be given credit for interest payments made to its own continental creditors after January 1, 1786. New Jersey, it will be recalled, had provided for such payments in its "revenue act" of December 20, 1783. "For this Voluntary Act to support the Credit of the United States and give relief to their Suffering Creditors in preference to our own [state creditors], what do we get?—the thanks of Congress?—No,— but their Severe *threats* in case we do the like in the future." Furthermore, he claimed, New Jersey's method of satisfying the public creditors was a sounder one than that proposed by Congress. Thus, more was behind New Jersey's refusal to honor the requisition of 1785 than mere anger at the tariff policies of New York. New Jersey's views on the impost question long antedated the erection of tariff walls by New York and Pennsylvania. Rather, the state had deep-seated grievances against the unfair and inadequate financial policies pursued by the Continental Congress, and the strong conviction that only with revenues derived from import duties could the Confederation equitably meet its obligations.

There was some sentiment within the state in favor of honoring the requisitions. When he learned that petitions calling upon the legislature to respond to the plea of Congress were being circulated, Clark aired his opinions in the press.[64] In reply, "Candidus" and "Federal" presented opposing arguments.[65] Pointing to the fact that New Jersey held a disproportionately large share of the public debt and would therefore receive a surplus of indents over and above the amount called for to meet the two-thirds of the requisition, they rea-

[64] "A Fellow Citizen" [Abraham Clark], *Political Intelligencer*, Jan. 11, 1786.
[65] *Political Intelligencer*, Feb. 1, 1786.

soned that it was decidedly to the advantage of the state to accept the proposition. The surplus indents could be sold in those states which lacked enough of them to fill their quotas, and the public creditors would thereby reap a return on their holdings. William Paterson approved of the measure because it would have a "direct Tendency to promote an *equal* Diffusion of Certificates through the Confederation." "The more the Interests of the States are intertwined," he believed, "the more close and perfect will be their Union; the more sure and permanent will be the Basis of national Credit & Honor. It is generally supposed, that New Jersey has a surplus of Certificates; and therefore it is emphatically the Interest of New Jersey to adopt the Resolution..." [66]

When the legislature convened in special session on February 15, 1786, it took time out from its debate over the loan-office bill to consider what action should be taken on the controversial requisition. On February 20, by a vote of thirty-two to three, the Assembly adopted a resolution prepared by Abraham Clark which decided the fate of the measure. A lengthy preamble recited the customary grievances of the state in terms similar to those employed by Clark in his letter of December 9. Essentially the resolution was a plea for the adoption of a continental impost. In conclusion it was

> *Resolved,* That this House cannot, consistent with the Duty they owe to their constituents, comply with the Requisition of Congress of the 27th of September last in the Mode therein directed, or agreeable to the Spirit thereof, or any other of a similar Nature requiring Specie, until all the States in the Union shall comply with the Requisition of April 1783 for an Impost and Revenue; or at least until the several States, having the Advantage of Commerce which they now enjoy solely from the joint Exertions of the United States, shall forbear exacting Duties or Imposts upon Goods and

[66] William Paterson, Draft of petition, [May, 1786], Paterson Papers (Bancroft Transcripts), NYPL.

Merchandise for the particular Benefit of their respective States, thereby drawing Revenues from other States whose local Situations and Circumstances will not admit their enjoying similar advantages from Commerce.[67]

Two weeks later both houses of the legislature approved a set of instructions to the state's delegates in Congress which had also been drafted by Abraham Clark. The belief was expressed that "neither Publick Credit...[could] be supported, the Publick Debts paid, or the Existence of the Union maintained, without the Impost-Revenue..." Accordingly the delegates were ordered to vote against any resolution that would produce any expense to New Jersey "for the Promotion or Security of the Commerce of these States, or any of them, from which neither the Union in general, nor this State in particular, derives any Advantage, until all the States shall effectually and substantially adopt and carry into Execution the Impost above mentioned." [68]

New Jersey's defiant refusal of the requisition was a great shock to Congress and deepened the pessimism which had come to dominate its deliberations. Several delegates feared that the action would have serious consequences. Nathaniel Gorham of Massachusetts, although he conceded that the state had grounds for complaint against its neighbors, characterized the refusal as "unjustifiable" and predicted that it might "work the end of all foederal Government." [69] John Beatty regarded the resolution as "extremely reprehensible" and thought it would tend "to the dissolving of a Union

---

[67] *Votes and Proceedings*, 10-2, pp. 12-13. The three men in the negative were Sinnickson (Salem), Swain (Cape May), and Whilden (Cumberland). The Council was not called to act in the matter. On February 22, it was resolved to resume the payment of interest to continental creditors in the state. *Ibid.*, 10-2, p. 17.

[68] *Ibid.*, 10-2, pp. 29-30, 34.

[69] Gorham to James Warren, Mar. 6, 1786, Burnett, *Letters*, VIII, p. 318. At the same time, Massachusetts had not complied with the requisition. Burnett, *Continental Congress*, p. 645.

already too feebly united." [70] Henry Lee of Virginia struck a different note. "Perhaps this intemperance in Jersey," he wrote to Washington, "may bring this state [New York] to acquiesce in a system of finance long ago approved by ten states and whose operation might have saved the difficultys which impend over the union." [71] James Monroe took some small comfort from the fact that the resolution was not an "express Act of Legislature, but merely the negative of a proposition to comply with the requisition in the branch with whom it sho[ul]d originate." [72] So concerned was Congress over the matter, that it appointed a three-man committee, composed of Charles Pinckney, Nathaniel Gorham, and William Grayson, to seek an audience with the New Jersey legislature "and represent to them, in the strongest terms, the fatal Consequences that must inevitably result to the said State, as well as to the rest of the Union, from their refusal to comply with the requisition of Congress of September, 1785." [73]

Armed with numerous documents that were intended to impress the lawmakers with the serious financial plight of the Confederation, the committee appeared before the legislature on March 13 to plead its case. [74] Charles Pinckney made the principal address. Although he attempted to answer point by point the objections on which New Jersey had based

[70] William A. Nelson, "Josiah Hornblower and the First Steam Engine in America," *PNJHS*, 2nd Ser., VII (1883), pp. 218-19.

[71] Lee to George Washington, Mar. 2, 1786, Burnett, *Letters*, VIII, p. 315.

[72] Monroe to James Madison, Mar. 19, 1786, Hamilton, ed., *Writings*, I, p. 124.

[73] *Journals of the Continental Congress*, pp. 95-97; Board of Treasury to Governor Livingston, Feb. 28, 1786; Charles Pinckney, Nathaniel Gorham, and William Grayson to Livingston, Mar. 12, 1786, Livingston Papers, MHS.

[74] Secretary of Congress to Pinckney, Gorham, and Grayson, Mar. 7, 1786, Burnett, *Letters*, VIII, p. 319; *Votes and Proceedings*, 10-2, pp. 49-50; *New Jersey Gazette*, Mar. 13, 1786.

its refusal, he stressed above all the necessity of preserving the union, and cautioned his listeners that small states would have much more to fear from disunion than large ones. He threw out the pregnant suggestion that if the state believed that the powers of the central government were inadequate, it ought immediately to instruct its delegates in Congress "to urge the calling of a general convention of the states, for the purpose of amending and revising the federal system." Pinckney declared himself ready to support such a move. In conclusion, he asked the members to rescind their resolution of February 20. "If they should not," he inquired, "in what other light can the united states view their conduct, than that of a breach of the confederation, and a solemn recession of this state from its union and protection..." [75] Pinckney was followed by Grayson, who warned that a new confederation would not accord the lesser states the position of equality that they then enjoyed. [76]

It now remained for the Assembly to decide whether or not it would heed the plea of the committee. On March 14, Abraham Clark indicated that he for one had not been moved to revise his opinions, for he offered a resolution restating New Jersey's grievances and reaffirming the inability of the state to comply with the requisition. [77] Three days later Thomas Clark of Gloucester proposed a substitute resolution which declared that notwithstanding the inequitable features of the requisition, the house was "willing to remove as far as in their power every Embarassment from the Counsels of the Union," and that the resolution of February 20 was rescinded. This motion was adopted without a record vote. [78] The capitulation was more one of form than of substance,

[75] Burnett, *Letters*, VIII, pp. 323-29; *American Museum*, II (1787), pp. 153-60; *Political Intelligencer*, Mar. 22, 1786.

[76] Burnett, *Letters*, VIII, pp. 329-30.

[77] *Votes and Proceedings*, 10-2, p. 57.

[78] *Ibid.*, 10-2, p. 66; *Journals of the Continental Congress*, XXX, p. 122.

however, for the Assembly took no steps whatsoever to fill the requisition, nor did it make any effort to raise funds in obedience to subsequent calls from Congress.[79] The policy of not contributing to the financial support of the Confederation, adopted in 1783, was never altered or abandoned.

New Jersey's refusal to comply with the requisition of 1785, coming at the time that it did, dealt the Confederation one of the worst blows it had yet received and raised widespread doubts about the future of the union. That the Confederation was at the end of its financial tether was apparent to all. Of the three million dollars which Congress had sought in September, 1785, less than a hundred thousand had been collected a year later.[80] In June, 1786, the Board of Treasury made the realistic report that there was "no reasonable hope" that the sums requisitioned would be forthcoming and flatly asserted that only the impost-revenue plan of April 18, 1783, could save the nation from bankruptcy.[81] To men like James Madison, the New Jersey episode taught a "salutary lesson." "Is it possible with such an example before our eyes of impotency in the federal system," he asked James Monroe, "to remain skeptical with regard to the necessity of infusing more energy into it?" Soon, he maintained, it must be decided whether the union was worth preserving.[82] William Grayson, on his return to Congress from his mission to New Jersey, noticed that there were "serious

[79] *Votes and Proceedings*, 10-2, p. 74; *ibid.*, 11-1, pp. 30-32, 63; *ibid.*, 12-2, pp. 9-10. On November 24, 1786, the legislature directed the delegates in Congress to be ruled by the instructions that had been adopted on March 2, and to point out to Congress the inability of the state to comply with its requisitions "so long as that Justice which we have long and loudly called for is denied us, and those unsisterly Oppressions against which we have hitherto unavailingly complained and remonstrated, are continued and increased."

[80] *Journals of the Continental Congress*, XXI, pp. 747-51.

[81] *Ibid.*, XXX, pp. 359-66. Not a single state complied with a requisition adopted in 1786. Burnett, *Continental Congress*, p. 689.

[82] Madison to Monroe, Apr. 9, 1786, Hunt, ed., *Writings*, II, p. 235.

thoughts in the minds of some of the Members of Congress to recommend to the States the meeting of a general Convention to consider an alteration of the Confederation..." [83] Doubtless his recent experiences influenced Charles Pinckney when in May he proposed that Congress should go into the committee of the whole on the state of the nation, a proposal which resulted two months later in the appointment of a grand committee to report such amendments to the Articles as would "render the federal government adequate to the ends for which it was instituted." [84]

THE SEAT OF CONGRESS

The question of the location of the permanent seat of the central government was another Confederation matter in which New Jersey had a particularly strong interest. A willing host to the perambulatory Continental Congress for two brief periods, the state cherished the justifiable hope that a site within its boundaries might be chosen as the capital of the new nation. It seemed for a time that this ambition would indeed be realized, but shifting sectional alignments within Congress prevented any conclusive determination of the issue, which was still undecided at the time of the adoption of the Federal Constitution.

It was as a result of the mutinous threats of a body of discontented soldiery that Congress in June, 1783, prudently removed from Philadelphia to Princeton. There, in makeshift accommodations provided by the hospitable inhabitants, the delegates remained from June 26 to November 3, holding their sessions in the library room of the college.[85] During

[83] Grayson to James Madison, Mar. 22, 1786, Burnett, *Letters*, VIII, p. 333.

[84] Burnett, *Continental Congress*, pp. 647, 663; *Journals of the Continental Congress*, XXX, p. 387n. For the report of the grand committee, see *ibid.*, XXXI, pp. 494-98.

[85] The story of Congress' residence at Princeton is related in abundant detail in Varnum Lansing Collins, *The Continental Congress at Princeton* (Princeton, 1908).

their residence in the small town, they received the welcome news of the signing of the definitive treaty with England, consulted with General Washington on the organization of the peacetime army, gave a formal reception to the newly arrived Dutch Ambassador, and debated at length where they should next take up their abode. They were ill-disposed to return to Philadelphia, the scene of their recent humiliation, and Princeton, although possessing many charms, lacked the facilities to house all the agencies of the government.

Congress was scarcely a popular body, but many states vied with one another for the honor of providing it with a home. The capital city would acquire a measure of prestige and would also be considerably enriched.[86] Furthermore, the location of the capital was expected to have an important bearing upon the relative weight of the principal sectional groups in the national scale. New Jersey was not hesitant in setting forth its pretensions. Even before the military disturbances in the Quaker City had come to a head, the citizens of the western part of Nottingham township in Burlington County had expressed their "hearty and sincere Desire" to place themselves under the jurisdiction of Congress.[87] At about the same time the legislature made a generous offer to cede control over twenty square miles of land and to give thirty thousand pounds in specie to Congress.[88] Subsequently Trenton, Princeton, New Brunswick, and Elizabeth Town extended warm invitations to Congress, and pointedly assured that "August Body" of protection against any insults or in-

[86] *Ibid.*, p. 167. Congress' presence in Philadelphia was estimated to be worth a hundred thousand dollars a year to that city; President Boudinot gave to one merchant a thousand dollars worth of business a month while at Princeton.

[87] Resolutions adopted by freeholders and inhabitants of the western part of Nottingham township, June 15, 1783, Papers of the Continental Congress, 46, Manuscripts Division, LC.

[88] *Votes and Proceedings*, 7-2, p. 147. This action was taken on June 18, 1783. The Philadelphia disturbances did not get under way until June 19.

dignities. Similar bids were made by towns in New York, Pennsylvania, Maryland, and Virginia.[89]

Congress had great difficulty in choosing among its many suitors. At last it decided on October 7 that the future capitol should be erected near the falls of the Delaware River.[90] Many members were influenced in their choice by the consideration that it would be best to give the honor to a small state, which could not "extend a dangerous influence into the public counsels." [91] The southern delegates were not pleased with the selection of the Delaware site, and on October 20— when Pennsylvania, New Jersey, and Delaware were temporarily unrepresented—they pushed through a vote in favor of having *two* capitals, one on the Delaware and the other on the Potomac. Until the buildings were completed, Congress would meet alternately in Annapolis and Trenton.[92] "I augur great evil from this measure," commented President Elias Boudinot, "and cannot help thinking of Rome and Constantinople." [93] The erratic David Howell of Rhode Island, on the other hand, saw great virtue in the unusual arrangement. "A perambulatory Congress," wrote the representative of the "otherwise-minded" state, "favors

[89] These invitations are preserved in the Papers of the Continental Congress, 46 (Proposals to Congress relative to locating the seat of government, 1783-1785), Manuscripts Division, LC.

[90] *Journals of the Continental Congress*, XXV, pp. 649-54, 657. The northern states, through Delaware, favored this decision. Maryland, Virginia, North Carolina, and South Carolina were opposed.

[91] David Howell to Thomas C. Hazard, Aug. 26, 1783, Burnett, *Letters*, VIII, p. 841.

[92] *Journals of the Continental Congress*, XXV, pp. 712-14. This maneuver was effected by a combination of New England delegations in co-operation with those of the South. Elbridge Gerry of Massachusetts is credited with having originated the two-capital idea to preserve harmony in the union. Massachusetts Delegates to Massachusetts Assembly, Oct. 23, 1783. Burnett, *Letters*, VII, p. 350. See also *ibid.*, VII, pp. 326, 331-32, 333, 373-74, 422n.

[93] Boudinot to R. R. Livingston, Oct. 23, 1786, *ibid.*, VII, p. 347.

republicanism—a permanent one tends to concentrate power, Aristocracy and Monarchy." [94]

After leaving Princeton, the delegates journeyed to Annapolis for a brief session, at the conclusion of which it was resolved to convene next in Trenton on October 30, 1784.[95] The New Jersey legislature in preparation for the event appropriated three hundred pounds to be used in refurnishing Jacob Bergen's "French Arms" tavern as a meeting place for Congress and in renovating the house of Stacy Potts as a residence for the President.[96] The congressmen were slow in coming together; not until November 29 were seven states represented. As soon as they had become settled, they decided in favor of an early removal, in part because they found many of the desirable accommodations taken up by members of the state legislature, which was then in session.[97] But they remained in town long enough to come to some important decisions respecting the location of a capital.

On December 20 they resolved to appropriate a hundred thousand dollars for the erection of federal buildings at not more than one place.[98] Three days later they took the additional steps of specifying that the federal town should be situated near the falls of the Delaware and of authorizing the appointment of commissioners to select the exact site and to enter into contracts for the construction of the necessary buildings. New York City, in the meantime, was to be the

[94] Howell to Governor William Greene, Dec. 24, 1783, *ibid.*, VII, p. 397.

[95] *Journals of the Continental Congress*, XXVI, p. 295.

[96] *Votes and Proceedings*, 8-2, p. 129. The details of the physical arrangements made for Congress' stay in Trenton may be gleaned from the bound volume of Continental Congress Papers in the New Jersey State Library.

[97] Burnett, *Continental Congress*, pp. 615-16; James Monroe to Governor Patrick Henry, Jan. 1, 1785, Burnett, *Letters*, VIII, p. 1.

[98] *Journals of the Continental Congress*, XXVI, p. 693.

temporary capital.[99] Seemingly the issue had been definitely settled. This impression was strengthened when in February, 1785, the commissioners were named.[100] Under the calm surface of Congressional harmony, however, treacherous crosscurrents, which were destined to wreck New Jersey's hopes, were developing. Virginia and Maryland had not abandoned their campaigns in behalf of Georgetown and Annapolis, respectively. Too, the parsimonious New Englanders began to have some misgivings about paying the costs of the project.[101] These dissident elements devoted their energies to having the appropriation item for the capital deleted from the requisition of 1785, and after several months of wrangling, they achieved their objective.[102] Thus the whole enterprise was brought to a standstill, where it remained for over two years.

The ratification of the Constitution by the ninth state, New Hampshire, on June 21, 1788, was the signal for the start of a bitter debate in Congress over the place where the new government should inaugurate its career. Philadelphia and New York were the leading competitors, but innumerable votes taken over a period of ten weeks found Congress so hopelessly at odds that no majority could be mustered for either.[103] Meanwhile the ordinance for putting the federal system into operation was delayed. One factor that accounted in part for the postponement of a prompt decision was the uncertainty of

[99] *Ibid.*, XXVII, p. 704. The Virginia delegates were mortified when their southern colleagues, contrary to their former inclinations, gave their support to the Delaware site. They explained that the "Southern gentlemen" had decided that when they left their native states, they wanted to go to a northern clime. Virginia Delegation to Governor Patrick Henry, Feb. 13, 1785, Burnett, *Letters*, VIII, p. 35.

[100] *Journals of the Continental Congress*, XXVIII, pp. 55, 58.

[101] Burnett, *Letters*, VIII, pp. 1, 16, 18, 26, 28, 29, 30, 47, 195.

[102] *Journals of the Continental Congress*, XXIX, pp. 734-45; Burnett, *Letters*, VIII, pp. 110, 110n.

[103] *Journals of the Continental Congress*, XXXIV, *passim*; Burnett, *Continental Congress*, pp. 712-19.

New York's stand on ratification.[104] New Jersey was divided over the question of which of its neighbors it should favor. It had by no means relinquished the hope that the national capital might eventually be established within its borders. The convention that assembled in December, 1787, to ratify the Constitution had recommended that the state should cede a tract ten miles square to the federal government for such a purpose.[105] The Continental Congress, however, could not designate a permanent site, and New Jersey was therefore presented with a choice between New York and Philadelphia as alternative temporary locations.

Abraham Clark was convinced that it would be sound strategy to designate New York as the first meeting place of the new government. He pointed out to Governor Livingston that "a removal to Philad[elphia] would be losing all Chance of having the permanent seat of Government fixed near the falls of the Delaware as formerly agreed to, which is an Object New Jersey ought not to lose sight of so long as

---

[104] Abraham Clark elaborated on this factor in a letter to Governor Livingston on August 26, 1789 (Livingston Papers, MHS). "The matter was taken up in Congress as soon as nine States had ratified," he explained, "but the Convention of New York being then sitting, in which two thirds of the members were opposed to the New Constitution, it was thought unadvisable to proceed in the business at that time . . . but the place of meeting was purposely delayed untill the New York Convention should come to some final determination: two reasons induced Congress to this delay, first that New York could not be fixed upon as the place unless they ratified; Secondly, to appoint any other place while they were deliberating would, in all probability, insure a final rejection, to prevent which it was suffered to pass as a very probable event, if not as a matter of Certainty, that in case they did adopt, New York would be the place of meeting;—this perhaps was one principle cause of their adopting, and without their being led into this opinion I believe they would have rejected the Constitution." See also, Spaulding, *New York*, pp. 270-71.

[105] *Minutes of the Convention of the State of New Jersey . . .*, reprinted by C. L. Traver (Trenton, 1888), p. 29.

a probable chance remains." [106] This viewpoint was not shared by many in West Jersey who felt a close tie with Philadelphia.[107] When the controversy within Congress was at its height, the legislature met in special session, principally to prepare for the election of Congressmen and presidential electors, and found itself subjected to pressure from forces favorable to one or the other of the two chief competing cities.

Alexander Hamilton, fearful of the possibility that the New Jersey delegates might be placed under instructions to vote for Philadelphia, sought to forestall such action by making a direct appeal to Governor Livingston. Advancing the same arguments that had been employed by Abraham Clark, he declared that there was "not a State in the Union so much interested in having the temporary residence at New York, as New Jersey," and warned the Governor not to "fall into the snares of Pennsylvania." [108] The wealthy New York merchant and banker, Nicholas Low, engaged Abraham Ogden of Newark as a lobbyist in behalf of New York. Ogden wrote to all his acquaintances who had influence with the legislature. "Their united Efforts, I hope," he informed Low, "have been abundantly sufficient to defeat the Schemes of the Pennsylvanians. Mr. Boudinot & many others of the Eastern Gentlemen," he added, "have enter'd very heartily into the

[106] Abraham Clark to Governor Livingston, Aug. 26, 1788, Livingston Papers, MHS. Clark reasoned that if Philadelphia was chosen, the capital would never move to the northward of that city but that it might move south from New York.

[107] Abraham Ogden to Nicholas Low, Sept. 6, 1788, Miscellaneous Manuscripts, RUL. One of New Jersey's delegates in Congress was Jonathan Elmer of Cumberland County. Elmer consistently voted contrary to Clark and Dayton, both of whom were from Essex County, on the capital-site question. *Journals of the Continental Congress*, XXXIV, pp. 359, 368, 384, 399, 400. Elmer left Congress around August 14, 1788, before the matter was finally decided. Burnett, *Letters*, VIII, p. xc.

[108] Alexander Hamilton to Governor Livingston, Aug. 29, 1788, *The Works of Alexander Hamilton...*, edited by John C. Hamilton (7 vols., New York, 1850-1851), I, p. 472.

Interests of New York." [109] Perhaps as a consequence of these machinations, the legislature issued no instructions to the state's delegates, who were clearly on record in favor of New York. Instead, an act was passed offering land to Congress for a federal district.[110] A few days later, on September 13, Congress finally broke the long-standing deadlock and resolved that the new government should be launched in New York.[111] This decision was particularly welcome to East Jersey, and it was generally regarded as leaving the way clear for an eventual location on the Delaware.[112] In all probability the hope of becoming host to the national government played some part in influencing New Jersey's attitude toward the union. Certainly the fact that the ratifying convention took special notice of the matter indicates that it was regarded as of some importance. Placed in its proper perspective, it was one of the several factors which made New Jersey strongly federalist.[113]

[109] Abraham Ogden to Nicholas Low, Sept. 6, 1788, Miscellaneous Manuscripts, RUL.

[110] *Votes and Proceedings*, 12-2, pp. 30, 32; *Session Laws*, 12-2, Act of Sept. 9, 1788. The action was unanimous in both houses.

[111] *Journals of the Continental Congress*, XXIV, p. 523. The New Jersey delegates supported this resolution.

[112] James Madison to George Washington, Sept. 14, 1788, Burnett, *Letters*, VIII, p. 795.

[113] One student has concluded that "it was the hope of New Jersey's securing the site of the Federal capital which perhaps more than anything else hastened its ratification of the Constitution." Jay S. Morris, "New Jersey and the Federal Constitution," typescript M.A. thesis (Columbia, 1931), p. 67. This is an exaggeration.

X

New Jersey and the Constitution

★★★

LONG aware of the necessity of strengthening the central government, New Jersey acted wholly in character in supporting the movement for a revision of the Articles of Confederation. The state had repeatedly evidenced its intense dissatisfaction with the Confederation and had as often indicated its willingness to grant important powers to Congress. Only through changes in the existing system could it hope to obtain the redress of the financial and commercial grievances of which it complained and to which it attributed a large share of its economic difficulties. One influential segment of the population had an additional reason for desiring a reconstituted union. This was the group that had become convinced as a result of the recent experiences with paper-money and debtor laws that the rule of the majority, if not somehow checked, would destroy all property rights and lead to "democratical license." What was wanted, therefore, was the imposition of external restraints upon the unlimited powers of the state government. Finally, there was the widespread belief that unless the states devised some means of ordering their general affairs, a promising experiment in republicanism—launched after an heroic war—would eventuate in failure.

THE ANNAPOLIS CONVENTION

Proposals for overhauling the Articles of Confederation had been made from time to time ever since 1779, but it was the Annapolis Convention, in which New Jersey played a significant role, that gave the final impetus to constitutional reform.[1] It was shortly after the Assembly had proclaimed its refusal to comply with the requisition of 1785 that Governor Livingston received from the Governor of Virginia the request that New Jersey send representatives to Annapolis to discuss with delegates from other states the implementation of Congress' power over trade.[2] The Governor promptly transmitted the invitation to the legislature, which lost no time in acting favorably upon it. Three commissioners —Abraham Clark, William Churchill Houston, and James Schureman—were appointed by the joint meeting and were authorized

> to take into Consideration the Trade of the United States; to examine the relative Situation and Trade of the said States, to consider how far an uniform System in their commercial Regulations *and other important Matters* may be necessary to their common Interest and permanent Harmony; and to report to the several States Such an Act relative to this grand Object, as when unanimously ratified by them will enable the United States in Congress assembled effectually to provide for the Exigencies of the Union ...[3]

[1] Burnett, *Continental Congress*, pp. 487, 507, 509, 614-15, 663-64.

[2] Governor Edmund Randolph to Governor Livingston, Feb. 19, 1786, Manuscript Collection, NJSL. At the instance of James Madison, the Virginia legislature had approved the calling of the convention on January 21, 1786. *Documents Illustrative of the Formation of the Union of the American States*, selected by Charles C. Tansill (Washington, D. C., 1927), p. 38.

[3] *Minutes of the Joint-Meeting*, Mar. 21, 1786; *Votes and Proceedings*, 10-2, pp. 72, 76. Italics supplied. The instructions, drafted by

The ambiguous phrase, "other important Matters," gave the commissioners the widest possible latitude and implied the hope that the convention would not restrict itself to its announced purpose. New Jersey, for one, was prepared to consider any suggestions for renovating the union.

That the state should have heartily endorsed the objectives of the Annapolis Convention is not surprising. In its "Representation" of 1778 it had recommended that "the sole and exclusive power of regulating the trade of the United States with foreign nations ought to be clearly vested in Congress." [4] Subsequently, when Congress sought limited powers to regulate commerce, New Jersey readily gave its assent.[5] It is equally understandable that the state should have indicated its interest in "other important Matters," for it had, perhaps more than any other member of the Confederation, abundant reasons for being discontented with the *status quo*.

With but five states represented, the convention met on September 11, 1786, and soon came to the conclusion that it could, under the circumstances, accomplish nothing.[6] The delegates were inspired, however, to propose in the report that they made to their legislatures that a second convention should be called. Moreover, they expressed their opinion "that the Idea of extending the powers of their deputies to other objects than those of Commerce, which has been adopted by the State of New Jersey, was an improvement on the original plan, and will deserve to be incorporated into

Sinnickson of Salem and R. S. Smith of Burlington, were approved unanimously.

[4] *Ibid.*, 2-2, pp. 143-48.

[5] *Journals of the Continental Congress*, XXVI, pp. 331-32; *Session Laws*, 10-1, Act of Nov. 26, 1785. See also *Votes and Proceedings*, 8-1, pp. 89-90; *Session Laws*, 9-1, Act of Nov. 4, 1784.

[6] The *New Jersey Gazette* on September 18, 1786, printed an extract of a letter from one of the Annapolis delegates, who stated it was improbable much could be done without at least six states in attendance.

that of a future Convention." Accordingly they recommended that a convention be held at Philadelphia the following May to consider such provisions as would "render the constitution of the Federal Government adequate to the exigencies of the Union." [7] After considerable hesitation, Congress on February 21, 1787, placed its qualified stamp of approval on the convention, at the same time limiting its function to the "sole and express purpose of revising the Articles of Confederation." [8] The "New Jersey Idea," emerging from the words, "other important Matters," had become the bridge between Annapolis and Philadelphia.[9]

THE CONSTITUTIONAL CONVENTION

New Jersey, having taken the lead in indicating the road to constitutional revision, was the first state to appoint delegates to the projected Philadelphia convention.[10] On November 23, 1786, the legislature in joint meeting elected David Brearly, William Paterson, William Churchill Houston, and John Neilson "to meet the Commissioners of the other States at Philadelphia, in May next on Commercial and other Matters." [11] Some months later, after Neilson had declined to

[7] *Journals of the Continental Congress*, XXXI, pp. 677-80. The term, "exigencies of the Union," had been employed in New Jersey's instructions to its delegates. It was not used in the original Virginia resolution.

[8] *Ibid.*, XXXII, pp. 73-74.

[9] Austin Scott, with his flair for picturesque metaphor, wrote that "when the States caught step on their final march to the Constitution, New Jersey whistled the tune." "The Share of New Jersey in Founding the American Constitution," *New Brunswick Historical Club Publications*, No. 1 (New Brunswick, 1887), p. 18.

[10] Virginia's legislature authorized the appointment of delegates on October 16, 1786, but the delegates were not named until December 4. The New Jersey delegates were appointed on November 23. *The Records of the Federal Convention of 1787*, edited by Max Farrand (3 vols., New Haven, 1911), III, pp. 559-63.

[11] *Minutes of the Joint-Meeting*, Nov. 23, 1786. On the following day the legislature by joint resolution defined the powers of the

serve and when it appeared likely that Houston's health would prevent his attendance, Governor William Livingston and Abraham Clark were added to the delegation.[12] Clark, who was then in Congress, did not choose to participate in the convention, and he was replaced by Jonathan Dayton.[13]

The four men who made up the New Jersey delegation—Brearly, Paterson, Livingston, and Dayton—were probably as able as any the state might have selected.[14] Chief Justice of the Supreme Court from 1779 until 1789, when he became a judge of the United States District Court in New Jersey, and Grand Master of the New Jersey Masonic Lodge, David Brearly had served briefly as a lieutenant colonel in the Revolution and had handed down the decision in the famous case of Holmes *versus* Walton. He was not a wealthy man and does not appear to have been a large security holder. Although

---

commissioners in terms similar to those used in the report of the Annapolis Convention, fixed their salaries at four dollars a day, and indicated that the delegation was to consist of not less than three men. *Votes and Proceedings,* 11-1, pp. 73-75.

[12] *Minutes of the Joint-Meeting,* May 18, 1787; *Votes and Proceedings,* 11-2, pp. 8-9; William Livingston to David Brearly, May 19, 1787 (copy by Theodore Sedgwick), Livingston Papers, MHS.

[13] *Minutes of the Joint-Meeting,* June 5, 1787; *Votes and Proceedings,* 11-2, p. 43. "Mr. Houston has formally resigned in consequence of his ill state of health," Dayton reported to David Brearly. "Mr. Clark has also resigned, but in his usual way that is very *informally,* because he thinks there is a kind of incompatibility in the two appointments. I am therefore unfortunately the only one on the list of Supernumeraries—" Dayton to Brearly, June [7?], 1787, Gratz Collection, Federal Convention, HSP.

[14] Houston was present in Philadelphia on May 25, but he was forced to withdraw because of ill health sometime between June 1 and June 6. Farrand, *Records,* III, p. 588; Petition of Brearly, Paterson, and Houston to the legislature, (in Houston's handwriting), Philadelphia, June 1, 1787, Loose Manuscripts, NJSL; Jonathan Dayton to David Brearly, June [7?], 1787, Gratz Collection, Federal Convention, HSP.

hardly a brilliant figure, he was capable and respected.[15] William Paterson, wartime attorney general of the state, and future governor, United States Senator, and Associate Justice of the Supreme Court, was a Princeton graduate and a distinguished lawyer. A rigid republican in his political beliefs, he was conservative in his economic thinking and became a thoroughgoing Federalist. He was a conscientious and indefatigable worker, a gifted orator, and a keen student of the law. Austere and formal in his personality, he possessed few of the attributes of the politician, but he commanded the admiration of his associates. His large practice brought him a good income, but he had yet to make his fortune. As the leading architect of the "New Jersey Plan," he became one of the outstanding members of the convention.[16]

William Livingston, who had retired to New Jersey on the eve of the Revolution after a successful but stormy legal and political career in New York, was a younger son of Philip, second lord of Livingston Manor, and the father-in-law of John Jay. As the first governor of the state from 1776 until his death in 1790, he displayed conspicuous fidelity to the Revolutionary cause and won renown as a rigorous Whig and as a devoted supporter of General Washington. He was a gifted satiric writer, an amateur poet, an inveterate pamphleteer. Once possessed of a comfortable fortune, he had seen his estate dwindle during the war as a result of currency depreciation and the confiscation by Vermont of the extensive

---

[15] Eli Field Cooley, *Genealogy of Early Settlers of Trenton and Ewing* (Trenton, 1883), pp. 15-16; *New Jersey Archives*, 1st Ser., XXXVI, p. 29; McGregor, "Freemasonry," pp. 145-46; Farrand, *Records*, III, p. 90; Charles A. Beard, *An Economic Interpretation of the Constitution of the United States* (New York, 1925), pp. 79-80; Austin Scott, "Holmes v. Walton: The New Jersey Precedent," *American Historical Review*, IV (1899), pp. 3-19. The sketch of Brearly in the DAB contains some serious errors.

[16] Gertrude S. Wood, *William Paterson of New Jersey, 1745-1806* (Fair Lawn, N. J., 1933), *passim;* Paterson Papers in RUL, PUL, and LC.

holdings he had there. At his death, his principal wealth was in lands in New York State. An aristocrat by birth and a democrat in his social sympathies, he, like Paterson, had a lawyer's respect for the rights of property and the sanctity of contracts. By 1787 he was in his declining years, and he had lost the combativeness for which he had once been distinguished. As one who believed that virtue was the essence of republicanism he was distressed by the tendencies of the times. "Our situation, sir," he wrote to a friend on the eve of the convention, "is truly deplorable, and without a speedy alteration of measures, I doubt whether you and I shall survive the existence of that liberty for which we have so strenuously contended." [17] Livingston did not take an active part in the debates at Philadelphia, but he was a member of important committees and, although he was not well known, "there was a predisposition in all to manifest the respect due to the celebrity of his name." [18]

One of the youngest men to sit in the convention, Jonathan Dayton at twenty-seven had graduated from Princeton, fought as a captain in the Continental Army, and served in the Assembly. The son of General Elias Dayton, first president of the Society of Cincinnati in New Jersey and a prosperous merchant, Dayton was to become speaker of the House of Representatives and a Senator before being forced into political eclipse because of his implication in the Burr scandal. A daring speculator, whose manipulations earned him wide notoriety, he was associated with John Cleves Symmes in the Miami enterprise and was one of the largest holders of public securities in the state. Politically, he was an ally of Abraham Clark, at least until 1790, but it is questionable whether his

[17] Sedgwick, *Memoir*, pp. 402-403 and *passim*; Macmillan, *War Governors*, *passim*; Harold W. Thatcher, "The Social and Economic Ideas of New Jersey's First Governor," *PNJHS*, LX (1942), pp. 225-38; *ibid.*, LXI (1943), pp. 31-46; Livingston Papers, MHS.

[18] James Madison to Theodore Sedgwick, Feb. 12, 1831; Farrand, *Records*, III, p. 496.

soaring ambition was tempered by any firm principles. Confessedly conscious of his youth and inexperience, he went to Philadelphia somewhat against his own wishes but with the hope that he might derive honor and improvement from the post.[19]

In the Constitutional Convention, the New Jersey delegates appeared most prominently as the champions of the small-state viewpoint.[20] Disturbed by those features of the Virginia plan which gave to the populous states power commensurate with their size, thus placing the small states in an inferior position, they supported the so-called Paterson plan.[21] This provided for the political equality of the states and did not in other respects constitute so drastic a departure from the form of the Confederation as did the Virginia plan. The Paterson plan was not the product of advance thought but was concocted, it would appear, to counteract the national tendencies evident in the convention. Probably none of the New Jersey delegates had given serious consideration to the matter of altering the structure of the government, for the state had been preoccupied with questions related to the powers of the government. The

[19] *DAB*, V, p. 166; Beard, *Economic Interpretation*, pp. 85-86; Bond, *Correspondence, passim*; Dayton to Brearly, June [7?], 1787, Gratz Collection, Federal Convention, HSP. Dayton subscribed over eleven thousand pounds in state securities to the funding loan of 1791 in New Jersey. Subscriptions toward a Loan, NJHS. There is evidence that he was speculating in depreciation notes while a member of the convention. Dayton to Gen. Elias Dayton, Sept. 9, 1787, Gratz Collection, Federal Convention, HSP. It is an interesting commentary on the "Beard thesis" that Dayton, who was a more extensive holder of securities than any of his colleagues, was less enthusiastic about the Constitution than they. Dayton to John Cleves Symmes, Oct. 22, 1788, Bond, *Correspondence*, pp. 206-207.

[20] Max Farrand, *The Framing of the Constitution of the United States* (New Haven, 1913), pp. 84-90.

[21] For a discussion of the different versions of the Paterson plan, see J. F. Jameson, "Studies in the History of the Federal Convention of 1787," *Annual Report of the American Historical Association*, 1902, I (Washington, 1903), pp. 133-43. Paterson's notes are printed in the *American Historical Review*, IX (1904), pp. 310-40.

Paterson plan was discarded, but the small states stubbornly continued to oppose proportional representation in Congress.[22] After a controversy that lasted over a month, they won the compromise by which they were accorded equal representation in the Senate.[23] "Give N. Jersey an equal vote, and she will dismiss her scruples, and concur in the Natil. system," Pinckney had predicted.[24] Such was indeed the case, for after the "Great Compromise" had been approved, the New Jersey delegates raised no formidable objections during the remainder of the deliberations. All four men signed the finished document, all became Federalists, and all except Livingston held office under the new government.[25]

While the convention was in progress, the press of the state reported current rumors about what was purportedly transpiring behind the closed doors in the Pennsylvania State House and expressed hope for the success of the meeting. Throughout the momentous summer, there was a striking absence of letters from pseudonymous subscribers, who apparently were content to wait in silence for the outcome of the Convention's labors. The available correspondence of contemporaries, too, throws little light on what was going

[22] One element of the Paterson plan found its way into the Constitution. This was the highly important "supreme law of the land" clause in article II, section 6. Scott, "Holmes v. Walton," pp. 14-15.

[23] On July 13, three days before the "Great Compromise" was achieved, Dayton wrote to Governor Livingston: "I have the mortification to inform your Excellency that, altho' we have been daily in Convention, we have not made the least progress in the business since you left us. It is unnecessary & would perhaps be improper, to relate here the causes of this delay, but they will very readily occur to your Excellency from your knowledge of them heretofore." Dayton to Livingston, July 13, 1787, Livingston Papers, MHS. Livingston was absent from the convention from July 3 to July 19. Farrand, *Records*, III, p. 589.

[24] *Ibid.*, I, p. 255.

[25] Paterson, who had left Philadelphia around August 1, returned only for the signing. Dayton to Livingston, July 13, 1787, Livingston Papers, MHS; Farrand, *Records*, III, p. 589.

on in men's minds as the future course of the nation was being planned. Judging from the brief newspaper comments, there was general agreement "that a strong and efficient executive power must be somewhere established."[26] "We have become so corrupt, so dishonest," editorialized Shepard Kollock, "that we must either form an efficient government for ourselves, suited in every respect to our exigencies and interests, or we must submit to having one imposed on us by accident or usurpation."[27] At the annual Fourth of July celebration in New Brunswick, patriotic citizens toasted "The Foederal Convention—may their deliberations be successful."[28] Late in September the long months of suspense ended, and the people were able to read in either of the state's two papers the full text of the document upon which they were soon to be asked to pass judgment.[29]

RATIFICATION OF THE CONSTITUTION

The process of ratifying the Constitution was carried through with the same high degree of unanimity that had characterized New Jersey's attitude toward Confederation problems in the past. The sectional and class feuds that prevailed in many other states were conspicuous by their absence. The traditional cleavage between East and West Jersey, which was usually apparent when purely local matters were under consideration, seemingly disappeared in an atmosphere of harmony. Even the divisive effects of the recent controversy over paper money were not manifest. Some students, perplexed by the absence of conflict, have found New Jersey's action "startling" and have resorted to speculation in an effort to explain away what appears to be a deviation from a general

[26] *New Jersey Journal*, May 30, 1787.
[27] *Ibid.*, June 6, 1787.
[28] *Brunswick Gazette*, July 10, 1787.
[29] *New Jersey Journal*, Sept. 26, 1787; *Brunswick Gazette*, Oct. 9, 16, 1787.

hypothesis.[30] But the simple fact is that the Constitution promised advantages to so many different groups within the state that any concerted opposition to the document would have been "startling."

The annual elections in October, 1787, provided the first opportunity for a test of public sentiment on the Constitution, but there is no evidence that ratification was made an issue. Popular interest in the campaign—as reflected in the newspapers—was almost exclusively centered on the fight to bring about the repeal of the objectionable state excise tax.[31] Except for the lone suggestion of "A Friend to Jersey" that "fit men" should be sent to the legislature because of the part that body would play in ratification, there was no discussion of the Constitution.[32] The results of the quietly conducted canvass brought about no significant changes in the composition of either the Assembly or the Council. It is particularly noteworthy that in the "paper-money" counties—Essex, Middlesex, Monmouth, Somerset, Hunterdon, Morris, and Sussex—twenty-five of the twenty-eight incumbents were returned to office. The friends of the loan office retained control in both houses.[33] No "counter-revolution" had as yet taken place.

Although ratification was not a controversial issue in the state election, it was a subject of lively public concern. Petitions were circulated in several counties requesting the legislature to call a convention without delay.[34] The inhabitants

[30] Beard, *Economic Interpretation*, p. 271; Wood, *Paterson*, p. 90.

[31] See above, pp. 114-15; also *Brunswick Gazette*, Sept. 14, 18, 25, Oct. 9, 30, 1787; *New Jersey Journal*, Aug. 29, Sept. 5, 19, 26, Oct. 3, 1787.

[32] *Brunswick Gazette*, Aug. 28, 1787; *New Jersey Journal*, Aug. 29, 1787.

[33] *Votes and Proceedings*, 12-1, p. 32. This point is important in view of the assertion that ratification was "pushed through ... without giving the agrarian party time to organize its forces ..." Beard, *Economic Interpretation*, p. 271.

[34] *Votes and Proceedings*, 12-1, p. 9.

of Salem voiced their belief that "nothing but the immediate adoption of... [the Constitution could] save the United States in General and this State in particular from absolute ruin." [35] This view was shared by leading citizens of Middlesex, who expressed their "entire satisfaction" with "the form of a foederal Government, agreed to by the Convention of Deputies..." [36] At meetings of the voters on election day in Essex, Somerset, and Burlington counties, it was unanimously resolved to instruct the members of the legislature to set in motion the machinery of ratification.[37] Shepard Kollock could announce with assurance that the Constitution met with the "greatest approbation" in the state.

Competent observers were in agreement in predicting speedy ratification. James Madison, following closely developments throughout the union, reported that New Jersey was "zealous" for the new charter.[38] Moore Furman, prominent merchant, was confident the document would be approved.[39] "New Jersey will not boggle about it," John Stevens, Jr., assured his father, who was to be the president of the ratifying convention.[40] The aristocratic Lambert Cadwallader, wealthy landowner and kin of the Dickinsons, expected that ratification would be unanimous:

> [The Constitution] is in my Opinion & that of all those with whom I have conversed a very excellent one [he wrote to a Delaware correspondent] & will make us if adopted

[35] Petition of Salem inhabitants, [Oct., 1787], Loose Manuscripts, NJSL.

[36] Petition of Middlesex subscribers, [Sept. 28], 1787, Manuscript Collection, NJSL. Among the eighty-three signers were Philip French, Jonathan Deare, John Chetwood, David Olden, John Dennis, John Neilson, Azariah Dunham, Richard Stockton, James Parker, Thomson Stelle, John Schuurman, and Shelly Arnett.

[37] *New Jersey Journal*, Oct. 24, 1787.

[38] Hunt, *Writings*, V, pp. 3-4, 10, 17, 78.

[39] *Letters of Moore Furman*, p. 74.

[40] John Stevens, Jr., to John Stevens, Sr., Oct. 27, 1787, Stevens Papers, SIT.

happy at home & respectable abroad & when I reflect that the smaller States are admitted to an equal Representation in the Senate with the larger it appears to me a Circumstance much more favorable than I could have expected . . .[41]

"Nothing is talked of here . . . but the new constitution," was the report from Salem, where only the few who had not paid their debts were hostile to ratification.[42] From no quarter did there come any intimation that sentiment in the state was not overwhelmingly federalist.

As soon as the legislators were assembled in Trenton, Governor Livingston laid before them a copy of the Constitution, together with a report of the delegates and a resolution of Congress authorizing the holding of conventions.[43] On October 26, acknowledging that it appeared to be "the earnest Wish of the good People of this State, that early and immediate Measures be taken to assemble a Convention . . . for the Purpose of deliberating and determining on said Constitution," the Assembly unanimously resolved that three "suitable persons" should be elected as delegates by each county on the fourth Tuesday in November and meet in Trenton on the second Tuesday in December. Three days later the Council concurred unanimously in this resolution.[44]

[41] Lambert Cadwallader to George Mitchell, Oct. 8, 1787, Emmet Collection, NYPL; William H. Rawle, "Colonel Lambert Cadwallader," *Pennsylvania Magazine of History and Biography*, X (1886), pp. 1-14.

[42] *Pennsylvania Packet*, Oct. 29, 1787.

[43] *Votes and Proceedings*, 12-1, pp. 9, 11; Report of commissioners, Oct. 25, 1787, Miscellaneous Manuscripts, NJSL. Livingston, Brearly, Houston, and Dayton—but not Paterson—signed the report, in which they stated that a plan of government had been agreed upon "after long and serious Deliberation, and with no small Difficulty . . ."

[44] *Votes and Proceedings*, 12-1, pp. 21, 24. On November 1, the resolution was given the formal sanction of law. *Ibid.*, 12-1, pp. 21, 25; *Journal of Council*, 12-1, p. 12; *Session Laws*, 12-1, Act of Nov. 1, 1787. Five hundred copies of the resolution were ordered to be printed. *Votes and Proceedings*, 12-1, pp. 25, 26. It was published also in the *New Jersey Journal*, Nov. 7, 1787.

The election was to be held in accordance with the same laws that regulated the choice of members of the legislature. Accordingly, all those who were worth fifty pounds proclamation money and could get to the polling places could vote.[45] Rejoicing in the prompt and unanimous manner in which the legislature had acted, Governor Livingston looked forward to the adoption of the Constitution with high hopes. "I think," he wrote with spiteful glee, "we shall soon make my native Country, New York, a little *sickish* of their opposition to it." [46]

In the weeks preceding the meeting of the ratifying convention, the newspapers carried numerous reports on public sentiment in other states but devoted little attention to the trend of events in New Jersey. Only two letters from correspondents, both of them favorable to ratification, were printed.[47] "Cassius" explained that the purposes of the Constitution were "to crush that malignant state of anarchy into which our confederation was like to fall... to secure the property of individuals from the encroachments of puerile legislators, [and to] ... lessen the expenses... of government." [48] "A Jerseyman" enumerated some of the advantages that could be expected under the new government. With commerce regulated properly, the treasury would be filled by the revenue from impost duties. Then the government could pay its debts and encourage industry and agriculture. There would at last be a uniform currency, for Congress alone would have the power to coin money. The

[45] For a complete description of the electoral system, see chapter IV. No qualifications were established for the delegates except that they should be "suitable persons."

[46] Livingston to Jedediah Morse, Nov. 1, 1787, Gratz Collection, Federal Convention, HSP.

[47] See the files of the *New Jersey Journal* and the *Brunswick Gazette*. The *Trenton Mercury* was also in existence at this time, but few issues have survived.

[48] *New Jersey Journal*, Oct. 31, 1787.

alternative to a strengthened union would be anarchy and disorder.[49] Doubtless many citizens in the state supplemented the meager intellectual diet offered in the local press by studying the lengthy essays that appeared in the New York and Philadelphia journals. Too, they may have read with particular interest the pamphlet, *Observations on Government* ..., written by John Stevens, Jr., under the pseudonym, "A Farmer of New Jersey."[50] In all probability, however, few arguments were needed to convince the average Jerseyman that the best interests of the state would be served by ratification.

On Tuesday, November 27, 1787, the election of delegates to the ratifying convention began under the favorable auspices of clear, cool weather. In some counties, where the poll was adjourned from place to place, the balloting continued for several days;[51] in others it could be completed within a few hours. There is no way of estimating how many votes were cast nor of learning who the opposing candidates were. It is reasonable to presume, however, that the election was not marked by bitter contests and that it was not generally regarded as a critical one.[52]

The thirty-nine men who were chosen to sit in the convention were almost without exception "early Whigs" who had held either civil or military offices during the Revolution and

[49] "A Jerseyman," *Pennsylvania Packet*, Nov. 15, 1787. Reprinted from the *Trenton Mercury*, Nov. 6, 1787. Printed also in *American Museum*, II (November, 1787), pp. 436-40.

[50] This pamphlet is generally attributed to William Livingston, but there can be little question that Stevens was the author. See *Note*, pp. 278-79.

[51] "Diary of Joseph Lewis," *PNJHS*, LXI (1941), p. 199.

[52] There is no indication in the press or in the correspondence of contemporary observers that the election found contending factions arrayed against one another. If there had been much vocal opposition to ratification, there would doubtless have been more pro-Constitution propaganda than appeared in the newspapers.

who occupied positions of respect in their local communities.[53] Almost all of them had been active in the militia, on revolutionary committees, or in the Provincial Congresses. Only one had been a member of the Colonial Assembly; another had been on the royal governor's Council. Nine had helped draft the state constitution in 1776, fifteen had been in the Assembly, eleven had been councilors, and seven had served in the Continental Congress. Sixteen had no legislative experience. One, David Brearly, was Chief Justice of the state; many were county judges. Six were members of the Order of Cincinnati. Notably absent were those men who had been politically active and prominent during the preceding three years. It would almost seem as though present or recent officeholders had been excluded from being candidates, for there were but two delegates who were at the same time members of the legislature. There was no conspicuous representative of the paper-money faction. Taken altogether, the group could best be described as conservative whigs.[54]

The delegates were men possessed of substantial estates, but they were not, in the main, the large security holders, the leading merchants, or the outstanding men of enterprise in the state.[55] John Neilson was the only member with extensive

[53] For a list of the members, see *Minutes of the Convention of the State of New Jersey* . . . , reprinted by C. L. Traver (Trenton, 1888).

[54] Biographical information about members of the convention has been gleaned from such a variety of sources that it would be impractical to list all the specific references. Especially useful were the various legislative journals, the contemporary newspapers, and the abstracts of wills published in the *New Jersey Archives*. There are biographical sketches of a majority of the delegates in the several county histories, in the footnotes of *New Jersey Archives*, and in numerous genealogical works.

[55] The original subscribers to the Society for Useful Manufactures may be taken as a fair guide to the economic "who's who" of New Jersey. Only one man—John Neilson—among some twenty-two Jerseymen who held stock in the SUM was a member of the convention. Davis, *Essays*, I, pp. 390-92.

commercial interests, although others may have been indirectly involved in trade. Four were lawyers, four were ministers, two were doctors, two were college presidents, four were engaged in the iron industry, and most of the remainder, as nearly as can be ascertained, were farmers and landowners. At least one-third were worth a thousand pounds or more as evidenced by the fact that they were at one time on the Council, and in all probability there were many others who had similar qualifications. The wealthiest man among them was undoubtedly John Stevens, Sr., who was also the lone proprietor. By his own estimate, Stevens' lands were valued at £62,500, and he had over twenty thousand pounds in loan-office certificates.[56] Aside from Stevens, few members held significant amounts of either continental or state securities.[57] It could not be asserted that the convention was dominated

[56] Hon. John Stevens' estimate of his real estate, April, 1789; Day Book of John Stevens, Sr. [April, 1784], Stevens Papers, SIT.

[57] The other principal continental creditors in the convention (as evidenced by holdings of 3 per cent funded stock in 1791) were John Beatty (£265), Frederick Frelinghuysen (£336), and John Chetwood (£28). These amounts were small when compared with the holdings of such nonmembers as Philemon Dickinson (£5,734), Cornelius Ten Broeck (£2,125), Archibald Mercer (£8,936), John Stevens, Jr., (£6,346), Joseph Lewis (£6,207), Charles Axford (£3,341), Robert Lettis Hooper (£3,973), Thomas Lowrey (£7,134), John Imlay (£11,273), Jacques Voorhees (£15,094), and many others. Samuel W. Stockton, who was appointed secretary to the convention, held £2,301 in 3 per cent stock. New Jersey Loan Office, Ledger C-2, Domestic Debt, Holdings of 3 per cent Stock (Funded 3 per cent Stock), July 1, 1791, National Archives. Those delegates owning state securities in 1791-1792 were John Fell (£102), Andrew Hunter (£789), Samuel Dick (£123), and Thomas Anderson (£660). On the other hand there were over fifteen nonmembers who held in excess of three thousand pounds each in state securities, and four—Ephraim Olden, Jonathan Dayton, Matthias Denman, and Jonas Stanbery—who held ten thousand pounds or more. Subscriptions toward a loan, NJHS. It should be noted that the information relative to security holdings is based on fragmentary records and applies to the years 1790-1792. Whether the picture would be the same if the holdings as of 1787 were known is problematical.

either by the mercantile or the public-creditor interest. On the other hand, the lower economic strata was not represented in the group.[58]

The delegates assembled at Francis Witt's "Blazing Star" tavern in Trenton on Tuesday, December 11, and on the following day elected officers and appointed a committee to draft a set of rules.[59] The elderly John Stevens, who had first entered political life as a member of the Assembly in 1751, was chosen president, and Samuel Witham Stockton, a non-delegate, was named secretary.[60] On the thirteenth, rules were adopted, and it was resolved that the Federal Constitution should be read and debated section by section, after which a vote should be taken on the general question, "Whether this Convention, in the Name and in Behalf of the People of this State, do ratify and confirm the said Constitution."[61]

[58] Although elected on the basis of limited suffrage, the delegates were more representative of the people of the state than were the members of the Constitutional Convention elected in June, 1947. In the latter group, for example, fifty of the eighty-one delegates were lawyers, only one was an active member of a labor union, and none was a farmer. "Biographies of Delegates," mimeographed, (New Brunswick, 1947).

[59] Thirty-eight delegates were present on December 12. One, Samuel Dick of Salem, did not attend the Convention. *Minutes... Convention*, p. 3.

[60] There is evidence that Stevens and his son were involved in speculating in securities. Two days before the convention met, John Stevens, Jr., wrote to his father from Hoboken to tell him that he had no information on the price of Condict's notes and that none were to be had either in New York or in his locality. On December 19 John Stevens, Sr., received in behalf of his son from John Cox some £28,000 worth of loan-office certificates that had been deposited with Cox several years before. John Stevens, Jr., to John Stevens, Sr., Dec. 9, 1787; Day Book of John Stevens, Sr., entry for Dec. 19, 1787, Stevens Papers, SIT.

[61] *Minutes... Convention*, pp. 7-9. Rule fourteen provided that any two members might require the yeas and nays on any question to be entered in the minutes. The fact that no votes are recorded would

Friday, Saturday, and Monday were spent in debate. According to a newspaper source, "many supposed exceptions were agitated," but Chief Justice Brearly "with a perspicuity of argument, and persuasive eloquence, which carried conviction with it, bore down all opposition." [62] On Tuesday, the eighteenth, the question of ratification was put to a vote and was "determined in the Affirmative unanimously." [63] The next day, after affixing their signatures to the form of ratification, the delegates marched in procession from the convention hall to the courthouse where the secretary announced to the assembled populace the welcome news that the Constitution had been adopted. While the citizens voiced their enthusiastic approval, a light-infantry company signalized the event by firing thirteen rounds, plus one each for Pennsylvania and Delaware.[64] The convention held its final session on December 20, at which time it went on record in favor of offering to the United States the cession of a district ten miles square as a site for a capital city.[65] Having acted with characteristic unanimity at every step in the process of creating a stronger union, New Jersey now looked forward expectantly and hopefully to the establishment of a government that would assure it the "equal Justice" that it had long sought in vain.

The months from January to June of 1788 were exciting ones for many Jerseymen as they anxiously followed the progress of ratification in other states. Shepard Kollock, a zealous friend of the Constitution, kept the readers of his paper closely

---

indicate that there was substantial agreement on all matters discussed in the convention.

[62] *New Jersey Journal*, Dec. 25, 1787. Although the convention met in open session, this is the only direct reference to its deliberations that has ever been found. The official *Minutes* give no hint as to what went on during the three days of debate.

[63] *Minutes... Convention*, p. 10.

[64] *New Jersey Journal*, Jan. 2, 1788.

[65] *Minutes... Convention*, p. 29.

abreast of developments and heralded with obvious joy each accession to the reconstituted union.[66] When, in April, the prospects for a ready acceptance of the new frame of government seemed dim, the presbytery of New Brunswick ordered a day of fasting and prayer and besought the Lord to "give a spirit of union to the United States of America to establish a free, energetic and permanent government." [67] The period of waiting ended late in June when it was learned that New Hampshire had become the ninth state to ratify.[68] The twelfth Independence Day was made the occasion for a dual celebration in many of the larger towns. In Newark, citizens responded to the toast, "May the New Constitution last until days come to an eternal pause, and Sun and Moon shall be no more." [69] The gentlemen of the Order of Cincinnati, assembled in Elizabeth Town for their annual meeting, listened to a sermon by the Reverend Mr. Austin on the appropriate text, "The Lord reigneth, let the earth rejoice," saw Governor Livingston review a "handsome legionnary corps" under the command of General Ogden, and then convened at the convivial board to toast the union.[70] When New York came into the federal fold, there was another series of demonstrations.[71] Everywhere there was evidence that the people looked forward with extravagant hopes to a new era.[72] The aging Governor Livingston, who a year earlier had despaired of the future of the republic, was full of confidence. "We are now arrived at that auspicious Era, which, I confess, I have

---

[66] *New Jersey Journal*, January-June, 1788.

[67] Minutes of the Presbytery of New Brunswick, Apr. 23, 1788, (typescript), RUL.

[68] *New Jersey Journal*, July 2, 1788; *Brunswick Gazette*, July 1, 1788.

[69] *New Jersey Journal*, July 9, 1788.

[70] *Ibid.*, July 9, 1788.

[71] *Brunswick Gazette*, July 29, 1788.

[72] Jonathan Dayton to John Cleves Symmes, Oct. 22, 1788, Bond, *Correspondence*, p. 206.

most earnestly wished to see," he told the legislature. "Thanks to God that I have lived to see it." [73]

The factors that motivated New Jersey to give such whole-hearted support to the Federal Constitution are not difficult to discover and assess. The state had long since come to believe that an extension of the powers of the central government, particularly in respect to finance, was essential to its economic well-being. It was to be expected, therefore, that all classes of citizens would enthusiastically approve of a government that could levy imposts, regulate trade, pay its debts, and control the sale of western lands. Less compelling, but nevertheless operative, was the strong desire of influential conservatives to see curbs placed on the power of the state legislature to the end that property rights might be safeguarded.

The one feature of the Constitution which probably more than any other guaranteed its ratification by New Jersey was the provision for tariff duties. As a public-creditor state, burdened with heavy taxes that could be raised only from assessments on land and compelled at the same time to contribute without recompense to the support of the governments of New York and Pennsylvania, New Jersey would profit immensely if the United States was granted the revenue from duties on imports. The landowner, large or small, would be relieved from taxation, and the public creditor would be assured of receiving the principal as well as the interest on his securities. Supplementing the tariff would be the income derived from the sale of the national domain. There was the prospect that the state would no longer have to tax itself to the extent of £31,259 annually to pay interest charges due to its continental creditors, to say nothing of the £12,500 it levied for servicing the state debt. Furthermore, there would

[73] Message of Governor Livingston to legislature, Aug. 29, 1788, Vault Manuscripts, NJSL.

be an end to requisitions. No taxpayer could fail to see the virtues of a constitution which promised such obvious financial advantages.[74] Federal regulation of commerce had been demanded for a decade, and it was particularly welcomed by the small merchant group. Annoying local barriers would be removed, and the general volume of trade would be expanded. "...we shall derive prodigious advantages from the Regulation of our Trade with foreign Powers who have taken the opportunity of our feeble State to turn everything to their own Benefit," predicted Lambert Cadwallader, "—by playing off one Nation against another we may bring them one after the other to some Consideration for us..."[75] Commercial considerations, however, were less important than the financial factor in determining New Jersey's attitude toward the Constitution.[76]

There can be little question that the most zealous advocates of the Constitution were those who believed in sound money and the sanctity of contracts and who foresaw that under the new government the state legislature would be effectively restrained by the provisions of article I, section 10, from impairing private property rights. The loan-office measure and the several acts for the relief of debtors had created an awareness

[74] Lambert Cadwallader to George Mitchell, Oct. 8, 1787, Emmet Collection, NYPL; Abraham Clark to John Cleves Symmes and Josiah Hornblower, Dec. 9, 1785, Miscellaneous Manuscripts, RUL; "A Jerseyman," *American Museum*, II (Nov., 1787), pp. 436-40; *New Jersey Journal*, Dec. 19, 1787.

[75] Cadwallader to Mitchell, Oct. 8, 1787, Emmet Collection, NYPL; Lewis Ogden to Messrs. Kemble and Spens, Feb. 18, 1788, Ogden Letter Book, NYPL.

[76] Hunter maintained that "To New Jersey herself the adjustment of her commercial difficulties overshadowed all other considerations." He arrived at this conclusion by misinterpreting the real basis of New Jersey's objections to the "exactions" of New York and Pennsylvania. Hunter, *Commercial Policy*, pp. 55-56. New Jersey wanted a federal tariff not so much to free its trade from the "shackles" imposed by New York and Pennsylvania but rather to obtain relief from taxation. See above, pp. 115-16.

of the need of such restraints.[77] Currency depreciation and the operation of *ex post facto* laws had taught a bitter lesson. The people were deficient in that sense of virtue which was deemed essential in a republic; consequently their representatives must be subjected to constitutional limitations.[78] Few men appreciated this fact more than Governor Livingston. In a message to the legislature soon after the Constitution had been adopted by the requisite nine states, he pointedly cautioned the lawmakers "to abstain, most religiously & inflexibly to abstain from enacting laws that have the least tendency to injure public credit or private contracts,—or aim at the relief of the distresses of some individuals at the expense & to the ruin of others." [79] Some years later William Paterson remarked on the "wonderful change" in the course of affairs that accompanied the inauguration of the new government. "Money became plenty, confidence was restored, and credit placed on its proper basis;" he observed, "for contracts were rendered sacred by the constitution, and paper-money was forever interdicted." [80] These were considerations of inestimable importance to conservatives and to men of substance.

A factor of indefinable weight in influencing popular sentiment toward ratification was the feeling that some drastic remedy was needed to prevent the experiment in independence from failing. Aside from their individual economic self-interest, people were genuinely distressed by the evident confusion and dissension that plagued their nation. "Nestor" expressed what must have been a prevalent belief. "The American war is over," he wrote when the Constitutional Convention was in

[77] See above, pp. 195-97.
[78] William Livingston, "Strictures of Liliput," *American Museum*, IX (1791), pp. 239-41; "Monitor," *Political Intelligencer*, Apr. 26, 1786; *New Jersey Journal*, June 6, 1787; "Cassius," *ibid.*, Oct. 31, 1787; "A Jerseyman," *American Museum*, II (1787), pp. 436-40.
[79] Message of Governor Livingston to legislature, Aug. 29, 1788; Vault Manuscripts, NJSL.
[80] "Aurelius," 8, William Paterson Essays, RUL.

prospect, "but this is far from being the case with the American revolution... It remains yet to establish and perfect our new forms of government, and to prepare the principles, morals and manners of our citizens." [81] Livingston, an ardent patriot and a devoted republican, felt that the country had been "in eminent danger of losing the great & important blessings to be expected from... Independence" because of the "want of an efficient national Government." "But from the Constitution now adopted," he exulted, "we have reason to hope for the re-establishment of public faith & private credit, of being respected abroad & revered at home." [82] A similar note of national pride was sounded by Chief Justice Brearly, who envisioned "the honor of the union vindicated, and America, from her reproach among the nations, rise into an empire of strength, beauty, and wide-extended renown." [83] The desire of men who had worked earnestly for the cause of independence to preserve and perfect their handiwork was one of the motivating forces that propelled the states toward a closer and stronger union.

That there were compelling reasons why New Jersey should have ratified the Constitution is apparent, but it is pertinent to inquire why there should have been such little controversy over the question. Why, in particular, was there no organized opposition from the former advocates of paper money and of debtor laws? For one thing, the paper-money agitation had reached its climax early in 1786. By the end of

[81] "Nestor," *New Jersey Gazette*, Nov. 6, 1786. See also William Peartree Smith to Elias Boudinot, Apr., 1783, *PNJHS*, IV (1849), pp. 122-24; William Livingston to Elijah Clark, Feb. 17, 1787, Sedgwick, *Memoir*, pp. 403-404; Walter Rutherfurd, State of the United States, May, 1786, Rutherfurd Manuscripts, NJHS; "Monitor," *Political Intelligencer*, Apr. 26, 1786; *New Jersey Journal*, June 6, 1787; "Cassius," *ibid.*, Oct. 31, 1787.

[82] Message of Governor Livingston to legislature, Aug. 29, 1788, Vault Manuscripts, NJSL.

[83] *New Jersey Journal*, July 9, 1788.

1787, the loan-office money had been in circulation for a year, and the period of sharpest economic discontent had passed. Even those who looked with disfavor on those sections of the Constitution that limited the powers of the states could favor the document as a whole because of the promise it gave of reducing their tax burden. There had never been anything other than substantial agreement on the subject of extending the powers of the central government. It should be remembered, too, that in the sections of the state where paper-money sentiment had been strongest, there was also the greatest concentration of public creditors, whose influence was exerted in favor of ratification. Finally, no leader came forth to rally the opposition. Abraham Clark might have essayed such a role, but he did not choose to do so.

Because Clark was the only man of political prominence in the state who was known to be lukewarm toward the Constitution, his views are of more than ordinary interest:

> I never liked the System in all its parts [he admitted in July, 1788]. I considered it from the first, more a Consolidated government than a federal, a government too expensive, and unnecessarily Oppressive in its Opperation; Creating a Judiciary undefined and unbounded.

In spite of these convictions, he was not willing to launch a campaign to defeat the document:

> I nevertheless wished it to go to the States from Congress just as it did, Without any Censure or Commendation, hoping that in case of a general Adoption, the Wisdom of the States would soon amend it in the exceptionable parts; Strong fears however remained on my mind untill I found the Custom of Recommending amendments with the Adoptions began to prevail. —This set my mind at ease ... I anxiously wish every state may come into the adoption in order to effect a measure with me so desireable; in which case, from the gen-

eral current of amendments proposed, we shall retain all the important parts in which New Jersey is interested.[84]

Although he was the chief sponsor of the loan-office bill and the author of the notorious "bull law," Clark, it should be noted, raised no direct objection to article I, section 10. Moreover, he took no worse than a neutral position on ratification. With their logical champion on the sidelines, the erstwhile paper-money host left the field in the complete possession of the forces of federalism.

It has been asserted that "New Jersey was among the states which pushed through ratification of the Constitution without giving the agrarian party time to organize its forces..."[85] No evidence is adduced to support such a conclusion. If ratification was indeed "pushed through," it was done by a legislature of essentially the same political complexion as that which had enacted the loan-office bill, a legislature in which the paper-money faction was sufficiently powerful to defeat a deflationary amendment to the loan-office measure.[86] If

[84] Abraham Clark to Thomas Sinnickson, July 23, 1788; Conarroe Collection, I, HSP. "When the plan of a new government appeared," Clark wrote later, "I found it not such as I had wished and expected; I perceived, as I supposed, some parts of it bearing too hard upon the liberties of the people, and giving some unnecessary powers to those who were to administer it..." At the same time, Clark denied that he had sought to prevent ratification by New Jersey. Clark to Shepard Kollock, *New Jersey Journal*, Feb. 4, 1789. For charges that Clark was anti-federalist, see the statement of Joseph Riggs in the *New Jersey Journal*, Feb. 4, 1789, and the statement of Adam Boyd in the *Brunswick Gazette*, Feb. 10, 1789.

[85] "Either there was a violent reaction against inflation," Professor Beard surmises, "or else the Federalist campaign had been highly organized." Beard, *Economic Interpretations*, p. 271. Another writer refers to the "high handed manner in which ratification was jammed through in New Jersey, without regard for the wishes of the inarticulate majority,—the farmers, the debtors, the paper-money classes." Wood, *Paterson*, p. 90.

[86] The Assembly by a vote of 21-17 killed a proposal that would have accelerated the rate of retiring the loan-office money. Jonathan

the advocates of paper money had chosen to oppose ratification, they certainly had abundant opportunity to do so, not only in the legislature but also in the state election of October, 1787, and in the election of delegates to the ratifying convention. They might also have employed that potent weapon of the "inarticulate majority," the petition, a weapon that had been used with telling effectiveness in 1786. The fact remains that the so-called agrarian party, for reasons that have been suggested, did not choose to "organize its forces" in opposition to the Constitution.[87]

Note

The authorship of the fifty-six page pamphlet, *Observations on Government, including some Animadversions on Mr. Adams's Defence of the Constitutions of Government of the United States of America, and on Mr. De Lolmes's Constitution of England*, by a "Farmer of New Jersey," published by William Ross of New York in 1787, has long been attributed to William Livingston.[88] Nowhere has any evidence been adduced to support such a conclusion. Theodore Sedgwick, Jr., Livingston's biographer, who identified many of the anonymous writings of the New Jersey governor, makes no mention of the *Observa-*

Dayton, interestingly enough, was the only East Jersey member in the negative. This vote was taken on the same day, November 1, that the bill authorizing the ratifying convention became law. *Votes and Proceedings*, 12-1, p. 32.

[87] It would be extremely difficult to apply what might be termed the Libby-Beard hypothesis to an analysis of the vote on ratification in New Jersey, even if the vote figures were available. Those counties which contained the greatest numbers of security holders were also the counties that voiced the loudest demand for paper money. Similarly, the nonsecurity holding counties were the sound-money counties.

[88] Both Evans and Sabin credit Livingston with the work. See also Beard, *Economic Interpretation*, pp. 202-203; Harold W. Thatcher, "The Political Ideas of New Jersey's First Governor," *PNJHS*, LX (1942), pp. 81-98, 184-99; and Thatcher, "Comments on American Government and on the Constitution by a New Jersey Member of the Federal Convention," *PNJHS*, LVI (1938), pp. 285-303. Thatcher bases his analysis of Livingston's political thought largely on the *Observations*.

tions. On the other hand, there is conclusive proof that the author was actually John Stevens, Jr., best known for his pioneering contributions in the field of steamboat and railroad transportation.[89]

Among the Stevens Papers in the Stevens Institute of Technology is a draft of the *Observations* in Stevens' hand (document number 5145-5151). Moreover, Stevens in his personal correspondence hinted at the authorship in such a way as to leave little doubt of the matter.[90] Finally, there is evidence that Stevens paid Ross for the publication of the pamphlet.[91]

There is no question but that Stevens was capable of writing the *Observations.* A graduate of Columbia College and a law student of James Duane's, he certainly had the requisite educational background. His interest in political subjects is attested to by the fact that in 1788 he drafted an elaborate constitution for New Jersey, which needless to say was never adopted.[92] He also wrote a series of articles on the Federal Constitution which appeared in the New York *Daily Advertiser* under the pseudonym, "Americanus," and may have authored other pieces at about the same time.[93] Although his greatest claim to fame is as an engineer, Stevens is entitled to rank among the minor political pamphleteers whose disquisitions on the Constitution molded public sentiment on the eve of the establishment of the new government.

[89] Archibald D. Turnbull was the first to establish Stevens' authorship of the *Observations.* See his *John Stevens: An American Record* (New York and London, 1928), pp. 90-94. The Library of Congress credits the *Observations* to Stevens.

[90] John Stevens, Jr., to John Stevens, Sr., Dec. 9, 1787, and Dec. 4, 1788; Stevens, Jr., to Benjamin Van Cleve, Nov. 21, 1788, Stevens Papers, SIT. Stevens sent the *Observations* and other productions of his pen to Van Cleve, who was Speaker of the Assembly at the time when he was soliciting support for his candidacy as a representative in the first Congress.

[91] William Ross to John Stevens, Jr., May 16, 1788, Stevens Papers, SIT. Ross acknowledged the receipt of £17.16.0, the balance of an account for printing five hundred copies of the *Observations.*

[92] The draft is among the Stevens Papers, number 4272, SIT.

[93] "Americanus," [New York] *Daily Advertiser*, Nov. 23, 30, Dec. 5, 12, 1787; John Stevens, Jr., to John Stevens, Sr., Dec. 14, 1787, Stevens Papers, SIT. An extract from the *Observations* appeared in the *Daily Advertiser*, Nov. 17, 1787.

XI

The Counterrevolution

****

THE adoption of the Federal Constitution did not result at once in drastic political or governmental changes in New Jersey, but there were obvious repercussions within the state. No longer was the majority to reign unchecked. An effective curb had been placed on the enactment of further laws violative of property rights. The conservative elements, heretofore divided and even disheartened by the trend of public affairs, were stimulated to mobilize their strength by the prospect of participating in the inauguration of what they confidently hoped would be a new era. It was they who stood to gain most from an alteration of the *status quo*. They soon demonstrated that their influence had revived, when they succeeded in gaining dominance in the legislature, crippling the loan office and capturing all four seats in the first Congressional election. A mild counterrevolution developed as the forces of the right assumed the helm.

REACTION AND DEFLATION

After 1787, the political balance, which for several years had been tipped in favor of East Jersey, swung to West

Jersey by a narrow but decisive margin. The effect of this shift in control was glaringly apparent in the actions of the legislature. As might have been expected, the inflationary monetary policies which the western counties had so long opposed in vain were brought under attack and reversed.

For more than a year after the loan-office bills had been put in circulation, there was little or no public controversy over the money question. Not until the summer of 1788, when the success of the Constitution seemed assured, were there outspoken demands for deflationary measures. Then loud complaints were raised against the evil of depreciation, debtors were once more accused of defrauding their creditors, and the latest experiment with legal tender was branded a failure. State paper was accepted in New York and Philadelphia only at a discount of 25 or 30 per cent. Private credit had been destroyed.[1] The gullible Frenchman, Brissot de Warville, was readily persuaded by those with whom he talked during a two-day visit to the state in August, 1788, that New Jersey was being "ravaged by a political scourge" more terrible than the mosquito. No man of sense, he was assured, would be fool enough to part with hard money in exchange for "depreciated rags." [2] The time had come, so many thought, to restore the currency of the state to a sound basis.

Concrete proposals for attaining this end were readily forthcoming. Abraham Clark, staunch friend of the loan office, conceded that it might have a "good effect" if the interest accruing to the treasury and any principal sums that

---

[1] "A Native of New Jersey," *Brunswick Gazette*, Apr. 1, 1788; "Correspondent," *ibid.*, Sept. 16, 1788; "J. Hamden," *Federal Post*, Sept. 6, 1788; "Horatius," 16, William Paterson Essays, RUL.

[2] J. P. Brissot de Warville, *New Travels in the United States of America, Performed in 1788* (2nd edition, corrected, London, 1794), I, pp. 142-51. His chief informants were William Livingston, son of the Governor, and Temple Franklin, neither of whom could be considered objective witnesses.

might be paid in were destroyed.[3] Some went further and suggested that the process of contracting the money supply should be hastened by additional taxation. The most extreme recommendation was that the loan-office mortgages should be transferred to any private purchasers who would pay up the principal and interest. This plan was advanced by a number of the leading citizens of Burlington, who claimed that it would "have a good Tendency and leave the borrowers of the money no room to Complain, they having received every benefit thereby intended by the Legislature." [4] Other groups petitioned their representatives to take steps to prevent further depreciation.[5]

Soon after the legislature met in August, 1788, a committee was appointed to study ways and means of restoring the value of the paper money. It reported its opinion that mortgagors should be permitted to pay off not less than one-fifth of their mortgages at any time, that no money should be reloaned, and that all bills received in payment of interest or principal, together with any unappropriated money in the treasury, should be cancelled.[6] A bill incorporating these provisions was drafted and was soon approved by both houses.[7] An effort was made by a combination of West Jersey members to attach an amendment to the effect that

[3] Clark to Thomas Sinnickson, July 23, 1788, Conarroe, I, HSP. Clark believed also that under the new government the state money would not be received by the Federal treasury or by citizens of other states, and that it would, therefore, cease to be full legal tender.

[4] Petition of inhabitants of Burlington [1788], Petitions of inhabitants of Burlington, Aug. 25, 1778, Loose Manuscripts, NJSL; *American Museum*, IV (July, 1788), p. 105; "A Native of New Jersey," *Brunswick Gazette*, Apr. 1, 1788.

[5] *Votes and Proceedings*, 12-2, p. 5.

[6] *Ibid.*, 12-2, p. 8.

[7] *Ibid.*, 12-2, pp. 16, 26; *Journal of Council*, 12-2, p. 8; *Session Laws*, 12-2, Act of Sept. 8, 1788. Opposed to this act in the Assembly were seven ardent paper-money men from Monmouth, Somerset, Morris, and Sussex.

paper money should not be legal tender for debts contracted in the future, but this move was easily defeated.[8] East Jersey was still supreme and would countenance only mildly deflationary measures.

The state election in October, 1788, had a significant effect on the relative strength of the rival sectional factions in the legislature. Two new councilors and five new assemblymen from counties that previously had given consistent support to paper money sided with the West Jersey conservatives, who were thereby able to control both houses by narrow margins.[9] The dominant western coalition promptly forced through an act which had as its main purpose the wholesale retirement of the loan-office bills.[10] Anyone who deposited twenty-five pounds or more in loan-office bills with one of the loan offices would be given a certificate entitling him to receive the interest and principal on that sum as it became due in the future. The money so deposited would be cancelled by the state. In effect, the income from the loan office, instead of going to the state treasury, would go to private individuals. At the same time, currency contraction would be hastened. From any point of view, this was ideal creditor legislation.

Despite the vehement attacks on the loan office, paper money continued to comprise the bulk of the circulating medium in East Jersey, where it passed at but a slight dis-

---

[8] *Votes and Proceedings*, 12-2, p. 14.

[9] Chetwood of Essex, and Manning of Middlesex in the Council, and James Schureman and Freeman of Middlesex, Hardenbergh of Somerset, and Taylor and Lambert of Hunterdon in the Assembly, were the men who swung the balance to West Jersey on monetary questions.

[10] *Votes and Proceedings*, 13-1, p. 66; *Journal of Council*, 13-1, p. 22; *Session Laws*, 13-1, Act of Nov. 24, 1788. The vote in the Assembly was twenty to seventeen. In the majority were solid delegations from Burlington, Gloucester, Salem, Cumberland, and Cape May; two members from Hunterdon; two from Middlesex; and one from Somerset.

count. In West Jersey and in the neighboring states it was accepted early in 1789 at three-fourths of its nominal value.[11] The most objectionable feature of the money to creditors was that it was legal tender. Many delayed pressing their debtors for payment because they did not wish to receive depreciated paper.[12] "It is not in my power to pay off my bond at present," explained John Stevens, Sr., to a wealthy New Yorker, "[because] the obligations due me are all in this State and Should I call them in it would at this time be a loss to me of all the depreciation on Jersey money."[13] Understandably enough, the abolition of legal tender was the next objective of the conservatives.[14]

The election of 1789 did not alter the complexion of the legislature; the West Jersey coalition remained in control by a few votes.[15] The lawmakers convened in October at Perth Amboy for the first time since the Revolution and immediately named a committee "to take into consideration the State of the Paper Money..." The remedy they proposed was to reduce the quantity of currency by cancelling not only all the loan-office bills that might come into the treasury but one-third of the revenue money as well.[16] These recommendations were included in the draft of a bill, together with a provision to curtail legal tender. For almost a month the

[11] Robert Morris to Tim Ford, Feb. 14, 1789, Robert Morris Papers, RUL.

[12] Joseph Bloomfield to Matthew Carey, May 25, 1789, Edward Carey Gardner Collection, HSP.

[13] John Stevens, Sr., to James Desbrosses, June 27, 1789, Stevens Papers, SIT.

[14] "Silver Money," *New Jersey Journal*, Oct. 7, 1789; "Correspondent," *ibid.*, Nov. 25, 1789.

[15] The five southern counties of Burlington, Gloucester, Cumberland, Salem, and Cape May formed a solid bloc with eighteen votes. Usually they were joined by one member each from Bergen, Middlesex, Somerset, Hunterdon, and Sussex. The northern counties could muster no more than seventeen votes. *Votes and Proceedings*, 14-1, pp. 30, 79, 85.

[16] *Ibid.*, 14-1, pp. 23-24.

measure was the subject of heated debate, with neither side apparently able to muster enough strength to force the issue.[17] David Brearly, former Chief Justice of the state and now a Federal judge, was exceedingly anxious that the legislature should not adjourn before it had taken proper action on the money problem. "Every Statesman, every Lawyer, every man of information and reflection," he wrote to his friend Jonathan Dayton, a member of the Council, "must *now* be sensible that the Tender for more than the real and current value of the bills, can be no longer supported." Contracts, he pointed out, could not be impaired under the new Constitution. It was his judgment that the opinion of the Federal courts would be "against the Tender for the nominal value." [18] Moved, perhaps, by such arguments as these, the opposition capitulated, and West Jersey had its victory.[19]

The law that was enacted provided for the retirement of a substantial portion of the revenue money and for the levying of a £12,500 tax to call in loan-office bills for cancellation. In addition, the loan-office commissioners were authorized to sell mortgages in their possession to private investors, who could select any mortgage they chose. Finally, and most important, it was decreed that future debts and contracts, whenever it was so stipulated, must be paid in gold or silver coin.[20] This was a notable triumph for the hard-money fac-

---

[17] *Ibid.*, 14-1, pp. 30, 72, 79, 85; *New Jersey Journal*, Nov. 11, 1789.

[18] Brearly to Dayton, Nov. 22, 1789, Gratz, Officers of the Revolution, HSP.

[19] *Votes and Proceedings*, 14-1, p. 102; *Journal of Council*, 14-1, p. 35. The sound-money men reportedly "had hard work and much manuvering to hurry the money Bill and [were] obliged to send Express for [Councilor] Newbold [of Burlington] who was absent sick." Walter Rutherfurd to John Stevens, Sr., Dec. 3, 1789, Stevens Papers, SIT.

[20] *Session Laws*, 14-1, Act of Nov. 30, 1789. The money which private purchasers paid for mortgages was to be cancelled as was any other loan-office money that came into the treasury.

tion. "Our Legislature have at last done some good," exulted one typical conservative. "I hope it will soon be in my power to bring some of my acquaintances to discharge their debts properly . . ." [21] Walter Rutherfurd rejoiced that New Jersey would "no longer [be] classed with Rhode Island." [22] The day of the debtor had been ended.

The measures that were adopted in 1788 and 1789 to hasten the retirement of the loan-office money were only moderately effective. Few men took advantage of the opportunity to purchase mortgages. Down to 1794 less than thirty thousand of the hundred thousand pounds that had been loaned was paid off. The bulk of the money was withdrawn from circulation between 1795 and 1799, when the scheduled annual payments of the principal fell due. Thus there was a gradual rather than an abrupt contraction of the currency.[23] The clamor against the loan office was stilled, however, because the inflationary trend had been reversed and the tender provision had been virtually eliminated. Depreciation had been halted, and creditors could now lend their money with a feeling of security.

It was in the field of currency legislation that the West Jersey coalition scored its most important successes. But the trend toward conservatism was evidenced by numerous other measures. The laws for the relief of insolvent debtors, passed in 1783 and 1786, were repealed.[24] The much-castigated "Clark's

[21] John Griffith to J. M. Wallace, Dec. 7, 1789, Wallace Papers, IV, HSP. Griffith added that monied men and merchants now planned to hold on to their paper until it should appreciate in value.

[22] Walter Rutherfurd to John Stevens, Sr., Dec. 17, 1789, Stevens Papers, SIT.

[23] See the Gloucester Loan-Office Book and the Somerset Loan-Office Book, NJSL, for examples of the operation of the loan office after 1787. The conclusions respecting the rate of retirement of the bills are based upon an analysis of the figures presented in conjunction with the annual report of the treasurer, which may be found in the *Votes and Proceedings* in November of each year.

[24] *Session Laws*, 12-1, Act of Nov. 3, 1787.

law" for regulating and shortening proceedings in courts of law was thoroughly revised.[25] Perth Amboy and Burlington, conservative strongholds and former centers of loyalism, were designated as the dual state capitals. The political restrictions that had been imposed upon tories during the war were abolished.[26] The counterrevolution was a reality. It had been brought about not by a wholesale reshuffling of political loyalties, but by the defection of a handful of East Jersey members from the traditional sectional alignment. Contributing to the movement to the right was the new psychology that developed out of the adoption of the Constitution. The opponents of "popular measures," no longer on the defensive, had the assurance that the power of the state to impair property rights had been limited. They had been vindicated in their contention that the rule of the majority must be restrained.

THE ELECTION OF 1789

The western-conservative coalition was a potent factor in the election that was held early in 1789 to choose New Jersey's first representatives in the Federal Congress. The canvass was a significant one despite the fact that no clear-cut issues were involved. For the first time, the people of the state were presented with the opportunity of voting as a whole on a set of candidates. Politics was raised above the county level; the scope of factional organization was correspondingly expanded. Although inconclusive in its results, the election provides an illuminating insight into the political behavior of Jerseymen as they brought to a close their experiment in independence.

The machinery for selecting the personnel of the new government was set in motion at the end of October, 1788, when the Council appointed a committee to draft a bill to provide for the choice of electors, senators, and representatives.[27]

[25] *Ibid.*, 13-1, Act of Nov. 26, 1788.
[26] *Ibid.*, 13-1, Act of Nov. 29, 1788.
[27] *Journal of Council*, 13-1, p. 7.

More than three weeks were spent in discussion of the measure. The controversy centered around the question of whether representatives should be voted for in a general or in district elections, with the western alliance favoring the general method. It was this plan which was finally adopted.[28] The law provided that any qualified voter might nominate four candidates by delivering a list of names to the clerk of the Court of Common Pleas in each county, who would in turn transmit them to the Governor for publication. The election was to be conducted by ballot in all counties under the same regulations that applied to state elections. The polls were to open on the second Wednesday in February; no date for their closing was fixed. To the Governor and his Privy Council was assigned the responsibility for counting the ballots and determining who were the successful candidates.[29] A week after this act had been approved, the law governing state elections was amended to increase the number of polling places in the state from twenty-nine to fifty-three. This change was especially important in the five lower counties, where it trebled the polling facilities.[30] West Jersey was anxious to garner the maximum votes for its ticket in the contest that lay ahead.

The appointment of presidential electors was left to the Governor and the Privy Council.[31] On January 7, 1789, six men—all of them prominent citizens whose fidelity to the Constitution was beyond doubt—were named.[32] The election

[28] Robert Lettis Hooper to Jonathan Dayton, Nov. 11, 1788, Miscellaneous Papers, NYPL; Elias Boudinot to James Kinsey, Nov. 20, 1788, New Jersey Manuscripts, III, NJHS; *Votes and Proceedings*, 13-1, p. 62; *Journal of Council*, 13-1, p. 18.

[29] *Session Laws*, 13-1, Act of Nov. 21, 1788.

[30] *Ibid.*, 8-1, Act of Dec. 16, 1783; *ibid.*, 13-1, Act of Nov. 29, 1788.

[31] *Ibid.*, 13-1, Act of Nov. 21, 1788. New Jersey was the only state to choose electors in this manner. Frank F. Stephens, *The Transitional Period, 1788-1789, in the Government of the United States* (*University of Missouri Studies, Social Science Series*, II, no. 4, 1909), p. 83.

[32] Minutes of the Governor's Privy Council, Jan. 7, 1789, NJSL.

of the state's first senators was entrusted to the joint meeting. William Paterson, Jonathan Elmer, Abraham Clark, and Elias Boudinot were placed in nomination when the two houses met together in the historic library room of Nassau Hall on November 25, 1788. Paterson and Elmer, the latter a distinguished physician from Cumberland County who had served numerous terms in the Continental Congress and in the legislature, were the victors.[33] Both men were "Federal characters" and both were highly acceptable to West Jersey.[34]

The character of the campaign that was to be waged over the election of four representatives to Congress became evident even before the legislature adjourned. Early in the session an agreement was effected among the political chieftains of West Jersey and a few powerful figures in East Jersey. This combination was responsible for the adoption of the general-election scheme and was active also in the senatorial canvass.[35] Its crowning achievement, however, was the plac-

---

Those selected were David Brearly, James Kinsey, John Neilson, David Moore, John Rutherfurd, and Matthias Ogden. Evidently the choice of these men was not free from controversy. John Mehelm to William Livingston, Feb. 20, 1789, Livingston Papers, MHS.

[33] *Minutes of the Joint-Meeting*, Nov. 25, 1788. The votes stood: Paterson, 45; Elmer, 29; Clark, 19; Boudinot, 7. *New Jersey Journal*, Dec. 3, 1788.

[34] Evidently the conservative faction in East Jersey, headed by Elias Boudinot, agreed to accede to West Jersey on the senatorial matter. "As to Senators, I am easy about," wrote Boudinot to James Kinsey, "provided C[lark] is kept out. This altogether depends on West Jersey. We have placed the Game entirely in their hands & they can do as they please." Boudinot to Kinsey, Nov. 20, 1788, New Jersey Manuscripts, III, NJHS. Boudinot's son-in-law, William Bradford, Jr., of Pennsylvania, was disappointed at the outcome. "I am surprised to find by the public prints that so unexpected a choice of Senators has been made in New Jersey," he wrote. "None of us here, can conjecture what direction of politics could have produced it." Bradford to Mrs. [Elias] Boudinot, Dec. 5, 1788, Wallace Papers, I, HSP.

[35] Elias Boudinot to James Kinsey, Nov. 20, 1788, New Jersey Manuscripts, III, NJHS.

ing in nomination, with the sanction of a large group in the
Assembly, of a four-man slate which became generally known
as the "Junto ticket" or the "West Jersey ticket." [36] The
quartet was made up of two men from East Jersey (Elias
Boudinot and James Schureman) and two from West Jersey
(Thomas Sinnickson and Lambert Cadwallader). All except
Sinnickson, who was a prosperous Salem merchant, had served
in the Continental Congress; all had been outspoken critics
of paper money; all were destined to become firm Federalists. The ticket was to receive almost universal support in the
western counties; Schureman alone was generally popular in
East Jersey. [37]

The politicos of East Jersey were unable to come to any
agreement on a slate which they could back in opposition to the
Junto. [38] Instead, many tickets were nominated in the northern
counties. Most of them included the names of Abraham Clark
and Jonathan Dayton. Others put forward as "local sons"
were John Witherspoon, Dr. Thomas Henderson, Josiah
Hornblower, Adam Hoops, and James Parker. [39] In some

[36] "A Freeholder," *New Jersey Journal*, Dec. 10, 1788; Samuel
Dick to William Livingston, Jan. 7, 1789, Livingston Papers, MHS;
John Stevens, Jr., to John Stevens, Sr., Dec. 23, 1788, Stevens Papers,
SIT.

[37] The original nomination list for the counties of Middlesex, Somerset, Sussex, Burlington, Gloucester, and Cumberland, preserved among
the papers of William Livingston in the Massachusetts Historical Society, detail the candidates nominated in each county and who nominated them. Consequently, they indicate the stand taken by important
individuals in the election and the relative strength of the different
candidates in various counties.

[38] John Mehelm to William Livingston, Feb. 20, 1789, Livingston
Papers, MHS.

[39] "A Freeholder," *New Jersey Journal*, Dec. 10, 1788; "A Free
Elector," *ibid.*, Jan. 7, 1789; "A Correspondent," *ibid.*, Jan. 21,
1789; *Brunswick Gazette*, Jan. 6, 27, 1789; Nomination lists, Middlesex, Somerset, and Sussex counties, Jan., 1789, Livingston Papers, MHS.
It is significant that many of the tickets proposed coupled the names of
Clark and Dayton with those of Schureman and Sinnickson. Too, some
of the most "respectable characters" placed Clark's name on their lists.

counties, strong combinations were formed in behalf of a particular group of candidates, but there was nothing comparable to the near-unanimity that prevailed in West Jersey. The friends of Dayton and Clark made common cause in East Jersey. Dayton alone of the non-Junto candidates had a small number of loyal campaigners in the southern part of the state.[40] In all, some fifty-four men were placed in nomination, although many subsequently announced their withdrawal from the race.[41]

The campaign was not characterized by debate over pertinent issues, but rather by attacks on personalities and by appeals to sectional jealousy. The Junto ticket was presented to the people as being staunchly Federalist and therefore deserving of their united support. An effort was made to depict the foes of the Junto, particularly Clark and Dayton, as unfriendly to the new Constitution. There is little evidence, however, that such a distinction in fact existed. ". . . I give all fears of Antifoederalism to the winds," remarked one competent observer, "and view it only as an Electioneering Phantom which will Vanish at the Approaching Dawn of an Energetic Government."[42] The question of where the seat of the Federal government should be located may have played some part in the contest, but it was not of major im-

---

[40] "Letters of Martin B. Bunn to Abraham Clark," *Brunswick Gazette*, Feb. 23 to Sept. 15, 1789. These letters, seven in number, were written by an opponent of Clark. They contain a wealth of veiled comment on the campaign in Somerset County and elsewhere and furnish one of the best sources on the election. The pseudonym, "Martin B. Bunn," was probably derived from Ephraim Martin, Robert Blair, and Edward Bunn, three legislators from Somerset who were friendly to Clark.

[41] *New Jersey Journal*, Jan. 21, 28, 1789; *Brunswick Gazette*, Jan. 27, 1789.

[42] Samuel Dick to William Livingston, Jan. 7, 1789, Livingston Papers, MHS. None of the surviving personal correspondence relating to the campaign would indicate that fidelity to the Constitution was a serious issue.

portance.[43] The principal active supporters of individual candidates were motivated by considerations of personal loyalty and friendship and by a desire to win power in the competition for office. Family alliances and close social relations among groups of leading men were at the basis of political factions. The electorate was influenced largely by sectional considerations. In essence, the contest was between the Junto slate of West Jersey and Clark and Dayton of East Jersey. It was the familiar contest that had long dominated Jersey politics.[44]

Rumors and accusations were actively propagated by all factions in the press, through handbills and by word of mouth. The Junto was condemned as a "secret cabal" of "great men" who should be taught not to meddle in politics.[45] Elias Boudinot was denounced for having drawn "many thousands of dollars out of the public treasury to decorate his palace, profusely furnish his table, and clatter through the streets in a chariot" while he was President of the Continental Congress.[46] Lambert Cadwallader was censured for having voted to surrender to Spain the navigation of the Mississippi.[47] The serious charge was made against Jonathan Dayton that he had been heavily involved in illegal trade during the war.[48] So general was the indulgence in vituperation that the editor of the *Brunswick Gazette* was moved to remark

---

[43] James Parker to English correspondent, [Mar. 1, 1789?], Parker, "Shipley," p. 117; Moore Furman to Joseph Edgar, Feb. 20, 1789, *Letters...Moore Furman*, p. 77.

[44] James Madison to Washington, Mar. 19, 1789, Hunt, *Writings*, V, p. 330; John Rutherfurd to Robert Morris, Jan. 13, [1789], Robert Morris Papers, RUL.

[45] "A Freeholder," *New Jersey Journal*, Dec. 10, 1788; "A Free Elector," *ibid.*, Jan. 7, 1789.

[46] "A Candid Enquirer," *New Jersey Journal*, Feb. 11, 1789.

[47] "Index," *New Jersey Journal*, Jan. 25, 1789.

[48] Joseph Bloomfield to Jonathan Dayton, Feb. 23, 1789, Gratz Collection, Governors of States, HSP.

that scarcely a single candidate "escaped the lash of some slanderous tongue." [49]

No one came in for more abuse than did Abraham Clark, the foremost political figure in East Jersey. Wide circulation was given to handbills containing sworn statements by Joseph Riggs of New York and former Assemblyman Adam Boyd of Hackensack to the effect that Clark had openly declared his hostility to the Constitution and to General Washington. [50] He was also accused of having tendered depreciated certificates in payment of a debt to Jacob Shotwell, a Quaker merchant of Rahway. [51] So serious were these charges that Clark felt called upon to answer them publicly. He readily admitted that he had had some early doubts about the Constitution but insisted that he had in no way opposed ratification and that he was willing to leave to Congress the matter of recommending amendments. He dismissed the insinuation that he was inimical to Washington and flatly denied the tender story. In his own behalf, he asserted that his letters had been "taken up and secreted, or the direction altered, and sent a contrary way" by his malicious opponents. Too, he scorned the erroneous report, printed in a Trenton paper, that he had withdrawn from the campaign. "Is this the way," he indignantly asked, "a certain gentleman [Elias Boudinot], once filling a high station, is to be brought forward in the election? And is he ... of the same principles with the chief author of the false reports against me?" [52] The campaign was obviously a heated one, with no holds barred.

It was in the manipulation of the actual election that political skulduggery reached its peak—or its depth. The Junto

[49] *Brunswick Gazette*, Mar. 24, 1789.

[50] The statements were also printed in the *New Jersey Journal*, Feb. 4, 1789, and in the *Brunswick Gazette*, Feb. 10, 1789.

[51] "Statement of Jacob Shotwell," *Brunswick Gazette*, Feb. 10, 1789.

[52] Two letters of Abraham Clark, *New Jersey Journal*, Feb. 4, 1789; *Brunswick Gazette*, Feb. 3, 1789.

had the superior organization and it spared no efforts, legal and otherwise, to garner votes. The key figure in the group was Joseph Ellis, a member of the Council from Gloucester, who was credited with having originated the whole plan.[53] Others who figured prominently in the inner workings of the machine were Elias Boudinot and his brother, Elisha; Richard Stockton, Boudinot's nephew; John Chetwood, close friend of Boudinot's and councilor from Essex; Joshua Maddox Wallace, John Lawrence, James Kinsey, Caleb and William Newbold, and Richard S. Smith of Burlington; and Franklin Davenport of Gloucester. Not a few of these men were tainted with toryism; all subsequently became Federalists.[54]

The strategy of the Junto was simple. Realizing that they would secure relatively few votes in East Jersey, they schemed to get every possible vote in the lower counties. In order that the managers in Burlington and Gloucester might be apprized of what was necessary to be done, a daily communication was maintained with Boudinot and Chetwood, who reported on the state of the polls in the northern counties. A printed ticket, probably an innovation, was prepared to be given to the voters. The electoral officials were chosen for their fidelity to the Junto in West Jersey, and they were not above refusing tickets that did not contain the prescribed four names. To insure a maximum vote, the polls were moved around the customary circuits not once but twice. Ballots were collected also at places not authorized by law.[55] "Everybody," wrote William Brad-

[53] Joseph Bloomfield to Jonathan Dayton, Feb. 28, 1789, Miscellaneous Manuscripts, RUL; "Triumph," *New Jersey Journal*, Mar. 18, 1789.

[54] Joshua Maddox Wallace to Elias Boudinot, Mar. 6, 1789, Wallace Papers, VI, HSP.

[55] Joseph Bloomfield to Jonathan Dayton, Feb. 23, 1789, Gratz Collection, Governors of States, HSP; John Lawrence to Elias Boudinot, Feb. 16, 1789, Emmet Collection, NYPL; J. M. Wallace to Elias Boudinot, Mar. 6, 1789, Wallace Papers, VI, HSP.

ford from Burlington, "seemed to be *positively* charged with the Electioneering Spirit, & ready to communicate it on the slightest approach." [56]

The greatest difficulty confronting the Junto was to persuade the rigid Quakers to turn out and vote.[57] The argument used to overcome this obstacle was that Dayton, Clark, and their cohorts were Presbyterians who would visit all sorts of oppression on the peaceable Quakers once they gained control of the government:

'Dayton and Clarke are bloody men, are men for war [so Joseph Bloomfield paraphrased the Junto appeal], they want another War, that they may make their fortunes by distress from the Quaquers, and, if they get into Congress, they will join with the New-England-Congress Men and we shall have War & Blood-shed immediately—the Gentlemen in our West-Jersey-Ticket, are good peaceable Men, they will oppose all War-measures. Congress will be brought to Phila., may be to Burlington and the Markets will then be good, we shall have no Paper Money.' The Poor Friend being alarmed at the situation of his Society, finds "Freedom" takes the Printed junto-Ticket, & away He goes, with such of his Neighbors as He can influence by telling them the same melancholy tale—to keep out the blood-thirsty Presbyterians and to prevent War, Blood & Slaughter.[58]

Such propaganda was extremely effective, even irresistible.

[56] Bradford to Elias Boudinot, Feb. 17, 1789, Wallace Papers, I, HSP.

[57] The Burlington Quarterly Meeting early in 1789 called the attention of Friends to the minute that had been adopted by the Philadelphia Yearly Meeting in 1758 warning Friends against holding public office. Many with "tender consciences" believed they should not participate in elections. Minutes of the Burlington Quarterly Meeting, Feb. 23, 1789, Friends Book Store; Michenor, *Retrospect*, p. 274; "John Hunt's Diary," *PNJHS*, LIII (1935), p. 111.

[58] Joseph Bloomfield to Jonathan Dayton, Feb. 28, 1789, Miscellaneous Manuscripts, RUL. This letter is printed in full in *The Journal of the Rutgers University Library*, IV (1941), pp. 48-50.

The supporters of Dayton were not idle in West Jersey, but their efforts were largely in vain. Joseph Bloomfield, Dr. John Ross, and some others from Burlington; the Reverend Andrew Hunter of Woodbury; the Ogdens and the Daytons of Elizabeth; Robert Lettis Hooper of Trenton; John Noble Cummings of Newark; and Jonathan Rhea of Monmouth visited the polls in the western counties and sought to bring in voters for their candidate.[59] All of these men were, with Dayton, members of the Cincinnati; several were former army comrades. Some of them later became Federalists (like Dayton), while others joined the Democratic-Republicans.[60] Personal loyalty as much as any other factor seems to have been the common denominator among Dayton's followers.

The climax of the election came late in February. The voting had begun throughout the state on the eleventh and, by the twenty-third, seven counties—all those to the northward of Trenton with the important exception of Essex—had closed their polls and reported their returns. The totals showed over five thousand for Schureman, approximately four thousand each for Clark and Dayton, and less than a thousand apiece for Boudinot, Cadwallader, and Sinnickson. The Junto ticket was clearly not popular in East Jersey.[61] The West Jersey politicos proved themselves more than equal to the occasion. They had originally assumed that the maximum vote in the five lower counties would be about five thousand, with Burlington providing fifteen hundred of that total.[62] When a courier from Boudinot in Elizabeth Town arrived in Burlington

[59] Joseph Bloomfield to Jonathan Dayton, Feb. 23, 1789, Gratz Collection, Governors of States, HSP; Bloomfield to Dayton, Feb. 28, 1789, Miscellaneous Manuscripts, RUL.

[60] List of the members of the Cincinnati Society in the State of New Jersey, July, 1788, File D:277, NJHS; Fee, *Transition, passim.*

[61] *New Jersey Journal*, Feb. 25, 1789; *Brunswick Gazette*, Mar. 3, 1789.

[62] James Kinsey to Elias Boudinot, Feb. 16, 1789, Miscellaneous Manuscripts, RUL.

with the final figures from East Jersey, the Junto managers went into action.

It had been planned to close the Burlington poll on the twenty-first of February, and that in Gloucester on the twenty-third. Instead, the ballot box was sent once more around the circuit in each county in order to round up sufficient votes to counterbalance the four thousand that Clark and Dayton already had in East Jersey plus the twenty-five hundred that they were expected to get from Essex. "The Bell-Weathers of Cadwallader & Boudinot are riding night and day for this purpose," Bloomfield informed Dayton. "If your Essex-Election is not closed," he advised, "You must turn out 3,000 votes, or I fear we shall not succeed in our wishes. Had the Polls in this County & Gloucester closed as first intended, there would not have remained a doubt of Mr. Clarks & Your Elections, as there would not have been more than 3,000 votes taken in this & Gloucester County." [63] His analysis was correct. Not until March 4 did the Burlington election end, by which date, 2,826 votes had been cast. "The fear of injuring a Cause which they were anxiously engaged to support," Joshua Maddox Wallace explained to Elias Boudinot, "induced our Inspectors to close the Poll. Unless more Votes than you expected are taken in Essex, The Western Ticket is safe." The polls were still open in Gloucester and Cumberland, but they had closed by March 12. [64]

Essex County, in the meantime, was fully aware of the de-

[63] Joseph Bloomfield to Jonathan Dayton, Feb. 23, 1789, Gratz Collection, Governors of States, HSP.

[64] J. M. Wallace to Elias Boudinot, Mar. 5, 1789, Wallace Papers, VI, HSP. According to Bloomfield, there had been 1,802 ballots cast in Burlington and about the same number in Gloucester up to February 23. When the election finally ended, the two counties had polled over 5,300 votes! This approximated the total combined vote of Bergen, Middlesex, Somerset, Monmouth, Morris, Hunterdon, and Sussex. The Burlington vote was equivalent to about 80 per cent of the adult white male population.

vices that were being employed in West Jersey to win victory for the Junto ticket, and the people there were determined not to be outdone. On March 12 the judges and inspectors in charge of the election in the county were petitioned by the citizens of Elizabeth Town to keep the poll open "so long as it is probable that the keeping it open will serve to counteract and frustrate the combination against us; as we wish to remain unrepresented, until we can have a Fair Election; rather than submit to a representation in which we have no confidence." [65] This request was granted, and not until April 27 did the balloting end.[66] The election had developed into a farce; James Madison was restrained when he commented on the "very singular manner" in which it was conducted. Walter Rutherfurd was more exact. "Poor Jersey," he lamented, "is made a laughing stock of." [67]

The complicated problem of determining the results of the election lay with the Governor and his Privy Council.[68] On March 3, when returns had been received from but seven counties, the Privy Council met and entered into a dispute over whether it should declare the results as final. This would have meant the election of Schureman, Clark, Dayton, and possibly Boudinot.[69] After some controversy, Governor Livingston decided to postpone any action until March 18, at

[65] *Brunswick Gazette*, Mar. 24, 1789.

[66] *New Jersey Journal*, Mar. 11, 1789; Essex election return, Apr. 30, 1789, Livingston Papers, MHS.

[67] Madison to Washington, Mar. 19, 1789, Hunt, *Writings*, V, p. 330; Rutherfurd to John Stevens, Sr., Mar. 13, 1789, Stevens Papers, SIT.

[68] The Privy Council, composed of members of the Council, met irregularly at the summons of the Governor to advise him on such matters as granting pardons, signing pay warrants, and issuing proclamations. It had never before had any part in determining elections. The Minutes of the Governor's Privy Council, 1777-1844, are preserved in manuscript in two bound volumes in the New Jersey State Library.

[69] *Brunswick Gazette*, Mar. 3, 1789.

which time another meeting of the Privy Council would be convened.[70]

When the Privy Council met again on March 18, the election scene had changed. The uninhibited endeavors of the Junto had given the Schureman-Cadwallader-Boudinot-Sinnickson ticket a majority of some seven thousand votes in the five lower counties. Sensing defeat for Clark and Dayton, Essex County refused to close its polls. The Privy Council had before it, then, the returns from twelve counties only. According to law, it was supposed to determine the four persons having "the greatest Number of Votes from the whole State, to be the Persons duly chosen" to represent the state in Congress.[71] Obviously it could not comply with the letter of the statute as long as Essex withheld its votes. With twelve members in attendance, the Privy Council wrestled with the knotty tangle and finally decided "to cast up the whole number of Votes from the twelve Counties . . . leaving the decision of the legality of the election of the four Persons who have the Majority of Voices from the twelve Counties . . . to those to whom it appurtains . . ." Thereupon, Schureman, Cadwallader, Boudinot, and Sinnickson were named as the four highest, and Governor Livingston was advised to issue a proclamation embodying the determination of the Privy Council. Vigorously dissenting from these actions were the councilors from Morris, Somerset, and Monmouth. They took the position that if March 3 had not been the proper time to decide the election, then the Privy Coun-

[70] The backers of Clark and Dayton attempted to pressure Livingston into declaring the election closed, but he refused to do so. There is no record of the March 3 meeting in the Minutes of the Governor's Privy Council, but a full account of the session is contained in "Evidence given before the Committee on [the] New Jersey Election, Aug. 13, 1789," (in the handwriting of Elias Boudinot) Livingston Papers, MHS.

[71] *Session Laws*, 13-1, Act of Nov. 21, 1788.

cil should wait until all of the counties had been heard from.[72] On the day following the meeting, Governor Livingston issued a proclamation announcing the verdict of the Privy Council and leaving the "decision of the legality of the election ... to whom it appertains." [73] Thus the final disposition of the matter was by implication left up to Congress.

The dubious victory scored by the Junto did not go unchallenged in East Jersey. The proceedings of the Privy Council were hotly debated in the press, and soon the inevitable petitions protesting against the illegality of the election were circulating through the northern counties.[74] Toward the end of April these petitions were presented to the House of Representatives, where they were promptly referred to the committee on elections.[75] Almost a month passed before the committee

[72] Minutes of the Governor's Privy Council, Mar. 18, 1789, NJSL. The vote totals from the twelve counties were: Schureman, 12,537; Cadwallader, 8,685; Boudinot, 8,603; and Sinnickson, 8,240. *Pennsylvania Packet*, Mar. 24, 1789. In the eight counties to the northward of Trenton the totals for the Junto candidates were: Schureman, 6,751; Cadwallader, 985; Boudinot, 1,462; and Sinnickson, 479. In the same eight counties the votes for Clark and Dayton were respectively 7,242 and 6,708. The belated returns from Essex, where some three thousand ballots were cast, were as follows: Clark, 2,762; Dayton, 2,984; Schureman, 1,274; Boudinot, 448; Cadwallader, 17; and Sinnickson, 124. These figures clearly indicate the sectional character of the election contest. *New Jersey Journal*, Feb. 25, 1789; Essex election return, Apr. 30, 1789, Livingston Papers, MHS.

[73] *Brunswick Gazette*, Mar. 19, 1789. Late in March both Boudinot and Schureman asked Livingston for formal commissions certifying to their election. There is a draft of a commission, dated March 21, 1789, in the Livingston Papers, but there is no evidence that it was ever issued. John Chetwood to Livingston, Mar. 26, 1789, James Schureman to Livingston, Mar. 28, 1789, Livingston Papers, MHS; "Essex," *New Jersey Journal*, Mar. 30, 1789.

[74] "Essex," *New Jersey Journal*, Mar. 18, Apr. 1, 1789; "Triumph," *ibid.*, Mar. 18, 1789; "A Lover of Order," *ibid.*, Mar. 25, 1789; *Brunswick Gazette*, Mar. 24, 1789.

[75] *The Debates and Proceedings in the Congress of the United States...*, compiled by Joseph Gales, Sr., (Washington, 1834), I, pp. 213, 231 (hereafter cited as *Annals of Congress*). Elias Boudinot

was empowered to conduct hearings and receive proofs and allegations from both sides.[76] Evidently the group was at a loss how to go about its task, for in July it inquired of the House what procedure should be followed in securing testimony from witnesses. Elias Boudinot, opposing the appointment of a travelling commission, innocently declared that neither he nor his colleagues had "been anywise concerned in any of the transactions at the election complained of." He insisted that the Governor's proclamation should be accepted as adequate. The suggestion that New Jersey judges should be authorized to take depositions met with little favor and no agreement could be reached on the appropriate manner for conducting a hearing before the House.[77] This was the first major election dispute to come before Congress, and that body, conscious of the fact that it would be creating precedents for the future, was inclined to move cautiously.

On August 13, 1789, the complainants were finally given an opportunity to appear with counsel before the committee on elections. The questions and the cross-examination were concerned mainly with the circumstances surrounding the meeting of the Privy Council on March 3. Little light was shed on the illegal conduct of the election.[78] On the

---

dismissed the petitions as "only designed to keep the People's Passions up for another Election next fall," but he nevertheless took the precaution of having counterpetitions circulated. Boudinot to Elisha Boudinot, Apr. 14, 1789, Gratz Collection, First Congress, HSP.

[76] *Annals of Congress*, I, pp. 396, 409. There is an incomplete account of Congressional action on the contested election in Matthew St. Clair Clark and David A. Hall, *Cases of Disputed Elections in Congress, 1789-1834* (Washington, 1834), pp. 38-44.

[77] *Annals of Congress*, I, pp. 637-42; "One of Seven Thousand," *New Jersey Journal*, Aug. 12, 1789.

[78] Evidence given before the Committee on [the] New Jersey Election, Aug. 13, 1789 (in the handwriting of Elias Boudinot), Livingston Papers, MHS; Elias Boudinot to Elisha Boudinot, Aug. 15, 1789, Boudinot Papers, III, HSP. Those who testified were Aaron Kitchell and Jacob Arnold, prominent political figures and legislators

eighteenth, the committee made its report, which was merely a brief statement of the chronological sequence of events in the election. No conclusions were drawn; no recommendations were made.[79] Two weeks later this report was taken under consideration by the House, and after a brief debate, a resolution was adopted declaring that the four Junto candidates had been "duly elected." [80] This decision was based on the reasoning that the Privy Council "would have been inexcusable if they had not delayed the Matter, when [on March 3] they found but 7 Counties had returned their Lists." [81] After almost six months of wrangling, the involved dispute had at last been settled. Many in East Jersey accepted the defeat with ill grace, while others looked confidently forward to the next contest with the Junto.[82]

The results of the bitterly fought election were indecisive. If the canvass had been conducted with normal honesty, Clark and Dayton would doubtless have been victorious, as they were in 1790. Federalism and fidelity to the new government were not issues. Rather the basis of conflict was the traditional sectional antagonism between East Jersey and West Jersey. The election was not, however, devoid of significance. For the first time, an approach was made toward the development of a state-wide political organization. A new

---

from Morris County, and Peter Haring, councilor from Bergen. "Their Testimony," according to Boudinot, "amounted to nothing more than to shew their Combination in a Party of determination to carry their Point at all Events."

[79] *Annals of Congress*, I, pp. 756-57; *New Jersey Journal*, Aug. 26, 1789; *Gazette of the United States*, Sept. 2, 5, 9, 1789; *Daily Advertiser*, Sept. 2, 3, 1789.

[80] *Annals of Congress*, I, pp. 834, 836; *New Jersey Journal*, Sept. 2, 16, 1789.

[81] Elias Boudinot to William Livingston, Sept. 2, 1789, Livingston Papers, MHS.

[82] *New Jersey Journal*, Sept. 9, 1789; *Brunswick Gazette*, Sept. 15, 1789.

element had been injected into the political life of the state, an element that was to assume increasing importance in the future. The crudity of the existent electoral machinery had been revealed in so dramatic a fashion as to arouse thought about the matter and lead eventually to constructive reforms. Finally, the contest had given rise to a dispute which created novel problems for the first Congress.

Inconclusive as was the outcome of the election, it did demonstrate that the conservative coalition in the state had acquired sufficient strength to challenge the rule of the East Jersey faction that had been responsible for the popular measures of the mid-eighties. By 1789 the leftward swing of the pendulum had been halted, and the swing to the right had begun. The counterrevolution, if such it can be called, was gradual and mild. But the change in the political scene was sufficiently obvious to indicate that the old era had ended and that a new one had begun.

XII

Conclusion

★★

THE "critical period" in New Jersey was not characterized by disintegration and disorder. It was, on the contrary, marked by progressive accomplishments in many fields. The immediate problems that arose out of the devastation that had been wrought by the war were met and solved. Homes, schools, churches, and business establishments were rebuilt or repaired. Educational, religious, and social organizations were rehabilitated and adapted to meet new conditions. The fabric of society, rent over the issue of independence, was mended. The vitality manifested by the people of the state in carrying out the heavy tasks of reconstruction is evidence of the fact that the postwar years were not ones of bleak despair.

Self-government, although subjected to rigorous tests, demonstrated its capacity to survive and develop. At no other period did the enfranchised citizens of the state have such power to determine the course of public affairs, for they were restrained neither by a rigid constitution nor by the external authority of a central government. From the viewpoint of conservative men of property, the unfettered rule of the majority was the greatest political evil of the day. From the vantage point of the present, however, it is not apparent that the majority was guilty of indulging in gross abuses of its powers. As the representative process assumed increased importance, consideration was given to the improvement of the crude electoral machinery that had been inherited from the colonial era, and significant advances were made.

Throughout the postwar decade, the fundamental basis of political division was the cleavage between East Jersey and West Jersey. The result of historical, geographical, social, cultural, and economic differences between the two regions, this sectional split was fairly clear-cut on all questions of internal policy. The balance between the rival sections was a delicate one, but during the mid-eighties East Jersey was in control. Not until after the adoption of the Federal Constitution did the western counties gain dominance. Because the spokesmen of East Jersey had been foremost in espousing popular measures, such as paper money, the political shift that occurred around 1788 was in some respects a counterrevolution.

The most critical problems of the period were financial. The sharp reduction in the money supply that resulted from the adoption of deflationary policies at the close of the war and from an unfavorable trade balance produced a grave currency shortage. At the same time, extraordinarily heavy taxes were levied to meet interest charges on the large debt burden that the state had assumed. It was to be expected that there would arise a strong popular demand for more money. To meet the crisis, the legislators resorted to the time-honored expedient of establishing a loan office and printing a hundred thousand pounds in paper bills. Their action was not, under the circumstances, radical, nor did it have disastrous consequences. It was violently opposed by the creditor group, which—remembering its experience with fiat money during the war—had little faith in the promises of a popularly controlled government. That same government, nevertheless, demonstrated remarkable concern for the welfare of public creditors by undertaking to service both the continental and the state debts. All in all, the legislators made valiant efforts to bring order out of the chaotic financial situation, and their endeavors are entitled to a more sympathetic appraisal than they customarily have been accorded by historians.

Responsible for many of New Jersey's financial difficulties were the weaknesses of the Articles of Confederation. From the first, the state had protested to Congress against the inequitable operation of the Articles and had put forward concrete proposals for strengthening the Confederation. It was particularly insistent that Congress should have control over the western lands and power to levy import duties. Because it had to rely exclusively on taxation to raise money to meet continental requisitions, it was desirous that the central government should have revenues derived from land sales and a tariff. Then the public debt could be serviced and landowners could be relieved of oppressive taxes. So determined was New Jersey on these points that it went to the length of flatly refusing to honor the requisition of 1785 and thereby precipitated a crisis which was probably at least as influential as the much-publicized Shays' Rebellion in stimulating the movement that resulted in the calling of the Constitutional Convention. At no time was the matter of revising the Confederation an object of controversy, for all classes and sections saw the benefits to be gained from a reconstituted union that would be able to meet its obligations without having to rely upon internal taxation. In addition, men of property welcomed the imposition of curbs on the state legislature. New Jersey concluded its experiment in independence by entering wholeheartedly into a federal union that promised enormous advantages in return for the acceptance of limitations on the sovereign powers of the state.

APPENDIX I

RECORD OF TAX RECEIPTS, 1784-1790 [1]

(shillings and pence omitted)

Year	New Emission and Certificates	New Emission	Specie	Revenue Money	Lawful Money	Continental
1784	£13,651	£2,662	£53,889	£15,132	—	$35,680
1785	1,414	1,537	17,333	14,104	—	45,535
1786	9,199	767	15,482	27,291	£ 8,339	2,546
1787	826	321	2,650	30,768	9,903	413
1788	1,413	18	4,453	34,414	17,098	—
1789	465	496	3,487	32,530	17,138	—
1790	406	613	652	27,168	36,052	—

[1] Compiled from the annual reports of the State Treasurer as printed in the *Votes and Proceedings*, usually in November of each year. The new emission and certificates were worth about one-third their face value. Lawful money included (in addition to specie) revenue money and loan-office money, which passed at a discount of not more than twenty-five per cent. Continental money after 1784 was worth perhaps one-half of one per cent of its face value.

APPENDIX II

RECORD OF INTEREST PAYMENTS, 1784-1789 [1]

(all figures in pounds; shillings and pence omitted)

Continental Obligations

	1784		1785		1786		1787		1788		1789	
	Specie	Paper	Specie	Paper	Specie	Paper	Specie	Paper	Specie	Paper	Specie	Paper
Loan office certificates	8,001	23,142	2,345	20,416	1,583	7,846	49	10,087	—	15,068	—	16,715
Thompson's notes	—	—	—	10,365	—	12,197	—	12,565	—	13,355	—	12,691
Pierce's notes	—	—	—	6,156	—	4,447	—	4,372	—	6,731	—	5,115
State Obligations												
Depreciation notes	6,029	—	2,491	—	1,265	—	—	1,428	—	4,208	—	3,718
Militia notes	—	—	—	—	—	—	—	—	—	1,791	—	2,462
Contractors' certificates	1,423	—	479	—	71	—	—	—	—	—	—	—
Surplus certificates	1,503	—	437	—	96	—	—	—	—	—	—	—
Demands vs. forf. estates	—	—	—	—	—	—	—	—	—	1,239	—	1,249
Condict's notes	—	—	—	—	—	—	—	—	—	5,161	—	5,151
Totals	16,956	23,142	5,762	36,937	3,015	24,490	49	28,452	—	47,553	—	47,061

[1] Compiled from the annual reports of the State Treasurer as printed in the *Votes and Proceedings*, usually in November of each year. The payments in paper were in revenue money or lawful money.

BIBLIOGRAPHY

★★★

MANUSCRIPTS

Friends Book Store, Arch Street, Philadelphia:
  Minutes of the Philadelphia Yearly Meeting, 1780-1790.
  Minutes of the Gloucester and Salem [Haddonfield] Quarterly Meeting, 1776-1794.
  Minutes of the Shrewsbury and Rahway Quarterly Meeting, 1757-1828.
  Minutes of the Quarterly Meeting of Burlington, 1770-1795.

Library of Congress, Manuscripts Division:
  Continental Congress Papers, series numbered 41, 42, 43, and 46.
  Papers of, or relating to, William Paterson, 1768-1806.
  Papers regarding the Ramapock Patent, 1787.

Massachusetts Historical Society:
  William Livingston Papers.

National Archives:
  New Jersey Loan Office, Ledger C-2, Domestic Debt, Holding of 3% Stock (Funded 3% Stock), July 1, 1791.

New Jersey Historical Society:
  Edwin A. Ely Collection.
  Miscellaneous Manuscripts.
  New Jersey Manuscripts.

William Nelson Manuscripts.

James Parker Papers.

Rutherfurd Family Papers.

Subscriptions towards a Loan to the United States as proposed by the Act of Congress of the 4th of August 1790 in the Office of James Ewing, Commissioner of Loans in the State of New Jersey, payable in Certificates of the Debt of the State of New Jersey.

New Jersey State Library, Trenton:

AM Papers, 13 boxes.

Continental Congress Papers (bound).

Damages by British and Americans, 6 vols., 1776-1782.

Gloucester Loan Office Book, 1786.

William Livingston Correspondence (transcripts), 7 vols., 1780-1782.

Loan Office Indentures, Somerset County, 1786-1798.

Loose Manuscripts, 10 boxes.

Manuscript Collection, 6 boxes.

Minutes of the Governor's Privy Council of New Jersey (bound), 1777-1795.

Miscellaneous Manuscripts.

Vault Manuscripts, 13 boxes.

New York Historical Society:

Elias Boudinot: Miscellaneous Letters.

Jonathan Dayton: Miscellaneous Letters.

Ellis Papers.

Diary of William North, 1786.

Joseph Reed Papers.

New York Public Library:

Elias Boudinot's Ledger, 1760-1814.

Emmet Collection.

New Jersey Box, Miscellaneous.

Letter Book of Lewis Ogden, 1787-1798.

Papers of William Paterson (Bancroft transcripts).

Stewart and Jones Papers.

Historical Society of Pennsylvania:

Elias Boudinot Papers.

Conarroe Collection.

Dreer Collection.
Etting Collection.
Edward Carey Gardner Collection, Carey Section.
Gratz Collection.
Society Collection.
Wallace Papers.

Princeton University Library:
Elias Boudinot Papers.
Elias Boudinot Letters.
Manuscript Minutes of the East Jersey Proprietors, 1786-1788.
New Jersey Treasurer's Receipt Books, 1783-1789.
William Paterson Papers.

Rutgers University Library:
William Churchill Houston—Robert Morris Letters.
Account Book of Robert Johnson, Salem, 1782-1790.
Minutes of the Presbytery of New Brunswick (typewritten copy).
Miscellaneous Manuscripts.
Robert Morris Papers.
Neilson Family Papers.
James Parker Papers.
William Paterson Papers.
Ten Eyck Papers.
Transactions of the Athenian Society.

Stevens Institute of Technology:
Stevens Family Papers.

Surveyor-General's Office, Burlington:
Minute Book of the Council of Proprietors of West Jersey, C and D, 1771-1800.

Newspapers and Periodicals

The American Museum or Repository of Ancient and Modern Fugitive Pieces, 1787-1792.
[Chatham] *The New Jersey Journal,* 1779-1783. Published by Shepard Kollock.
The Christian's, Scholar's, and Farmer's Magazine, 1789-1791. Published at Elizabeth Town by Shepard Kollock.

The Columbian Magazine or Monthly Miscellany, 1786-1788.

[Elizabeth Town] *The Political Intelligencer. And New-Jersey Advertiser*, 1785-1786. Removed from New Brunswick to Elizabeth Town in April, 1785.

[Elizabeth Town] *The New-Jersey Journal, and Political Intelligencer*, 1786-1792. Continuation of above with changed title.

[New Brunswick] *The Brunswick Gazette*, 1789-1792. Published by Shelly Arnett until November, 1789; thereafter by Abraham Blauvelt.

[New Brunswick] *The New-Brunswick Gazette, and Weekly Monitor*, 1787-1789. Predecessor of above.

[New Brunswick] *The Political Intelligencer. And New-Jersey Advertiser*, 1783-1785. Established in 1783 by Shelly Arnett and Shepard Kollock. Kollock became the sole proprietor in July, 1784, and moved the paper to Elizabeth Town in April, 1785.

The New Jersey Magazine, 1786-1787. Published in New Brunswick by Frederick C. Quequelle and James Prange.

[New York] *The Daily Advertiser*, 1787-1788.

[Philadelphia] *The Pennsylvania Packet*, 1787-1789.

Princeton Packet, 1786-1787. Published by James Tod.

[Trenton] *Federal Post*, 1788-1789. Published by Frederick C. Quequelle and George M. Wilson until November, 1788; thereafter by Quequelle alone.

[Trenton] *The New-Jersey Gazette*, 1781-1786. Published by Isaac Collins.

OFFICIAL PUBLICATIONS

Acts of the Council and General Assembly of the State of New Jersey, from the Establishment of the present Government, and Declaration of Independence, to the End of the first Sitting of the eighth Session, on the 24th day of December, 1783 ..., compiled by Peter Wilson (Trenton, 1784).

Acts of the General Assembly of the Province of New Jersey, from the Surrender of the Government to Queen Anne ... to the 14th Day of January, 1776, compiled by Samuel Allinson (Burlington, 1776).

Acts of the ... General Assembly of the State of New Jersey, 1776-1790. Generally cited as *Session Laws*, the acts of the legislature were published in pamphlet form at various places, usually at the end of each sitting of the legislature. The most complete collection is in the New Jersey State Library.

American State Papers: Finance, II (Washington, 1832).

Archives of the State of New Jersey, First Series, vols. XXXIV-XXXIX (Trenton, 1931-1936), *Second Series* (5 vols., Trenton, 1901-1917).

Biographical Directory of the American Congress, 1774-1927 (69th Congress, 2d Session, House Document No. 783, Washington, 1928).

Collections of the New Jersey Historical Society, IX (Newark, 1916).

The Debates and Proceedings in the Congress of the United States (*Annals of Congress*), I, compiled by Joseph Gales, Sr., (Washington, 1834).

Hood, John. *Index of Colonial and State Laws of New Jersey between the Years 1663 and 1903 Inclusive* (Camden, 1905).

Journals of the Continental Congress, 1774-1789, ed. by Worthington C. Ford *et al.* (34 vols., Washington, 1904-1937).

Journal of the Proceedings of the Legislative-Council of the State of New-Jersey, 1776-1790. Published at various places at conclusion of sittings.

Laws of the State of New-Jersey; Revised and Published under the Authority of the Legislature, by William Paterson (New Brunswick, 1800).

Minutes of the Convention of the State of New-Jersey, Holden at Trenton the 11th Day of December 1787, reprinted by Clayton L. Traver (Trenton, 1888).

Minutes and Proceedings of the Council and General Assembly of the State of New-Jersey in Joint-Meeting, 1776-1790. Published at various places at irregular intervals.

Minutes of the Provincial Congress and the Council of Safety of the State of New Jersey (Trenton, 1879).

Selections from the Correspondence of the Executive of New Jersey, from 1776 to 1786 (Newark, 1848).

Votes and Proceedings of the General Assembly of the State of New-Jersey, 1776-1799. Published at various places at the close of each sitting. The *Votes and Proceedings,* the *Journal of the Council,* and the *Minutes of the Joint-Meeting* are available on microfilm from the Library of Congress.

PRINTED SOURCES

American Husbandry, ed. by Harry J. Carman (New York, 1939).

An address from the Council of Proprietors of the Western Division of New-Jersey, to the Occupiers of Lands Within the Angle. To which are added Remarks on the said Address by Aristides (n. p., 1795)..

"Additional Letters of the Reverend Abraham Beach, 1772-1791," ed. by Walter H. Stowe, *Historical Magazine of the Protestant Episcopal Church*, V (1936), pp. 122-41.

Bond, Beverley W. *The Correspondence of John Cleves Symmes* (New York, 1926).

"Letters of Phineas Bond," *Annual Report of the American Historical Association*, I (1916), pp. 513-59.

Boudinot, J. J., ed. *The Life, Public Services, Addresses and Letters of Elias Boudinot* (Boston and New York, 1896).

Brissot de Warville, Jean P. *New Travels in the United States of America, performed in MDCCLXXXVIII* (2 vols., 2nd ed., corrected, London, 1794).

Burnett, Edmund C. *Letters of Members of the Continental Congress* (8 vols., Washington, 1921-1936).

The Journal and Biography of Nicholas Collin, 1746-1831, translated by Amandus Johnson (Philadelphia, 1936).

A Concise View of the Controversy between the Proprietors of East and West-Jersey: Being An Explanation of the Bill presented by the Western Proprietors to the Legislature of New-Jersey; published with a Design to remove the Misrepresentations contained in a Pamphlet, entitled "The Petitions and Memorials of the Proprietors of East and West-Jersey" ... [probably the work of Richard Stockton] (Philadelphia, 1785).

Documents Illustrative of the Formation of the Union of the American States, selected, edited, and indexed by Charles C. Tansill (Washington, 1927).

Edwards, Morgan. *Materials towards a History of the Baptists in Jersey*, II (Philadelphia, 1792).

An Enquiry into Public Abuses, Arising for want of a Due Execution of laws, provided for the Suppression of vice in the State of New-Jersey (Philadelphia, 1784).

Farrand, Max. *The Records of the Federal Convention of 1787* (3 vols., New Haven, 1911).

"Diary of Timothy Ford," *South Carolina Historical and Genealogical Magazine*, XIII (1912).

The Letters of Moore Furman, Deputy Quarter-Master General of New Jersey in the Revolution, compiled and edited by the Historical Research Committee of the New Jersey Society of the Colonial Dames (New York, 1912).

Green, Ashbel. *The Life of Ashbel Green,* prepared for the press by Joseph H. Jones (New York, 1849).

Guest, Moses. *Poems ... to which are annexed, Extracts from a Journal Kept by the author while he followed the sea* (Cincinnati, 2nd ed., 1824).

The Works of Alexander Hamilton, ed. by John C. Hamilton (7 vols., New York, 1850-1851).

"John Hunt's Diary," ed. by Edward A. Fuhlbruegge, *Proceedings of the New Jersey Historical Society,* LII (1934), pp. 177-93, 223-39; LIII (1935), pp. 26-43.

The Correspondence and Public Papers of John Jay, ed. by Henry P. Johnston (4 vols., New York, 1890-1893).

Journals of the General Conventions of the Protestant Episcopal Church in the United States of America, 1784-1814 (Philadelphia, 1817).

Journals of the Conventions of the Protestant Episcopal Church of the State of New Jersey, 1785-1816 (New York, 1890).

"Diary of Joseph Lewis," *Proceedings of the New Jersey Historical Society,* LIX (1941), LX (1942), LXI (1943), LXII (1944).

The Writings of James Madison, comprising his public papers and his private correspondence, 1769-1836, ed. by Gaillard Hunt (9 vols., New York, 1902).

Monaghan, Frank. "Unpublished Correspondence of William Livingston and John Jay," *Proceedings of the New Jersey Historical Society,* LII (1934), pp. 141-62.

The Writings of James Monroe, ed. by Stanislaus M. Hamilton (7 vols., New York, 1898-1903).

Morse, Jedidiah. *The American Geography* (Elizabeth Town, 1789).

Records of the Town of Newark, New Jersey ... (Collections of the New Jersey Historical Society, VI, Newark, N. J., 1864).

"Objections of New Jersey to the Articles of Confederation, submitted to the American Congress, June 23, 1778," *Proceedings of the New Jersey Historical Society,* X (1865), pp. 173-76.

Observations on Government; including some Animadversions on Mr. Adams's Defence of the Constitutions of Government of the United States of America, and on De Lolme's Constitution of England. By a Farmer of New Jersey [John Stevens] (New York, 1787).

"The Cornelia (Bell) Paterson Letters," *Proceedings of the New Jersey Historical Society,* New Ser., XVI (1931), pp. 186-201.

"Papers of William Paterson on the Federal Convention," *American Historical Review,* IX (1904), pp. 310-40.

Records of the Presbyterian Church in the United States of America (Philadelphia, 1841).

Reed, William B. *Life and Correspondence of Joseph Reed* (2 vols., Philadelphia, 1847).

The Rise, Minutes, and Proceedings of the New Jersey Medical Society (Newark, 1875).

Robin, C. C. *New Travels through North-America*, translated by Philip Freneau (Boston, 1784).

Rutherfurd, John. "Notes on the State of New Jersey," *Proceedings of the New Jersey Historical Society*, 2nd Ser., I (1867), pp. 79-89.

[Rutherfurd, John]. *The Petitions and Memorials of the Proprietors of West and East-Jersey to the Legislature of New-Jersey, together with a Map of the State of New-Jersey, and the Country adjacent: and also An Appendix: Containing Extracts from several original papers* ... (New York, 1784 and 1786).

Schoepf, J. D. *Travels in the Confederation, 1783-1784*, translated and edited by A. J. Morrison (2 vols., Philadelphia, 1911).

Sedgwick, Theodore. *A Memoir of the Life of William Livingston* (New York, 1833).

Sheffield, John, Lord. *Observations on the Commerce of the United States* (new ed., Dublin, 1784).

Shinn, Henry C. "An Early New Jersey Poll List," *Pennsylvania Magazine of History and Biography*, XLIV (1920), pp. 77-81.

Shreve, Col. Israel. "Journal From Jersey to the Monongahela, Aug. 11, 1788," *Pennsylvania Magazine of History and Biography*, LII (1928).

Smyth, J. F. D. *Tour in the United States of America* (2 vols., London, 1794).

"Somerset Civil List, 1688-1799," *Somerset County Historical Quarterly*, VIII (1919), pp. 33-37, 119-23.

[Varlo, Charles]. *Miscellany of Knowledge* (London, 1792).

The Writings of George Washington from the Original Manuscript Sources, 1754-1799, ed. by John C. Fitzpatrick, XXII-XXVII (Washington, 1937-1938).

Webster, Noah. *A Collection of Essays and Fugitive Writings on Moral, Historical, Political, and Literary Subjects* (Boston, 1790).

Winterbotham, William. *An Historical, Geographical, Commercial, and Philosophical View of the United States of America* (New York, 1796).

[Witherspoon, John]. *Essay on Money, as a Medium of Commerce* ... By a Citizen of the United States (Philadelphia, 1786).

Witherspoon, John. *The Works of John Witherspoon, D. D.* (9 vols., Edinburgh, 1804).

SECONDARY WORKS

Abernethy, Thomas P. *Western Lands and the American Revolution* (New York, 1937).

Alexander, Samuel Davies. *Princeton College during the Eighteenth Century* (New York, 1872).

Atkinson, John. *Memorials of Methodism in New Jersey from the Foundation of the first society in the State in 1770, to the completion of the first Twenty Years of its History* (Philadelphia, 1860).

Atkinson, Joseph. *The History of Newark, New Jersey* (Newark, 1878).

Bancroft, George. *History of the Formation of the Constitution of the United States of America* (2 vols., New York, 1882).

Beard, Charles A. *An Economic Interpretation of the Constitution* (New York, 1913).

Bemis, Samuel F. *Pinckney's Treaty* (Baltimore, 1926).

Benedict, William H. *New Brunswick in History* (New Brunswick, 1925).

Bi-Centennial Celebration of the Board of American Proprietors of East New Jersey, at Perth Amboy, Tuesday, November 25, 1884 (Newark, 1885).

Bining, Arthur C. *Pennsylvania Iron Manufacture in the Eighteenth Century* (Harrisburg, 1938).

Bishop, C. F. *History of Elections in the American Colonies* (*Columbia University Studies in History, Economics, and Public Law*, III, No. 1, New York, 1893).

Bishop, J. L. *A History of American Manufactures From 1608 to 1860* (Philadelphia, 1866).

Bolles, Albert S. *The Financial History of the United States, 1774-1789* (4th ed., New York, 1896).

Boyer, Charles S. *Early Forges and Furnaces in New Jersey* (Philadelphia, 1931).

Brace, Rev. F. R. "New Jersey Chaplains in the Army of the Revolution," *Proceedings of the New Jersey Historical Society*, 3rd Ser., VI (1907), pp. 1-11.

Brown, Allen Henry. *An Outline History of the Presbyterian Church in West or South Jersey from 1700 to 1865* (Philadelphia, 1869).

Brunhouse, Robert L. *The Counter-Revolution in Pennsylvania, 1776-1790* (Harrisburg, 1942).

Bullock, Charles Jesse. *The Finances of the United States from 1775 to 1789 with Especial Reference to the Budget* (*Bulletin of the University of Wisconsin, Economics, Political Science, and History Series*, I, No. 2, Madison, Wisconsin, June, 1895).

Burnett, Edmund C. *The Continental Congress* (New York, 1941).

Burr, Nelson R. *Education in New Jersey, 1630-1871* (Princeton, 1942).

A Century of Population Growth, From the First Census of the United States to the Twelfth, 1790-1900 (Department of Commerce and Labor, Bureau of the Census, Washington, 1909).

Chambers, T. F. *The Early Germans of New Jersey* (Dover, 1895).

Clarke, Matthew St. Clair and Hall, David A. *Cases of Disputed Elections in Congress, 1789-1834* (Washington, 1834).

Clayton, W. W. and Nelson, William. *History of Bergen and Passaic Counties* (Philadelphia, 1882).

Clement, John. *Notes and Memoranda relating to the West New Jersey Society* (Camden, 1880).

Cochran, T. C. *New York in the Confederation* (Philadelphia, 1932).

Cole, Arthur Harrison. *Wholesale Commodity Prices in the United States, 1700-1861* (Cambridge, 1938).

Collins, Varnum Lansing. *President Witherspoon, A Biography* (2 vols., Princeton, 1925).

———. *The Continental Congress at Princeton* (Princeton, 1908).

Cooley, Eli Field. *Early Settlers of Trenton and Ewing* (Trenton, 1883).

Cooley, Henry S. *A Study of Slavery in New Jersey* (*Johns Hopkins University Studies in Historical and Political Science*, 14th Ser., IX-X, Baltimore, 1896).

Channing, Edward A. *History of the United States*, III (New York, 1912).

Corwin, Edward T. *A Manual of the Reformed Church in America, 1628-1902* (4th ed., New York, 1902).

Crowl, Philip A. *Maryland During and After the Revolution: A Political and Economic Study* (*Johns Hopkins University Studies in Historical and Political Science*, Ser. LXI, No. 1, Baltimore, 1943).

Davidson, Rev. Robert. *A Historical Sketch of the First Presbyterian Church in the City of New Brunswick* (New Brunswick, 1852).

Davis, Joseph S. *Essays in the Earlier History of American Corporations* (2 vols., Cambridge, 1917).

Demarest, William H. S. *A History of Rutgers College, 1766-1924* (New Brunswick, 1924).

Dictionary of American Biography, ed. by Allen Johnson and Dumas Malone (20 vols., New York, 1928-1936).

Domett, Henry W. *A History of the Bank of New York, 1784-1884* (3rd ed., n. p., [1884]).

Dunaway, W. F. "The English Settlers in Colonial Pennsylvania," *Pennsylvania Magazine of History and Biography*, LII (1928), pp. 317-41.

East, Robert A. *Business Enterprise in the American Revolutionary Era* (New York, 1938).

Ellis, Franklin. *History of Monmouth County, New Jersey* (Philadelphia, 1885).

Elmer, Lucius Q. C. *Constitution and Government of the Province and State of New Jersey, with Biographical Sketches of the Governors from 1776 to 1845, and Reminiscences of the Bench and Bar, during more than Half a Century* (Newark, 1872).

Erdman, Charles R. *The New Jersey Constitution of 1776* (Princeton, 1929).

Farrand, Max. *The Framing of the Constitution of the United States* (New Haven, 1913).

Fee, Walter R. *The Transition from Aristocracy to Democracy in New Jersey, 1789-1829* (Somerville, 1933).

Fisher, Edgar J. *New Jersey as a Royal Province, 1738-1776* (New York, 1911).

Fiske, John. *The Critical Period of American History, 1783-1789* (Boston, 1888).

Fitch, Asa. "The Hessian Fly," *Transactions of the New-York State Agricultural Society*, VI (1846), pp. 316-73.

Fuhlbruegge, Edward A. "New Jersey Finances During the American Revolution," *Proceedings of the New Jersey Historical Society*, LV (1937), pp. 167-90.

Gardner, D. H. "The Emancipation of Slaves in New Jersey," *Proceedings of the New Jersey Historical Society*, NS, IX (1924), pp. 1-21.

Gavin, Frank. "The Reverend Thomas Bradbury Chandler in the Light of his (Unpublished) Diary, 1777-1785," reprint from *Church History* (June, 1932), pp. 3-19.

Giesecke, A. A. *American Commercial Regulation Before 1789* (Philadelphia, 1910).

Given, Lois V. "The Sixth Query: A Study of the Friends of Burlington County During the Revolutionary War, 1774-1784," typed manuscript in possession of author, Moorestown, New Jersey.

Glenn, Thomas. *William Churchill Houston* (Norristown, 1903).

Gordon, Thomas F. *The History of New Jersey from its Discovery by Europeans to the Adoption of the Federal Constitution* (Trenton, 1834).

Gordon, William. *The History of the...Independence of the United States of America*...(3 vols., 3rd ed., New York, 1801).

Gouge, William M. *A Short History of Paper Money and Banking in the United States*...(Philadelphia, 1833).

Griffith, William. *Annual Law Register of the United States*, IV (Burlington, 1822).

Hageman, John F. *History of Princeton and its Institutions* (2 vols., Philadelphia, 1879).

Hall, John. *History of the Presbyterian Church in Trenton, N. J.* (2nd ed., Trenton, 1912).

Harlow, Richard V. "Aspects of Revolutionary Finance," *American Historical Review*, XXXV (1929), pp. 46-68.

Hart, Ann Clark. *Abraham Clark, Signer of the Declaration of Independence* (San Francisco, 1923).

Hart, Charles Henry. "Colonel Robert Lettis Hooper, Deputy Quarter Master General in the Continental Army and Vice President of New Jersey," *Pennsylvania Magazine of History and Biography*, XXXVI (1912), pp. 60-91.

Hatch, Louis C. *The Administration of the American Revolutionary Army* (New York, 1904).

Heusser, Albert H. *The Forgotten General, Robert Erskine, F. R. S.* (Paterson, 1928).

Hepburn, A. Barton. *History of Coinage and Currency in the United States and the Perennial Contest for Sound Money* (New York, 1903).

A History of Trenton, 1679-1929, published under the auspices of the Trenton Historical Society (2 vols., Princeton, 1929).

Hodge, Charles. *The Constitutional History of the Presbyterian Church in the United States of America* (2 vols., Philadelphia, 1840).

Hooker, Joseph. "Thomas Bradbury Chandler," *The Church Eclectic*, XVIII (1890), pp. 289-302.

Honeyman, A. Van Doren. "Concerning the New Jersey Loyalists in the Revolution," *Proceedings of the New Jersey Historical Society*, XLI (1933), pp. 117-33.

———. "The Early Scotch Element of Somerset, Middlesex and

Monmouth Counties," *Somerset County Historical Quarterly*, VI (1917), pp. 1-23.

Hunter, William C. *The Commercial Policy of New Jersey under the Confederation, 1783-1789* (Princeton, 1922).

Jameson, J. F. "Studies in the History of the Federal Convention of 1787," *Annual Report of the American Historical Association*, 1902, I (Washington, 1903), pp. 89-167.

Jensen, Merrill. *The Articles of Confederation* (Madison, 1940).

———. "The Cessions of the Old Northwest," *Mississippi Valley Historical Review*, XXIII (1936), pp. 27-48.

———. "The Creation of the National Domain, 1781-1784," *Mississippi Valley Historical Review*, XXVI (1939), pp. 323-42.

Johnson, Robert Gibbon. *An Historical Account of the First Settlement of Salem*... (Philadelphia, 1839).

Jones, E. A. *The Loyalists of New Jersey, their memorials, petitions, claims, etc. from English records* (Newark, 1927).

Jones, Rufus M. *The Quakers in the American Colonies* (London, 1911).

Kemmerer, Donald L. *Path to Freedom* (Princeton, 1940).

———. "The Colonial Loan-Office System in New Jersey," *Journal of Political Economy*, XLVII (1939), pp. 867-74.

———. "The Suffrage Franchise in Colonial New Jersey," *Proceedings of the New Jersey Historical Society*, LII (1934), pp. 166-73.

Kull, Irving S., ed. *New Jersey—a History* (6 vols., New York, 1930-1932).

Lane, Wheaton J. *From Indian Trail to Iron Horse* (Princeton, 1939).

Lee, Francis B. *New Jersey as a Colony and as a State* (4 vols., New York, 1903).

Lester, Richard A. "Currency Issues to Overcome Depressions in Delaware, New Jersey, New York and Maryland, 1715-1723," *Journal of Political Economy*, XLVII (1939), pp. 182-217.

Lewis, George E. *The Indiana Company, 1763-1798* (Glendale, 1941).

Libby, Orin G. *Geographical Distribution of the Vote of the Thirteen States on the Federal Constitution, 1787-8* (Madison, 1894).

Livermore, Shaw. *Early American Land Companies* (New York, 1939).

Lundin, Leonard. *Cockpit of the Revolution* (Princeton, 1940).

MacKay, R. A. "New Jersey in the Confederation," unpublished thesis, 1922, Princeton University Library.

McConnell, S. D. *History of the American Episcopal Church* (New York, 1899).

McCormick, Edward J. "New Jersey Supplies the Revolutionary Army," unpublished master's thesis, 1937, Rutgers University Library.

McCormick, Richard P. "The First Election of Governor William Livingston," *Proceedings of the New Jersey Historical Society*, LXV (1947), pp. 92-100.

————. "The West Jersey Estate of Sir Robert Barker," *Proceedings of the New Jersey Historical Society*, LXIV (1946), pp. 119-55.

McGregor, David. "History of Freemasonry in New Jersey," *Proceedings of the Grand Lodge . . . of Free and Accepted Masons for the State of New Jersey*, XL (1937), pp. 75-217.

McKinley, Albert E. *The Suffrage Franchise in the Thirteen English Colonies in America* (*Publications of the University of Pennsylvania, Series in History*, No. 2, Philadelphia, 1905).

McLaughlin, Andrew C. *The Confederation and the Constitution* (New York, 1905).

Macmillan, Margaret. *The War Governors in the American Revolution* (New York, 1943).

"Sketch of Colonel Ephraim Martin, of the New Jersey Continental Line," *Pennsylvania Magazine of History and Biography*, XXXII (1910), pp. 480-83.

Messler, Abraham. *Centennial History of Somerset County* (Somerville, N. J., 1878).

————. *First Things in Old Somerset* (Somerville, N. J., 1899).

Michener, Ezra. *A Retrospect of Early Quakerism, being extracts from the records of Philadelphia Yearly Meeting and the meetings composing it* (Philadelphia, 1860).

Miller, Harry E. *Banking Theories in the United States Before 1860* (Cambridge, 1927).

Morris, Jay S. "New Jersey and the Federal Constitution," unpublished master's thesis, 1931, Columbia University Library.

Mott, George S. "The First Century of Hunterdon County," *Proceedings of the New Jersey Historical Society*, 2nd Ser., V (1877), pp. 60-111.

Murray, Nicholas. *Notes, Historical and Biographical Concerning Elizabethtown, . . .* (Elizabethtown, 1844).

Nevins, Allan. *The American States During and After the Revolution, 1775-1789* (New York, 1924).

Parker, R. Wayne. "Taxes and Money in New Jersey Before the Revolution," *Proceedings of the New Jersey Historical Society*, 2nd Ser., VII (1883), pp. 143-57.

Phillips, Henry. *Historical Sketches of the Paper Currency of the American Colonies, Prior to the Adoption of the Federal Constitution,* 1st Ser. (Roxbury, Mass., 1865).

Rawle, William H. "Colonel Lambert Cadwallader," *Pennsylvania Magazine of History and Biography,* X (1886), pp. 1-14.

Report of the Committee of the Council of Proprietors of West New Jersey in Relation to the Province Line between East and West New Jersey (Camden, 1888).

"Report of Committee on Linguistic and National Stocks in the Population of the United States," *Annual Report of the American Historical Association* (1931), pp. 107-441.

Roome, William. *The Early Days and Early Surveys of East New Jersey* (Morristown, N. J., 1883).

Rutherfurd, Livingston. *Family Records and Events compiled principally from the Original Manuscripts of the Rutherfurd Collection* (New York, 1894).

Salter, Edwin. *A History of Monmouth and Ocean Counties...* (Bayonne, 1890).

Savelle, Max. *George Morgan, Colony Builder* (New York, 1932).

Schuyler, Hamilton. *A History of St. Michael's Church, Trenton* (Princeton, 1926).

Scott, Austin. "Blazing the Way to Final Victory—1781," *Proceedings of the New Jersey Historical Society,* New Ser., VI (1921), pp. 1-10.

———. "The Early Cities of New Jersey," *Proceedings of the New Jersey Historical Society,* 2nd Ser., IX (1887), pp. 151-73.

———. "Holmes v. Walton—The New Jersey Precedent," *American Historical Review,* IV (1899), pp. 3-19.

———. "The Share of New Jersey in Founding the American Constitution," *New Brunswick Historical Club Publications,* No. 1 (New Brunswick, 1887).

Shourds, Thomas. *History and Genealogy of Fenwick's Colony* (Bridgeton, N. J., 1876).

Sickler, Joseph S. *The History of Salem County, New Jersey* (Salem, N. J., 1927).

Smith, R. Morris. *The Burlington Smiths, a Family History* (Philadelphia, 1877).

Snell, J. P. *History of Hunterdon and Somerset Counties, New Jersey* (Philadelphia, 1888).

Swick, Minor. "A Dutch Migration from the Raritan Valley to New

York State in 1785 and Later," *Somerset County Historical Quarterly*, IV (1915), pp. 21-25.

Spaulding, E. Wilder. *New York in the Critical Period, 1783-1789* (New York, 1932).

Stephens, Frank F. *The Transitional Period, 1788-1789, in the Government of the United States* (*University of Missouri Studies, Social Science Series*, II, No. 4, 1909).

Stewart, Frank H. *Notes on Old Gloucester County, New Jersey*, I (n. p., 1917).

Stowe, Walter H. "The Corporation for the Relief of Widows and Children of Clergymen," *Historical Magazine of the Protestant Episcopal Church*, III (1934), pp. 19-33.

———. "The Reverend Abraham Beach, D.D.," *Historical Magazine of the Protestant Episcopal Church*, III (1934), pp. 76-95.

Sumner, William G. *A History of American Currency* (New York, 1884).

Tanner, Edwin P. *The Province of New Jersey, 1664-1738* (New York, 1908).

Thatcher, Harold W. "Comments on American Government and on the Constitution by a New Jersey Member of the Federal Convention," *Proceedings of the New Jersey Historical Society*, LVI (1938), pp. 285-303.

———. "The Political Ideas of New Jersey's First Governor," *Proceedings of the New Jersey Historical Society*, LX (1942), pp. 81-98, 184-99.

———. "The Social and Economic Ideas of New Jersey's First Governor," *Proceedings of the New Jersey Historical Society*, LXI (1943), pp. 31-46.

———. *The Biographical Encyclopaedia of New Jersey of the Nineteenth Century* (Philadelphia, 1877).

Thompson, Robert T. *Colonel James Neilson, A Business Man of the Early Machine Age in New Jersey, 1784-1862* (New Brunswick, 1940).

Turnbull, Archibald D. *John Stevens, an American Record* (New York, 1928).

Tuttle, Joseph F. "Biographical Sketch of General William Winds," *Proceedings of the New Jersey Historical Society*, VII (1853), pp. 15-37.

———. "The Early History of Morris County, New Jersey," *Proceedings of the New Jersey Historical Society*, 2nd Ser., II (1870), pp. 17-53.

————. "Hibernia Furnace and the Surrounding Country in the Revolutionary War," *Proceedings of the New Jersey Historical Society*, 2nd Ser., VI (1881), pp. 148-73.

————. "Reverend Jacob Green of Hanover, New Jersey . . . ," *Proceedings of the New Jersey Historical Society*, 2nd Ser., XII (1893), 191-241.

Van Tyne, Claude H. *The Loyalists in the American Revolution* (New York, 1902).

Vedder, Henry C. *A History of the Baptists in the Middle States* (Philadelphia, 1898).

Vermeule, C. C. "The Active Loyalists of New Jersey," *Proceedings of the New Jersey Historical Society*, LII (1934), pp. 87-95.

Volwiler, A. T. *George Croghan and the Westward Movement, 1741-1782* (Cleveland, 1926).

Werner, G. V. "The Fiscal History of Colonial New Jersey (with special references to the taxation of real estate)," unpublished master's thesis, 1934, Rutgers University Library.

Westcott, Thompson. *The Life of John Fitch, the Inventor of the Steamboat* (Philadelphia, 1878).

Whitaker, Arthur P. *The Spanish American Frontier: 1783-1795* (Boston, 1927).

Wickes, Stephen. *History of Medicine in New Jersey and of its Medical Men . . .* [to 1800] (Newark, 1879).

Winfield, Charles H. "Life and Public Services of John Cleves Symmes," *Proceedings of the New Jersey Historical Society*, 2nd Ser., V (1877), pp. 22-43.

Wood, Gertrude S. *William Paterson of New Jersey, 1745-1806* (Fair Lawn, N. J., 1933).

Woodward, Carl R. *Ploughs and Politics; Charles Read of New Jersey and His Notes on Agriculture, 1715-1774* (New Brunswick, 1941).

Woody, Thomas. *Quaker Education in the Colony and State of New Jersey* (Philadelphia, 1923).

Wynkoop, Richard. *Schuremans, of New Jersey* (2nd ed., New York, 1902).

INDEX

****

Abbott, Benjamin, 54
Agriculture: pattern of, 42-43; depression in, 189; price movements in, 197n
"A Jerseyman," 265
Allentown 11, 56n
Allison, Burgess, 57
American Museum, 60
"Americanus," 279; *see also* John Stevens, Jr.
Amwell, 11
Anderson, George, 92n
Anderson, Thomas, 130, 231n, 268n
Anglican Church, 44; *see also* Episcopal Church
Annapolis, 246, 247, 248
Annapolis Convention, 253-55
Arnett, Shelly, 30, 59, 263n
Arnold, Jacob, 130, 301n
Asbury, Bishop Francis, 45, 54
Asgill, Capt. Charles, 8
Ashfield, Richard, 142n
Assleck, Com. Sir Edmund, 15
"Association," 10, 35

Athenian Society, 167
Axford, Charles, 268n

Bache, Theoph., 141n
Bacon, John, 7
Baker, John, 200
Ball, Aaron, 57
Ball, Joseph, 144
Baptist Church, 44, 53
Barney, Capt. Joshua, 13
Barton, J., 141n, 142n
Beach, Rev. Abraham, 49, 50
Beatty, John, 225, 240, 268n
Bell, Andrew, 14, 29
Benezet, Anthony, 55
Bergen County, 20, 32n, 33, 34, 35n, 36, 41, 87n, 127, 198, 200, 212
Biddle, Clement, 149-57
Biddle, John, 92n
Bingham, William, 145
Bispham, John, 143n
Bispham, John, Jr., 143n
Blair, Robert, 291n

Bland, I., 141n

"Blazing Star" (tavern), 269

Bloomfield, Joseph, 98, 130, 152, 230, 231n, 232n, 296, 297

Bloomfield, Moses, 153

Bond, Phineas, 145

Borden, Joseph, 174

Bordentown, 11, 56n, 57

Boudinot, Elias: 15, 18, 46, 113n, 137, 230, 231n, 232, 245n, 246, 250, 289; and peace negotiations, 12; retirement in 1783, 16-17; and government securities, 216; and first Congressional election, 289n, 290ff

Boudinot, Elisha, 97, 98, 113n, 141n, 230, 231n, 294

Boyd, Adam, 293

Bradford, William, 231n, 294-95

Brearly, David: 62n, 70n, 232n, 264n, 267, 270, 275, 289n; appointed to Constitutional Convention, 255-56; attitude toward paper money, 285

Brissot de Warville, J. P., 281

Bunn, Edward, 291n

Burlington, City of: 11, 38, 42, 49, 56n, 61, 92, 118, 122, 143; designated "free port," 31, 117-20; chartered as city, 122-23; and location of state capital, 125-26; designated state capital, 287

Burlington County: 7, 20, 32n, 35n, 55, 87n, 127, 128, 166, 192, 198, 263, 282, 294; election of 1784 in, 38, 86; election of 1783 in, 77; election of 1782 in, 81; voting in, 90; contested elections in, 91-93; in first Congressional election, 297

Burnet, John, 231n

Burnet, William, 137n, 138n, 141n, 231n

Butland, James, 144

Cadwallader, Lambert; 227, 263, 273; and first Congressional election, 290ff

Camp, Nathan, 231n

"Candidus," 238

Canfield, Israel, 231n

Cape May County, 32n, 35n, 87n, 198

Carleton, Sir Guy, 5, 9

"Cassius," 265

Chandler, Rev. Dr. Thomas Bradbury, 29

Chetwood, John, 263n, 268n, 294

Christian's, Scholar's and Farmer's Magazine (Elizabeth Town), 60

Cities: and the "free-ports" project, 116-20; movement for incorporation of, 122-24; location of state capital, 125-26, 287

Clark, Abraham: 21, 46, 99, 139, 168, 185n, 204, 206, 214n, 226, 253, 258, 281, 282n, 289, 289n; candidate for governor, 96; and legal reform, 181; and paper money, 193; sponsors loan-office measure, 198-202; sponsors "bull law," 205; and the debt problem, 208; opposes payment of Continental requisition, 209; and the Mississippi question, 228; and rejection of Continental requisition of 1786, 236-44; favors New York as temporary capital, 249-50; appointed to Constitutional Convention, 256; views on Federal Constitution, 276-77; and first Congressional election, 290ff

Clark, Thomas, 96, 143n, 242

Clements, Samuel, 143n

Coetus, 53

College of New Jersey (Princeton University), 45, 54, 57, 58-59

Collin, Nicholas, 44

Collins, Isaac, 59, 64

Commerce: during Revolution, 9-12, 105-06; postwar condition of, 105-08; foreign, efforts to create, 109-11; and free-trade policy, 111-12; and tariff policy, 112-16; and "free-ports" project, 116-20; and Federal Constitution, 272-73; *see also* Tariff

Committee for the Promotion of Trade in New Jersey, 116

Condict, Silas, 207

Confederation, New Jersey and the: 112, 173, 175, 218, 306; financial relations, 176-79, 233; "Representation" of 1778, 218-20; western land problem, 220-27; Mississippi question, 227-29; land companies, 229-33; refusal of requisition of 1785, 233-44; location of capital, 244-51, 270; *see also* Continental Congress

Conferentie, 53

Confiscated estates: 27; legal procedure on, 31-32; financial returns from, 32-33, 35; postwar action on, 33-34

Constitution, Federal: 248, 249n, 251n; delegates to Constitutional Convention, 255-59; and Paterson plan, 259-60; reception of, 260-61; general enthusiasm for, 262-64; ratification of, 265-70; ratification reconsidered, 272-78, 306

Constitution of 1776, 70-71, 74, 80

Continental Congress: 11, 14; at Princeton (1783), 16, 244-45; and financial plan of 1780, 159; and financial plan of 1783, 175; and requisition of 1785, 208-09, 211; New Jersey's views on powers of, 218-20; Committee appeals to New Jersey legislature, 241-44; and location of capital, 245-51; *see also* Confederation, New Jersey and the

Cooper, Benjamin B., 145n

Corporation for the Relief of Widows and Children of Clergymen, 51

Corshon, Joshua, 62n

Cox, John, 17, 129, 211, 215, 232n, 269n

Coxe, Daniel, 34, 143, 143n

Coxe, John, 92n

Cowell, Ebenezer, 148n; and dividing-line controversy, 149-57

Cumberland County, 32n, 35n, 87, 198

Cummings, John Noble, 231n, 296

"Curtius," 72

Cuyler, Henry, 34, 137n, 141n

Cuyler, Henry, Jr., 141n

Davenport, Franklin, 204n, 231n, 294

Dayton, Gen. Elias, 96, 113n, 230, 231n, 258

Dayton, Jonathan: 46, 113, 214n, 216n, 228, 229, 230, 232, 250n, 260n, 264n, 268n, 285; appointed to Constitutional Convention, 256, 258-59; and first Congressional election, 290ff

Deare, Jonathan, 263n

Debtor laws: and tender laws, 180; and the "£12 law," 180-81; and legal reform, 181; and currency depreciation, 181-82; and securities-tender law, 182-

Debtor laws—cont'd
84; in 1786, 204-06; repeal of, 286-87

Debts (Continental): amount owed to New Jersey, 172-73; interest payments made by New Jersey on, 173-78, 206, 209, 238, 308; and requisition of 1785, 208-09, 236-40; proposal for funding, 211-12; holders of, 212-14, 213n, 214n, 268; speculation in, 215-16; 269n; and Federal Constitution, 272

Debts (state): amount of, 172-73; interest payments on, 179, 206, 308; and adjustment of contractors' certificates, 206-09; plans for servicing, 208, 209, 211-12; provision for servicing, 212; holders of, 268n; and Federal Constitution, 272

de Gardoqui, Don Diego, 227

Delancy, John, 141n

Delancy, Oliver, 34, 137n

Denman, Matthias, 231n, 268n

Dennis, John, 263n

Dick, Samuel, 268n

Dickinson, Philemon, 268n

Dover, 84

Drake, James, 202

Duane, James, 279

Dunham, Aaron, 232n

Dunham, Azariah, 138n, 141n, 142n, 263n

Dunlap, William, 126n

Dutch, 41

Dutch Reformed Church, 44, 53

East Jersey: and effects of war, 20; distinctiveness of, 24, 43; heterogeneous population in, 42; political alignment, 85, 100, 305; voting practices in, 87;

attitude on postwar currency problems, 164ff; and the money question, 185; loses political supremacy, 280-81; and first Congressional election, 290ff

East Jersey, Board of Proprietors of, 135ff; and dividing-line controversy, 147-57; *see also* Proprietors

East Jersey Company, 232

Education: Quaker interest in, 55-56; academies, 56-57; colleges, 58-59

Egbert, Abraham, 132

Egbert, Thomas, 202

Election, Federal: law governing, 287-88; and presidential electors, 288-89; and Federal Senators, 289; and "Junto ticket," 289-90; and nominations, 290-91; and character of Congressional campaign, 291-96; political manipulation in, 296-99; determination of results of, 299-300; contested, 300-02

Election machinery: 70, 71; importance of, 73; nominations, 75-79; suffrage qualifications, 80-82; control of, 82; polling facilities, 82-86; voting practices, 86-88; size of electorate, 89-91; contested elections, 91-95; estimate of, 101-02; and Congressional election of 1789, 287-89, 296-303

Elections: by joint-meeting, 95-98; of ratifying Convention, 264-68

Elections, county: in Somerset County (1782), 76; in Burlington County; (1782), 81, 91-92; (1783), 77, 92-93; (1784), 86; in Hunterdon County: (1784), 78; (1788), 82, 93-94

Elections, state: (1783), 167; (1784), 167-68; (1785), 78, 192, 199n; (1786), 204; (1787), 262; (1788), 283; (1789), 284
Elizabeth Town: 9, 29, 42, 46, 56n, 57, 61, 117, 122, 139, 201, 232, 245, 271, 298; Presbyterian Church in, 46-47
Elizabeth Town Associates, 139
Ellis, Daniel: 143n; and dividing-line controversy, 149-57
Ellis, Joseph, 204n, 294
Elmer, Eli, 231n
Elmer, Dr. Jonathan, 62, 250n, 289
English, 41
Episcopal Church, postwar conditions, 49-52
"Equality," 224
Erskine, Robert, 128
Essex County: 20, 32, 35n, 87n, 105, 132, 165, 183, 192, 201, 212, 214n, 263, 296; voting in, 90; in first Congressional election, 296, 299, 300n
Estaugh, John, 143n
Ewing, James, 98
Ewing, Maskell, 62n, 98

Faesch, John Jacob, 128, 130
"Farmer of New Jersey," 266, 278; see John Stevens, Jr.
"Federal," 238
Fell, John, 268n
Fenimore, Thomas, 92n
Forman, Daniel, 6, 28
Forman, David, 94n
Franklin, Temple, 281n
Freehold, 56n
Frelinghuysen, Frederick, 93, 98, 232n, 268n
French, 41
French, Philip, 263n

Furman, Moore, 105, 110, 263
Furman, Richard Way, 132

Georgetown, 248
Georgia, state of, 235
German Reformed Church, 44
Germans, 41
Gerry, Elbridge, 246n
Gibbs, Joel, 232n
Gloucester County: 32n, 35n, 38, 44, 55, 87, 127, 166, 198, 294; loan-office in, 203-04; in first Congressional election, 297
Gorham, Nathaniel, 240, 241
Grayson, William, 241, 242, 243
Green, Ashbel, 45
Greene, Gen. Nathanael, 129
Greenwich, 49
Griffith, John, 286n

Hackensack, 56n
Hackensack Academy, 56
Haines, Josiah, 92n
Hall, Clement, 183
Hamilton, Alexander, 250
Hankinson, Kenneth, 142n
Haring, Peter, 202, 302n
Hasenclever, Peter, 127
Heard, Gen. Nathaniel, 28
Henderson, Dr. Thomas, 94n, 290
Hendrickson, Daniel, 94n, 153
Hessian fly, 189, 189n
Hewlings, Abraham, 143n
Hinchman, John, 29
Hooper, Robert Lettis, 62n, 128n, 130, 201, 268n, 296
Hoops, Adam, 290
Hope, 58
Hopkins, John Estaugh, 143n
Hornblower, Josiah, 227, 290
Hough, John, 222n
Hough, William, 222n

Houston, William Churchill: 17, 64, 97, 227n, 253, 264n; and dividing-line controversy, 151-57; appointed to Constitutional Convention, 255-56

Howell, David, 246

Howell, Maj. Richard, 98

Howell, Silas, 231n

Huddy, Capt. Joshua, 8

Hughes, Hugh, 130

Humanitarianism: and anti-slavery, 63-66; and entail and primogeniture, 66-67; and intemperance, 67

Hunt, John, 143

Hunter, Andrew, 268n, 296

Hunterdon County: 32, 35n, 38, 41, 84-85, 87n, 131, 166, 182; election of 1784 in, 78; election of 1788 in, 82, 93-94; voting in, 90

Hyler, Capt. Adam, 8

Imlay, John, 268n

Indiana Company, 221-23, 225-27

Irish, 41

Iron industry: origins of, 127-28; postwar conditions in, 128-31

Jay, John, 227-29, 257

Johnes (Jones), Rev. Timothy, 188, 231n

Johnston, Andrew, 141n

Johnston, Heathcote, 137n

Johnston, John, 138n

Johnston, John L., 137n, 138n

Kay, Isaac, 143n

Kearney, Isabella, 142n

Kingwood, 11

Kinney, Thomas, 231n

Kinsey, James, 152, 289n, 294

Kitchell, Aaron, 301n

Knott, David, 141n

Knott, P., 142n

Kollock, Sheppard, 30, 59, 60, 61, 64, 204, 261, 263, 270

Lambert, John, 155n, 199n

Lamberton, 117, 118

Lamington, 56n

Lawrence, E., 141n

Lawrence, John, 147, 294

Lawrence, Dr. John, 29

Lawrence's line, 148, 149, 151

Leake, Samuel, 183

Leddell, William, 62n

Lee, Henry, 241

Lewis, Joseph, 188, 190, 215, 231n, 268n

Little, John, 130

Little Egg Harbor, 147, 148

Livingston, Dr. John H., 53

Livingston, P. V. B., 141n

Livingston, R. R., 141n

Livingston, Gov. William: 4, 14, 15, 45, 46, 60, 67, 72, 177n, 190, 202, 207, 249, 250, 253, 260n, 264, 265, 266n, 281n; and peace treaty, 13; and postwar prospects, 18-19; and confiscated estates, 33n; and tories, 37; attitude toward slavery, 64-65; defines ideal legislator, 75; election to governorship, 95-97; views on commerce, 111; and the currency problem, 160-61; and currency depreciation, 169; denounces loan-office plan, 195-96; appointed to Constitutional Convention, 256-58; on ratification of Constitution, 271-72; and prospects of Federal government, 274-75; and authorship of *Observations on*

Government, 278-79; and first Congressional election, 298-300

Loan Office: in colonial times, 190-91; agitation for and against, 192-97; legislative action on, 197-202, 210; provision for, 202-03; operation of, 203; in retrospect, 216-17; and Federal Constitution, 273-74, 275-76; efforts to curtail, 281-86; *see also* Money

London Company, 127, 128

Low, Nicholas, 250

Lowrey, Maj. William, 231n, 268n

Loyalists: postwar attitudes toward, 26-29; invitations to return, 29-31, 118-19; confiscated property of, 31ff; postwar political status of, 35-37; removal of disabilities on, 37-39, 287; *see also* Confiscated estates

Lutheran Church, 44

MacWhorter, Dr. Alexander, 46

Madison, James, 228, 243, 253n, 263, 298

Mansfield Neck, 49

Manufacturing: feeble condition of, 131-32; efforts to stimulate, 132-33

Marsh, Daniel, 62n, 113, 214n, 230, 231n

Martin, Ephraim, 204n, 291n

"Martin B. Bunn," 291n

Maryland, 248

Masonic Grand Lodge, 62

Massachusetts Medical Society, 62

Medical College of Philadelphia, 62

Mercer, Archibald, 231n, 268n

Methodist Church, 44, 54

Miami Company, 229-32

Middlesex County, 20, 32, 35n, 87, 166, 180n, 212, 263

Mississippi question, 227-29

Money: flows to New York and Philadelphia, 104, 112; deranged condition of, 160-61; "new emission" of 1780, 159, 161-64, 170; controversy over depreciation of "new emissions," 164-69; and deflation, 170-71, 187; "revenue money," 176, 210; loan-office, 190ff, 210, 216-17, 281-86; decline of debate over, 204; and Federal Constitution, 273-74; *see also* Loan Office; *and* Taxation

Monmouth County: 32n, 35n, 87n, 121, 127, 164, 192, 212; disorders in, 6; corrupt election of 1785 in, 94

Monroe, James, 228, 241, 243

Monrow, John, 143n

Moore, David, 289n

Moravian Church, 44

Morgan, George, 221-23, 225-27, 232

Morris, Richard, 141n

Morris, Robert, 17, 38, 137, 138n, 141n, 145, 157n, 161, 185n, 187n, 227n

Morris County, 20, 32n, 35n, 41, 87n, 117, 127, 132, 188, 190, 192, 204

Morristown, 137, 231

Mott, James, 98

Mount Bethel, 46

Negroes, 41

Neilson, Col. John: 21, 105, 113n, 263n, 267, 289n; trading ventures, 109-10; supports "free-ports" proposal, 116-20; appointed to Constitutional Convention, 255-56

"Nestor," 274

Newark, 42, 45, 55, 56n, 131, 132, 201, 271

Newbold, Caleb, 294

Newbold, Clayton, 96, 232n

Newbold, Joseph, 232n

Newbold, William, 92n, 96, 232n, 294

New Brunswick: 5, 7, 8, 42, 56n, 105, 117, 122, 167, 183, 192, 245, 261, 271; mercantile convention at, 30; Presbyterian Church in, 46-47; Episcopal Church in, 49-51; polling place at, 84; chartered as city, 122-23; and location of state capital, 125-26

New Jersey Gazette (Trenton), 59

New Jersey Journal (Chatham), 59

New Jersey Land Society, 232

New Jersey Magazine, The (New Brunswick), 60

New Jersey Medical Society, 61

New Jersey Society for Promoting Agriculture, Commerce and Arts, 62

New Madrid, 232

Newspapers and Magazines, 59-61

New York, City of: 43, 247, 248, 281; illegal trade with, 9, 12; trade with, 104-08, 112, 120; and location of the capital, 248-51

New York, State of: 235, 272; tariff policies of, 115, 120-21; boundary with New Jersey, 147-48

New York Presbytery, 48

Nottingham, 11, 245

Observations on Government, 266, 278-79

Ogden, Abraham, 250

Ogden, David, 137n

Ogden, Matthias, 113n, 214n, 230, 231n, 289n

Ogden, Samuel, 129

Ogden, Rev. Uzal, 44, 46, 52

Ohio Company, 230

Olden, David, 263n

Olden, Ephraim, 268n

Orange-Dale, 56n, 215

Parker, James: 29, 113, 137, 138, 140n, 141n, 142, 157n, 263n, 290; urges return of tories, 29; elected mayor of Perth Amboy, 38; supports "free-ports" proposal, 116-22; and the incorporation movement, 124; and location of state capital, 125-26; and dividing-line controversy, 149-57

Parker, John, 138n

Paterson, Cornelia Bell, 14

Paterson, William: 15, 21, 67, 88, 93-94, 113n, 169, 190, 260, 264n, 274; retirement of in 1783, 6; and peace treaty, 13; and tories, 28; defines republicanism, 71-72; estimate of eligible voters, 90n; and dividing-line controversy, 151-57; opposes loan-office plan, 196; and the requisition of 1785, 239; appointed to Constitutional Convention, 255-57; Paterson plan, 259-60; elected to Senate, 289

Paterson plan, 259-60

Pemberton, James, 64

Penn, Richard, 141n

Pennsylvania, 272; tariff policies of, 115

Perth, Earl of, 141n

Perth Amboy: 38, 42, 56n, 117, 118, 122; Episcopal Church in, 50; designated "free port," 31, 117-20; chartered as city, 122-24; and location of state capital, 125-26; designated state capital, 287

"Perth Amboy group," 71

Pettit, Charles, 129

Philadelphia: 43, 51, 244, 245, 248, 281; trade with, 104-08, 112, 120; and the location of the capital, 248-51

Philadelphia Merchants' Committee, 116

Philadelphia Presbytery, 48

Philadelphia Yearly Meeting, 55

Pinckney, Charles, 241-44, 260

"Pine Robbers," 7

Piscataway, 55, 117

Plainfield, 55

Political behavior: 137, 140, 154-55, 156-57, 168-69, 187, 206, 261, 304-05; affected by Revolution, 23-24, 35-39, 79; and republicanism, 71-73, 274-75; and election campaigns, 76-79; factors influencing, 99-101, 305; on money question, 185, 197ff; and security holding, 212-14; and Federal Constitution, 275-78; conservative trend after 1787, 281ff; in first Congressional election, 289ff; *see also* Election, Federal; Election machinery; *and* Elections

Political Intelligencer. And New Jersey Advertiser, The (New Brunswick and Elizabeth), 29, 59, 60

Population: size of, 40; national origins of, 41-42; distribution of, 42

Presbyterian Church, 44, 295; postwar problems, 46-48

Princeton: 5, 11, 14, 16, 56n, 117; Continental Congress at, 244-47

Princeton University, *see* College of New Jersey

Proprietors: 135-36; of East Jersey, effects of Revolution on, 137-38; and Elizabeth Town Associates, 139-40; dividend by, 140-43; of West Jersey, effect of Revolution on, 143; boundary between East and West Jersey, 147-49; controversy over the dividing-line, 149-56; *see also* East Jersey, Board of Proprietors of; West Jersey, Council of Proprietors of; *and* West Jersey Society

Provincial Congress, defines suffrage qualifications, 80

Quakers (Society of Friends): 44; postwar condition, 48-49; schools founded by, 55; attitude toward slavery, 63-66; attitude toward intemperance, 67; debarred from officeholding 74-75; behavior in Revolution, 100-01; in first Congressional election, 295

Queen's College (Rutgers University): 54, 167; postwar revival, 58

Rahway, 55

Ramapo Tract, 141, 150n

Rattoone, John, 138n, 141n, 142n

Read, Charles, 127, 128

Reed, Bowes, 150

Reed, Joseph: and West Jersey Society, 143-45; and dividing-line controversy, 149-57

Reid, John, 141n

Religion: major denominations, 44; postwar condition of, 44-46; Presbyterian Church, 46-48; Society of Friends, 48-49; Episcopal Church, 49-52; Dutch Reformed Church, 53; Baptist Church, 53; Methodist Church, 54; *see also* specific denominations

Remsen, Henry, 14

"Retaliators," 6, 28, 36, 77

Revolutionary War: concluding phases of in New Jersey, 4ff; and civil dissensions, 6-7; illegal trade during, 9-12; effects of, 20-24

Reynolds, Thomas, 130

Rhea, Jonathan, 296

Rhode Island, 234, 286

Riggs, Joseph, 293

Rodman, Thomas, 143n

Roman Catholic Church, 44

Ross, John, 296

"Rusticus," 78

Rutgers University, *see* Queen's College

Rutherfurd, C., 141n

Rutherfurd, John: 29, 55, 113, 138n, 191, 289n; views on commerce, 111; views on manufacturing, 132; and dividing-line controversy, 151-57; author of *Petitions and Memorials*, 151n

Rutherfurd, Walter: 29, 137, 137n, 138n, 139, 141n, 286, 298; and dividing-line controversy, 149-57

St. Eustatius, 109

Salem, 56n

Salem County: 32n, 35n, 41, 44, 55, 87n, 166, 192, 197n, 198, 263, 264

Sandy Hook: 7; lighthouse taxed at, 121

Schenck, Peter, 94n

Schoepf, Dr. Johann D., 15, 130

Schureman, James: 99, 204, 253; leads opposition to loan-office measure, 199-202; and first Congressional election, 290ff

Schuurman, John, 263n

Scotch, 41

Scotch-Irish, 41

Sergeant, Jonathan D., and dividing-line controversy, 149-57

Sharp, Anthony, 130, 153, 199n

Sharp, Isaac, 141n

Sharp, Joseph, 141n

Shaw, John, 14

Shotwell, Jacob, 293

Shreve, Caleb, 92n

Shreve, Israel, 92n

Shrewsbury, 127

Sinnickson, Andrew, 183

Sinnickson, Thomas: 290n; and first Congressional election, 290ff

Skinner, Cortlandt, 137n

Skinner, Stephen, 137n

Slavery: attitude of Quakers toward, 63ff; attacks on, 64-65; legislation relating to, 64, 66

Smith, Isaac, 232n

Smith, Richard S., 294

Smith, Samuel, 201

Smith, Dr. Samuel Stanhope, 59

Smith, William, 143n

Smith, William Peartree, 17, 26

Smyth, J. F. D., 15

Smyth, John, 137n

Smythe, Frederick, 28

Society for the Propagation of the Gospel, 50

Society of Cincinnati, 62

Somerset County: 20, 32n, 35n,

41, 87n, 192, 197n, 200n, 263;
election of 1782 in, 76; loan-
office in, 204
Sons of St. Tammany, 62
Springfield, 56n, 132
Stafford, 84
Stanbery, Jonas, 268n
Stelle, Thompson, 263n
Stevens, E., 141n
Stevens, John: 17, 78, 137, 138n,
139, 140, 141n, 149n, 157n,
284; and dividing-line contro-
versy, 149-57; president of
ratifying convention, 268-69
Stevens, John, Jr.: 138, 141n,
263, 268n, 269n; author of
Observations on Government,
266, 278-79
Stirling, Lord, 137
Stockton, Richard, 98, 154, 231n,
232n, 263n, 294
Stockton, Samuel Witham, 97,
231n, 232n, 268n, 269
Sussex County, 32n, 34, 35n, 41,
87n, 127, 131, 192
Swedes, 41
Swedish Lutheran Church, 44
Symmes, Daniel, 231n
Symmes, John Cleves: 190, 228,
229, 231n, 258; and the Miami
Company, 230-32

Tabor-Kempe, John, 34
Tallman, Peter, 92n
Tariff: movement to enact state,
112-14; excise as indirect, 114-
15; protests against New York
and Pennsylvania, 115-16, 120-
21; and the "free-ports" project, 116-20; desire for a continental impost, 121, 133, 176,
233ff; and support for Constitution, 272-73
Taxation: for retirement of con-

tinental money, 161-62; and
the "new emission," 165-68,
170; amount of (1779-1784),
170-71; in 1783, 174; for continental creditors, 176ff; and
money shortage, 187-88, 190;
proposals for, 210, 211; for
servicing state debts, 212; and
Federal Constitution, 272-73;
receipts (1784-1790), 307
Ten Broeck, Cornelius, 268n
Thompson, Benjamin, 129, 177,
207, 207n
Thompson, Mark, 130
Throop, Amos, 57
Toms River, 84
Treaty of Peace, 1783: reception
of in New Jersey, 13-14; and
the end of "the lines," 14-16;
and retirement of prominent
leaders, 16-17; sober reflections
on, 17-19
Trent, William, 221-23, 225-27
Trenton: 4, 10, 42, 56n, 61, 105,
117, 118, 122, 132, 245, 246;
and location of state capital,
126; Continental Congress at,
247
Trenton Academy, 56
Trenton Society for Improvement
in Useful Knowledge, 62
Tucker, Samuel, 96, 155n

Upper Evesham, 49
Upper Springfield, 49

Van Cleve, Benjamin, 99, 153,
199n, 202, 279n
Vandalia Company, 220
Vandike, Henry, 232n
Van Winkle, Enist, 232n
Vardon, Daniel, 232n
Vermont, 257

Virginia: 248; and western land claims, 222-26

Voorhees, Jacques, 215, 268n

Wadsworth, Jeremiah, 145

Wallace, Joshua Maddox, 294, 297

Washington, Gen. George, 4, 9, 11, 12, 14, 245, 257

Webster, Noah, 100

West Indies, trade with, 104

West Jersey: 212, 214, 215n; and effects of war, 20; distinctiveness of, 24, 43; political alignment, 85, 100, 305; voting practices in, 87; attitude on postwar currency problems, 164ff, 185, 282-83; gains political supremacy, 280-81; and first Congressional election, 287ff

West Jersey, Council of Proprietors of: 135ff; and dividing-line controversy, 147-57; see also Proprietors

West Jersey Society, postwar problems of, 143-45

Wharton, Samuel, 222n

Whig Societies, 11, 36, 163

White, Rev. Dr. William, 51

"Willing to Learn": defines republicanism, 73; defends loan-office money, 193-94

Witherspoon, John, 17, 18, 59, 72, 191, 196, 234n, 290

Witt, Francis, 269

Woodbridge, 28, 55, 84, 117

Woodbury, 49, 56n

Woolman, John, 55

BOOK   CARL SANDBURG COLLEGE
Experiment in independence McCormick, R
STACKS F138.M2

05613   05613
                    F   138   •M2
F   WITHDRAWN
138   MCCORMICK   R
•M2
         EXPERIMENT IN INDEPENDENCE

Sandburg College
Learning Resource Center
Galesburg, IL 61401

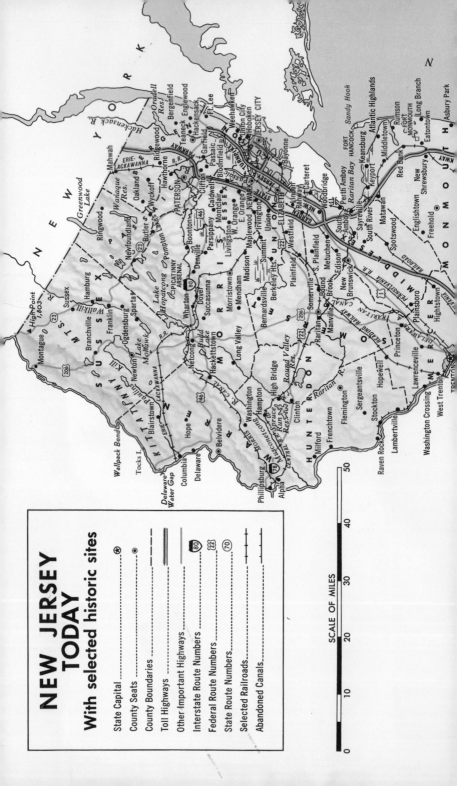

NEW JERSEY TODAY
With selected historic sites

State Capital .... ⊛
County Seats .... ⊙
County Boundaries ....
Toll Highways ....
Other Important Highways ....
Interstate Route Numbers ... 🛡80
Federal Route Numbers ..... 🛡202
State Route Numbers .... 🛡70
Selected Railroads ....
Abandoned Canals ....

SCALE OF MILES

0   10   20   30   40   50